SELKIRK
PROTOCOL BOOKS
1511–1547

DEDICATION

This book is dedicated to the memory of Bruce and Walter Mason who did so much to preserve the history of Selkirk and the Borders. Without their foresight this book would never have appeared.

THE STAIR SOCIETY

SELKIRK
PROTOCOL BOOKS
1511–1547

The Protocol Books of
John Chepman, 1511–36 and 1545–47,
Sir John Chepman, 1536–43,
John and Ninian Brydin and Other Notaries, 1526–36
and John Brydin, 1530–37

Transcribed and Edited

by

TERESA MALEY and WALTER ELLIOT

with an

INTRODUCTION

by

PETER SYMMS

EDINBURGH
THE STAIR SOCIETY AND THE WALTER MASON TRUST
1993

Jointly Published by

The Stair Society
16 Charlotte Square
Edinburgh
EH2 4YS

and

The Walter Mason Trust
Municipal Buildings
High Street
Selkirk
TD7 4BU

First published 1993

ISBN 1 872517 04 8

This publication has been financially supported by a
Glenfiddich Living Scotland Award

British Library Cataloguing-in-Publication Data

A catalogue record for this book is available from the British
Library.

Typeset by Computing Services (University of Glasgow) Limited.

Printed by Martins the Printers Ltd, Berwick-upon-Tweed.

CONTENTS

PREFACE

The Walter Mason Collection and the Walter Mason Trust

This publication is an important step for the Walter Mason Trust as it represents more than three years work involving conservation, research, transcription and editing of the four Protocol Books which make up this volume. Hopefully this is only the first volume in a series of transcripts from the Selkirk Protocol Books as there are still another ten remaining. The Protocol Books themselves only represent a very small proportion of the large and important collection of manuscripts which has become known as the Walter Mason Collection and which dates from 1511.

The history of this collection and the manner in which it was saved from destruction and then later returned to public ownership is a story in itself worth telling. The archive relating to the Royal Burgh of Selkirk would have lain with the town clerks who, throughout the Burgh's history, were also solicitors practising in Selkirk. When the Town Council acquired an administration headquarters in what is now the Municipal Buildings their minute books and other archives should have been transferred from the office of Peter Rodger, Writer, High Street to these new premises. However, not all were taken and many remained in the High Street attic even when the Commercial Bank moved into these premises in 1887. Here the manuscripts stayed until about 1940 when, due to the fear of air raids, the bank manager was ordered to destroy all possible incendiary hazards in the building. This directive was taken too literally when the manager instructed a member of his bank staff to remove all the 'old papers in the attic' and burn them. Next to the bank was the firm of J.S. Mason, Bakers, owned at that time by the brothers Bruce and Walter Mason. Both brothers were keen antiquarians and collectors and they immediately recognised the significance of the manuscripts about to be destroyed. Despite being told of the importance of the collection the bank manager insisted that the documents be burned. The Masons were then forced to indulge in some slightly underhand action; while the bank employee returned to the attic from the fire to bring down more manuscripts to burn, the Mason brothers quickly removed what they recognised as being the most important manuscripts. This way they rescued protocol books covering the period 1511 to 1668, loose pages from the Burgh of Selkirk Court Book and a large number of legal transactions, royal proclamations and letters, tax demands, militia lists, legal correspondence and posters. Although the collection all originated from Selkirk the geographic area they relate to goes beyond the boundaries of the current Borders Region.

As Bruce and Walter Mason had obtained the manuscripts in rather dubious circumstances they kept the fact that the collection was safely stored in their baker's shop attic a fairly closely guarded secret. Carefully selected material was only shown to close friends or to individuals they knew were carrying out research on topics covered by papers in the collection.

The Collection remained a secret until the death of Walter Mason in 1988, Bruce having died some 25 years before. It was then that the archive came into the care of Ettrick and Lauderdale District Council who were in fact the legal owners of much of it. Despite the collection's age and the fact that it had spent years in attics it was in relatively good condition. Nevertheless the oldest material, and particularly the protocol books, required conservation before any attempt could be made to examine their contents and find out more about life in the late medieval Borders. Although the District Council were able to commit funds to the project it was obvious the level of support they could give would only allow a very limited programme of conservation, transcription and cataloguing. To speed up matters and to ensure a safe future for the collection the Walter Mason Trust was established in May 1989. The main aims of the Trust are to raise money to fund the conservation of the collection and to enable the information contained therein to be made available to as wide an audience as possible.

This project is a perfect example of these aims; the first four Protocol Books have been conserved, they have been transcribed and now they are being published along with an introduction, putting them in their historical context, and an extensive index which allows access to the information. The funds raised by the Walter Mason Trust have ensured that all of the Protocol Books have been conserved along with many of the loose manuscripts and a start has been made on the transcription and cataloguing of this most valuable collection.

Further support is necessary if the work of the Trust is to continue and other Protocol Books are to be published. The Walter Mason Trust welcomes all contributions and further information can be obtained by writing to the Secretary, The Walter Mason Trust, Municipal Buildings, High Street, Selkirk TD7 4JX.

Ian Brown,
Secretary to the Walter Mason Trust

ACKNOWLEDGEMENTS

The Walter Mason Trust and Ettrick and Lauderdale District Council wish to acknowledge the help received from the following in making this publication possible.

Dr. John Imrie and Dr. John Durkan for their efforts checking our transcriptions against the original Protocol Books and also their valuable advice and suggestions.

The Scottish Record Office for advice and support.

Tom Valentine and his staff for the conservation work they have undertaken on the Walter Mason manuscripts.

Debbie Gordon for typing the manuscript.

All of our earlier donors and sponsors whose support enabled us to fund the conservation and transcription of these four Protocol Books, especially the following who have all given donations or awards of £500 or more;
> The Scottish Museums Council
> The Pilgrim Trust
> The Royal Bank of Scotland
> Mr & Mrs J Cruickshank
> The Buccleuch Charitable Foundation
> The Buccleuch and Queensberry Trust
> The Columba Trust
> The Esmee Fairbairn Charitable Trust
> The Marc Fitch Trust
> Morton Ward Associates
> The National Manuscripts Conservation Trust
> The Radcliffe Trust
> Selkirk Common Good Fund
> Selkirkshire Antiquarian Society
> Andrew Stevenson Fund
> The Wolfson Trust
> Norman Wright
> Walter Wright

The Walter Mason Trust is especially grateful to the Glenfiddich Living Scotland Awards scheme for its financial support which has contributed to the publication of this volume.

EDITORS' NOTES

In translating and transcribing the text which follows we have attempted to achieve some consistency of style without detracting from the individual character of each book. The formal entries vary little in style from notary to notary but many items are not formal. Although the majority are recorded loosely in the style of an instrument many are nothing more than a note in cobbled-together Scots and Latin. It was our intention to retain such quirks rather than edit them out. As a general rule we have abridged the formal documents written in Latin unless their style was particularly obscure but those written in Scots have been transcribed in full and indicated by quotation marks. Where the poor condition of the page was a consideration, we have recorded what remains of an instrument or note only when sense could be made of it.

A preliminary study of the paper used in the volumes revealed a variety of watermarks. Those we were able to check indicate a northern French provenance as might have been expected.

The following textual abbreviations have been employed.

Round brackets to describe the condition of the text e.g. (p/t) for page torn, (blank), etc.

Square brackets to indicate supplied information e.g. [Ker] of Lyntoun. In general this has been supplied from information found elsewhere in the text. Additionally, *The Burgh Court Book of Selkirk*, eds. J. Imrie, T.I. Rae and W.D. Ritchie (Scottish Record Society, 2 vols, 1960, 1969), *The Register of the Great Seal of Scotland*, eds. J. Maitland Thomson and others (reprinted Clark Constable, Edinburgh 1984) and T. Craig-Brown's *History of Selkirkshire* (Edinburgh 1886) were most helpful in filling gaps. We are sorry that time did not permit full cross-referencing as the Burgh Court Book in particular provides numerous parallel or complementary items.

Christian names have been modernised but surnames, place names (except Edinburgh and Selkirk) and sobriquets are kept in the form found in the text.

We have retained the notarial titles, although they are now numbered and printed in bold, followed by the date. Old style dating has been modernised e.g. February 1534 appears as February 1534/5. We have modernised the medieval forms of the letters 'y' to 'th' and 'z' to 'y' unless they are retained in modern spelling e.g. Cadzow.

Finally, of the many people who have helped us, we would like to thank in particular John Imrie and John Durkan for checking our text and making numerous suggestions and improvements and to Donald Galbraith for compiling the indexes and for his support throughout the project.

All errors in the edited text are our own.

Teresa Maley
Walter Elliot
Selkirk, October 1992

The Selkirk Protocol Books – their Importance in Historical Research

On the face of it, the discovery, transcription and publication of four more protocol books of the sixteenth century does not look like a major milestone in Scottish history. After all, the definition of a notary's protocol book as a collection of the essential details of legal transactions does not suggest, except to genuine enthusiasts, anything but a summary of the humdrum and commonplace. Such a view is understandable, and until the contents of a protocol book are seen in context, the humdrum and commonplace will obscure the real value of such records as rich sources of evidence about everyday life and community affairs. In his essay on the early Scottish notary, John Durkan looked at the value of notaries' records, which when used in conjunction with other public records, 'seldom fail to throw light on the complexities of human relationships within kin groups, between masters and servants, churchmen and laymen, and even between a vicar and his God'.[1]

Notaries

In common with almost all Scottish notaries before the Reformation, the Selkirk notaries of the sixteenth century were in holy orders. Indeed a common occupation for priests was that of notary public, and since the better educated clergy were generally trained in the law, this was 'one of the major services that the Church could offer to the community at large',[2] and something that gave priests an opportunity to earn a good living, free from dependence on stipend or altarage fees. Until the sixteenth century the lay notary was almost unknown, and priestly notaries were closely involved with many aspects of the daily lives of those around them. Cowan argues that the legal duties performed by priests and chaplains for members of the laity, who were often fellow burgesses and possibly even kinsfolk, had the effect of 'cementing bonds between them',[3] and there is no doubt that their literacy and knowledge gave them an important place in the community. Sometimes the skill and degree of literacy of the notary may have been little better than that of his clients, but 'in the country of the blind, the one-eyed man is king', and any knowledge of the law in a society much addicted to litigation must have been regarded as a marketable commodity. One writer claimed that 'the work of the notary reflects the life of his period in all its phases – in the family, in commerce, in trade, in the country and in the

---

1. I.B. Cowan and D. Shaw (eds.), *The Renaissance and Reformation in Scotland – Essays in honour of Gordon Donaldson* (Edinburgh 1983), 40.
2. I.B. Cowan, *The Scottish Reformation* (London 1982), 20.
3. I.B. Cowan, *Scottish Reformation*, 21–22.

town, in civil, in ecclesiastical and in criminal matters'.[4] The truth of this statement is apparent from documentary sources, which show notaries dealing with matters ranging from marriage settlements to apprenticeships, and from sasines to testaments. The importance of the notary to the authentication of documents can be seen in the saying 'no document in Scotland is an instrument that is not under the hand of a notary'.[5]

A notary's licence to practice came from the Pope, the Holy Roman Emperor, or both, or in some cases after the Act 1469 c.30 (*A.P.S.*, ii, 95, c.6) from the crown. The notary apostolic had 'the greatest field in which to operate',[6] not restricted in any way by geographical area, and this was therefore the most favoured designation. The financial rewards open to a notary sometimes led to fraudulent use of a notarial designation, or to the more serious offence of falsely pretending to be a notary. This was enough of a problem in 1503 for parliament to discuss complaints against false notaries and to order bishops to call together and examine all those in their dioceses claiming to be notaries, punishing those found to be impostors.[7]

The Selkirk Notaries

From the surnames of the Selkirk priests and notaries we can assume that many of them were from local families, and further evidence of local connections is provided by wills and records of land transactions. It has been said that 'the clergy were thoroughly involved in everyday life. Clerics were expected to advance the interests of their kinsmen, take part in their quarrels, occasionally in their crimes, draw up their legal business, become sureties for their debts'.[8] In fact, they were so closely involved with the ordinary, everyday activities of their communities that their very worldliness was seen by some critics as a major factor in the decline of the pre-Reformation church.

The Selkirk records show the clergy in their familiar roles as priests and notaries, carrying out the duties of the literate few in a largely illiterate society.[9] The records also show us the clergy in some of their other activi-

---

4.   D. Murray, *Legal Practice in Ayr and the West of Scotland in the 15th and 16th centuries* (Glasgow 1910), 2.

5.   D. Murray, *Legal Practice*, 17. Notarial instruments are defined (*Dictionary of the Older Scottish Tongue*, iii, 288) as 'formal and duly authenticated records of any proceedings or transaction drawn up by a notary public, and similar records made by the scribe of a court'. The records commonly include the phrases 'he asked an instrument', or 'he took an instrument'.

6.   G. Donaldson (ed.), *Protocol Book of James Young 1485–1515*, (Scottish Record Society, Edinburgh 1952), v.

7.   T. Thomson and C. Innes (eds.), *The Acts of the Parliaments of Scotland* [*A.P.S.*], ii, 250.

8.   M.H.B. Sanderson, 'Some aspects of the church in Scottish society in the era of the Reformation', *Scottish Church History*, xvii (1970), 91.

9.   Those requiring instruments, and unable to write or even sign their own names, would signify that a document was theirs by touching the notary's pen. Thus, 'In wytnes of the quhilk thing I have tweychit the pen with my hande in presens of sir Niniane Brydin and Jhone Chepman, bailye of the burgh for the

ties, and since most of the clergy in Selkirk were notaries, it is interesting to
see how they managed to combine several roles in order to earn a living.
The common clerk, Ninian Brydin, was said in 1532 to be in possession of a
rig of land on 'the knowe', and while there is no evidence that he farmed
this land in person, there was nothing to stop a priest devoting a major part
of his time and energy to farming. It has also been suggested that some
priests were even engaged in trade,[10] and although there is no record of this
occurring in Selkirk there is an interesting reference to a priest carrying out
manual work. In giving evidence in a hearing of a dispute over the ownership of a cupboard, John Michelhill, chaplain, gave his priestly word, 'verbis
sacerdotis', that he fitted the cupboard with locks and bands at the request
of one of the people claiming ownership.[11] He does not appear again in the
role of craftsman, so perhaps this should be regarded as an abnormal activ-
ity for a priest. Another unusual entry records the appointment of the
common clerk as an ale-conner.[12] Unless Ninian Brydin managed to carry
out this duty without the extensive ale tasting that was expected, it is
difficult to see how he could both do the job, and maintain some measure
of priestly dignity.

However, these two examples do not represent the normal role for the
clergy of Selkirk. They were very much involved in the daily life of the community, but because of their education and social standing, and their unique
relationship to the laity in religious matters, they occupied a special position. They were, in a sense, members of a professional class, and as such,
were socially different from the mass of the laity, and their special status
was even marked by distinctive dress. Chaplains were expected to wear a
gown or cassock of a dark coloured cloth, a white linen shirt and a round
bonnet (biretta). To further distinguish them from the laity they were
expected to be clean-shaven.[13] However, these distinguishing features of
appearance, education (although the education was often to a very basic
standard), skills of literacy and, commonly, legal training, would not have
brought about much social distancing in a small community. The obvious
local family connections of the majority of the Selkirk clergy must have created a sense of identity between them and the burgh, so that their social
position, like that of the wealthier members of the community, was always
subject to the checks and balances of the wide range of close personal relationships within which they had to work.

We can see from the records that the Selkirk clergy were often called
upon to act as procurators, representing litigants before the burgh court.

9...   time, and Jhone Jonsone, sir Vylliem Chapman, chapellane, David Jonsone
    with utheris divers'. The Burgh Court Book of Selkirk, 1503–1545, undated.
    See also the instruments A67 and A78 below. It was also possible for the
    notary to guide the hand of his client to form a signature on a document, as
    apparently in the writing following the instrument D71.
10.   M.H.B. Sanderson, 'Some aspects of the church', 91.
11.   The Burgh Court Book of Selkirk, 3 March 1531.
12.   The Burgh Court Book of Selkirk, 7 December 1529.
13.   D. McRoberts (ed.), Essays on the Scottish Reformation, (Glasgow 1962), 90.

They were also appointed to arbitrate between individuals in disputes,[14] and to act as oversmen (umpires) in the event of disagreement between arbiters.[15] These duties were carried out in addition to the work that many of the clergy did as notaries, but it should be noted that laymen also acted as procurators, arbiters and oversmen. However, neighbours in dispute would tend to look towards the leading men of the burgh for arbitration and advice, and it seems clear that the clergy were regarded in that light, a further pointer towards their special position in the community. The role of those clergy who were notaries involved them in almost every aspect of inter-personal relationships that were to be found in any community.

Transactions Involving Notaries

Landholding

Ownership of property, and in particular the ownership or tenancy of land, provided a force for continuity and cohesiveness, while at the same time creating opportunities for tension and disputes. Ownership or occupation of the land were such important factors in burgh life that one of the earliest burgh laws regards the burgess as 'essentially a land-holder'.[16] 'Burgage was held in chief or in subtenancy, usually for a money rent',[17] but as royal burghs developed, and became firmly established as viable communities, the definition of burgess status was widened, so that toft-holding was no longer essential, and burgesses could be created by 'admission by existing burgesses'.[18] However, in a small community like Selkirk, land tenure and the procedures, disputes and settlements over land and its use and transfer, occupied much time in the burgh court, creating professional opportunities for the burgh's notaries.

By the early sixteenth century legal custom and practice relating to land was well developed, and urban communities devoted considerable effort to monitoring and controlling its ownership and use. Land repre-sented wealth and status which was significant not only to individuals and families but also to the community at large. The orderly ownership, transfer and use of land was essential to both economic and social life, and gave

---

14. The Burgh Court Book of Selkirk, 17 November 1528. 'Ve ordand sir Villiem Chepman to declair and decerne the mater movit betuex Robert Chepman and Maiyone Almuir one Thirsday next to cum quhidder scho coft the almery in hir husbandis lyfetyme or efter'. William Chepman was a chaplain and a notary.
15. The Burgh Court Book of Selkirk, undated, but lying between the entries for 16 February 1530 and 26 April 1530. The vicar, William Brydin, who was also a notary, was appointed as oversman in a dispute between John Hawe and Thomas Minto.
16. G.S. Pryde, 'Scots burgh finances prior to 1707' (unpublished Ph.D. thesis, University of St Andrews, 1926), 109, referring to A.P.S., i, 333.
17. G.C.H. Paton (ed.) An Introduction to Scottish Legal History, (Stair Society, Edinburgh 1958), 152.
18. R.L.C. Hunter, 'Corporate personality and the Scottish burgh' in G.W.S. Barrow (ed.), The Scottish Tradition (Edinburgh 1974), 236.

stability and continuity to the community. This helps to explain the importance that was attached to the use of ritual and procedure in transactions involving land, which were matters of public interest, and such, openly dealt with.[19]

Delivery of Sasine

The public nature of the ceremony of delivery of sasine illustrates the part played by the community in witnessing transfers of land, notwithstanding the fact that individual burgage holders in a royal burgh held their lands direct of the crown, and not of the community.[20] The ceremony of delivery of sasine in burghs had two elements. First, the land was resigned by the owner, normally through a procurator, and accepted by a bailie. The bailie then gave sasine to the new owner, normally through the new owner's legal representatives. These two acts were then set down in one instrument, the instrument of sasine, evidencing completion of the new owner's right. The bailie's role was that of crown representative, and the common clerk recorded the delivery of sasine, and obtained the marks or signatures of the witnesses on each page. The common or town clerk was supposed to have the monopoly of acting as notary in sasines,[21] but it seems that other notaries could become involved. In 1565 it was necessary for the bailies and council of Peebles to order that notaries should not record infeftments without the presence of the town clerk, who would read sasine from the 'regester of the toun', so that the 'jugis for the tyme may knaw the werritte'.[22]

An important part of the ceremony of giving sasine was the delivery of symbols, which were handed by the bailie to the new proprietor on the ground in question. Sasine of houses within the burgh was represented by a hasp and staple; annualrent of lands by earth, stone and a penny piece and the ownership of lands by earth and stone.[23] No doubt the ceremony of giving sasine became a mere formality, since it was performed so often in any urban community, but because it was a public act, public opinion was always likely to be invoked in disputes over land. Sometimes sasine was a completely straightforward matter, amounting to formal completion of the

19.   *Ancient Laws and Customs of the Burghs of Scotland*, (Scottish Burgh Records Society [S.B.R.S.], Edinburgh 1868–1910), i, 54. 'Gif sesyng be geyffin in burgh befor the nychtburis of the burgh thocht it be ututh the courte na forspokyn thar in, it sall suffice wele inoch'.

20.   J. Burns, *Handbook of Conveyancing* (5th edn. reprinted, Edinburgh 1960), 223.

21.   J. Burns, *Handbook of Conveyancing*, 225.

22.   W. Chambers (ed.), *Charters and Extracts from the Records of the Burgh of Peebles, A.D. 1165–1710*, (S.B.R.S., Edinburgh 1872), i, 298–99.

23.   G. Watson (ed.), *Bell's Dictionary and Digest of the Law of Scotland* (7th edn., Edinburgh 1890), 1060. Other symbols of sasine were a staff and baton, representing resignations of lands by a vassal to a superior; clap and happer (grain hopper and its shaking mechanism) for mills; net and coble for fishings; oar and water for ferry rights; a sheaf of corn for teinds (tithes) and a psalm book and the keys of the church for the patronage of a church living.

right established by an heir to his or her land.[24] Confirmation of the existence of the right was usually simple, but occasionally it was necessary for
the burgh court to investigate a claim more fully.

In case of alienation, when property was disposed of voluntarily, completion of the right was marked by delivery of sasine to the new owner.
Charters of alienation were first drawn up, being regarded as necessary by
the burgh court before sasine could be granted.[25]

Rights in Security

The completion of rights in land by the ceremony of delivery of sasine was
not confined to ownership, but also applied to rights in security of various
kinds, particularly wadsets and reversions. In a fairly complex wadset agreement,[26] drawn up in 1535, three rigs of land in and around Selkirk were
disponed to secure a debt of three pounds. The agreement provided that if
repayment of the debt took place before a specified day the wadsetter
would pay the debtor three firlots of meal and bere (a primitive form of
barley). If the debt was not settled by the due day the three pounds still had
to be repaid, but the wadsetter, his heirs or assignees were entitled to
remain on the land for four years on payment of a rental of meal and bere.
As a final act, the wadsetter was formally given sasine of the land before
witnesses.[27]

Kindly Tenancies

The ceremony of giving sasine on the transfer of land was also associated
with the grant and transfer of 'kindly' tenancy rights. 'Kindly tenancy was
not how the tenant held but why he held',[28] and such holding was related
to the belief in the inherent rightness of possession by inheritance, usually
because of close kinship to the previous tenant. A kindly tenancy right was
sold in Selkirk on 27 June 1527 when Marion Moyes gave 'our hir kyndnes
of hir part of tenement' for the sum of eight merks.[29] Payment was to be
made in instalments, with 20s being paid at Lammas and the balance at
Beltane (1 August and 1 May respectively), and four ells of good brown
cloth immediately or at Yule, and 'ane auld curche (cap or kerchief) and
ane coller'.

---

24. The Burgh Court Book of Selkirk, 14 February 1515. The inquest found
     Elspeth Tait to be the lawful heir of William Tait, and a bailie gave her sasine.
25. The Burgh Court Book of Selkirk, 6 November 1520. The court examined a
     charter of alienation given by one burgess to another. Since both men were
     dead, sasine was given to a relative of the recipient, and another relative was
     named as heir.
26. To wadset land was to grant away land as a security for debt. The wadsetter
     held the land until the debtor settled the debt. (*Chambers Scots Dictionary*
     (1977), 649).
27. The Burgh Court Book of Selkirk, 12 October 1535.
28. M.H.B. Sanderson, *Scottish Rural Society in the Sixteenth Century* (Edinburgh
     1982), 58.
29. The Burgh Court Book of Selkirk, 27 June 1527.

Litigation and Arbitration

Burgh lands were the subject of an intricate network of ownership, tenancy and sub-tenancy, regulated by an equally complex structure of rules, traditions and custom and practice. Indeed this may be said of all aspects of urban life. Land ownership and use were governed by some nationally accepted rules, and a variety of practices that had either developed to suit particular local needs, or had been borrowed or adapted from other communities. The notary was usually a local man, and fully understood the custom and practice of his own community. In case of disputes the aim of the community, as in all matters relating to property, was to provide a forum, (the burgh court), where both parties to the dispute could put their cases, and, when circumstances demanded, a decision could be given that would settle the point at issue, if both parties were prepared to submit to the decision. Tenancy disputes often arose over failure to pay rent, and the burgh court usually tried to establish the facts by asking to see the tenancy agreements.

Notaries' protocol books sometimes also record the outcome of arbitration. Arbitration was a method frequently employed even by burgh courts as a means of settling disputes, and rules existed to ensure that a fairly standardised procedure was followed. Arbiters were appointed by a court as 'jugis and amycabill compositouris', or by the parties to a dispute. To avoid deadlock an odd number of arbiters was considered most suitable,[30] but in practice it appears that four arbiters were usually appointed, sometimes with an oversman supervising their deliberations and where necessary giving the casting vote.

Because arbitration commanded respect as a method of dealing with potentially disruptive breakdowns in inter-personal relationships in a calm and socially acceptable manner, one can appreciate why communities took care to follow established rules and procedures, and why care was taken to select arbiters of good reputation and standing, and, in particular, to appoint suitable oversmen. Thus, we may find the clergy and sometimes local lairds acting as oversmen.

Recording of Transactions

On the basis of the evidence from burgh court records and notaries' protocol books, it would be possible to imagine that litigation was the most popular pastime in urban communities of the sixteenth century, and that inter-personal relationships were marked only by disagreement. There is no doubt that the pattern of urban life, based on trade and barter, with the ownership of property being of such importance to the stability and prosperity of both families and the community, was bound to give rise to the need for procedures for dealing with disputes, but it is also likely that many business arrangements were settled amicably, without recourse to any form

---

30.   Lord Cooper (ed.), *Regiam Majestatem and Quoniam Attachiamenta*, (Stair Society, Edinburgh 1947), 108. 'Submissions should be made to an odd and not an even number of arbiters...for God delights in odd numbers'.

of public discussion or decision-making by a public forum such as a burgh court. It is also apparent from the evidence that many matters brought before the courts with the aid of notaries were not matters in dispute, but were made public in order to record the details of agreements or to acknowledge indebtedness.

Procuratories

Despite familiarity with the traditions and procedures which governed the various aspects of inter-personal relationships, people would commonly choose to appoint procurators to act on their behalf, rather than appear in person to argue cases. Sometimes the procurator was a priest, who was likely to be literate, and who probably also practised as a notary. It is worth noting that communities might attempt to curb the use of professional lawyers as procurators except in inheritance cases, because of fears about 'outside' influences.[31]

Marriage Contracts

Another significant task for the notary was to draw up marriage contracts and settlements. Kinship ties were of great importance to the social and economic life of the Borders, and family connections were as significant in the life of a burgh as clan loyalties were to the highlander. Apart from this aspect of loyalty to a family name or kinship group, which was to some extent matched in the burghs by a wider loyalty to the community and its interests, it is also true to say that family connections were closely bound up with the ownership of land, property and money. Families with land and property saw the marriage contract or marriage settlement as a opportunity for consolidating and increasing family wealth and power.

Marriage contracts were also concerned with land, indeed it has been said that 'half or more of the lands in Scotland were held under marriage contracts at the end of the nineteenth century',[32] which suggests that the ownership of land and its significance to family relationships remained as a major factor well into the modern period. The fact that land was transferred in this way in urban communities reminds us that townsfolk were often farmers as well as craftmen or merchants. This was particularly true of a small burgh like Selkirk where many of the inhabitants farmed land both inside and outside the confines of the burgh. In Selkirk, as in all other burghs, land ownership conferred wealth, and consequently power and status on its owners, and the records provide evidence that land was not

---

31. *Extracts from the Records of the Burgh of Peebles*, (S.B.R.S., 1872), i, 215–16. 'No neighbours shall solicit or cause men of law to come to act as procurators one against another for whatsoever action, except brieves of heritage only, under pain of losing their freedom for ever'. W.C. Dickinson, in 'Burgh life from burgh records', *Aberdeen University Review* xxi, (1944–46), 214 at p. 217 suggests that the burgh community saw 'outsider' lawyers in much the same light as local lairds or the nobility – a threat to the established power hierarchy of the burgh.

32. G.C.H. Paton (ed.), *An Introduction to Scottish Legal History*, 114.

necessarily farmed by its owners, but was sometimes let out to provide a cash income. So important was land to the wealth and continuity of families that land transfer as a result of marriage contracts was, perhaps, the most important part of any contract, and this gave added significance to the role of the notary in arranging and recording these agreements.

Wills and Inheritance

Finally, in this brief review of the part played by the notary in sixteenth century communities, there is the important area of wills and inheritance.

Much of the evidence on succession by inheritance contained in protocol books refers to moveable goods, which, unlike land, could be the subject of testaments, and appear in the documentary sources in the form of inventories. Sometimes the records provide examples of succession to heritable property,[33] mainly land, and we also find frequent references to heirship goods, which passed to the heir rather than the executor to ensure that the heir did not inherit an empty house, shop or farm without the means to live and work.

This evidence can be looked on as a valuable source of material about domestic property and furnishings, which gives us an insight into domestic life, as well as providing an impression of the relative wealth of individuals. It may also be seen as a source of information about inter-personal relationships in an aspect of daily life which was of great importance to individuals, and as suggested above, continuity and stability could flow outwards from the family to the community itself. Because the community had an interest in individual inheritance, it tended to involve itself publicly in ways that were both practical and symbolic. The rights of heirs were established in the sight of the community, often before the burgh courts.[35] Disputes over land and goods were aired publicly, and agreements about the division of property were reached openly, with neighbours acting as witnesses. Inventories of goods were recorded so that all were able to know what was involved, and the interests of children in inheritance were protected by the community.[36]

33. D.M. Walker, *The Oxford Companion to Law* (Oxford 1980), 564. Heritable property normally passed undivided to the owner's male heir, whereas moveable property passed to the executor for division among the next of kin.

34. M.H.B. Sanderson, *Scottish Rural Society in the Sixteenth Century* (Edinburgh 1982), 172.

35. M. Bateson (ed.), *Borough Customs* (London 1906), ii, p. cxxxviii. Although referring to English borough courts, the observation is also valid for Scotland. 'That the will should be made known in the borough court was desirable for the sake of publicity and certainty of record, and, when land was devised, to secure delivery of seisin in court'.

36. The Burgh Court Book of Selkirk, 5 June 1515. The burgh court found that a 'barne of Robert Gillies that was producit in curt nerest and lauchful ayr to hir fader'. In another example, from 30 April 1533, the court book records that Janet Fairle was found to be the lawful heir of her father, tha late John Fairle, the younger, but it was decided to postpone a final decision until 'discretfull men of law' advised whether or not Adam Fairle was heir to his niece, Janet. On 20 May 1533 the judgement was given that Adam Fairle was 'naixt and lau-

Cases of disputed succession sometimes took many months to settle, providing welcome regular income for the notaries involved. A graphic illustration of such a case relates to the estate of John Brydin, priest and notary of Selkirk, whose protocol book for the years 1530 to 1537 is contained in this volume, and whose testament is referred to later in this introduction. In July 1539 James Scot and his wife disputed a tenement of land left by the priest, claiming that it was theirs, and not the property of another John Brydin, a priest of Glasgow. Brydin was represented in his absence by George Tait, and Scot chose as his procurator another Scot. Later in July Scot and his party agreed to accept the common clerk, Ninian Brydin, as clerk in the case, a decision, perhaps, made necessary by the clerk's kinship to Scot's adversary. On 2 December 1539 there was further discussion of the case in the burgh court, with an argument put forward by George Tait that he should be accepted as John Brydin's procurator, and that the common clerk, and other court officers, should take part in the proceedings. James Scot countered this argument by objecting to the presence of the common clerk and the dempster.[37] Finally, another Tait, this time Alexander, appearing as procurator for John Brydin, agreed to the decision of the bailies, (John Mithag and another John Brydin), that the case should be heard in fifteen days, with all members of the court being chosen by the bailies. When the court met again within fifteen days, yet another Brydin, this time William, vicar of Selkirk, appeared as procurator for John Brydin to answer a complaint from the Scot family about Brydin's failure to attend court. William Brydin explained to the court that Brydin could not travel from Glasgow because 'all the vatteris are of flud', and the case was continued. The case came before the court again on 20 January 1540, and James Scot agreed to the composition of the court. The matter was finally settled before the burgh court on 27 January 1540 when John Brydin of Glasgow was found to be the nearest and lawful heir to John Brydin of Selkirk, the proof being found in the protocol book of William Brydin, who was a notary as well as being the vicar of Selkirk.

Transactions outside Selkirk

Although the Selkirk protocol books often deal with matters affecting the burgh of Selkirk and its inhabitants, there are also frequent entries that make it clear that the Selkirk notaries had many clients outside the burgh. In a case heard before the Selkirk Sheriff court on 1 June 1535, John Michelhill and Ninian Brydin acted as notaries in a case between some of the leading landowning families of the Borders, Hume and Douglas on the one side and Rutherford on the other.[38] Other landowning names appear frequently, for

---

36... full air to his broder dochter, Jenot Fairlie, quhilk vas air to Jhone Fairle, yonger'.
37.   The dempster, or deemster, was an officer of a court responsible for pronouncing the 'dooms' or judgements of a court.
38.   The Protocol Book of John Brydin, 1530–1537, D99–101. This case was clearly an important one, and involved a procurator acting for 'Margaret, Queen of Scots, lady of Ettrick Forest, and her spouse Henry, laird of Methven'.

example the family of Hoppringill (later to become the Pringles), were regular clients of the Selkirk notaries, using them to conduct land transactions, as well as more unusual business.[39] The notaries can be seen to have travelled widely within the central Borders, visiting clients in their homes, and conducting business for them there or in the local church or chapel. Two inventories of the goods of deceased Selkirk notaries of the sixteenth century survive. Both inventories refer to horses or saddlery, suggesting that clients were not only to be found in the burgh. The notary James Johnson, also described as a priest, left spurs, saddle and bridle, as well as sword and buckler and a whinger or short sword.[40] John Brydin, referred to above, left a horse and other goods to Robert Brydin his nephew, out of which his natural daughter, Margaret Brydin was to receive twenty merks and his 'goods and gear, the heirship excepted'.[41]

Selkirk and the Sixteenth Century Burgh

The life and work of the Selkirk notaries must be seen in the context of the sixteenth century burgh. It is necessary to see Selkirk within the context of this general setting of the smaller royal burghs of the early sixteenth century. It shared a number of common features with other burghs in terms of economic function, trading privileges and the special position of burgesses. It dominated trade in its landward area and operated as a marketing centre. It was of use to the crown as a source of revenue and when the need arose, as a source of military manpower.

Although Peebles had a larger population and because of its location was less vulnerable to English attack, and although Jedburgh was more significant as an administrative centre, Selkirk was a border burgh of some importance to the crown. It was used by James V as a wool depot for the annual clip from his flocks in the Ettrick Forest and it shared with Peebles the rather doubtful privilege of being used as a meeting place for levies of troops raised to suppress the unruly parts of the Borders.[42] In most respects it was a typical border burgh, apart from the extent of its common lands, which were perhaps the largest in the country.

39. The Protocol Book of John Brydin, Ninian Brydin and others, 1526–1536, C95. The banns of marriage between a Rutherford and a Hoppringle were challenged in the chapel of Galashiels by Adam Rutherford, burgess of Jedburgh. This challenge led to the production of a dispensation from Rome, allowing the marriage to take place despite the two parties being 'within the prohibited bands of consanguinity'.

40. P.S.M. Symms, 'Social control in a sixteenth century burgh: a study of the Burgh Court Book of Selkirk, 1503–1545', (unpublished Ph.D. thesis, University of Edinburgh, 1986), appendix xi, 434.

41. In P.S.M. Symms, 'Social control in a sixteenth century burgh', appendix xi, 435–436. This cites an unpublished manuscript, now in the Walter Mason collection, which records the inventory of the property of John Brydin, priest and notary public in Selkirk.

42. D.L.W. Tough, *The Last Years of a Frontier* (Oxford 1928), 19. Peebles and Selkirk were seen as suitable places for levies to meet. Jedburgh was 'well inhabited and frequented', and Kelso and Hawick were described as 'towns of some importance'.

Selkirk is thought to have grown up as a settlement to serve the needs of Selkirk Castle, which was built for David, Earl of Huntingdon, on a good defensive site beside the Haining Loch.[43] By June 1328 the sheriff of Selkirk accounted to the exchequer for rent due from free tenants and burgesses,[44] and Pryde dates Selkirk's existence as a royal burgh from this exchequer roll-entry.[45] In fact, the burgh was simply a king's burgh during its early life, a title denoting that it stood on royal land and paid rent to the crown. The term *burgus regalis* or royal burgh, began to be used in the fifteenth century to distinguish between royal foundations and burghs of barony.[46] By the sixteenth century, when Selkirk's status as a royal burgh was confirmed by James V,[47] the community had survived the Wars of Independence, and the decline and eventual ruin of Selkirk Castle. The burgh was burned during an English raid in 1418[48] and again in 1502 by a raiding party of English and Scots led by Sir John Musgrave.[49]

The first half of the sixteenth century was not an easy time for the community, which was relatively poor and under-populated, and economically weak compared with some of the larger and wealthier burghs. During this period the burgh continued to face the effects of war, sharing with all communities the impact of the battle of Flodden in 1513, as well as further English raiding. The extent and nature of the common land gave rise to almost continuous disputes with the burgh's neighbours, plague and animal disease periodically threatened its stability and economy, and an increasing burden of taxation affected most burgesses and indwellers, even those who might have been considered too poor to pay by other communities. Against this difficult background the burgh was able to remain a viable community, with a rich and vigorous social life, and a strong sense of community identity which comes out clearly from the evidence contained in the burgh court records and the protocol books of the Selkirk notaries.

The Population of Selkirk

Selkirk was a small community, even in the context of the low population density of the Borders. It has been estimated that the total population of the Middle Marches was around 20,000, compared with over 10,000 for the Eastern Marches and 14,000 for the Western Marches.[50] These figures can

43.   J.W. Elliot and J. Gilbert, 'The early Middle Ages', in J. Gilbert (ed.), *Flower of the Forest; Selkirk; a new history*, (Galashiels 1985), 25.
44.   J. Stuart and others (eds.), *The Exchequer Rolls of Scotland* (Edinburgh 1878–1908), i, 105.
45.   G.S. Pryde, *The Burghs of Scotland: A Critical List* (London 1965), 21.
46.   J.W. Elliot and J. Gilbert, 'The Early Middle Ages', in *Flower of the Forest*, 27.
47.   J.M. Thomson and others (eds.), *Registrum Magni Sigilli Regum Scotorum* (Edinburgh 1882–1914), iii, 1555.
48.   T. Craig-Brown, *The History of Selkirkshire, or Chronicles of the Ettrick Forest* (Edinburgh 1886), ii, 13.
49.   R. Pitcairn (ed.), *Criminal Trials in Scotland from 1488–1624* (Edinburgh 1833), i, *35.
50.   D.L.W. Tough, *The Last Years*, 28. Tough's estimates of population are for the year 1600, and should be seen against his estimate of a population of 600,000 for Scotland as a whole.

only be regarded as guesses, and must therefore be treated with some caution. The same caution is necessary when attempting to arrive at a population estimate for Selkirk. The best evidence for this comes from taxation records, but certain assumptions are usually made about taxation roll estimates which do not necessarily apply to Selkirk. For example, two writers on Edinburgh have taken figures from taxation rolls and based their calculation on indications that approximately 30% of householders were burgesses,[51] or that males predominate on the tax rolls and that those listed make up some 30% of the adult male population.[52] A multiplier is then applied to arrive at an estimate of the total population.[53] From the evidence of the Selkirk taxation rolls it appears that the proportion of people paying tax, although often at a very low rate, was perhaps higher than in Edinburgh. If 50% of the population were burgesses and paid tax the figure of 110 burghal tenures cited for 1426,[54] using a multiplier of 4.5 persons per household, produces a population figure of 990. This would seem to be somewhat high, and it may be that more than 50% of the population paid tax in this community. The stent rolls continued in the burgh court book provide the following totals of names:–

January 1521	122 names
3 March 1531	86 names
22 April 1535	118 names
20 July 1535	123 names
17 March 1536	117 names
9 April 1538	126 names
6 September 1539	153 names

51.   M. Lynch, *Edinburgh and the Reformation* (Edinburgh 1981), 10.
52.   J.J. Brown, 'The social political and economic influence of the Edinburgh merchant elite' (unpublished Ph.D. thesis, University of Edinburgh, 1985), 12.
53.   Opinions vary as to the size of the multiplier that should be used to represent the average number of people per household. In a chapter entitled 'Poverty and urban development in early modern Europe', Thomas Riis claims that analysis of population figures for cities compared with smaller towns and the countryside shows that the cities tend to have smaller households than the towns, and the towns smaller households than the countryside. He cites the example of Florence where the ratio of people to hearths rose from 4.19 in 1380 to 6.21 in 1552, suggesting that household size does not remain constant but is influenced by the economic situation, the effect of epidemics and by the political climate (Thomas Riis (ed.), *Aspects of Poverty in Early Modern Europe* (Florence 1981), 6). Susan Reynolds in *An Introduction to the History of English Medieval Towns* (Oxford 1977), 36 cites a multiplier of 'about 5' used by H.C. Darby and his colleagues in calculating the population of a town from the number of burgesses (H.C. Darby and others (eds.), *The Domesday Geographies of England* (Cambridge 1954–1967)) . A multiplier of 4.75 is used by T.P.R. Laslett in 'Size and structure of the household in England over three centuries', *Population Studies* xxiii, no.2 (1969), 207, 211, whilst D.V. Glass and D.E.C. Eversley suggest a figure of 4.2 in *Population in History: Essays in Historical Demography* (London 1965), 177. In the light of all this advice, a multiplier of 4.5 has been used to calculate the likely population of Selkirk.
54.   S.G.E. Lythe and J. Butt, *An Economic History of Scotland 1100–1939* (Glasgow 1975), 5.

The last stent roll was prefaced by the words 'Ane stent cassyne throu all the communite',[55] and using the multiplier of 4.5, this produces a population figure of 688. There are two more lists of names in the burgh court records which may represent all householders, rather than just taxpayers. The first, dated 25 May 1513, is headed with the words *'Communitas burgi de Selkyrk'* and contains 160 names, which gives a population figure of 720, and the second, undated but appearing after an entry for 6 October 1523, has 180 names, which suggests a population of 810. It would, therefore, seem reasonable to suggest that Selkirk had a population of between 700 and 800 during the first half of the sixteenth century.

Occupations

This population followed the wide variety of trades and occupations typical of the smaller burghs, in which burgesses and indwellers combined their urban occupations with the rural work of growing crops and raising livestock. The burgh was largely self-sufficient in simple manufactured goods such as clothing, footwear, tools, implements and weapons, with the relatively unsophisticated needs of a small community being met by local craftsmen. As inventories show, it was possible to find luxury items in some households, and these were not produced locally, but were from the larger burghs or from abroad.[56] The burgh's food supplies came from the produce of individual holdings of land both inside and outwith the perimeter dykes, and from grazings on the extensive common lands. Food was also brought in from the burgh's hinterland, to be bought and sold in the weekly market, and at fair days, which also gave the burgesses a chance to trade with a wider area, and to buy specialist and luxury items brought in from further afield.

Selkirk and the Surrounding Countryside

The fact that the community was largely self-sufficient was related to the economic base of burgh life being built on this mixture of trade and agriculture. It is possible to see Selkirk as an isolated pocket of urban life surrounded by an alien and often hostile rural area, but such a view fails to take account of the way in which the life of the burgh was closely linked with the life of the countryside. Outside the burghs, 'these little scattered, vigorous, contentious and monopolising towns, lay the open country',[57] but it was a countryside that was understood and used by the townsman in ways that would only disappear with the advent of large-scale industrialisation. The life and work of the Selkirk notaries was closely integrated into this 'vigorous and contentious' community, and into its network of relationships with the surrounding countryside, and it is this integration that makes these documents valuable new sources in our understanding of sixteenth century communities.

---

55.   The Burgh Court Book of Selkirk, 6 September 1539.
56.   A number of Selkirk inventories include luxury items. An inventory dated 8 November 1534 refers to a carved bed, probably imported, and a 'Flanders counter with the formes,' which was probably a counting table.
57.   J. Clapham, *A Concise Economic History of Britain* (Cambridge 1957), 149.

Book A
The Protocol Book of John Chepman, 1511–36, 1545–47.

[In left margin of page one "liber d[omi]n[u]s Jo. Haw [et] d[omi]n[u]s Jo. Chepman".]

1.   No title, no date. Fragment of a sample style of appointment of procurators.

2.   No title. No date. Fragment of an instrument narrating that John Bulman resigns his tenement of land with pertinents from himself, his heirs [and assignees] in favour of William Mayne in the hands of George Scot bailie of Selkirk, requesting the bailie to give heritable state, sasine and possession of the said tenement to William Mayne personally present and accepting by delivery of earth [and stones] according to the tenor of a charter of the said John shown and delivered before to the said William. Before witnesses Thomas Jhonson, [?Robert] Chepman, John Cadzow, William Lermont, Nicholas Hendirsone, (p/t) Lawson.

3.   No title. 28 [Oct? 1511.] (p/t) that on the 10 November (p/t) to his kirk of Selkirk in the hands (p/t) made clear in a certain instrument on behalf of the said master [Walter?] (p/t) on the ninth day from the date of these presents the said master Walter resigns, renounces and solemnly demits all ownership and possession he has, had or will have in or to the clerkship of the said kirk of Selkirk. Witnesses Robert Dwne, master William Ker.

4.   ***Dowglass*** 23 Nov 1511 ...before me notary public and witnesses underwritten, Charles Dowglass not moved by force or fallen in error but of his own pure and spontaneous will resigns demits and renounces forever all ownership and possession which he has, had or will have to clerkship of the parish kirk of Bowdene in the hands of (p/t) and that in the same resignation, demission and renunciation fraud, guile, simony, persuasion ["labes"] or preference ["convens"] was not [committed?] about which James Dowglass son (p/t) for his interest asked instrument or instruments from me notary public. Done at the kirk of Bowdene around 11 am... before Andrew (p/t), sir Nycolas Ker, master Adam Scot vicar of B[owden?], and Thomas Ruthirfurd, etc.

And I John Chepman priest of Glasgow (p/t) the said resignation, renunciation and demission (p/t) all and whole being done, seen, understood and heard (p/t) as this present instrument written in my own hand (p/t) reduced into the form of a public instrument, signed and (p/t) in faith and witness of the abovewritten.

5.   Fragment of an instrument narrating that the clerkship [of the parish of
      Bowdene?] with effect was given to the young man James [Dowglass]
      (p/t) Charles [Dowglass] which clerkship the said Charles resigned on
      the 23rd day of November year as above as was shown before me
      notary public in the hands of the [procurators "prorourum"] of the
      same and resigns and demits all right and claim, ownership and pos-
      session in favour of the said James, of which a note follows. Witnesses
      Andrew Ker of Sesfurd, sir Nycolas Ker, William Armstrong, Thomas
      (p/t), Andrew Bannantyn.

6.   *Huntar* (p/t) March 1511/12 Before me notary public and witnesses
      underwritten, Elizabeth Huntar relict of the deceased [Thomas] Huntar
      of Wilyemlaw, put into the hands of the notary a certain letter of asse-
      dation of the venerable man in Christ Barnard Bell, by divine permis-
      sion lord abbot of Melrose, and his monks written on parchment and
      sealed with the common seal of that place without erasures (p/t) or
      spoilt in any part as appeared on first sight, to read out and make
      public and with mature understanding the said Elizabeth...with con-
      sent of her [firstborn] son, Robert Huntar, gave the said letter of asse-
      dation to her [sons] James Huntar and William Huntar in these words
      "You are my boys ["pueri"] and for the filial [love] which I bear you
      make and ordain you my true and lawful assignees in all and whole
      the terms and years contained in the letter of assedation made to the
      deceased Thomas Huntar my spouse and to me (p/t) after my
      decease". James and William asked instrument. Done at Yare at 1 pm
      before [William] Ker rector of Lindene, William Ker in Yare elder,
      William Ker in Selkirk, Robert Ramsa in Wylecleucht, Andrew
      Ormstoun, William Bannantyn.

7.   Same day. (p/t) brother-german (p/t) bind (p/t) for Elizabeth Huntar
      relict [of the deceased Thomas Huntar] (p/t) regarding the possession
      of her terce (p/t) for her lifetime undisturbed (p/t). [Elizabeth] asked
      instrument or instruments. Done at the place of Yair in the hall of the
      same around 1 pm before witnesses William Ker rector of Lindene,
      William Ker in Yair elder, William Ker in Selkirk, Robert Ramsay in
      Wylescleucht, Andrew Ormston, (p/t) Ormston and William
      Bannantyne.

8.   *Ker* 8, 9, 11 Feb 15 [11/12 – eighth indiction of Julius II] It was clearly
      shown to me notary public that (p/t) relict of the deceased John Furd,
      Gilbert Furd, Isabella Furd, (?) Furd (blank) children of the said
      deceased (p/t) declare that they are content and paid of the sum of 50
      (p/t) from William Ker in Yair...and the same William Ker debtor and
      surety for the deceased Ralph Ker (p/t) through amicable agreement
      concerning the cruel murder of the said (p/t). About which William
      Ker asked instrument. Done on the grounds of Yair and le
      Cawfschaws within the land of W(p/t) around 3 pm on the 8th, (p/t)
      on the 9th and 2 pm on the 11th day before Thomas Hoppringill, (p/t)

in Torwodlie, William Hoppringill in (p/t) chaplain, Roger Hoppringill, William Bannantyn.

9. Fragment of an instrument narrating that (illegible) Melross gives his younger son for the sake of filial love that he has for him his [moveable and immoveable?] goods and that they should be delivered after the decease of the said Marion. Thomas Melrose asked instrument before (p/t) Chepman, Robert Chepman, John Chepman, James Chepman, (p/t) Chepman and Janet Scot.

10. *Murraye* (p/t) April 1512 (p/t) [John] Murray of Fawlahill came to the principal dwellinghouse of 2 [husband]lands with pertinents lying in the town and land of Bold and within the sheriffdom of Peebles and there presented a precept of sasine of our supreme lord king...under testimony of his great seal in hands of William Hair bailie...and for the execution of the same precept...the notary made a sworn copy as follows: (illegible) and to his bailies of Peebles and Selkirk also...to William Hair and Thomas Cogburn and (illegible) of Peebles and Selkirk in that part...greetings. (illegible) to our lovit John Murray of Fawlahill all the husbandlands of Bold with pertinents (p/t) of old extent lying in the sheriffdom of Peebles with (the next part of the deed is missing or badly decayed)...after our recognition made before to the said (p/t) from William Cogburn and John Murray and all others [contained] in our letter of citation to hear (illegible) the said lands to pertain to us by reason of forfeiture...and handed over by the lords of council all the said lands pertaining to us and [returned] to our possession by our own free will as was proven clearly by [the lords of council?] as is contained in the earlier decreet made before to the said John...and we command you (p/t) John Murray or his lawful attorney to take [sasine] of the said lands of Bold and of Phillophauch with pertinents [called] Quhitlawislandes according to the tenor of our said charter made from us...without delay...from our [bailies] of Selkirk and Peebles in that part...(p/t) under testimony of the great seal at Edinburgh, (p/t) March 1510 and of our reign xxiii [1510/11]. After reading out and making public the said precept, William Hair bailie in that part, delivered earth and stones on the ground of the said lands to John Murray personally present and according to the tenor of his charter, saving the right of anyone. Witnesses George Dikesone, John (p/t), (p/t) Scot, Alexander Tait of Pyrne.

11. Fragment of an instrument narrating that [Stephen Lauder] burgess of the burgh of Selkirk presented a precept of sasine written on parchment and with [red] and white seals appended of [John Lord Hay] of Yester to [David Broun] bailie in that part requesting him to execute the same and the said David took it and handed it to me notary public to read out as follows: John Lord Hay of Yester and baron of the barony of Oliverscastell to John Cokburn, William Gresoune, Thomas Paterson, Simon Geddes and David Broun and whomsoever of them

jointly and severally, my bailies in that part specially constituted greetings, we have given and granted to Stephen Lauder burgess of the
burgh of Selkirk all the lands of Todrig with the manor and dwelling
house thereof and pertinents lying in the said barony of Olivercastell
in the sheriffdom of Selkirk as is more fully contained in his charter
made before. Therefore we charge you jointly and severally and firmly
command you...without delay to give heritable state sasine and possession...of the lands etc to the said Stephen or his lawful attorney
according to the tenor of the charter, saving the rights of
anyone...which was done under testimony of the seal of these presents at Edinburgh (p/t) Aug 1512. After the same was read out [the
bailie gave sasine of the same to Stephen Lauder]. Witnesses Richard
Lauder, John Reid, William Reid, (?) Schortreid, Thomas Robson.

12. 27 (p/t) Patrick Elphinstone [procurator] (p/t) of the diocese and university of St Andrews (p/t) of Morbottill (illegible) to these stalls
["stalli"] [before] master George Ker canon of Glasgow (p/t) and
diverse others.

13. *Ker* 26 July [1514?] [George] Ker vicar of Morbottill instituted and
invested master [Thomas] Ker in and to the archdeaconry of
Teviotdale by handing him the chalice and other priestly vestments at
the kirk of Morbottil before witnesses William Ker of Corbethouse,
Robert Ker, Alan (p/t), Robert Alexander, William Spenss, Thomas
Tailyor.

14. *Ker* 2 Aug [1514?] master Thomas Ker (p/t) protested that his removal
from the choir of Glasgow should not turn to his hurt because of his
obediences and divine services [performed] by him in his right and
claim to the Archdeaconry of Teviotdale before witnesses Patrick
Colquhoune rector of Stobo, master Martin Reid (p/t), [master Thomas]
Forsyth, sir Alan Smyth, sir Thomas Smyth, sir William Hammilton,
William Cunynghame of Craganis.

15. *Ker* 6 Aug [1514?] George Ker... constitutes masters William Ker and
Thomas Ker...principal intromitters with his goods [to dispose of
them] as they wish...before David Patersone.

16. Fragment of an instrument, date missing [*temp.* Pope Leo but year not
known] narrating that master George Ker canon of Glasgow and
prebendary of [Morebattle] of his own free will constitutes and ordains
Angelus of Censis, Barnard of Bartonis, James Cortesius, Thomas
Midri, John Hay, Adam (?)sone, William Lame...his procurators in all
writings, acts and special and general messengers...and in appointing
as depute and assignee his brother-german [Thomas Ker?] to the
canonical prebend of auldroxburgh with future succession to the same
in the event of his decease. Done at the house of the said master
[George Ker] between 11 and 12 am before (p/t) Ker, Thomas Ker
clerk, George Ker, James Ker.

17. **Ker** 21 Nov 1514 George Ker [son] of the deceased James Ker of Lynton appoints [master Thomas] Ker canon of Glasgow his procurator and assignee of the fruits and profits of the archdeaconry of Teviotdale [by letter of] assedation made to him from master Thomas (p/t) of Morbottill. Witnesses Thomas Scot, James Elwand.

18. **Elwand** 27 July 1516 Dispensation to marry within the prohibited bounds of consanguinity in the fourth degree, given by master Thomas Ker, [Arch]deacon of Teviotdale to Ingran Elwand and Elizabeth Scot before witnesses Thomas Scot, Alexander Scot and (p/t).

19. **Sandelandes** 20 July 1517 Fragment of a dispensation to marry given by master Thomas Ker. Witnesses George Ormston, William (p/t), and Thomas Dickinson.

20. **Ormston** Sept 1517 Dispensation to marry within prohibited bounds of consanguinity in the fourth degree, given by master Thomas Ker archdeacon of Teviotdale to George Ormston and Elizabeth Scot before witnesses master George Ker canon of Glasgow, George Ker of Lynton, Gilbert Furd and John Ker.

21. [4] April 1518 Thomas Dikesone [son of] Thomas Dikesone of Ormstoune and heir apparent of the same, came to the principal dwelling house of Ormstoune and there broke a certain sasine of the lands of Ormstoune formerly given to (p/t) Dickson second born son of the said Thomas...declaring that the said sasine given before should not prejudice him in his enjoyment or his heirs in time to come. Witnesses John Sandelandis, Adam Bennet, George Vache, (p/t) Robeson, John Mur, Richard Wat, James Steile.

22. **Watson** Sept 1513 (*sic*) John Watsone son and heir of Archebald Watsone burgess in Selkirk, came to a tenement...between the lands of William Patersone elder on the east and (p/t) on the west and there of his own free will, resigned one and a half rigs with "le Mabillis" (p/t) to one of the bailies who...gave sasine to James Watsone before William Trumbill, John Caidzow, James Hall, James Murray, (?) Hall, John Portus, John Hall, Thomas Brydyn, Thomas Portus and James (?).

23. **Ker** 19 June 1518 master George Ker canon of Glasgow [presented] a certain letter of acquittance of Margaret, Queen of Scots [written] as follows: " Regina, we grant ws to haif fra oure servand Master George Ker in the Farnele [the sum] of auchtene pundis and five shillings of our maile of the said (p/t) and discharges the said Master George of all the (p/t) this present wrytt subscrivit wyth oure hand at Ed[inburgh] the xxiiii day of September in the yeir of God 15 (p/t). Margaret R". Witnesses master Richard Bothwell rector of Askirk, sir (p/t), sir William Braidfut, William Hoppringill.

24. **Doby** 31 May 1516 Fragment narrating that John Doby rector of
     Ankrum (p/t) for the works by the said master (p/t) to the same John
     for the said master (p/t) and this on his own confession. Witnesses sir
     David Scot vicar of [Ashkirk], Alexander Robertoun, sir Andrew
     Chrystyson, Mungo (p/t). Done around 2 pm [in the house of] the
     said master John in Glesgw.

25. **Hoppringill** May 1516 Dispensation to marry within the prohibited
     bounds of consanguinity in the third and fourth degree, given by
     master Thomas Ker Archdeacon of Teviotdale to Adam Hoppringill
     and Janet Dalgless before witnesses master George Ker canon of
     Glasgow, sir John Ker and Herbert Hoppringill.

26. **Davisone** Same day May 1516 Dispensation to marry within the pro-
     hibited bounds of consanguinity given by master Thomas Ker
     archdeacon of Teviotdale to (?) Davisone and Janet Hoppringill.
     Witnesses as above.

27. **Ker** (?) June 1518 ["in the same year" i.e. 1516 scored out]. Fragment
     referring to master Thomas Ker who appealed to [James?] by divine
     permission Archbishop of Glasgow before witnesses master James
     Steward canon of M[oravia?], Robert [Elphinstoun] rector of Kincardine,
     John Reid, James Neilsone James (p/t), sir Robert Hill, Robert Durens,
     William Hoppringill, William Tait.

28. **Ker** 28 July 1516 Fragment mentioning master Thomas Ker, master
     Thomas Couttis and witnesses John Keyne, Thomas Tulcis.

29. **Ker** 7 Dec 1517 (p/t) Ker of Lynton declared that he was compelled
     by royal letters to desist from intromitting with and receiving the rents
     and lands of (p/t) and Wester Blaklawis, protesting that the same
     should not prejudice him from pursuing his right and claim at a con-
     venient time and place. Witnesses Andrew Ker of Farnell, (p/t)
     Ruthirfurd of Hundalee, George Dowgless of Bonjedward, Lancelot
     Ker, William Davidsone, Adam Ruthirfurd, Cristall Davidsone.

30. **Ker** 7 Dec 1517 master Thomas Ker Archdeacon of Teviotdale procu-
     rator for master [George Ker?] canon of Glasgow, compeared and
     declared that the said act [or deed] was between George Ker of Lynton
     and Robert Ker of Sundirlandhaw and Robert Ker in Selkirk (p/t) it
     should not prejudice him in respect of his right and claim and that he
     was not called to the said courts, before witness above.

     [Same day] George Ker of Lynton affixed the seal of master George
     [Ker of auldrox]burgh to the said letter of assedation. Witnesses James
     Ker, master Thomas Ker, William Hoppringill, (?) Bradfut.

31. **Ker** 6 May 1516 master [George] Ker prebendary of Auldroxburgh and
     rector ‧ of the parish kirk of Thankartoun in the diocese of
     Glasgow...appointed, created and ordained his true undoubted and

lawful actors, factors and managers of all his transactions underwritten and messengers special and general viz. the venerable men masters and sirs Andrew Sybald canon of Glasgow, Andrew Marschell prebendary of Moffat, Stephen Douglass [commissary] of Teviotdale absent and present...so that...he may resign, renounce and demit his rectory of Thankartoun to the reverend in Christ and lord archbishop James of the diocese of Glasgow purely and simply...all fraud and guile...excluded... (illegible) and for whatever reason...he might have in the future...and they bind themselves [under pain of] their moveable and immoveable goods present and to come. George Ker asked instrument or instruments. Done at Farnilee before witnesses Andrew Elwand, Robert Ker, Robert Boyd.

32. **Haw** (p/t) June 1519 John Jhonsone procurator in the name of Janet Robesone spouse of Thomas Robesone declared that on Tuesday [9?] June 1519, Janet Robesone had provided evidents viz. a charter and sasine of a tenement now occupied by the said Thomas [Henresone?] before the bailies of Selkirk and the bailies had assigned to the said Thomas Henresone on Tuesday 15 next immediately following to produce the evidents he has for the tenement the said day coming and the bailies sitting...the said Thomas did not produce evidents to defend his claim. John Jhonson asked instrument. Done in the court house of Selkirk around 11 before witnesses Andrew Ker of Primsydlocht, Robert Ker in Selkirk, Stephen Lauder, sir David Chapman, Alexander Scot, Thomas Jhonson, Thomas Jhonson.

33. **Baillies and Community of Selkirk** On the same day, Andrew Ker of Primsydloucht of his own free will...came to his mill of Hadirle and there he resigned the said mill with "le bullis heucht" and other pertinents, by delivery of earth and stones, delivered the mill with all its pertinents to Robert Ker procurator and in the name of the burgh of Selkirk, heirs and assignees forever the said bailies and community rendering 24 merks usual money at the terms of [Whitsunday and Martinmas]. Done at the mill of Hadirle around 3 pm before sir David Chepman, Alexander Scot, Adam Wilkeson, Thomas Wilkeson, John Sanderson, Thomas Portuus, Alexander Gray, Symone Farle, Alan Keyne, Richard Robeson.

34. **Ker** Same day and witnesses. Robert Ker of Selkirk procurator in the name of [the whole] community of Selkirk, promised the foresaid Andrew Ker he would not set in tack the [said] mill without his consent. Andrew Ker asked instrument. Done at the said mill at 3 pm before witnesses as abovewritten.

35. **Ormstoune** 19 May 1520 Andrew Ker of Primsydloucht acknowledged that he had a letter of premonition from John Ormstoun of Wester Meirdene to compear at the kirk of McKarstoun at the altar of Blessed Mary of the same kirk on 9 Nov bypast and there to receive in

his hands £40 scots and a certain letter of tack for the space of three
years under the tenor and form of a reversion of his father to him
John, made and dated at the said altar [before?] John Ormstoune with
the letter of compromise and letter (p/t) with all the points and articles contained in it to be considered more fully and now he has
received the sum of £40 with the letter of assedation for three years
and the said Andrew declares he is well content and paid by John
Ormstoun, his heirs and assignees...and after receipt of the same, the
said Andrew quitclaimed and resigned all the lands of Statherik and
Nethirlongtoune with the charter and sasine and all evidents made by
Ralph Ker, his father and Andrew Ker...to John Ormstoun, his heirs
and assignees by staff and baton as is the custom and the said
Andrew, his heirs and assignees delivers all right claim etc in and to
the lands of Statherik and Nethir Longtoun...forever. Also Andrews
binds himself his heirs and assignees to [render] discharge, defend,
depone and serve their heirs and assignees at the [hand?] of the lady
of (p/t) [relict?] of the deceased Ralph Ker his father (p/t) interest to
the said sum of £40 and the letter of assedation. Witnesses John
Hoppringill of Galloschelis, Walter Trumbill of Mynto, Alexander Gray,
William Hoppringill of Tofts, Andrew Tait and George McDowell.

36. **Ker** 11 June 1520 William Atkin, Roger Tait and William Wode
acknowledged that they owe master George Ker, rector of
Aldroxburgh the sum of money and victuals below :

£15 arrears of 20 bolls barley from 1518. Item 5 firlots barley tithes [or
teinds] of the same year. Item 14 bolls oats from 1519. Item 2 bolls
barley from 1519. Item 12 bolls corn from 1519. Item 3 equal parts of
a share of 50 shillings. Item 3 bolls willows.

Which confession George Ker asked from me notary public. Done at
the chapel of Farnele at 3 pm before witnesses sir William Bradfut,
Andrew Ker and Henry Elwand.

37. **Kirkhope** 29 July 1520 Fragment of a declaration by Thomas
Kirkhope that he made an examination of a letter from James archbishop of Glasgow at Aldroxburgh Kirk at the time of High Mass
before witnesses Andrew Ker, Thomas Dwne, John Jak, (p/t) Martyn,
James Ker.

38. **Penvene** 5 Aug 1520 master Robert Penman curate of Aldroxburgh
showed the abovementioned letter before the parish at the time of
High Mass at (p/t) before witnesses William Ker, James Ker, John Jak,
Thomas Dwne, William Atkin, Patrick Wod.

39. **Ker** 2 Oct 1520 master George Ker rector of ald roxburgh renounces
the incorporation of the perpetual vicarage of aldroxburgh together
with the rectory thereof in favour of William Brydin which vicarage
was annexed to the said rectory by apostolic bulls dated 1492 in the

eighth year of the pope Innocent 8th and by which he has, had and will have right of title in and to the said vicarage by reason of the said incorporation...and he relinquishes the same as above from the said rectory. George Ker asked instrument or instruments before witnesses master Thomas Ker archdeacon of Teviotdale, sir William Braidfut.

40. 1520 Dispensation to marry within the prohibited bounds of consanguinity in the third degree given by Thomas Ker archdeacon of Teviotdale to Adam (p/t) and Janet Scot according to a letter of Andrew archbishop of St Andrews legate before witnesses Robert Ker in Selkirk, sir John Hudson, sir David Wethirburn, sir William Furd.

41. *Michelson* 13 Jan 1521 Dispensation to marry within the prohibited bounds of consanguinity in the fourth degree given by master Thomas Ker to Simon Michelsone and Katherine Davidsone [by the same authority as above] before witnesses sir David Logan, John Daveson, William Daveson.

42. *Scot* 26 Jan 1522 Dispensation to marry within the prohibited bounds of consanguinity in the fifth and fourth degrees given by master Thomas Ker to George Scot and Margaret Trumbill before witnesses William Hoppringill and William Tait.

43. *Scot* 30 Nov 1520 Dispensation to marry within the prohibited bounds of consanguinity in the fourth degree given by master Thomas Ker archdeacon of Teviotdale to Adam Scot and Elizabeth Scot [by same authority as no. **40**] before witnesses William Tait, James Donaldson, John Vallance.

44. *Ker* 27 April 1523 George Ker and James Ker brothers-german bind themselves to George Ker of [?Lynton] against all men, the king and Andrew Ker excepted. Witnesses master George Ker canon of Glasgow, Thomas Ker archdeacon of Teviotdale.

45. Year month and day as above [i.e. no. **44**] the same G[eorge] Ker binds himself to Lancelot Ker, George Ker and (p/t) Ker in form and style as follows and binds himself in the sum of 300 merks scots to a marriage contract god willing with Isabel Ker daughter of Lancelot Ker between this and the feast of St John next and immediately following. Witnesses as [**44**].

46. *Ker* 16 Feb 1523 master George Ker canon [of Glasgow] and prebendary of Aldroxburgh healthy in mind [sick] in body, to his certain knowledge, made his testament in the following way:

Item first he ordains William and Thomas Ker and sir William Brydin his executors and intromittors with his goods [jointly] to dispose of his goods and things and to complete his legacy as they wished to [answer] before God.

Item first (*sic*) he wills and ordains that his executors erect and found his chapel in the kirk of the Blessed Virgin Mary of Calco in honour of St Salvator and Blessed Mary of Pity and for this £12 and he also chooses sir John Chepman chaplain of the said chapel.

Item he ordains the old images to be burnt at the said altar of the Salutation, three images viz. one larger image of St Salvator, one of the Salutation of Blessed Mary and one of St John the Baptist and the image of the Blessed Mary to be painted anew in the best way possible and [put] in a place near the said altar which might be most convenient.

Item he ordains that the choir be re-built of the kirk of Blessed Mary of Roxburgh and there is to be made "le sylor [ceiling] de estland burd" from one [?side] to the other and the walls of the choir to be painted and [be given] to it a chalice of 18 ounces of silver of double gilt and one [vestment] of black colour with fringe of gold. [In the kirk at] Morbottill one chalice of silver of 18 ounces and vestments of [?black] with gold fringe and in the kirk of Lyndene [a chalice] of silver of 18 ounces and double gilt. Before witnesses George Elwand and John Elwand.

47. ***Ker of Yair*** 10 Nov 1523 (1 Adrian) Thomas Ker in Yair came to the principal dwelling house of one third of his lands of Stevinston lying in the sheriffdom of Peebles and the regality of Dalketht of which lands with pertinents, his grandfather died last vest and seised and there on the grounds of the same the said Thomas presented a precept of sasine of the noble and potent lord James Earl of Morton, lord of Dalketh written on parchment and sealed with his seal impressed on white wax in hands of James D[owglass] requiring the said James [bailie] in that [part] to execute the same. James accepted the precept and read it out (p/t) as follows: James earl of Morton lord [of Dalketht] to his bailie specially constituted in that part greetings. It has been clearly shown to us that William Ker of Yair grandfather of the [said] Thomas died last vest and seised and at the faith and peace of our lord king of one third part of lands of Stevistoun with pertinents...and that the said Thomas is lawful and nearest heir to those lands of the deceased William his grandfather...to the [said] lands...and he is of lawful estate and that the said lands are held of us in chief and have been in our hands since the death of the said William...therefore we order you to give heritable sasine state and possession of the third of the said lands without delay to the said Thomas as lawful and nearest heir of the deceased William... or his lawful attorney following the tenor of the infeftment...saving the right of anyone...in testimony of which we append our seal at Dalketht 17 Sept 1523. When the precept had been read out, the bailie delivered sasine. Done at the principal dwelling house of Stevinston before witnesses James Ker, Robert

Ker, (p/t) his son, John Hoppringill, David [?Hoppringill]), (p/t) Hoppringill, Edward Huntar, Thomas Huntar, Gilbert Sollomanes.

48. **Hall** 23 Dec 152[3?] the young man John [Hall], grandson of Thomas Hall elder came to the tenement of Thomas Hall his grandfather and there on the ground of the same, broke a dish ["discum"] for a sign of breaking sasine [protesting] that his grandfather said (p/t) or granted the said sasine on the said tenement on his own authority to Robert Hall his son [and] that it would turn to prejudice of his right in time to come. Witnesses Andrew Makdowell, Walter Hall, Robert Hall and James Ker.

49. **Ker** 8 Oct 1524 Ann Cre[nstoun?] spouse of Andrew Ker of Cesfurd not [moved by force] or fallen in error...of her own free will...resigned all right and claim which she has or will have in and to [her] conjunct fee of lands or tenement of (p/t) Selkirk with pertinents as is contained fully in the charter made thereon in favour of master George Ker canon of Glasgow. Robert Ker brother-german of George Ker of Lyntoun procurator and in name of master George Ker asked instrument or instruments. Done at the tower of Halydene. Witnesses Andrew Elwand, sir Cuthbert Claperton, Thomas Wolsoun.

50. **Quhytheid** 2 June 1525 George Ker of Lynton tutor of the children of the deceased John Lyddaill his uncle assigns or delivers to Margaret Quhytheid relict of the said deceased John Lyddaill her third part of the lands of the deceased John Lyddail [viz.] 4 merks in the north part of Castletoun [in the hands?] of (p/t) Smyth. Item 40 shillings of Dowg (p/t) on the east side of Espertoun which John (p/t) occupies. Item 13 merks on the north side (p/t) viz. 4 merks occupied by John Smyth and Alexander Ra and 3 merks [occupied] by John Waldarstoun. Item 2 merks occupied by (p/t) myll and John Gyrnlaw. Item half merk of Marion (p/t) in Casteltoun. Witnesses Alexander Tait of Pyrne, (p/t) Ramsay, Robert Lyddaile, John Symsone, John Smyth and John Br[oun].

51. **Ker Tait** 4 June 1525 George Ker of Lyn[ton] and Alexander Tait of Pyrne being personally present before me notary public and witnesses underwritten, the said George Ker binds himself to compear before the official of Edinburgh and there to create and ordain the said Alexander Tait tutor to the children of the deceased John Lyddaill of Halkarstone receiving the rents and holding courts for the said children and Alexander binds himself to compear [before] the judge to this effect and on wednesday at (p/t) to provide to the said George Ker of Lyntoun (p/t) tutor of the said children sufficient and more security (p/t) than the said George knew to provide by reason and right of (p/t) for relieving and indemnifying the servants of the said George against creditors of the same deceased John Lyddail. Done at Farnele at 1 pm before witnesses master Thomas Ker archdeacon of

Teviotdale, Robert Lyddaill, Antony Tait, James Kyrkhope, Thomas
Freir, William Freir.

52. **Ker** 12 May 1526 master Thomas Ker of Sunderlandhall refutes and
denies that he has accepted certain evidents viz. a charter and precept
of sasine of 5 merklands at Wester Blaklaw with pertinents from
master George Ker rector of Aldroxburgh in hope of an agreement
between himself and George Ker of Lyntoun heir of the said lands.
Done in the chamber of master George Ker in Farnele at 11 am before
witnesses sir William Brydin vicar of Selkirk, George Elwand chaplain,
John Elwand and Thomas Robson.

53. **Symsone** 19 Aug 1525 George Ker of Lynton [tutor?] of the children of
the deceased John Lyddaill binds himself on his faith to warrant and
confirm a certain assedation under the seal of John Symsone of
Espertoun with his sign manual...to the said John [Lyddaill] for a term
of five years. Done "at my chamber in Farnele" around 11 am and
noon before Robert Ker german of the said George, James Tait, Henry
Kyrkhope [or possibly Elwand].

54. **Ker Turnbull** 27 July 1528 George Trumbill layman of the diocese of
Glasgow and Christian Ker of the same diocese desiring to contract a
marriage within the third and fourth degrees of consanguinity handed
to me notary public a certain letter of dispensation [without] impediment to read out as follows: To all and singular of the [faithful?] of the
holy mother church to whom these present notices by letter come
John Dingwall protonotary of the Holy Apostolic See, provost of the
collegiate kirk of the Holy Trinity near [Edinburgh] and chancellor of
the cathedral church of Aberdeen and apostolic commissioner in that
part specially constituted greetings in the lord for eternity. George
Turnbull layman of the diocese of Glasgow and Christian Ker [of the
same] diocese have brought us a petition that they desire to be joined
in holy matrimony but because they descend from common stock in
the fourth and [fifth?] degrees of consanguinity their desire is [to
obtain] a lawful dispensation. In this instance they require as procurators John Huntar in the name of William Trumbill and sir James
Newtoun chaplain in the name of Christian Ker whose mandates of
attorney are clearly established to us by impressions of the seals and
subscriptions of sir James C[hepman] and sir John Chepman priests of
the diocese of Glasgow..., also George and Christian have been
dignified with a merciful dispensation in the following tenor. We
therefore (text ends here)

55. 29 (?Jan) 1529/30 master Thomas Ker of Sunderlandhall gave sasine to
the heirs (p/t) with pertinents to George Ker of Lyntoun according to
the tenor of the charter. Witnesses master William Ker rector of
Aldroxburgh, Robert Ker vicar of Lyndene, John Hoppringill, James

Ker in Sunderlandhall, James Ker in Aldroxburgh, William Tait and William Haldane. Done at the dwelling place at Farnele around 1 pm.

The same day the said George Ker and master Thomas [Ker] in Sunderlandhall bound themselves to implement all agreements or evidents between them not implemented by the year day and month of these presents. Witnesses as above.

56. ***Parishioners of Stow*** 3 Feb 1530 the honourable persons, James Hoppringill, William Tait, Stephen Turnour, John Tait, James Turnour, William Inglis, James Thomson, William Hoppringill, David Hoppringill, John Fawla, Thomas Lawsoun, John Murray, John Ethingtoune, Robert Thorbrand, John Ednem, George Chisholm of that ilk, George Hoppringill, James Dalgless, Thomas Dalgless, George Dalgless, Gavin Quhit, Henry Knox, Robert Broun, William Donaldsoun, William Thomson, James Thomson, John Arcas [Arres], Richard Broun, John Blyth, Thomas Blyth, Bartholomew Cowane, James Law, John Jhonsone, William Hiltsoun, Alexander Hiltsoun, Robert Hoppringill, Andrew Ailmur, Robert Harvy, Robert Portar, (p/t) Donaldsoun, William Thomson, Thomas Thomson, (p/t), Nicholas Gray, Thomas Cowane, John Gray, John (p/t), (p/t) Donaldsoun, David Thomson, John Patersoun, (p/t) Quhit, Charles Thomson, William Cruk, David (p/t), (p/t) Tailyour, James Thomson, Adam Dikkesoun, William (p/t), (p/t) Schort, John Portus, Robert Clerk, Marion Tait, Janet Turnour, Helen Murray, Janet W(p/t), Margaret Brewhouss, Margaret Gray, Alison Burn, and He[len] Rouththeid tenants and occupiers of the lands of the lordship of [Stow in] Weddaill lying in the parish of Stow within the diocese of St Andrew pertaining to the reverend father in Christ James archbishop of the same and primate of the realm of Scotland by reason of the said office of archbishop and explained and declared that it had recently come to their notice (p/t) how considerations arising from a question moved in a cause in the Roman Curia between the said reverend father on the one hand and the noble and potent Lord Borthwik on the other concerning a lease of all and singular the said lands of the lordship of Stow made to the said Lord Borthwick for the space of 19 years by the deceased Andrew* archbishop of St Andrews and which if put into effect they would be forcibly removed from their fields and possessions, territory and houses which they and their predecessors had occupied without harm from time immemorial...and reduce them to extreme poverty. The which persons compeared acting and defending their own interest in the said cause depending in the Roman Curia. Done within the bounds of the said parish of Stow in a succession of hours between 7 am and 5 pm before witnesses Robert Tait, George (p/t), (p/t) Millar, William Murray, Robert Wythman, sir Thomas Hoppringill.

*i.e. Andrew Forman 1514 –1521.

57.   *Hoppringill* 3 Feb 1531 Margaret Lundy spouse of David Hoppringill of Smaillem asserts that the said David has a marriage contract of George Brown of Colstone...and the said Margaret requests that he take in marriage either Janet or Margaret Hoppringill, her daughters, as pleases the said David. Margaret in the name of her spouse asked instrument. Done here [i.e. Smailholm] at 9 am before witnesses sir David Gray and Thomas Hoppringill chaplains, James Ker, Thomas Bykkertoun and Thomas Fergref laymen.

58.   *Ker* 8 May 1531 Walter Ker of Cesfurd came to the principal dwelling house of the lands of Hassindenbank with pertinents lying in the sheriffdom of Roxburgh...of which the deceased Andrew Ker of Cesfurd his father died last vest and seised and there gave a certain precept of sasine of the noble Sir William Cunygham, feudal lord of the lands of Glencarn and superior of Hassindenbank sealed with red and white seals and bearing sign manual to [?Robert] Chepman bailie in that part which was handed to the notary to read out as follows: William Cunygham knight feudal lord of the lands and [said] barony and superior of the underwritten lands to...Robert Chepman and my bailies in that part specially constituted conjunctly and severally...greetings. Because it is clearly shown to me by evidents and documents that the deceased Andrew Ker of Cesfurd father of the said Walter Ker died last vest and seised at peace and faith of our lord king of all the lands of Hassindenbank with pertinents lying within the sheriffdom of Roxburgh and that the said Walter is the nearest and lawful heir to his father in the said lands with pertinents and that he is of lawful age and that it is held in chief of me as superior, I command you or your lawful attorney without delay to give sasine of the said lands according to the tenor of the old infeftment made before to the said Walter or his lawful attorney...saving the right of anyone, taking security for doing [this] to me as superior of the said [lands] that it is held to be done by [law]...in testimony of which I append my sign manual and seal at Streviling on 1 May 1531. Witnesses master John Colden, John Boid, Troilus McGw and master John Peblis notary public.

Note below "Wilym master [of] Glencarn".

59.   *Ker* (p/t) Feb 1531 Patrick [Murray] of Fawlahill declared that he owed 100 teind sheaves of corn to Mark Ker tacksman [to the kirk] of St Mary of the forest from his [lands] of Hangingschaw for the payment of which the said Patrick made the said Mark Ker his assignee to uplift the payment...from his husbandlands of Selkirk £10 scots at Whitsunday next to come after the day and date of these presents and 10 merks of the same money uplifted at Martinmas next and immediately following and 10 merks at the feast of Whitsunday next and immediately following. Mark Ker asked instrument. Done at Carterhauch at 10 am or thereabouts before witnesses master William

Ker rector of Aldroxburgh, Thomas Ker of Sunderlandhall, James Ker his brother-german, George Ker of Lynton and William Ker.

60. **Halyburton** 26 May 1531 Roland Trottar bailie in that part for the honourable women and men Marion Home, with consent of her spouse George Lord Home, and Margaret Ker, with consent of her spouse George Ker, tutor of Cesfurd, came to the principal dwelling place of Boltoun and there on their command asked to speak to Patrick Hebburn master of Halis in which the son of Patrick master of Halis in the name of the [said] Patrick, with certain servants of theirs obstructed the said Rolland saying that he could not enter until (p/t) he saw hitherto. Done at the door of the said place [i.e. Boltoun] at around 9 am before witnesses James Ker, Andrew Mudy, Thomas Synklar, John Gray.

61. **Ker in Yair** 27 July 1531 Thomas Ker in Yair respectfully requested Patrick Murray of Fawlahill to give him state possession and sasine of the lands of Crenstounryddaill with pertinents as lord superior of these lands which at that time Patrick Murray refused to do [because] he wished [them] to belong to friends. Thomas Ker asked instrument. Done near the door of Farnele at around 2 pm before witnesses George Ker of Lynton, James Ker, William Tait, David Murray and William Ker.

62. **Ker** August 1531 sir Laurence Jhonson in name of master Thomas Ker, requests Patrick Murray of Fawlahill to give sasine of his lands of Crenstoun Ryddaill with pertinents which the said Patrick refused to do. Sir Laurence asked instrument. Done at hall of Farnele around 3 pm before John Mathosone, William Ker, William Tait, James Dowglass.

63. **Ker** 8 Oct 1531 William Vaiche on the part of Thomas Ker of Yair requested Patrick Murray of Fawlahill superior of the lands of Crenstounryddaill to give sasine of the same to Thomas Ker and Patrick Murray asserted that he did not wish to deny him sasine but wishes to know whether the said Thomas has sufficient evidents of the said lands or not. Done at Byrkindalyschank before witnesses Thomas Murray, James Murray, James Murray and James Vaiche.

64. **Patrick Murray of Fawlahill** 8 Oct 1531 This entry is very faint. It seems to record that William Vaiche on part of Thomas Ker asked Patrick Murray to give sasine of the above lands to Thomas Ker and Patrick enquired by whose command he asked and that he had no mandate unless on the word or precept of the king. Patrick Murray asked instrument. Done at Byrkindalyschank before witnesses Thomas Murray, James Murray, John Vaiche.

65. **Rutherfurd** 9 April 1532 [The first part of this instrument is mainly illegible] David Hoppringill (p/t) and superior of the lands of

[Cavirhill?] on his own free will revokes renounces and annuls ward relief and a marriage contract [given] on the [lands] of Caverhill with pertinents so that...by whatever right on such terms that (illegible) after which revocation...of the above ward etc of the lands of Caverhill with pertinents belonging to him and [held from] his superior (blank) Ruthirfurd of Honthill he gives and freely hands over (p/t). Done at the hall of Galloschelles at 9 am before witnesses John Hoppringill son and apparent heir of the said David, George Preston of Cragmillar, David Farle of Cranstoun, Archibald Cunygham, William Synklar, sir Thomas Hoppringill.

66. **_Hoppringill_** 15 April 1532 sir Thomas Hoppringill in the name of David Hoppringill of Smallame had in his hands a certain form of appeal to the papal see which he handed to me notary public to [make public] as follows: "As an appeal or notice of objection etc". After reading out which the said sir Thomas Hoppringill on part of the said David Hoppringill has from the abbot and convent of Melrose and his (p/t) and executors against (illegible) an appeal to the [pope] Clement at the holy see. Witnesses George Ker of Lyntoune, James Ker of Farnele, Barnard Ker and John Hog of (illegible).

67. **_Scot of Howpaslot_** 23 April 1532 Walter Scot bailie in that part of Janet Scot, daughter and heir of the deceased [Walter] Scot of Howpaslot, holds in his hands a precept of sasine written on parchment with the seal of the said Janet and her spouse Thomas Makdowell and handed it to me notary public to read out in the following way: Janet Scot daughter and heir of the deceased Walter Scot of Howpaslot and her spouse Thomas Makdowell of Mak[er]stoun to Walter Scot etc my bailie in that part specially constituted greetings. Because with consent and assent of my spouse I have sold and alienated heritably all my ten merklands of Berkinsyd with pertinents lying in the sheriffdom of Berwick as contained fully in a charter to the said [Robert], I therefore command you to give heritable [state] sasine and possession to Robert Scot or his lawful attorney according to the tenor of the said charter...in testimony of which I append my seal and the seal of my spouse at Edinburgh 20 March 1532.

Janet Scot with my hand at the pen. Thomas Makdowell of Makerstoun with my hand at the pen.

Alexander Young notary public in witness of the above.

After which...the bailie gave heritable state, sasine and possession of the said ten merklands of Byrkinsyd with pertinents to Robert Scot personally present and accepting...according to the charter made thereon saving the right of anyone. Robert Scot asked instrument or instruments. Done on the ground of the same around 10 am before witnesses Adam Hoppringill, William Bannantyn, Henry Wynterhope, Gilbert Wynter, Thomas Gibson, Thomas Gibson officer.

68. ***Dykesone*** 21 May 1533 William Dykesone came to the principal dwelling house of Ormstoun and there gave all of the ten poundlands of Ormstoun with tower and pertinents to his cousin John Dykesone following letters of command of the king before witnesses Ralph Ker, Bernard Ker, James Tait, William Steill, John Lawson, Alexander Carstars, William Jhonson and James Jhonson.

69. ***Jhonson*** 28 May 1533 Thomas Jhonsone burgess of the burgh of Selkirk freely resigns all his tenement to Thomas Jhonsone younger, son of John Jhonsone, his heir by delivery of earth and stones reserving liferent to himself and his spouse. Witnesses sir Ninian Brydin, sir William Brydin vicar of [Selkirk] and Robert Chepman.

70. ***Ker*** (p/t) Dec 1534 James [Matho?] and Marion Lermont his spouse declared themselves well content that Robert Ker will have half of all the profits of their 5 merklands if the said Robert will acquire "le steding" for his debts and also pay the expenses of litigation in bringing the said lawsuit in court before the bailies of Calco. Done in the kirk of Calco before witnesses Thomas Matho chaplain, William Ker, Mark Ker.

71. ***Ker*** 26 March 1535 Andrew Young produced his instrument of the parish clerkship of Morbottill confirmed by deceased master George Ker canon of Glasgow and handed it to the notary public to be read out. After which the said George Ker of Corbethouss protested that this instrument should not turn to his prejudice in respect of any right or claim which he had or might have to the parish clerkship of Morbottill. Done in the kirkyard of Morbottill around 9 am before witnesses sir John Ker vicar of Morbottil, John Young of Sesfurd, Robert of Crukit Schawis.

72. ***Ker*** 2 April 1535 William Wod younger procurator in the name of Thomas [Ker] of Yair, came to the principal dwelling house of master George Hay and there warned the said master George to compear within 40 days in the collegiate church of St Giles in Edinburgh and there on the altar of St James to receive the sum of 100 merks scots and this for the redemption of a [fifth?] part of the lands of Stenstoun according to the tenor of his letter of reversion made before to the said Thomas. Done in the dwelling place of the said master George before witnesses George Ker of Corbethouse and William Wode elder.

73. ***Lundy*** [10?] Feb 1536/7 before me notary public and witnesses underwritten, compeared in the court house of Lawder, George Wethirheid sheriff depute for the court [and] sir Thomas Hoppringill on the part of Margaret Lundy relict of the deceased David Hoppringill of Smallam and of the conjunct fee of Pilmuir...asked the said George as depute to prove his power to sit in the said court in place of the sheriff and the said George refused and he said that he proposed to sit with the power he had of death and mutilation. Secondly sir Thomas alleges they were [not] lawfully arrested by a precept of the sheriff (p/t) and the same did not proceed and was not in his name. Thirdly he alleges that he has paid the rents and customary dues of the said Margaret Lundy for the tenants also that [there elapsed] from the said judgement 100 days to his calling to warrant the said tenants which he denied. Fourthly, the same protests because he was acting in the court on that day, it turned to the prejudice of his rights. Fifthly he was questioned by master James Crenstoun advocate for the opponent on whose part he was proxy who ren[dered?] on part of William Murray sometime factor of the rector of Lawder. Sixthly the same accepts the exception against the judgement of the deputy alleging that the same was deputy for the lord of Haltoun who was judge, also he suspected that half the mill belonged to the lord of Halton.

sir Thomas Hoppringill asked instrument. Done in the court house at Lawder at 12 am before witnesses Thomas Crenstoun of Dodds, Cuthbert Crenstoun, Richard Lawder, master James Crenstoun, George Wauchthop, Charles Murray, sir Peter Hyltsone notary public.

74. **Ker** 13 May 1536 master Robert Ker vicar of Lyndene [next part scored out but narrates that he had a letter of donation of Walter Ker of Cesfurd of the preceptory of "le masyndew" near Roxburgh written on parchment and sealed with red and white seals impressed on wax and handed to the same notary to read out] came to the preceptory or hospital of Masindew [near] Roxburgh and handed a (p/t [letter of donation]) from his father [Walter Ker] of Cesfurd to sir Thomas Kirkhope curate of (p/t) asking him to execute the said letters and sir Thomas handed them to me notary public to read out in the following way: "To all and sundry etc", after which sir Thomas invested master Robert Ker canon of the said hospital or preceptory by taking chalice, books, vestments and missals of the said preceptory forever according to the tenor of the said donation and master Thomas curate handed over real actual and corporeal possession of the preceptory forever. Done at the high altar of the said preceptory. [No witnesses given.]

75. **Ker in Yair** 22 April 1536 William Wod younger procurator for Thomas Ker in Yair, came to the presence of John Sandelandis and personally apprehended as possessor of the 6 husbandlands of Bold to compear (blank) May next at Blessed Mary the Virgin of Selkirk and there to receive payment of the said sum of 240 merks scots in the church of St Bride, at the High Altar of the same to receive payment of the sum of 120 merks as specified in a letter of reversion to the same Thomas under a redemption. Done at the chapel of Saint Mary Magdalene at Bold at 11 am before witnesses Hector Crenstoun, Thomas Paterson, Adam Vallance, George Purves.

76. Same day and hour John Sandelandis enquired from William Wod concerning which lands he was warned to receive the money. William

said for the six husbandlands. John Sandelandis asked instrument. Done in the same place before witnesses above [no. **75**].

A number of pages are missing from the text here.

77. ***Ryddaill Ker*** 5 May 1545 James Ryddaill younger son of John Ryddaill of that ilk, came to his lands of "le ester place" and there gave state and sasine of 30 shillings of land with half the houses, buildings and easements with other pertinents to his wife Janet Ker in liferent, the said Janet being personally present and accepting delivery of staff and baton. Janet asked instrument. Done in the said place at 9 am before witnesses George Ker of Gait Schaw, Walter Ryddaill heir apparent of the lord of Ryddaill and [John?] Ryddaill.

The same day John Ryddaill of that ilk, superior of the lands of ester place, declared that he ratified and confirmed the said sasine before the above witnesses.

78. 16 July 1526 [3 Clement VII] John Bard, lord of Posso and Janet Scot, daughter of the deceased Walter Scot, lord of Howpaslot brought to me notary public, a marriage contract between them having no impediment etc by reason of a dispensation to marry and appoints the priests sir [William] Braidfut and sir John Keyne together with William Lawder, (p/t) Hendersone, William Askirk, William Haw, Thomas Jhonsone...actors, factors etc to act jointly on their behalf and to receive the said dispensation on their behalf to prove the legitimacy of their descendants before the reverend in Christ master Gilbert Strathathquhan, commissary in that part. Done at Farnele at [blank] am. John Chepman notary public with his own hand.

I sir John Chepman priest of the diocese of Glasgow and notary public subscribe my signet and sign manual on this present letter of assignation of special mandate A of B not knowing how to write with his hand placed on the pen.

79. [The first part of this deed is missing]. 5 May 1547

...the lawful and nearest...heirs of the said Andrew [Hoppringill] and failing this the nearest heir...to all our 5 merklands and town of Nethirblanislee with houses, buildings and yard thereupon called Le Roun and with crofts...lying in runrig which the said Andrew occupies with his subtenants and family in the sheriffdom of Roxburgh and lordship of Melrose, whatsoever land and town of Nethirblanislee within these boundaries and divisions above mentioned and limits and [?markers] that is to say from the west descending to a burn called "Le Mossburn" and from there ascending and extending towards the east to "Le Hollitcarne" and from there ascending and extending towards the east to the stone called "Le Standingdstane in Routhrig" and from here descending and extending towards the east to the wall called the

March Dyk or otherwise the Monksdyke and from here extending towards the north to the chapel walls called the Chapel Walls or alias "Cheildkellis Chapell Wallis" and from there extending and descending through the burn called Mylsyburn and from here extending towards the south and ascending to that cross called "Liells Corce" and from here extending and ascending towards the south to that cross called the Hie Cross and from here extending and descending towards the south to that part of the burn called "Helburinsfurd" and from here extending and descending through the said burn towards the east to the lands called "Wilkynishaugh" and from here extending and descending towards the south to the old aqueduct called the "Ald Watirgang de Mydstreyme de Ledir" and from here extending and descending towards the south from the said aqueduct and in the middle of the same to the boundary called the "Erliss Aker" and from here extending and ascending towards the west through the burn called Hawik Scheilburn to that loch called the Oair Loucht and from here extending and ascending towards the west to the public highway called the "Common Mercate Gait" and from here extending and descending towards the west to the said place the "Willebush" near the old dyke called the "Ald Dyk in Wyndelawcruke" and from here extending and ascending towards the north through the burn called the Blackburn to the Blakfurd of the same burn and from here extending and ascending towards the north to the middle of the "Helmoss" and from here extending and descending towards the north through the middle of the Helmoss to the same burn called "Le Mosburne" lying as it comes (illegible) in the lordship of Melrose within the sheriffdom of Roxburgh between the lands of the forest of Lauder on the north part, of the lands of the monastery of Dryburgh on the south, the lands of the Lord of Halton called Quhitslaide and the lands of the said Dryburgh monastry and lands of Byrkkinsyde towards the east and the lands of the said monastery of Melross called Colmsliehill and Threpwodschaw towards the west.

Now we therefore command you to give sasine and possession without delay of all the 5 merklands and town of Nethirblanisle with houses etc and a yard thereto called "Le Rone" with crofts and part of the same lands lying in runrig to the said Andrew his subtenants occupied with all rights and privileges and pertinents by the said Andrew in free holding or liferent for his lifetime. Also he delivers heritable sasine thereupon to the said George or his lawful attorney according to the tenor of the charter made before...with no omissions...in testimony of which our seal and sign manual also the seal of our head court and sign manual of the convent is appended at our monastery of Melross 5 May 1547 with the subscription of James commendator of Melross, Richard Patonson subprior, Thomas Mercer, John Watson, Mungo Purves, David Hoppringill, John Hogart, Bernard Bowston, William Fylpe, Richard Chatto and John Foross. After reading out the precept the bailie in that part John Fledschair by virtue of his office gave heritable state sasine and possession of the 5 merklands of Nethirblanislie called "lie Rone" with pertinents to Andrew Hoppringill and his heirs personally present and accepting by delivery of earth and stones on the ground of the same...saving the right of anyone. Andrew Hoppringill asked instrument. Done at "Le Rone Hall" at 10 am before witnesses George Daveson, James Swynhouss, James Swynhouss, John Swynhouss, William Hall and William Stirling.

80. ***Hoppringill of Trynillin Know*** 21 May 1547 Alexander Hoppringill of Trynnilinknowe says that Queen Mary's officer summoned or commanded Adam Gray to appear before the lords of council to implement a certain contract between him and Janet Liddaile lady of Halkerstoun, about which no letters or even a copy of letters testify. Witnesses John Hoppringill of Smailhame, George Hoppringill of Torwodlie, James Hoppringill of Quhitbank, Robert Hoppringill of Blyndlee, sir Stephen Synklar.

81. ***Mathosone*** 29 May 1547 Andrew Mathosone acknowledged he is content and...fully paid for a certain cow which was sold by him to his brother David Mathosone in Yair except for an ell of "albepannii" [= white cloth?] to make him a pair of hose worth 3 shillings...and quitclaims the same cow to his brother. David asked instrument. Done at the valley of Farnele at 6 pm. Witnesses James Freir, William Freir and Richard Freir.

82. ***Hoppringill of Smailhame*** 11 June 1547 Thomas Huntar in Hawkburn came to the five merklands and town of Nethirblanisle in the lordship of Melross within the sheriffdom of Roxburgh then occupied by Thomas Smyth with part of the said lands lying in runrig and gave sasine of 32 shilling lands of the said five merklands and town etc to John Hoppringill of Smailhame and Margaret Gordone his spouse in conjunct fee and their heirs...and assignees personally present and accepting by delivery of earth and stones according to the form of a charter by the said Thomas made thereon saving the right of anyone. John and Margaret asked instruments. Done at the principal dwelling place of the 5 merklands and town of Nethirblanisle at 10 am before master Robert Hoppringill rector of Moirhame, John Spottiswod, William Hoppringill, William Spottiswode and Thomas Huntar younger.

The same day John Hoppringill enquired of the said Thomas Huntar elder if that was his own seal appended to his charter of the above 32 shilling lands delivered to him and his spouse, which the said Thomas affirmed. Also the said Thomas promised to pay John and Margaret whichever lives longer and their heirs 8 bolls of barley on the feast of the purification of our lady yearly as a rent on the 32 shilling lands before witnesses as above.

83. *Ker of Dalcoif* 13 Aug 1547 Robert Newton attorney in the name of
Adam Ker of Schaw and Janet Newton lady of Dalcoif his spouse,
whose power of attorney is clearly shown to me notary public, came
to the lands of Merssyntoun lying in the sheriffdom of Berwik and
there on the grounds of the same handed a precept of sasine of our
lady queen under testimony of the great seal to the bailie in that part
Alexander Strang ensign ["signifero"] requesting he execute the
same…and the bailie handed it to me notary public to read out as follows: Mary by the grace of God queen of Scots to her sheriffs and
bailies of Berwik and Roxburgh also to Alexander Strang ["maser"?]
greetings. Because we have given and granted to Adam Ker of Schaw
and his spouse Janet Newton lady of Dalcoif, whichever lives longer,
in conjunct fee all the lands of Marsingtoun with pertinents extending
to 20 pound lands of old extent and now worth £100 yearly lying in
our sheriffdom of Berwik, 23 shillings and 11 penny worths of land of
old extent and 10 merk lands of Cesfurd Mains now worth £5 19s 7d
and 21 shillings of land of old extent of Cesfurd Mains within the sheriffdom of Roxburgh which were owned by James Ker of Marsington
and apprised for a debt in the sum of £2119 8s 4d which was recovered from the said Adam Ker and Janet Newton together with the
sheriffs fee of £105 and which lacking moveable goods to distrain
from the said James Ker the said sums were assigned to Adam and
Janet in accordance with an Act of Parliament and royal letters as contained fully in the charter made before, we therefore command you
Adam and Janet to take sasine of the said lands without delay according to the tenor of our charter dated under the testimony of the great
seal at Edinburgh on 4 July 1547. After which the bailie gave sasine of
the said lands to the attorney Robert Newton by delivery of earth and
stones on the ground of the same saving the right of anyone. Robert
asked instrument. Done on the ground of the lands of Marsingtoun
around 10 am before Cuthbert Curror, Alexander Strang, Robert Hwme
living in Eklis.

Final page : "Liber Dominus Johannes Chepman [11 times]
"Hic liber est meus possum producere testes/ si quis me querit Johannes
mihi nomen erit/ Chepman iungatur mihi nominatur/ iam fert totum per
Iesum Christum da mihi [potu..?]".

Book B
The Protocol Book of Sir John Chepman,
Notary Public, 1536–43

1. 2 June 15 (p/t) John Sandelandis of that ilk enquired whether Thomas
    Ker in Yair or the same John Sandelandes (p/t) the husbandlands of
    [Mert scored out] Dalcoff in (p/t) six husbandlands of Bold or not
    which [Thomas] Ker acknowledged that the said John had the six hus-
    bandlands of Dalcoff [contained] in a clause of warrandice of the said
    6 husbandlands of Bold. Also on the same day the said Thomas Ker in
    Yair acknowledged he had received six pounds scots from John
    Sandelandis for two years rent on a half of the husbandlands lying in
    the town and bounds of Bold the which six pounds the said Thomas
    quitclaims forever to the said John, his heirs and assignees. John
    asked instrument. Done at the Chapel of Bold around 11 pm before
    George Tait of Pirne, (p/t) Crenstoun, James Crenstoun his son,
    William [Wod], Thomas Patersone, John Lowis and John Borthik.

    Same day and hour. Thomas Ker in Yair inquired of John Sandelandis
    if he was paid and content of the sum of 18 score of merks scots for
    the redemption and relaxation of the six 6 husbandlands of Bold per-
    taining to Thomas in heritable fee and he acknowledged himself well
    paid and quitclaimed the said Thomas, his heirs and assignees forever.
    Thomas Ker asked instrument. Done on the same day and hour
    before witnesses abovewritten.

2. ***Hwme*** 13 July 1536 John Hoppringill brother of George Hoppringill
    of Torwodlee having authority for the purpose invested and gave
    sasine to Robert Symsone attorney for George Hwm of Wethirburne of
    all the lands of Blakhauch with pertinents. Witnesses John Hoppringill
    in New Hall, William Jhonsone, Andrew Michelsoun, Robert
    Wychtman and Hector Wychtman.

3. ***Ker of Lyntoun*** 10 Dec 1537 John Hog of Lyntoun attorney and in
    the name of James Ker son and apparent heir of George Ker of
    Lyntoun whose power of attorney is clearly established to me notary
    public came to five pound lands of Primsyde lying in "le ryndaill" with
    lands (p/t) of Sproustoun and within the sheriffdom of Roxburgh (p/t)
    and required Adam Wauchope bailie in that part to execute a precept
    of sasine of Walter Ker of Cesford with red and white seals appended
    and the bailie handed it to me notary public to read out as follows:
    Walter Ker of Cesford and lord of the lands of Primsyde to Adam
    Wauchhope my bailie in that part lawfully constituted greetings.
    Knowing that I have given and by a charter granted to my cousin
    James Ker apparent heir of George Ker of Lyntoun all my five [pound]
    lands lying in "ly ryndaill" with the lands of Lancelot (p/t) in the lord-

ship of Primsyde for service used and wont. Therefore I command you to give heritable state [sasine] and possession without delay of the [said] lands to James Ker or his lawful attorney in the terms of his charter which he has of me...saving the rights of anyone. In testimony of which I append my seal at Haldane on the 26 Nov 1537 with my subscription "Walter Ker of Cesfurd". After which the bailie by virtue of his office gave sasine of all the five poundlands of Primsyde. John attorney for the said James asked instrument. Done at the house of Thomas Richartsoun on the ground of the said lands around 11 am, before Thomas Mathosone, George Trumbull, James Gilcryst, Thomas Richartsoun, Thomas Leidhouse, John Ker, William Ker and others.

4. ***Ker of Lyntoun*** 3 Dec 1537 before me notary public and witnesses underwritten was transumed and extracted a protocol certified by worthy men cited for that purpose before Sir William Newton commissioner of the ["Raris..inis?"] of which protocol the tenor follows: AD 1509 August seventh William Lermont bailie of David Somervell openly gave heritable sasine to George Ker son and heir to the deceased James Ker of Lyntoun of lands underwritten viz. "le Couttwallis" with the orchard thereof, of Holdane, Hyndelaw and "le Park" and 7 husbandlands lying in the town of Lyntoun within the sheriffdom of Roxburgh by delivery of earth and stones according to the tenor of the old charter on a precept of David Somervell. Done at (illegible) Wallis before George Dowglass of Bon Jedburcht, George (p/t), (p/t) Dowglass, John Hog, Robert Thomsone, John (p/t), (p/t) Ker, John Vaiche, Robert Termerid, James Rutherfurd and Henry Trumbull .

5. ***Ker of Sunderlande Hall*** 15 June 153[8] [III Paul 3] James [?Dow]glass of Cavers acknowledged that he had promised [master Thomas] Ker in Sunderlandhall by a precept of the first of June (p/t) to receive a sum of money viz. 80 (p/t) scots by the fifteenth June for the redemption of the lands of Esschebank. Master Thomas asked instrument. Done at the monastery church of (p/t) at the altar of blessed Mary around 3 pm before William Alesone, Adam Rutherfurd, Andrew Ker, (p/t) Roxburcht, sir James Bernet and Edward Morton.

Same day James Dowglas of Cavers produced a letter of reversion (p/t) of Esshebank written on parchment with the seal of [master Thomas] Ker of Sundirlande impressed in red and white wax and asserted that the seal was not that of the deceased Robert [Ker?] nor were the letters under his subscription manual as the witnesses clearly showed on which he asserts that the land of Esschebank was not lawfully his (p/t) or pertaining heritably to him. Witnesses as above [no. **5**].

6. ***Ker*** 20 Feb 1538/9 George Davesone attorney and in the name of the Robert Ker and Elesabeth Harvy his spouse...came to the lands of

Estir Blaiklaw lying in the barony of Lyntoun and within the sheriffdom of Roxburgh and there required George Ker son of Robert Ker in
Crukit Schaw and bailie in that part of George Ker of Lyntoun to execute a certain precept of sasine of the said lands signed by the said
George in his own hand...the which precept the bailie gave to me
notary public to be made public as follows: George Ker of Lyntoun to
George Ker son of Robert Ker in Crukitshaw greetings. Because I have
given and granted to my brother-german Robert Ker and Elesabeth
Harvy his spouse...in conjunct fee...and their heirs lawfully procreated, on account of brotherly love...all the lands (p/t) [Estir] Blacklaw
with pertinents lying in the barony of Lyntoun, sheriffdom of
Roxburgh...to be held of me, my heirs (p/t) as in my charter to Robert
and Elesabeth made thereon.

Therefore I order you...to give state, sasine and possession without
delay of the said lands of Estir Blaiklaw with pertinents to Robert and
Elisabeth whichever lives longer in conjunct fee or to their lawful
attorney according to the tenor of my charter made before to
them...in testimony of which I append my seal and sign manual at
Edinburgh, 6 Feb 1538. Before witnesses master Robert Ker vicar of
Lyndeyn, sir William Bradfut chaplain, James Ker and James Ker.

The bailie gave sasine of Estir Blaiklaw to George Davesone attorney
by delivery of earth and stone according to the tenor of the said pre-
cept. George asked instrument. Done at the principal dwelling house
of the said lands around 10 am, before Symon Wolsone, James
Wolsone, Henry Davesone, Andrew Curror, James Curror and Robert
Ker in Crukit Shaw and the bailie gave sasine to Robert and
Elesabecht in Crukit Shaw before William Daveson, John Daveson,
Thomas Daveson, James Rannyk and John Rannyk his son.

7. **Ker** 28 March 1539 master William Ker rector of Aldroxburgh showed
    a copy of a royal letter specifying that the said master William was
    under censure of the church on account of non-payment of a certain
    ferme of our supreme lord king from which he appealed on the
    grounds that he paid the amount and has the acquittance to prove it.
    Witnesses Gilbert Ker of Primsyde, James Ker in Grenheid, master
    Thomas Ker, James Borthik, William Thomson and others.

8. **Ker** 8 May 1539 it is appointed and agreed between Robert Ker
    burgess of Edinburgh on the one part and Christian Murray relict of
    the deceased Thomas Murray of Bowhill on the other in this following
    way viz. the said Christian leased a third part of the said place of
    North Bowhill belonging to her to the said Robert Ker in return for a
    fourth part and that the same Christian after the end of the tack of the
    teind sheaves of the forsaid place of Bowhill belonging to Christian
    herself from the abbot and convent of the monastery of Calco, she
    resigned all right and claim she has or could have in future...in favour

of the same (p/t) and Robert Ker pays 8 merks scots to Christian
Murray. Done at the house of George Vallance before G(p/t)amn,
John Fergreiff, Andrew Bell and others.

9. ***Lyddaill of Hairtherne*** 4 Feb 1539/40 James Reid sheriff in that part
    of our supreme lord King James V put in the hands of the notary a
    certain precept of sasine...under the testimony of the great seal...in
    the following manner: James by grace of God King of Scots to his
    sheriff and bailies in Selkirk and to James Reid (blank – then p/t) and
    severally to our sheriffs of Selkirk in that part greeting. Because (illegi-
    ble) after having reached perfect age (25 years) and following general
    revocation with the (p/t) and consent of our comptroller we have
    given and granted in heritable feu ferme to Robert Lyddaill all [the
    lands of] Hairtherne with pertinents lying in the lordship of Selkirk in
    our sheriffdom of Selkirk extending yearly (p/t) in rent in all profits to
    30 [?pounds] scots as contained in our charter made thereupon.

    We order and command Robert [Lyddaill] or his sure attorney to have
    this present sasine of the lands with pertinents according to the tenor
    of the charter he has from us...under the testimony of the great seal at
    Edinburgh 27 July, 25th year of James V. After reading the precept the
    bailie by virtue and vigour of his office gave sasine of all the lands of
    Hairtherne with pertinents to Robert Lyddaill who asked this instru-
    ment from me notary public. Done at the principal dwelling house of
    Hairtherne called "Le Peill" about 10 am, before George Hall, William
    Patersone and James Sandelandis.

10. ***Ker*** 20 Feb 1538/9 [George] Ker son of Robert Ker in Crukit Schaw
    bailie to George Ker of Lyntoun on account of his precept of sasine
    [and] letters of the office of bailie sealed with red and white seals
    impressed in wax and with sign manual...came to the [lands] of Ester
    Blaklaw with pertinents lying in the barony of [Lyntoun] within the
    sheriffdom of Roxburght and there handed the said precept to the
    notary to read out as follows: George Ker of Lyntoun to... George Ker
    son of Robert Ker in Crukitschaw and my bailies specially constituted
    in that part conjunctly and severally greetings. Because I have given
    and granted to my brother-german Robert Ker and Elisabeth Harvy his
    spouse whichever of them lives longer in conjunct fee and their heirs
    lawfully procreated for the brotherly affection and love we have for
    one another and other good deeds and favours... all my lands of Ester
    Blaklaw with pertinents holding them from me as contained fully in
    my charter to the said Robert and Elisabeth thereon. Therefore we
    command you to deliver sasine of the said lands to the said Robert
    and Elisabeth without delay according to the tenor of my charter
    made thereon... in testimony of which I append my seal and sign
    manual at Edinburght 6 Feb 1538. Before master Robert Ker vicar of
    Lyndeyn, sir William Braidfut chaplain, James Ker and James Ker.

The subscription of George Ker thus George Ker of Lyntoun

After which, the bailie gave sasine.

11. [This item has been inserted as a loose sheet in the main body of the text]

20 Feb 1538/9 George Davidsone attorney in name of Robert Ker and Elisabeth Harvy his spouse came to the lands of Estir Blaiklaw lying in the barony of Lyntoun within the sheriffdom of Roxburgh and there demanded from George Ker son of Robert Ker in Crukit Schaw bailie in that part of George Ker of Lyntoun that a certain precept of sasine regarding those lands be executed. The bailie received the precept and handed it to the notary public who read it out. Then George Ker after the precept...was made public...by vigour and virtue of his office of bailie gave sasine of all the above lands to George Davidsone attorney for Robert and Elisabeth and in their name George Davidsone attorney asked instrument. Done at the principal dwelling house of the said lands at 10 am before Simon Wolsone, James Wolsone, Henry Davidsone, Andrew Curror, James Curror and Robert Ker in Crukit Schaw.

Same day at the hour of eleven, the bailie invested the said Robert and Elisabeth in the lands of Dennerles according to the tenor of another precept for a term of [?nineteen] years before Robert Ker in Crukit Schaw, William Daveson, John Daveson, Thomas Daveson, James Rannyk and John Rannyk his son.

[Reverse : this may complete No. 10].

of a precept, state, heritable sasine and possession...of all the said lands of Estir Blaklaw with pertinents to George Daveson who accepts as attorney on behalf of Robert and Elesabeth by letters of our lord king under the great seal as is clearly shown to me notary public and to whoever lives longer in conjunct fee by delivery of earth and stones. Done at the principal dwelling house of the said lands at around 10 am before witnesses Simone Wolsone, James Wolsone, Henry Davidson, Andrew Curror, James Curror and Robert Ker in Crukit Schaw.

12. (p/t) Jan 1539/40 [Robert Scot] of Howpaslot on his own confession acknowledged that he had received from Janet Scot relict of deceased Robert Elwand of [Toungtis?] the sum of 120 pounds scots in counted money for which sum the same Robert Scot sent his seal to the venerable man John Scot vicar of Hawik to make and seal evidents of the said Janet viz. a charter and precept of sasine of his lands of Apiltrehall in "le mains" called "le cot rig" now occupied by William Bell for 20 bolls [as] rent to the same Janet provided always the said

Robert Scott his heirs and assignees pay or will pay the said Janet the sum of 120 pounds.

The said Robert Scott binds himself faithfully after coming to his house from Edinburgh to act for his heirs and assignees in the books of the commissary of Teviotdale to guarantee peaceful possession of the lands or rent always and until the complete [payment] of the same to Janet Scot, her heirs and assignees. Janet asked instrument. Done at Fawsyde around 8 am before Simon Scot, James Scot, William Scot in Hartwodmyers, Roland Scot, John Dowglass and Thomas Andersone.

13. **Hall** 1 Feb [1539/40] Alexander Tait on the one part and [Alexander Hall in] Selkirk on the other bound themselves in the following form and effect viz. [Alexander] Hall and Isabella Tait daughter of the same Alexander Tait to solemmize the act of marriage in face of kirk...at such a convenient time as occurs and under penalty of a double dowry or "le touchquhir guds" to be paid by the party in breach of contract. John Mithag burgess of Selkirk in name and on the part of the said Alexander Hall asked instrument which was done at the house of James Anderson at Farnele about 2 pm before James Bard, John Hall in Selkirk, John Greif, John Watson in Yair, Janet [? Trent.]

14. **Feirgreiff** 25 Feb 15 [39/40] [Patrick?] Feirgreiff dwelling in Ankrum faithfully binds himself his heirs executors and assignees to pay Thomas Feirgreiff living in Braidmedois his (p/t) yearly and [?for five years] a boll of flour stacked (p/t) of malt provided always the said Patrick his heirs (p/t) pay to the said Thomas Feirgreiff his heirs and assignees the sum of 21 pounds and this on account of (p/t) for a husbandland lying in the barony of Ankrum (p/t) belonging to him by law he delivers (p/t) on the lands should the money be lacking. Thomas Feirgreiff asked instrument. Done at the parish church of Blessed Mary of Selkirk in the aisle of St. John the Baptist on the north side of the church before sir John Michelhill and Thomas Skwne chaplains and others.

15. **Ker** 22 March 15 [39/40] Robert Ker burgess of Edinburgh in name and on the part of "Margrete" the old Queen leased "le steding" of North Bowhill to John Jhonson for 32 pounds scots and the said John will render the rent of the said place to the lady queen or her factors before sir George Elwand chaplain and William Tait.

16. **Ker of Corbethouse** 27 May 1540 George Ker of Lyntoun affirmed a certain letter of assedation made with the consent of James Ker his apparent heir sealed and subscribed by the same George and James. (p/t) to the honourable man George Ker of Corbethouse of his 50 shillinglands of Crukitschaws and so George Ker of Lyntoun annulled broke and destroyed a protocol of an instrument written on the back of the said letter of assedation bearing [on it] that George Ker of Corbethouss his heirs and subtenants shall enjoy the 50 shilling lands

for all terms in the said assedation. George Ker of Corbethouss asked instrument. Done in the inner chapel of Farnele at midday before John Hog of Lyntoun, George Davidsone in Throgdane and sir William Young chaplain and others.

17. **Ker of Lyntoun** 18 June 1540 it was agreed between [George] Ker of Lyntoun on the one part and William Ker of [Quhitmurhall] and Janet Ker relict of William Ker of Quhitmurhall in following form and effect viz. George Ker of Lyntoun declares that he is content that Janet Ker accepts the place of Quhitmuirhall [for] the son and heir of the same William Ker and his heirs from the factors of Calco in tack and so the same Janet Ker relict of the foresaid binds herself that...if she should contract a marriage in any way she will renounce all right and claim forever that she has or will have in future in favour of her son and [his] heirs. George Ker asked instrument. Done at Farnele around 4 pm before Thomas Ker in Yair amd James Ker in Farnele.

18. **Ker of Quhitmuirhall** Same day George Ker of Lyntoun and William Ker of Schaw bind themselves, their heirs and assignees that they will not interfere with the place of Quhitmuirhall until the perfect and lawful age of the offspring of the deceased William Ker of Quhitmuirhall unless with the unanimous consent of the same George and William Ker and their heirs and that the same have leased the said place of Quhitmuirhall with consent as said...to the use and utility of the said offspring. Janet asked instrument at Farnele as above.

19. **Ker** 27 Sept 1540 sir William Brydin vicar of Aldroxburgh freely and in the certain knowledge of better things renounces his office of the vicarage of Aldroxburgh with all rights and pertinents into the hands of the father in Christ, lord Gavin archbishop of Glasgow, ordinary of the place in favour of the venerable man Thomas Ker clerk of the diocese of Glasgow before Gilbert Ker of Primsyd, [George] Ker of Lyntoun, master Thomas Ker in Sunderlandhall, [Andrew] Ker in Aldroxburght, William Tait.

20. **Brydin Vicar of Selkirk** Same day Gilbert Ker of Prumsyd, master William Ker rector of Aldroxburcht and George Ker of Lyntoun jointly and severally of their own free will faithfully bound themselves to pay the venerable man sir William Brydin vicar of Selkirk and his assignees the sum of 12 pounds scots yearly and for the year until complete payment of 60 (blank) pounds (blank) will be made or at least until Thomas Ker vicar of Aldroxburgh gives satisfaction to the said sir William in other ways...and for greater security he promises to act himself in the books of the dean of Teviotdale for the payment of this sum to the vicar of Selkirk before witnesses master Thomas Ker in Sunderlandhall and Andrew [Ker] in Aldroxburgh.

21. **Ker** (p/t) master Thomas Ker in Sunderlandhall requested the honourable man [George] Ker of Lyntoun to fulfil a contract in all its [arti-

cles] made between them (p/t) which George was prepared to do in all things...both parties asked instrument. Done at the chapel of Farnele at about 1 pm before Gilbert Ker of Prumsyde, master William Ker rector of Aldroxburgh and Andrew Ker in Aldroxburgh.

22. **Ker** 7 March 1540/1 sir Thomas Kirkhope chaplain of the diocese of Glasgow by touching the door of the parish church of Aldroxburgh, baptistery, altar, chalice, book and ornaments of the same invested Thomas Ker, acolyte...in real actual and corporeal possession of the fruits and emoluments of the perpetual vicarage of the same [i.e. Aldroxburgh] endowed and inducted him with all the uses etc adjoined in form previously written.

Thomas Ker acolyte asked instrument in the aforesaid church before Andrew Ker in Aldroxburgh, William Dwne, Thomas Dwne, James Smyth, Walter Hog.

23. **Ker "quinto"** 20 Feb 1538/9 George Ker son of Robert Ker in Crukitschaw bailie in that part of George Ker of Lyntoun by his precept of sasine or letters of bailiary sealed with a red pendant and impressed seal and corroborated with sign manual on parchment came to the lands of Dennerles with pertinents lying in the barony of Lyntoun within the sheriffdom of Roxburgh and there delivered into the hands of me notary public the said precept of which the tenor follows: "George Ker of Lyntoun to my lovittis George Ker sone to Robert Ker in Crukit Schaw and Rawff Ker and ilkane of yow coniunctlie and severally my bailies in that part specially constitute greting Forsamekill as I have sett in assedatioun to my weilbelovit brothir Robert Ker and Elesabeth Harvy his spouse and to the langar levand of thai twa yair aires and subtenentes ane or ma all and haill tha my landis and steding callit Dennerles wyth the pertinentis liand in the barony of Lyntoun within the sheriffdome of Roxburgh for all the days and termes of nyntene yeiris as at mair leintht is contenit in my lettres of assedatioun maid and gevin to thaim thereupon heirfor I charge yow straitlie and commandis that incontinent this my precept sene ye or ony of yow that beis requirit therewyt pass and giff stait possession and saising corporal actual and real of all thai my saidis landis of Dennerles wyth the [pertinents] to the saidis Robert my brother, Elesabecht [his spouse] and to the langar levand of thaim twa airis [and subtennentis] forsaids induring the saidis nyntene yeires of my forsaids lettres of assedatioun maid to thame thereupon and this one na wys ye leif undone as ye will answer to me upone the execution of your office. The quhilk to do I comitt to yow and to every ilkane of yow coniunctlie and severalie my full power be this my precept subscribed wyth hand my seill is affixet at Edinburgh the 7 day of Februar the yeir of God 1538 yeirs before thir witness maister William Ker parsone of Aldroxburgh, maister Robert Ker vicar of Lyndene, sir William

Braidfut chaplain to James Ker in Farnylee, James Ker in Grenheid". The subscription of the said George is thus "George Ker of Lintoun".

After reading out the precept of sasine George Ker bailie as above by virtue of his office gave sasine of all the lands of Dennerlees with pertinents to George Davidsone present and accepting as attorney, constituted by royal letters under testimony of the great seal of Robert and Elisabeth, for them and whichever of them lives longer and their heirs and subtenants for the space of 19 years by delivery of earth and stones on the ground of the same according to the tenor of letters of assedation by the said [George] Ker of Lyntoun to Robert and Elisabeth.

George Davidsone [attorney] as above asked instrument. Done on the ground of the lands of Dennerles around 11 am before witnesses Robert Ker in Crukitschaw William Davidsone John Davidsone Thomas Davidsone James Rannyk and John Rannyk his son.

24. **Dikeson of Ormstoun** 20 April 1541 John Dikesone of Ormstoun came to the presence of William Stewart of Tracquair and warned him to compear at the chapel of blessed Mary of Peblis to receive a certain sum of money for the redemption of his 6 merklands according to the form and tenor of his reversion before George Tait of [Ca...lecht], John Crenstoun, John Franche, William Vache and Thomas Patersone.

25. **Hoppringill** 19 May 1541 Adam Hoppringill brother-german of Robert Hoppringill of Blindlee and cessioner and assignee of [Sir Ninian] Seton of Tulibody knight as letters patent show came to the principal dwelling house of William Carncroce in Comesle and there warned the said William personally apprehended with all the inhabitants and occupiers of two husbandlands lying in "Le Fawins" within the sheriffdom of Berwik apprised to the deceased Sir John Streviling of Ker knight for the sum of (blank) scots to compear in the consistorial aisle upon the altar of the same of the collegiate church of the blessed St. Giles in Edinburgh on the 1st June next to receive a certain sum (blank) to redeem the said two husbandlands also for expenses made for the said Sir John Streviling...and said Adam cessioner as above came to the principal dwelling house of the lands lying in Fawins and at same time warned William Carncroce and all the inhabitants etc.

Done at Comesle around 3 pm before Robert Hoppringill in Murcleucht, John Carncroce brother-german of William, George Murray, David Patersone, Thomas Tait. Done in Fawins about 6 pm before David Burnet, Jhon Browis, William Purves.

26. **Dikesone of Ormstoun** 29 May 1541 William Stewart of Tracquair acknowledged he had accepted from John Dikesone of Ormstoun the sum of 100 merks scots for the redemption and relaxation of (p/t) his

lands of Ormstoun to him from the above William (p/t) which William delivered to him...in a sasine (p/t) of the said lands. Also the said William Stewart renounces (p/t) his right and claim forever and possession which he has or he, his heirs and assignees will have in the future to the said 6 merks of lands with pertinents...of the sum of 100 merks the said William declares that he is content and paid and has quitclaimed and discharged the said John Dikeson his heirs and assignees for the same.

John Dikeson asked instrument. Done at Tracquair in the new tower around 5 pm before John Sandelandes of Bold, William Sandelandes, James Stewart, Alexander Stewart, Adam Vaiche, John Crenstoun, Thomas Ker in Yair, master Robert Ker vicar of Lyndeyn

27. **Stewart** Same day and place John Dikesone of Ormstoun discharged and quitclaimed William Stewart of Tracquair his heirs and all his associates from wrongful occupation of the lands of Ormstoun in times past up to this present before all witnesses abovewritten. John Dikesone binds himself to show to the said William Stewart his instrument of sasine of the lands of Ormstoun so he can know the same and if John is lawful heir and lord of the lands of Ormstoun or not before Thomas Ker in Yair and master Robert Ker vicar of Lyndeyn.

28. **Carncroce** (p/t) May 1541 William Carncroce of Comesle alleges that he has not been (p/t) warned to receive a sum (blank) for the redemption of his (p/t) husbandlands lying in Fawins apprised to...Sir John Streviling of Keyir knight from him and that he was not warned on 40 days. Before witnesses Robert Hoppringill in Morcleucht, John Carncroce, George Murray, Davide Patersone and Thomas Tait.

29. **Hoppringill** 8 June 1541 Alexander Hoppringill of Cragleche asked if James Ker of Mersyntoun or Ralph Ker his brother-german had any bonds or contracts of the same Alexander or from the deceased Robert Hoppringill his father which the said Ralph then produced and also Alexander Carmaige officer and serjeant in that part of the noble lady queen Margaret having in his hand a precept under her signet and sign manual also corroborated with the subscription of her spouse Henry Stewart came to the dwelling house of Williamhope to eject the tenants thereof and after the precept was read out Alexander alleged that in the precept no mention was made of [removing them from their?] houses and the said Alexander Hoppringill also alleged he had not made "le forcement" from him in that he had letters of the king and queen maintaining him in possession. Then James Syntoun shepherd of our supreme lord king in Hartherne said that one of the associates of Ralph Ker attacked him with injurious words saying that one of them would grieve if the said James did not wish to allow sheep on his pasture. Witnesses John Achesone, Gilbert Scot, John Jhonesone, William Crawfurd, Richard Palmar and Simon Tait.

30. *Ker* Same day and place James Ker of Mersintoun protested [Alexander Hopprin]gill of Craglethe had no evidents (p/t) from the said James Ker that he could produce before the judges (p/t) in the court of the queen and to him ought to be rendered as the law [requires?] (p/t). Afterwards, the said Alexander sent out sheep and cows and kept them on the [lands] of Williamhope which Alexander Carmaig officer and serjeant in that part of a noble lady queen Margaret held by the said precept having power by precept to put down and remove the goods of the said Alexander and his tenants of Williamhop on account of which the said Alexander made "le force-ment" and he said Alexander Carmaig by virtue of his office came and requested entry to the principal dwelling houses of Williamhope at which Alexander ordered the wives that they should not open the doors which they did…Alexander Carmaig put Ralph Ker german (*sic*) of the same James Ker in a house with his friends and also put three cattle viz. "ane hawkit stot, ane garit stot and ane garit quy" on the same land and demitted possession of the same by virtue of his pre-cept and finally Alexander Hoppringill said he did not want to [see] any letters from him to Ralph. Before witnesses Gilbert Scot, John Achesone, John Jhonsone, William Thomson.

31. *Dwnne* 18 June 1541 master Michael Scot, William Scot in Bowhill, William Rennyk and John Hog conjunctly and severally bind them-selves…to abide by all points and articles contained in a contract between them and (p/t) Ninian Brydin notary public. [?Walter] Dwnne asked this instrument. Done here under the mercat cross of Selkirk at about 4 pm before John Clerk in Quhithauchbra, James Chepman my german [i.e. brother or close relative of sir John Chepman – the notary] Cuthbert Curror and William Scot in Hartwodburn.

32. *Hay of Tracquair* 1 Aug 1541 master Robert Ker vicar of Lyndeyn acknowledged that Agnes Hay spouse of William Stewart laboured and made all her diligence to make an agreement between her spouse and the same John Dikesone. Witnesses George Ker of Lyntoun, William Dikesone, William Tait.

33. *Spottiswod* 13 August 1541 Elisabeth Spottiswod relict of the deceased John Hoppringill of Blindlee relinquishes all right and claim to the steding of Blindlee after the expiry of her tack to Robert Hoppringill her first born son and heir. Said Robert asked instrument. Done in the lower part of Blindlie around 9 am before friar John Dwn, friar William Symson, sir George Elwand curate of Lindeyn and John Hoppringill.

34. *Hoppringill* Same day and place Elesabeth constituted, made, created and [ordained] sir Ninian Spotiswod (p/t) [brother?] german and James Hoppringill her son [her executors] and assignees after her death for the enjoyment and occupation through the years and terms of her tacks in future of the place of Blindle. Done before friar John Dwnn, friar William Symson, sir George Ellwand curate, sir Thomas Ranaldsoun and John Hoppringill her son.

35. *Jamesone of Lyndeyn* Same day Thomas Ker in Yair enquired of John Hall burgess of Selkirk if the same was content that George Jameson in Lyndeyn had freedom to consume grain pertaining to half a husbandland which the same John Hall has from Thomas Ker in tack, and for agreed times. Regarding which John Hall declared he was [content].

George Jameson asked this instrument. Done in the market place of Selkirk about 3 pm before sir James Bennet.

36. *Hoppringill* (?) August 1541 Adam son of Robert Hoppringill of Blindlee assignee of and in the name of Ninian Setoun of Tulibody knight in and to the redemption of those two husbandlands of Fawins with pertinents lying within the sheriffdom of Barwik lawfully apprised to James Muschat of Colgarh for the sum of 60 pounds and to Robert Oliphant ensign king's sheriff in that part for 3 pounds personally came before William Carncroce in Comsle and William warned Adam to appear in the collegiate church of St. Giles in Edinburgh, at the altar of St. Katherine the Virgin founded there on the 20th of this month of August at the hour of 10 to receive the sum of 63 pounds, also the expenses incurred on the same by the deceased Sir John Streveling of Keir knight in his infeftment, for the redemption of the said lands of Fawins with pertinents...and William promises the said Adam shall receive the 2 husbandlands for the sum of money.

Adam Hoppringill asked instrument. Done at the dwelling place of William at Commslee before John Carncroce brother-german of William, George Carncroce son of said William and John Thomson gardener.

37. *Braidfut* 17 Jan 1541/2 Before me notary public and witnesses sir Ninian Brydin notary public (p/t) said he had a certain instrument in the form of a contract...between (p/t) and James Braidfut and Isabella Haldane his spouse (p/t). James Braidfut asked instrument here in the courthouse of Selkirk before the "well known man Walter Scot provost of Selkirk", John Brydin bailie, Lancelot Ker, Symon Farle and others.

38. *Chepman* 31 Jan 1541/2 John Brydin one of the bailies of Selkirk came to the tenement of the deceased Robert Chepman and there gave sasine of all the tenement front and back to his son and heir John Chepman in accordance with an old infeftment of the said Robert. Then the said bailie came to the tenement of Thomas Grahame in Peilgait and invested the said John Chepman in an annualrent of 5 shillings scots uplifted from the same tenement and then came to the tenement of William Flegschar and there invested him in

an annualrent of 5 shillings uplifted from the said tenement and after to the tenement of John Braidfut and gave him an annualrent of 5 shillings uplifted from it yearly in two terms a year [Whitsunday and Martinmas] and lastly came to a rig of land under "le know" and there invested John Chepman with the rig of land according to the tenor of an old infeftment from his deceased mother Elisabeth Jhonsone. Done at the said places around 3 pm before Robert Scot [brother] german of Walter Scot of Edschaw, Peter Stodart, John Mouss, Thomas Melrose, John Melrose his son, George Smyth, David Todryg, John Smyth and Alexander Brown in Sunderland.

39. *[H]yltsone Achesone* (?) Feb 1541/2 (p/t) Achesone and Thomas Hyltson discharged all actions and claims between them, by their own free will, up to this present day. Thomas Hylston asked instrument. Done in my own chamber* of Farnele at about 3 pm before John Barre, James Tait, Ninian Chepman and others.

*i.e. of sir John Chepman.

40. *Ker Harvy* 5 April 1542 George Ker son of Robert Ker in Crukit Schaw attorney and in the name of Robert Ker burgess of Edinburgh and Elisabeth Harvy his wife...came to the lands of Hyndlaw lying in the barony of Lyntoun and sheriffdom of Roxburgh...and there presented to John Hog of Lyntoun bailie in that part of George Ker in Lyntoun a precept of sasine of the said lands of Hyndlaw under seal...and sign manual of said George and required it to be executed. The said bailie received the precept...and handed it to the notary to make public. After making public the precept, the bailie gave sasine and possession of the fourth part of the lands of Hyndlaw then occupied by (p/t) Wolsone and William Wolsone to George Ker in the name of the above. Done on the ground of Hyndlaw around 10 am before William Hog, sir William Corbet, notary, William Wolsone, John Almiss, James Lowry.

41. *Ker* 26 June 1542 William Dwne in Aldroxburgh acknowledged he had been well paid from the hands of master Robert Ker vicar of Lyndene of the sum of 40 merks scots in complete payment of his dowry ["dotis"] which sum the said master Robert promised to pay William. Master Robert asked instrument, done at Farnele around 4 pm before sir Thomas Ker, vicar of Roxburgh, James Ker in Quhitmur, John Ker there.

42. *Andersone* 13 April [1542] sir William Chepman came to his [tenement] lying in the burgh of Selkirk between the tenement of Stephen Loremer on the west, the land of John Ross on the [south], the land of Gilbert Ker of Primsyde on the east and the common way which leads to the loch on the north and freely resigned the tenement...in favour of Patrick Andersone in the hands of John Brydin bailie of Selkirk who gave sasine of the same to the said Patrick in accordance with

the tenor of a charter by the sir William to the said Patrick. Done on the ground of the same around 7 am before James Hall smith, John Brownne, John Thomsone, David Todrig.

43. **Ker** (p/t) April [1542] sir John Michelhill notary public and clerk of the sheriff court of Selkirk acknowledged that Patrick Murray sheriff principal of Selkirk had created by oath John Sandelandis of Bold his depute with the consent of those present and took instruments. The said John Sandelandis his depute was consulted by trustworthy persons regarding a royal letter and declared by virtue of his office that he would continue this court to the twentieth day following. Patrick Murray sheriff principal rose and took the letter from his depute and deprived him of his office and asserted that he would obey the said royal letter notwithstanding that James Ker of Mersingtoun alleged acts of Parliament in the contrary and that a private royal letter should not take place over acts of Parliament in all these matters. The said John depute as above and deprived of his office declared he was willing to obey the said royal letter in all points. James Ker of Mersyntoun for his interest asked instrument. Done on the land of James Bradfut, burgess of Selkirk around 1 pm in the presence of David Ker, James Bradfut, Ralph Ker, George Michelhill.

44. **Lyddaill** 5 May [1542] "Jonet of Lyddaill spouss to Niniane of Lyddaill lard of Halkarstoun allegeand (p/t) hir said spouss and scho had lauchtfullie w[arnit] (p/t) precept Thome of Dalgless, Jame Lyddaile and (p/t) to remove and flyt fra our steding of Alebank (p/t) the said Jonet of hir favor and benevolens [had] tholit the said Thomas Dalgless to pastur his gudis (p/t) beand one the ground quhill flitting fryday nixt to cum and na mair of his gudis to be brocht apone the groun quhill that day and than he to remove and red himself servandis and gudis plesandlie of the ground the quhilk to do he oblist him be his hand and fath of body". Janet asked instrument. Done at the place of Alebank before witnesses William Wod, Mark Ker, James Lyddail, Alexander Liddaill,John Watsone and James Liddaill.

45. **Dalglese** Same day Thomas Dalgless alleges that he is the old tenant and in possession of one fourth part of the place of Alebank before witnesses above.

46. **Wod** Same day William Wod enquired "quhilke haf quarter of Alebank scho ressavit him tenent to and scho said to the half quarter that Jame Lyddail occupiet". William Wod asked instrument before witnesses above.

47. **Davidsone** (?) June 1542 Andrew [Davidsone] came to his tenement lying in the burgh of Selkirk between the tenement of Andrew Loucht on the east, the land or tenement of Janet Lydderdaill on the west, the king's street which leads to the well on the south and the land or tenement of Marion Hoppringill lady of Grenheid on the north and there

freely gave all the tenement to his brother-german Richard Davidsone
by resigning it in hands of Peter Moffet bailie of Selkirk who gave
sasine to Richard in accordance with the tenor of a charter by Andrew
to Richard. Richard Davidsone asked instrument. Done at the tenement around 4 pm before Andrew Loucht, David Ker, cousin (p/t)
George Lydderdaill, William Henderson, Thomas (p/t), James Turnor,
John Dunhope and others.

48. **Symsone** 22 June 1542 John Symsone came to a husbandland commonly called Lammes Land lying in the lordship of Selkirk within the
sheriffdom thereof and there upon a croft of the said husbandland he
presented to George Mowat sheriff depute in that part a certain precept of sasine of our chancery of our lord the King under the testimony of the great seal requiring the said George to execute the deed.
The sheriff received the precept and [gave it] to me notary public for
reading as follows: James by grace of God etc...to his sheriff and
bailies of Selkirk and George Mowat our sheriff of Selkirk in that part
greetings. Because we have given and granted to John Symsone heritably for his good faithful deeds and acts in our service...and for several sums of money paid to our treasury all the lands called "Lammes
landis" with pertinents lying in the liberty of the burgh of Selkirk and
in the lordship, "le mains" and the sheriffdom of the same which first
belonged heritably to the said John Symsone and were held by him
immediately in chief ("in capite") of Archibald formerly Earl of Angus
and now belong to us and are in our hands by escheat following the
forfeiture of the said Archibald for several acts of treason and lesion of
our [majesty] committed by him and of which he was judicially con-
victed by [due] process and forfeiture duly decreed against him (p/t)
our charter thereon more fully bears. Now we command you to give
the said John sasine of the said lands according to the tenor of the
charter he has from us without delay dated under testimony of the
great seal at Edinburgh 10 June 1542". Whereupon the said George
gave heritable sasine in accordance with the said precept and charter
to the said John saving the right of anyone. John asked instrument.
Done on the ground of the croft around 10 am before Thomas
Symsone in Smailhame, John Brydin, John Mowat, Thomas Mowat.

49. **Lyddaill** 27 May 1542 William Liddaill brother-german of Ninian
Liddaill of Halkarstoun [acknowledged?] and it was clearly established
to me that he and Janet spouse of the said Ninian removed the household things and utensils (p/t) and their servants of the houses in
Alebank and (p/t) viz. cows viz. "le nowt" and sixty sheep of the said
place of Alebank. William Liddaill in name and part of Ninian Lyddaill
his brother asked this instrument. Done on the ground of the said
place around 10 am before Adam Gray, James Liddaill and James
Liddaill, John Watsone,Robert Watsone and Archibald Thyne.

50. **Lyddaill Gray** 29 June 1542 " Adam Gray, John Watson, Robert
Watsone, Thomas Burnton, Patrick Leiss, Arche Thyne (blank – gap
for more names?) tenentis of Alebank band and oblist thaim coniunctlie and severalie till ane honorabill man Niniane Lyddaill lard of
Halkarstoun and fewar of the said steding of Alebank that thai suld do
thair uter deligence for keping of his wod of Alebank that thai nor
never ane of thaim suld cut distroy surfetlie nor thoill it to be cuttit
nor distroyit be thaim self nor nane other personis wittandlie nor wil-
fullie under the pane of forfaltin of thair takkis And gyff thai mystir
ony wod grath for beting of or bigging of thair houses thai to cum till
him and ask leiff and he to cause servandis of his to cum and deliver
it to thaim at thair mystir (p/t)…cuttis or distroyis the said wod aganis
(p/t) [his] wills one force than thay sall pleyne to thair maister William
Stewart of thai persones and gyf thair maister re(p/t) it nocht the
tenents sall incur na danger therfor". Ninian Liddaill and the above
tenants asked instrument at Farnele about 9 am, before William
Liddaill, George Ker, Robert Ker.

51. **Gordoun** 18 July 1542 William Hoppringill procurator and in the
name of John Hoppringill of Smalem under a command signed and
sealed by John Hoppringill came to all of the tenements subscribed
lying in the burgh of Lawder from which John Hoppringill receives
certain annualrents levied as follows:

> The tenement of William Joly 13s 4d lying between the lands of
> George Dewar on west and George Brodostanis on east and
> kings highway on south.

> Annualrent of 18s from the tenement of David Hereot lying
> between the land of John Brown on west, Patrick Diksone on
> east and kings highway on south.

> Annualrent (p/t) from the tenement of deceased Alexander
> Brown lying between Charles [?Murray] on the west and lands of
> John Brodostanis on the east.

> Annualrent of 13s 4d from the tenement of Charles Murray lying
> [between] the lands of the deceased John Scheill on west and
> lands of (p/t) on east.

> Annualrent of 6s 8d from the tenement of the deceased John
> Scheill lying between the lands of John Michell on west and
> Charles Murray on east.

> Annualrent 6s 8d from the tenement of John Michell between the
> lands of sir John Gyll on the west and deceased John Scheill on
> east.

Annualrent of 13s 4d from the tenement of deceased sir John Gyll between the lands of John Mersour on west and lands of John Michell on east.

Annualrent of 13s 4d from the tenement of John Mersour between the lands of William Hoppringill on west and sir John Gyll on the east.

Annualrent of 13s 4d from the tenement of the deceased James Lychtbody between the lands of Andrew Diksone on west and lands of Nycolas Sandelandes on east

and there William Hoppringill, procurator resigned the sum of above annualrents into the hands of George Wauchthope one of the bailies of the burgh of Lawder and he by vigour and virtue of his office gave sasine of the annualrents to Roger Gordoun attorney for the honourable woman [Margaret] Gordoun. Roger Gordoun asked this instrument. Done in the said burgh at said tenements around 11 am, before Hugh Crenstoun, David Hoppringill, Robert Tait, Thomas Mersour, John Tait.

52. **Gordoun** Same day Roger Gordoun attorney for Margaret Gordoun daughter of William Gordoun of Crauchlew whose power of attorney is clearly established came to the lands of Murhouss, Blackchester, Nether Commone and Hawkarland extending to five pound lands of old extent with pertinents lying in the lordship of Lawderdaill in the sheriffdom of Berwick and there William Hoppringill bailie of John Hoppringill of Smailhame presented a precept of sasine of the said lands under the seal and subscription of the said John and the bailie gave it to me notary public to make public as follows: John Hoppringill to William Hoppringill and my bailies conjunctly and severally greetings. Because I have given and granted to Margaret Gordoun, daughter of William of Crauchlew now in her pure virginity ["nunc in sua pura virginitate"] in liferent for her lifetime all my lands of Murhouss, Blackchester, Nethir Commone and Halkarland extending to 5 poundlands of old extent with pertinents...held of our lord king and his successors as contained fully in my charter to the said Margaret therefore we command you without delay to give sasine of the [above] lands to the said Margaret in liferent or to her lawful attorney according to the tenor of my charter. In testimony of which I append my seal and subscription at Edinburgh on the 17th June 1542 before witnesses [master] Barnard Bailie rector of Lammyngtoun, master (p/t) Hoppringill rector of Morhame, Roger Gordoun, (p/t) [Ban]nantyne, Thomas Lame and master Thomas Keyne notary public". After reading out the precept William Hoppringill bailie gave sasine of the said lands to Roger attorney of Margaret Gordoun personally present and accepting the tenor of the charter made thereon and saving the right of anyone. Roger asked instrument. Done at the

principal dwelling house of Murhouss around 2 pm, before David Hoppringill, Robert Tait, Robert Tait,William Staig, Robert Weddaill and John Wod.

53. *Scot* 19 January 1543 sir Simon Schortreid chaplain came to his tenement lying in the burgh of Selkirk on the south of the road which leads to the loch between the tenement of Thomas Prechour on the east and the lands of (p/t) on the west and "le bog" on the south and there on the ground of the said tenement he resigns the said tenement with pertinents in favour of William Scot in the hands of John Brydin bailie of Selkirk according to the tenor of sir Symone's old infeftment. Done on the grounds of the said tenement around 3 pm before John Dwn merchant, John Fairle younger, James Newlandes, Alexander Gledstanes, John McDowell, Thomas Hendry and Robert Mithag.

54. *Angus* Same day and hour, the said bailie infefted John Angus in the same tenement with pertinents by the resignation and request of the said William Scot before abovewritten witnesses .

55. *Borthik* (p/t) December 1543 Thomas Knox [in name of] and on the part of the noble and potent lord John Borthik protested that the said act in giving sasine to Walter Ker of Cesfurd of the lands of Torsonis, Cordlaue, Penplocht and Murhouss with the mill of Stow with pertinents should not turn to his loss or prejudice of the marches or bounds of his lordship or "le stedingis" adjacent to the said lands. Thomas Knokis asked instrument. Done on the motte or "le Know" near the place of Torsonss at about 11 am before Walter Ker of Cesfurd, Gilbert Ker of Primsyde, George Ker of Lyntoun Thomas Ker in Yair, James Ker in Quhitmuir, Robert Ker of Loucht and Adam Wauchthope.

56. *Hoppringill* Same day and hour sir James (blank) chaplain in name and on part of John Hoppringill in Torsonis broke a dish ["discum" i.e. broke sasine] protesting that the act done or to be done in not giving the sasine of the lands of Torsonis, Coadlaue, Penplotht, Murhouss with mill of Stow and pertinents to Walter Ker of Cesfurd should not turn to John Hoppringill's loss in prejudice to his right and possession of the same lands. Sir James (blank) asked instrument. Done on the ground of the lands of Stow before witnesses abovewritten.

END

Book C
The Protocol Book of John and Ninian Brydin
and Other Notaries, 1526–36

1.   This volume is bound in a parchment document being a dispensation
      to marry within prohibited bounds of consanquinity between Elisabeth
      Cranstoun and (?) c 1500. [Following repair the original cover is sepa-
      rate].

2.   **Devotion to Our Lady of Pity.** The first four folios of this book con-
      tain an office of nine lessons for the late-medieval devotion of the
      Compassion of the Blessed Virgin, known more generally in Scotland
      as 'Our Lady of Pity'. It has not been thought necessary to reproduce
      the text as it is primarily of interest to students of liturgy.

      Though the sorrow of Our Lady at the foot of the Cross was a popular
      subject of personal devotion, only four examples of an appropriate
      office, such as might form part of the formal worship of a church,
      have appeared hitherto in British sources. Of these, two, both similar,
      are associated with Aberdeen. The Selkirk office, which is different
      from all of them, was clearly of continental origin and seems to have
      been particularly associated with the Dominicans.

      The metrical parts of the office are those of one of ten offices for the
      Compassio noted by G.M. Dreves in *Analecta Hymnica Medii Aevii*,
      xxiv (Leipzig 1896), pp. 122–52. (The material of the Selkirk office,
      beginning 'O Maria, stans sub cruce' is on pp. 122–25, and that of the
      Aberdeen office is on pp. 142–46.)

      The discovery of the office suggests that this devotion was not
      confined to the eastern seaboard of Scotland, which was of course the
      part of the country to which continental innovations in worship could
      most easily penetrate. Given the disparity between the two countries
      in the quantity of surviving evidence, it further suggests that, like
      other late-medieval devotions, the *Compassio* took root more readily
      in Scotland than in England. [J.D.G.]

3.   *"Littera Bannorum"* sir John B[rydin?] of S[elkirk?] has made and
      claimed three times in our kirk of S[elkirk?] that J.S. and M of He (p/t)
      of this parish have no impediment which might prevent the
      abovewritten persons [from making?] a lawful marriage...in witness of
      which they affix their seals at S[elkirk?] Page cut here. No date.

4.   *Smaill* 7 September 1526 James Mithag bailie of the burgh of Selkirk
      came at instance of Richard Young to [a portion of] land there with
      pertinents. Richard resigned one portion of the land in hands of the
      bailie asking the said James by virtue of his office to give sasine to

John Smail of the portion of his tenement with pertinents lying between the tenement of James Mithag by (p/t) lying in length and breadth by all right (p/t) old and devised with consent of his spouse. Before sir William Brydin, Ninian Brydin, Robert Melross, (p/t) Ker and others.

5. **Master James Jonsone** 26 July 1526 Robert Brydin and John Chapman bailies constituted in that part in the name of Robert [?Cadzow] came to a portion of land of his tenement lying in the burgh of Selkirk between the lands of Simon Fairle on the south and the tenement of (p/t) Jonsone on the east and the bailies gave sasine to master James Jonsone and his heirs forever before sir David Chapman, Thomas Portus, John Jonsone and others.

6. **John Portus** 25 Sept 15[26] Simon Fairle bailie came to the tenement of Adam Fairle held of sir William Bradfut in marriage ["maritagium"] and gave sasine to John Portus with the consent of sir William Bradfut and Adam Fairle of half of his tenement lying on the west of the Peilgate between the lands of master John Chapman on the east and on the other part of the said tenement which belonged to John Mithag on the west as it lies in length and breadth by all right ancient and devised bounds and the said John Portus paying yearly to William Bradfut and his heirs 10s scots at Whitsunday and Martinmas. Done at 2 pm before witnesses John Scott, James Curror, William Lermont.

7. **Mouss** 2 June 1526 Simon Fairle bailie went to the principal place of the deceased John Mouss lying in the burgh of Selkirk between the lands of John Hawe on the east and the lands of David Brydin on the south and there by virtue of his office, gave sasine to Marion and Helen Mouss true lawful and nearest living heirs of the said deceased who died last vest and seised, before witnesses James Scott, Thomas Portus, William Loremer, and a portion of land lying near Taittis Croft which is held of the Lord of Hanyng, paying 3 shillings 9 pence yearly.

8. **Ker** 5 Aug 1526 Janet Scot wife of Alexander Scott her (p/t) in New Vork for that time came to the principal dwelling house of two husbandlands lying in the lordship of [Selkirk] called the lands of the lord of Philiphaugh or the lands of the lord [sheriff?] (illegible) for a certain time and there on the ground of the same (p/t) Janet Scott presented a precept of sasine of Alexander Scot her spouse with his manual subscription on parchment cancelled with his seal in red wax impressed on white, in the hands of John Chepman burgess in Selkirk there present, requesting him as bailie in that part...to execute the same...and the bailie received the precept with due reverence and handed it to me notary public undersigned to be taken and read, whose tenor is word for word as follows: Alexander Scot burgess of Selkirk and lord of two husbandlands in the lordship lying in the said burgh to my

beloved Robert Thomp[sone], John Chepman and Robert Brydin my bailies in that part specially constituted greeting. Because I have given, granted to my beloved spouse Janet Ker for all her life or as I promised to her at the time of our marriage contract, all my two husbandlands with pertinents lying in the burgh bounds of the said burgh of Selkirk, therefore...jointly and severally...I firmly ordain and command that you by virtue of these presents give sasine in conjunct fee and liferent and personal possession of all the said lands with pertinents for all her life to the said Janet Ker or to her sure attorney to hold lawfully, doing this and making delivery without delay and leaving nothing undone... which being done (p/t) you jointly and severally [with] my irrevocable powers (p/t) according to the tenor of these presents in witness of which I have [placed] my own seal [and] the seal of sir William Brydin vicar pensioner [of Selkirk] and to these presents appended and also [subscribed?] on the 25 July 1526 before Michael Scott, John Ker, David Scott, John Fergref and (p/t) [the bailie?] by virtue of his office gave sasine to Janet (p/t).

9. **Margaret Ker** 16 Oct 1526 James Murray, sheriff of Selkirk came to the lands of Philiphaugh which belonged to the deceased Ralph Trumbull and there acknowledged and entered Mark Ker attorney for Margaret Ker, relict of the deceased Ralph whose power of attorney was plainly evident to me notary public, to her lawful third share of the lands and to a third of the dwelling house and tenement of the same on the sunny side according to the form of a retour following a brieve of terce for the same Margaret served before the said sheriff as is customary in such things and which third part the deceased Janet (*sic*) Turnbull held and possessed. Mark Ker asked instrument. Done on the ground of the lands of Philophauch between 11 am and noon before John Murray of Lewynshoupe and Andrew Gilcrist.

10. **John Chepman** 5 Jan 1526/27 John Chepman bailie of Selkirk at the instance and request of sir John Chepman heir of the deceased Richard Chepman his father burgess in Selkirk came to the tenement of the said Richard Chepman with pertinents lying between the lands of James Brydin on the west, lands of John Freir on the east, the king's street on the north and a third part of the yard of James Brydin younger on the south and there in the forehouse of the same, the bailie by virtue of his office gave sasine to sir John Chepman before witnesses sir William Chepman, Thomas Skune, George Michilhill, Thomas Portuus, Martin Pot. As the law requires the bailie ascended to the principal dwelling house or tenement of his father Richard and there on the ground of the same...gave sasine to sir John [Chepman] chaplain well known heir personally accepting. And soon the said [sir] John...of his own free will out of brotherly love gave earth and stones in hands of the bailie asking that the same give and resign all the tenement to Robert Chepman heritably forever rendering 5 shillings at two customary terms and burgh [ferme] to the lord of Gargunnok from

him his heirs and assignees...by all right ancient and devised [bounds] as it lies in length and breadth between the lands of Stephen Lauder on the south and the tenement of John Brydin on the north. Robert asked instrument. Done (p/t) before sir William Chepman, James [Helme].

11. *Chepman* Same day and hour the said bailies of Selkirk ascended to another tenement in the Peilgait between the tenement of Stephen Loremer on the west, the tenement of Andrew Ker on the east and the king's street on the other side and gave sasine to sir John chaplain, who for the sake of brotherly love of his own free will resigned it in the hands of the bailie who gave it to his brother-german sir William Chepman and his heirs and assignees forever by all its old bounds and divisions as it lies in length and breadth. Sir William asked instrument. Done on the ground of the same before witnesses John Melross, James Helme, David Mithag.

12. *Helme* 15 Jan 1526/27 John Chepmen bailie of Selkirk came at the request of John Melross heir to the deceased John Melross his father to a tenement with pertinents lying between the lands of John Mithag on the north, the tenement of John Lermont on the south, the yard of Patrick Wilkeson on the east and the wide vennel ["vastica"– Kyrk Wynd?] on the west and there on the ground of the same, the bailie gave sasine to John Melross, son and heir of the deceased John Melross paying annual dues and customs and burgh ferme, before witnesses Thomas Portuus, James Helme, sir John Chepman, William Chepman. On the same day and hour, bailie John Johnsone came at the request of John Melross heir of the deceased John his father, to the tenement of James Helme with pertinents in the Peilgait between the lands of John Cadzow on the west, the tenement of John Bradfut on the north and the king's street on the east and there on the ground of the same the said John by delivery of a penny, resigned an annualrent of 6 shillings on the same in hands of the bailie and he gave sasine of the annualrent to James Helme personally present and accepting before witnesses Patrick Sweit, Thomas Trumbull and Richard Yong.

13. *Sir John Chepman* 12 Feb 1526/27 in plain court before alderman and bailies of [?Selkirk] the said John asserted that a royal letter which Robert Trumbull showed was written by himself and was given to him last year viz. 1525[/6] and of our reign 13, before witnesses sir David Chepman, Andrew Keyn and all [the court].

14. [13?] Feb 1526/27 sir John Scott interlocutor for Robert Trumbull asked instrument there in plain court before the alderman and bailies and he presented an instrument of assedation which he had obtained from Janet Huntar relict of the deceased Thomas Trumbull living in Coldengam for his lifetime and another instrument newly made on paper cancelled or drawn up with sign manual of sir John Howme

notary public and a royal letter commanding the alderman and bailies that they should maintain the same Robert in possession of said annualrents unless he is expelled lawfully by right. The said John asked instrument. Done in plain court around noon before witnesses sir David Chepman, Andrew Keyne, James Brydin, Simon Fairle and the whole inquest.

15. **Wilsone and Others** 19 Feb 1526/27 William Wilsone in Galoschelis liable to escheat and arrest at the instance of the lord of Pyrne or his lawful subjects for buying ewes in the public market place from John Penman and John Scott in Beut [or Bent?] and the said alienors were unwilling to find caution for the said buyer and the pursuers knew the said William carried away the said ewes from a house near the market place whither he was led at the 10th hour of the day. William Wilsone in the presence of Adam Scott and lord of Pyrne and his pursuers asked this instrument that he discharged himself of the said ewes to John Penman and John Scott of Beut and discharged himself from the goods and asserted that if anyone wished to escheat him that it should be presented at the burgh court and that the said purchase of ewes would not result in his hurt. Done before John Chepman, John Jonsone, Thomas [Bell?].

16. **Best** 20 Jan 1526/27 John Jonsone bailie came to the tenement of William Robesone lying in the vennel which leads to St Mary's well [Wellwynd] within the bounds of Selkirk between the tenement of David Brydin on the east, the tenement of John Brydin on the south and the king's street on the north and resigned the tenement in hands of the bailie who gave sasine to John Best personally accepting... paying yearly to William Ker 13s 4d and burgh ferme. Before (p/t) Lumsden, William Robesone, William Hoppringill.

17. **sir John Michilhill** 2 March 1526/27 Stephen Lauder compeared before the notary public and witnesses underwritten and acknowledged that he has received and was paid in counted money from sir John Michilhill chaplain the sum of 20 pounds scots for the redemption of one husbandland with pertinents in the lordship of Selkirk which James Murray of Fallowhill now has. The said Stephen quitclaimed and discharged all right and claim to the ownership of his husbandland and ratified that place in the lordship of Ettrick by delivery of and receiving of the said sum according to the tenor of the reversion. Sir John in the name of James Murray asked instrument. Done in the hall of Stephen Lauder before the witnesses sirs James Craik, David Chepman, William Crenstoun, Ninian Crenston.

18. **Walter Scott in Branxhelm, knight** 16 March 1526/27 John Chepman and John Jonsone bailies of Selkirk came with their client ["cliente"] to the principal cross and there proclaimed royal letters of the date 8 March under signet or privy seal and sign manual of the

king warning the underwritten Archibald, Earl of [Angus], James Earl of Araynne and lord of Fleurs and James Hamylton knight of Finnart not to molest or invade Walter Scot of Branxhelm knight or John Crenstoun of that ilk and Walter Scot of Synton or his kinsmen and men under penalty of escheat or forfeiture. Walter Scot asked instrument. Done at the cross around 10 am before John Chepman, John Jonsone, Thomas Scot, Master Michael Scot, sir Richard parson of Sowdone, David Scot of Ashkirk vicar. On the same day Walter Scot declared to all having an interest that the said lords had attacked him and his kinsmen and that he and his kinsmen on behalf of his excellency the king had expelled them into their own parts.

19. *[?Ker]* 21 March 1526/27 John Unis serjeant of the honourable man Robert Bruss burgess of Edinburgh and sheriff of the high commission of our lord king, sheriff of Selkirk specially deputed in that part, appeared and came to the market cross of the said burgh of Selkirk and there on a certain brieve of the chapel royal [chancery] requested by master Thomas Ker, son and heir of the deceased Robert Ker in Sinderlandhall before the great gathering of people on the market day publicly proclaimed and made public to assign a court to the service of the brieve at the tolbooth of Edinburgh before Robert Bruss sheriff of Selkirk deputed in that part on the 5 April next to come for swearing in and holding of the same and the said serjeant by virtue of his office warned and intimated to all those having interest or likely to have to compear on the said day assigned in the said tolbooth and moreover the said John Unys serjeant of the said Robert Bruss sheriff deputed by commission in that part, by virtue and right of his office summoned all the undermentioned persons personally apprehended viz. John Jonsone, John Chepman, bailies of Selkirk, Simon Fairle, James Mithag, John Mithag burgesses of the said burgh, Simon Jamsone, George Jamsone, John Wod, George Ellot, George Freir, William Vynterhoup before Robert Bruss sheriff of Selkirk in that part constituted by commission sitting in judgement to pass to ["transeundum"?] the service of a brieve of the chapel royal requested by master Thomas Ker under pain of £10 scots to each person summoned as is contained fully in the commission of Robert Bruss. Before witnesses James Bell, Thomas Wod, John Archibald.

20. *Master Thomas Ker* Same day place and hour John Unis serjeant of the honourable man Robert Bruss burgess of Edinburgh and sheriff by commission in that part of the sheriffdom of Selkirk, cited the undermentioned personally apprehended Thomas Ker, Robert Dalgless, John Sandelandes, David and John Spottiswood and the underwritten persons to that place viz. William Wods of Hairtherne, Hector Crenstoun of Bold, William Sandelandis of Bold, Alexander Hoppringill of Trowis, Robert Hoppringill of New Hall, George Hoppringill of Torwoodlee, Alexander Franche of [Bukham?] to compear before the said Robert Bruss at a court to be held 5 April next at

the tolbooth of Edinburgh and to pass to an inquest concerning a brieve of the chapel royal requested by master Thomas Ker son and heir of Robert Ker of Suderland Hall under a pain of 10 pounds Scots. Master Thomas Ker asked instrument. Done at the hours of 10, 12 and 1 before the above witnesses.

21. *Haw* (illegible) April 1527 John Lumisden with consent of Marion his spouse and John Brown with consent of his spouse Janet Hawe acknowledged that they had given and granted all right and claim, evidents, ownership and possession which they had or will have to a tenement lying in Selkirk on the south side between the tenement of Thomas Jonsone on the west and north and the common gate called the Fulbrig and the loaning on the south, to John Hawe son and heir of the deceased Thomas Hawe younger and elder his heirs and assignees forever without recall or revocation under penalty of 40 pounds. John Haw asked instrument before witnesses John Chepman bailie, John Brydin, William Ker in Schaw, sir Andrew [Keyne]; concerning the same the court may be held 9 April.

Same day suits called and the court lawfully fenced the parties appeared and manifested by this present instrument that by law James Keyne in the name of John Hawe paid £8: 6s: 8d in gold and silver coins to John Lumisden and John Brown and their spouses to resign all right, claim, letters and evidents to the above which he has or could have before the above inquest.

On the same day place and hour, John Lumisden and John Brown with the consent of their spouses asked this instrument that they made this alienation not for money but for love and affection because said John is nearest heir to Thomas Hawe younger and John Hawe elder his grandfather.

22. *Jonsone* 4 June 1527 John Jonsone bailie came at request of Richard Brydin to the principal dwelling house of Thomas Jonsone burgess of Selkirk lying in the vennel which is commonly called [Ful]brig between the tenement of Thomas Jonsone on the east, the yard of Simon Fairle on the west, part of the lands of master James Jonsone on the north and the king's street leading to the common loaning on the east, and there at the door of the forehouse, the said Richard resigned an annualrent of 7s 6d by delivery of one penny in hands of John Jonsone bailie who gave sasine of the annualrent to Thomas Jonsone. Thomas asked instrument. Done before witnesses George Michilhill, John Scot, James Downe.

23. *Sir David Scot* 5 June 1527 John Jonsone bailie at request of John Smail burgess of Selkirk came to his tenement lying in Pelgait on the south side of the king's street between the yard of William Mithag on the east, the Bog on the south, the tenement of John Mithag on the west and the king's street on the north and there on the ground of the

same the said John Smail... resigned the above tenement with house and yard in the hands of the bailie who gave sasine to sir David Scot vicar of Askyrk paying yearly 32 pence and burgh ferme to Thomas Johnsone. sir David asked instrument before witnesses James Helme, Robert Toddryk, David Jonsone, William Portuus, John Farle.

24. **Master James Jonsone** 12 June 1527 John Chepman, burgess of Selkirk in name of Robert Cadzow living in Davyk whose authority as procurator was plainly evident to me notary public, came to a tenement of land once belonging to William Cadzow now deceased [father?] of the said Robert, lying near the Fulbrig in the said town of Selkirk between the tenement of John and Simon Fairle on the west and north, the tenement of Thomas Jonsone on the south and the king's street on the east, and there John Chepman, procurator in the name of the above, resigned half of the front part and third of the rear of the tenement with pertinents discharging all right and claim to possession of the same which he has or will have in hands of the bailie who gave sasine to master James Jonson, vicar of Valestoun [Walston].

25. **Vinterhoup** 30 April 1527 John Chepman bailie at request of William Vynterhoup heir of the deceased Andrew Vynterhoup came to his tenement lying in the vennel called Goslynne Rawe between the tenement of Robert Brydin on the south, the tenement of Robert Bennat on the east, the tenement of Janet Gray on the north and the yard of Helen Lydderdaill on the west and there at the door of the said forehouse the said bailie gave sasine to William Vynterhoup his heirs and successors personally by touching staff [and baton]. William asked instrument before witnesses underwritten.

At the same place day and hour the said bailie came to the tenement of Janet Gray lying in the south part of the said vennel near the cross with the tenement of Katherine Mychelhill on the north, the king's street on the east and the tenement of Robert Bennat on the south and there on the ground of the same gave sasine of an annualrent of 10 shillings uplifted from the said tenement to William Vynterhoup and his heirs forever by delivery of a penny according to the tenor of his instrument produced in plain court. William asked instrument. Done around 1 pm before witnesses sir Thomas Skune, George Scot, Thomas Doune, Thomas Portuus.

26. **William Chepman** 26 June 1527 John Jonsone one of the bailies at the request of master John Chepmen heir of the deceased James Chepman came to his tenement lying in Pelgait on the north side of the king's street between the tenement of John Portuus on the west and half of the said tenement now in hands of John Chepman on the north, the king's street on the south and the smithy of Stephen Loremer on the east and there at the door of the upper house the said master John Chepman resigned the upper part of the said tenement

with pertinents in hands of the bailie who gave sasine to William Chepman personally accepting by earth and stones and to his heirs and assignees male and female paying to master John his heirs and assignees 20 shillings which will revert to master John if males be wanting. William asked instrument. Done around 6 am before sir William Chepman, James Chepman, Thomas (blank) John Curror and others.

27. **Bennat** 5 June 1527 John Jonsone bailie came at request of Robert Bennat to two back houses of his tenements lying in the burgh of Selkirk between the tenement of William Vynterhoup on the east on the one part, the tenement of Robert Brydin on the south, the tenement and yard of Helen Lidderdaill on the west and the tenement of Katherine Michilhill on the north and there on the ground of the same the said Robert Bennat resigned his two houses in hands of the bailie John Jonsone who gave sasine to Ysabella Benna (*sic*) his spouse in conjunct fee and liferent with free entry and ish paying 12d annualrent to the Lords of Glenrath.

The same day place and hour, the said Ysabella with consent of her spouse Robert Bennat resigned her conjunct fee and liferent of two houses in favour of John her second [son] for graces and services as is contained specifically in the burgh book. John Bennat asked instrument. Done around 6 am before Thomas Portuus, serjeant, Cuthbert Lidderdaill, Thomas Ker, George Michilhill, William Vaich.

28. **Gibsone** 11 June 1527 on St Barnabas day, John Vollson, special mandatary of Robert Scot of Howpasloit acknowledged that he had received a ferme or grassum of £20 scots duly paid by his servants and tenants for the five years immediately following and by the same authority quitclaimed the said servants now and forever. Thomas Gibsone with consent of his friends asked instrument. Done before Robert Brydyn, James Bradfut, John Smyth, William Brydyn, Thomas Ker.

29. **Melross** 9 July 1527. [No text.]

30. **Smaill** 4 [or 5] July 1527 Janet Smaill widow of the deceased George Scot on account of causes urging her soul renounces and admits the conditions and all points made between herself and William Smaill, her brother-german about half a husbandland with pertinents lying in the town and bounds of Lellescleiff within the sheriffdom of Roxburgh for this reason that the assedation and claim pertain to the children of the said Janet Smaill on the decease of her husband George Scot. Janet Smaill asked instrument. Done before sir William Brydyn vicar of Auldroxburgh, George Scot of Blyndhauch, John Middilmest, Adam Boill, William Ailmur, Ninian Smyth.

31. **Forest** 26 July 1527 John Jonsone bailie at request of William Cadzow
     burgess of Selkirk came to a tenement of land of the same William
     with pertinents lying in Selkirk in the street commonly called
     Fulbregrawe on the east side of the same between the tenement of
     James Mouss on the north, the lands of master John Chepman on the
     other side, the king's street on the west and the lands of William Ker
     on the east and there on the ground of the same William Cadzow and
     James Bradfut procurators and in name of David Cadzow resigned all
     the tenement in hands of the bailie who gave sasine of the same to
     Thomas Forest according to the tenor of his charter.

     The same day place and hour, John Jonsone bailie at request of
     William Cadzow burgess came to a portion of the lands on the east of
     the king's street which leads to Selkirk hill between the lands
     commonly called Le Denysland on the north and the other portion
     called the lands of Ladyland on the south and there on the ground of
     the same William Cadzow freely resigned the lands in hands of the
     bailie who gave sasine to Thomas Forest for his lifetime in corporal
     possession paying yearly in 2 equal portions 20 shillings scots at
     Whitsunday and Martinmas at the altar of St Salvator in Calco. Thomas
     Forest asked instrument. Done on the ground of the same around 10
     am before George Mayne, Thomas Jonsone, James Bradfut, James
     Mouss, Robert Trumbull, Andrew MacDuell, James Keyne, David
     Jonsone.

32. **Scot** 16 Aug 1527 James Bessat sheriff in that part compeared at the
     mercat cross of Selkirk and there publicly proclaimed and summoned
     Walter Scot of Branxhelm to compear on Thursday viz. 24 October fol-
     lowing the form and tenor of a royal brieve made thereon…also sum-
     moned John Chepman, John Jonsone bailies of Selkirk to give faithful
     testimony of refusal before witnesses sir David Scot vicar of Askirk,
     Mungo Almur, George Michilhill, Thomas Portuus, Cuthbert
     McLauchlene, Thomas Lame.

     Scot Same day sir David Scot chaplain in the name of his master
     Walter Scot knight requested James Bessat in the name and authority
     of the king for a copy of the said royal letter which the said James
     denied for a time and withheld. Sir David asked instrument before
     John Jonsone, John Chepman, sir David Scot vicar of Askirk, Mungo
     Almuir, William Bennat, William Scot, Thomas Lidderdaill, William
     Brydin, sir William Lidderdaill. On the same day James Bessat declared
     and warned that he had express command from his lord to recite pub-
     licly the king's letters as commanded above before witnesses. Sir
     David asked instrument at the front door of Robert Brydin.

33. **Mynto** 19 Aug 1527 Thomas Mynto burgess of Selkirk came to his ten-
     ement with pertinents and one portion of land lying in "Le Knowe"
     which lies between the tenement of John Brydin on the east of the

town, the tenement of John Scot on the west, the king's street leading to the Milburn on the third side and near to the Ettrik Water on the north and the said Thomas freely resigned the said tenement and portion of land lying over "Le Knowe" between the lands of Thomas Jonsone on the east and the lands of John Keir on the west in hands of bailie John Jonsone who by virtue of his office gave sasine to Elizabeth Notman his spouse in conjunct fee paying burgh ferme viz. 5d and after the decease of the said Elizabeth the tenement reverts to the heirs and successors of the said Thomas. Elizabeth asked instrument before witnesses below.

The same day Thomas Mynto came to the tenement of David Mynto lying on the east of the said burgh between the lands of John Hawe on the east, the lands of Janet Broun on the west, the king's street on the south and the riverbank near Ettrik on the north and there the said Thomas at the front door of the house by delivery of a penny resigned an annualrent of 16 shillings in the hands of John Jonsone bailie who gave sasine to Elizabeth his spouse for her lifetime and after her decease the same reverts to the heirs of the said Thomas. Elizabeth asked instrument. Done before witnesses Thomas Portuus, Cuthbert Haw, John Trumbull.

34. **Trumbull** 25 Aug 1527 Robert Trumbull of Houdene personally present before witnesses below assigned, renounced and quitclaimed all right and claim which he has or he might have hereafter against James Trumbull his cousin in Philophaucht in respect of his wardship, relief and marriage contract done in his own interest, returns royal letters in the hands of said James so that the said James should make humble homage to him as the rest of his subtenants. Moreover I admit the homage and service done and to be done to James Murray so that he will not trouble me in doing my services. James Trumbull asked instrument. Done in the house of William Trumbull before William Trumbull, Robert Sowter, Patrik Fausit, Thomas Ker.

35. **Helme** 26 Aug 1527 James Helme burgess of the burgh of Selkirk asserts that he had entertained a thieving robber in his house and after had brought the same to the sheriff James Murray. James asked instrument that it would not turn to his prejudice afterwards. Done in the said burgh about the hour of 9 before John Chepman, John Jonson, George Haudene, Robert (?).

36. **Haudene** 27 Aug 1527 George Hauden in plain court intimated and declared to William Ker of Schawe personally present and in presence of bailies and witnesses that William alleges that the tenement which I have bought from the heirs of John Mouss owes him those annualrents not paid in the time of the deceased John Mouss and now I make known to the said William and all you having an interest that the said tenement or ground is in itself distrainable ["stringibile"] and

equivalent to the said rents and I protest that firstly at the time of purchase the Lord of Schawe or his heirs should not disturb me in my peaceful possession and that the said annualrent should not come to my prejudice. George Hauden asked instrument before bailies John Jonsone, John Chepman, Stephen Lauder, James Helme and the whole inquest.

37. *Ker of Shaw ("Luco")* Same day. William Ker lord of Shaw in the name of Adam Ker discharged George Hauden in the matter of the said tenement and neither George nor the woman who lawfully sold [it] to him be open to question about state or sasine. William asked instrument before witnesses above.

38. *Hoppringill* No details, Page [15] missing.

39. *Fairle* 13 Sept 1527 John Chepman bailie came at the request of Christian Crukshankis to a tenement lying near the mercat cross of the burgh of Selkirk between the tenement of David Broun on the east, the tenement of the blessed Virgin Mary on the south, the tenement of the heirs of the deceased William Ker on the west, the king's street or the court house on the north and there on the ground of the same Christian Crukshankis with the consent of her heir Thomas Crukeshanke and assent of his heir Mungo Crukeshankis resigned the annualrent of 20s uplifted from all the tenement in hands of the bailie by delivery of a penny who gave sasine of the annualrent to Simon Farle, his heirs and assignees provided always that Christian and her heirs pay £16 to Simon and his heirs and assignees between sun rise and set. Simon Farle asked instrument. Done on the ground of the same around 10 am before William Houp, Thomas Portuus, Thomas Ker, William Turnbull.

[Next side blank.]

40. *Alexander Scot* 23 March 1527. [No text].

41. *Nochtman* 11 Oct 1527 James Mouss burgess of the burgh of Selkirk came to half of a fourth part of his lands of Est Haning which he has in wadset ["vadimonio"] from the heirs of Robert Scot for the sum of twelve and a half pounds scots and there on the ground of the same James resigned the said half of the fourth part of his lands in hands of the bailie who gave sasine to Matthew Nochtman of the said lands and the wadset with all right and claim he has or will have in future provided always that the said heirs of Robert Scot pay twelve pounds and ten shillings to the said Matthew between the rising and setting of the sun. Matthew asked instrument before James Keyn, Andrew McDuell, James Crawfurd, John Lauder.

42. *Wilkesone* 9 Nov 1527 sir Stephen Wilkesone procurator and in name of Isabel, Elizabeth and Agnes Haitle humbly requested John

Crenstoun of that ilk to [be] personally at his principal dwelling house of Kirkhoup on account of a sasine and interest in all of 6 merklands lying in the bounds and lordship of Smalam and the said John asserted and publicly declared in the hearing of the underwritten that the women and heirs of the said lands retain their interest in the said lands when the said John will be called before any judge or judges without fraud or guile of any kind. Stephen asked instrument. Done here at the appointed place before sir William Lidderdaill chaplain at Crenston.

43. *Spottiswod* 16 Dec 1527 sir Ninian archdeacon of the Chapel Royal ["preposaitus (*sic*) capelle regie"] required David Spottiswod son and heir of the deceased Archibald Spottiswod because I am his tutor and have his promise of marriage in my hands and require him from David Hoppringill at this instant and protest before witnesses that his detention should not turn to my prejudice regarding his food and clothing in future nor in time past. sir Ninian asked instrument, done around 1 pm before witnesses sir George Dikesone, chaplain, John Ruderfurd. Also sir Ninian requested the presence of said David as he wanted to (illegible) with him or not and all this he asked David Hoppringill.

44. *Hoppringill* On which day David Hoppringill of Gallochellis denied that he held David Spotsvod by gift of his deceased father but by gift of my firstborn son John Hoppringill and apparent heir; the said John held the said David by gift of the deceased, and afterwards the said young man splendidly and honourably had victuals and clothing from me because my son did not have a place in his own right and straightaway at your request I shall deliver the said David with the approval of my son and I now make demand on the said sir Ninian Spotsvod for his expenses in times past. David Hoppringill asked instrument before witnesses sir George Diksone, John Ruderfurd and others.

45. *Ker* 31 Dec 1527 John Ker and Janet Brown his spouse came to their two tenements lying in the burgh of Selkirk between the tenement of John Acheson on the east, the tenement of William Ker on the west, the croft of master John Chepman on the south and the king's street on the north, and there on the ground of the same John Ker and Janet Brown resigned an annualrent of 20 shillings pertaining to the two tenements with pertinents in hands of the bailie Simon Fairle who gave sasine of the annualrents to Lancelot Ker burgess of Selkirk according to the tenor of the charter from John and Janet saving the right of anyone. Lancelot Ker asked instrument before witnesses Thomas Portuis, George Michilhill serjeant, Alan Keyn, Thomas Mynto, Henry Young.

46. *Lance Ker of Gatschaw* Same day, place, hour Simon Fairle bailie at request of James Haw burgess came to the main dwelling house or

tenement of the same lying in the east of Selkirk between the tenement of Thomas Mynto on the east, the king's street on the south, the
tenement of David Mynto on the west and the riverbank of the Atric
on the north and there on the ground of the same resigned an annualrent of 20 shillings uplifted yearly from the said tenement in the hands
of the bailie Simon Fairle who gave sasine of the annualrent to Lance
Ker according to the charter of John Haw. Lance asked instrument
before witnesses above.

47. **Janet Smyth** 14 Jan 1527/8 Janet Smyth spouse of John Mithag
protested in plain court before alderman, bailies, inquisitors for the
day and witnesses underwritten that the deliberation of an inquest
against her brother John Smyth younger son of the deceased John
Smyth burgess of Selkirk would not come in prejudice of my heirs and
assignees hereafter for reasons given or to be given. Janet Smyth
asked instrument before sir Richard Brydin, William Chepman, George
Michilhill alderman and all the inquest and bailies.

48. **Ker** Same day, place and hour Robert [Ker] interlocutor and procurator for John Smyth son and heir apparent of the deceased John Smyth
his father burgess of Selkirk, publicly declared before the above
inquest that Janet Smyth renounced, demitted and gave away all right
and claim to ownership and possession of all her tenements, annualrents, possessions of which John Smyth died seised and vest. Before
same witnesses.

49. **Robert Ker, procurator in the name of John Smyth** 14 Jan 1527/8
Simon Fairle bailie came to the tenement of the deceased John Smyth
burgess of Selkirk with pertinents lying in the said burgh on the north
of the burgh court house and there on the ground of same gave
sasine of a tenement with pertinents viz. of a croft of the same, one
rig under Know over "le Milschot", two rigs near "le suar (or fuar)
furd", one rig over the west side of "Vosterlais" and one rig over the
east side of "Wosterlais" to John Smyth son and heir of the deceased
John Smyth his father personally present and accepting by delivery of
earth and stones. Robert Ker asked instrument before witnesses sir
Stephen Vilkesone chaplain, John Craw, Adam Vilkesone and others.

Same day and hour before witnesses the said bailies came at request
of Robert Ker procurator to the tenement then inhabited by Christian
Crukshankis on the south side of the burgh near the court house...and
there the bailie Simon Fairle gave sasine of an annualrent of 10
shillings from the tenement to John Smyth younger and his heirs and
assignees according to the tenor of an instrument made thereon and
assigned to him for £8 scots on one day between the rising and setting of the sun. Robert asked instrument before the above witnesses

50. **Achesone** 7 Feb 1526 (*sic*) Robert Brydin bailie of the burgh of
Selkirk came to a tenement of John Achesone lying in the bounds of

the burgh of Selkirk between the tenement of John Trumbull in the
east, the tenement of William Ker on the second side, the king's street
on the south and the waterbank of Etric on the third side, and on the
ground of same there the bailie gave sasine to John Achesone of all
the tenement as lawful heir of James Achesone by delivery of earth
and stones and on the same day, the bailie came to a rig lying over
"le Gosloodaillis" between the lands of the Earl of Angus and
there...gave sasine to said John Achesone as his lawful heir. [John]
asked instrument before witnesses John Lumisden, William
Chesholme, James Lumisden, John Brydin, Andrew Brydin.

51. **William Ker** 7 Feb 1526/27 Robert Brydin one of the bailies of Selkirk
at the request of John Achesone came to his tenement lying in the
said burgh between the tenement of John Trumbull on the east, the
tenement of William Ker on the west, the king's street on the south
and the waterbank of the Etric on the north and there on the ground
of the same resigned the tenement with pertinents in hands of the
bailie requiring the bailie to give sasine provided always that the said
John Achesone, his heirs and anyone in his name, delivers and pays
18 merks to William Ker, his heirs and assignees and also the said
John pays the customary ferme to sir John Chepman or the servant of
St Salvator situate in the monastery of Calco [Kelso] and another 20
shillings to William Ker paid yearly and after relaxation and to this
effect the said William Ker (illegible) before the above witnesses.

52. **Thomsone** Same day, place and hour Robert Brydin bailie at the
request of John Achesone went to a rig of his land lying in
"Gosloodails" between the lands of the Earl of Angus, the lands of
Thomas Jonsone younger on the north and the lands of George
Hauden on the south, the king's street on the east and Charles (illegible) on the west* and there on the ground of the same John Achesone
resigned the rig in hands of the bailie who gave sasine of all the rig to
Robert Thomesone his wife's brother ["leviro"] and John Achesone his
heirs and assignees pay 4 pounds scots to Robert Thomesone his heirs
and assignees and moreover that Robert Thomesone pays 12 pence to
lord of Haining his heirs and assignees yearly. Before witnesses
above.

* [the boundary clause has been entered later.]

53. **Hauden** 27 (April – scored out) February 1527/28 John Jonsone bailie
at the request of Helen Mouss one of the heirs of John Mouss burgess
of Selkirk came to a tenement and the front side of the same, lying
between the tenement of John Haw on the east, the tenement of
David Brydin on the west, the lands of master John Chepman on the
south and the king's street on the north and there at the back of the
tenement Helen resigned the same in hands of the bailie who gave
sasine to George Hauden of all the forepart [as firmly chosen? "fortis

electionis"] of the said tenement paying according to the charter of
John Mouss 16 shillings in name of annualrent to Adam Ker and burgh
ferme to our lord king. George Hauden asked instrument. Done
around 7 am before witnesses George Michilhill, serjeant, John Brydin,
John Brydin elder, Thomas Mynto, John Lumisden, John Chepmen.

54.   **Hauden** 18 Feb 1527/8 Robert Brydin one of the bailies of the burgh
of Selkirk came at the request of Marion Mouss daughter and one of
the heirs of the deceased John Mouss to the back of the same tenement lying between lands or tenements of John Hawe on the east, the
tenement of David Brydin on the west, the lands of master John
Chepman on the south and the king's street on the north and there on
the ground of the same the said Marion resigned the said back of a
tenement in hands of the bailie who gave sasine of the said back of
tenement to George Haudene following the charter of her father, John
Mouss, paying yearly to Adam Ker or his heirs and assignees 16
shillings scots in the name of annualrent and burgh ferme to the king.
George asked instrument before witnesses underwritten.

On the same day, the bailies at the request of Marion Mouss came to a
portion of land in the open fields lying in the bounds of the town of
Selkirk between the lands of Elizabeth Tait in "Taittis hyll" and
between the lands of the lord of Schaw and there on the ground of
the same Marion resigned the portion with pertinents in hands of the
bailie who gave it to George Haudene, his heirs and assignees paying
yearly to Thomas Scot son and heir apparent of the deceased Robert
Scot in Haning 3s 9d. George asked instrument before witnesses John
Chepman, John Bryden younger, John Brydene elder, George
Michilhill serjeant, Thomas Lassibe [Lazenby], Thomas Scot.

55.   **Sir M Ker** 26 Feb 1527/28 Andrew Ker in Grenheid agrees to comply
with royal letters in hands of James Murray of Faulophauch sheriff of
Selkirk, the tenor of which was that a justiciar or his depute compear
at a court at Selkirk on the third day of session...to consider...all the
contents of the said letter. Andrew Ker asked instrument before witnesses sir William Brydin vicar in Aldroxburgh, James Laynge, John
Rankinge chaplain, Mungo Robsone, Thomas Ker, William Ker, James
Scot and others.

56.   **[David] Chepman, John Chepman, Robert Melross in the name
      of Thomas Scot** 10 March 1527/28 John Chepman burgess of Selkirk
discharged and commended to their memory the conscience of the
honourable man Stephen Lauder burgess of the said burgh, how he
had willed [to draw up] his testament for the salvation of his soul and
and the profit of his children and the same Stephen not in due form
(p/t) sound in his mind but labouring in his final pains on his bed
plainly showed as he made signs that he wished to ratify the testament made by him and all that was in it. John Chepman asked instru-

ment on behalf of his brother before John Chepman elder, James Bell, Thomas Ker.

57. **Fairle** 19 March 1527/28 Robert Brydin bailie came at the request of Alan Keyne burgess of Selkirk to his croft lying in the north of the burgh between the lands of the Earl of Angus or James Murray in the east and west and the loaning in the north and the lands of Elizabeth Scot heir of the deceased [?Robert] Scot in the south and there on the ground of the same Alan Keyne resigned the upper part of the croft with pertinents in hands of the bailie who gave sasine of the same to Simon Fairle his heirs and assignees provided always that the said Alan his heirs and assignees pay £7 scots to the said Simon. Simon asked instrument before witnesses Henry Young, Thomas Ker, John Farle.

58. **sir John** [Title only.]

59. **Mithag** 21 April 1528 Robert Brydin one of the bailies of Selkirk came to the tenement with pertinents of the deceased James Mithag burgess of the burgh of Selkirk, lying within the said burgh in Pelgait on the south side of the burgh between the tenement of John Mithag elder on the east, the common called "Le Bog" on the south, the tenement of William Lermonth on the west and the king's street which leads to the loch on the north and there on the ground of the same the bailie gave sasine to John Mithag younger son and heir of James Mithag paying annualrent yearly and burgh ferme. John Mithag asked instrument before witnesses Robert Melross, John Jonsone, John Scot in Pelgat, John Mithag, John Melross and others.

Same day Robert Brydin bailie at the request and special command of John Mithag came to the said tenement and John resigned it in hands of the bailie who gave sasine to Alan Mithag his brother-german, his heirs and assignees forever after the death of Margaret Mithag their mother, paying annualrent and burgh ferme following the tenor of their charter to sir John Chepman chaplain for service to the altar of our Saviour situate in the monastery of Calco. Alan asked instrument before above witnesses.

Same day the said John [and] Alan Mithag resigned the said tenement for a sasine in liferent to Margaret Mithag his mother for favours and deeds etc, before witnesses above and the said Margaret asked it be entered in my protocol book.

Same day before witnesses above, Robert Brydin bailie came to a tenement of the deceased James Mithag which lies in the west of the burgh between the tenement of Andrew Davidson inhabited at that time by John Loremer on the east, the tenement and yard of sir William Bradfut heir of the deceased James Bradfut on the south, the tenement of Robert Brydin on the west and the king's street leading to

Moryss Hill on the north, and there on the ground of the same the bailie gave sasine to John Mithag son and heir of James Mithag paying an annualrent and burgh ferme according to the tenor of the charter made thereon. John asked instrument before witnesses James Bradfut, John Mithag elder, Alan Mithag, John Ross, George Michilhill serjeant, Thomas Ker and others.

60. **Forest** 21 April 1528 Robert Trumbull in Howden set forth in plain court after deliberation of an inquest that he discharged, set forth and quitclaimed to Thomas Forest concerning his intromission with a portion of untilled land ["terre virginalis"] commonly called Ladylands, provided always that the said William Cadzow [?agrees]. Before witnesses James Bradfut, Thomas Johnson, sir John Michilhill, George Michilhill serjeant and all the inquest.

61. **Hog** 23 April 1527 John Hog apparent heir and brother-german to James Hog lately deceased compeared before me notary public and witnesses underwritten [declaring] that James inhabited and held two husbandlands of common land in rental of lord Gawin archbishop of Glasgow lying in the town and bounds of Lillescleff within the sheriffdom of Roxburgh and for friendship and favours done the said John (*sic*) Hog resigned all right and claim he has or will have to said husbandlands with pertinents for his service as serjeant, his constant and special friendship to John Hog through many graces and benefits bestowed in my urgent need and to his heirs and assignees forever. John Hog asked instrument before witnesses William Reddall, William Middilmest, William Trumbull, William Ailmer, John Blaike, David Mithag.

62. **Scot** 16 April 1528 John Scot in Myrris or Vest Manes in Lillescleff acknowledged that he had received from John Scot in Beulie one of the sums of £40 scots in complete payment of the greater sum for the time for 3 portions of land viz. "ye est halff of the vest manes of Lillescleffe" of which sum of £40 I John Scot in Vest Manes hold me · well paid and I discharge the said John Scot in Beulie his heirs and executors forever. John asked instrument before witnesses William Brydin vicar of Selkirk, sir Richard Brydin, David Ker, Robert Chesholm, done at the chamber of James Brydin at around 1 pm.

63. **Lanclus Ker** 30 April 1528 Robert Brydin one of the bailies of Selkirk came at the request of Christian Crukshankis to the fore booth of her tenement with pertinents lying in the burgh of Selkirk on the south of the mercat street between the tenement of William Ker on the west and the tenement of David Brown on the east and the lands inhabited by Alesone Wilkeson on the [south] and the said mercat Street on the [north], and there on the ground of the same she resigned the fore booth with the consent of (illegible) Crukshankis her son and apparent heir in the hands of the bailie who gave sasine to Lancelot Ker, his

heirs and assignees provided always that the said Christian and her son pay Lancelot Ker his heirs and assignees £10 scots. Lancelot asked instrument before witnesses Henry Young, James Richertsone, Thomas Ker.

64. **Scot** 26 May 1528 Simon Fairle one of the bailies of Selkirk came at the request of John Scot in Pelgait to the principal dwellinghouse of his tenement lying between the tenement of Robert Toddryk on the east, the tenement of the deceased James Mithag on the west, the bog on the south and the king's street leading to the loch on the north and there on the ground of the same the said John Scot resigned the said tenement in hands of the bailie Simon Fairle, who gave sasine to Walter Scot his son personally present and accepting, his heirs and his assignees. Walter asked instrument before witnesses John Mithag elder, Robert [Toddryk], David Toddryk his son, Robert Melross and (illegible) Ker.

65. **Margaret Howme** 2 June 1528 James Murray of Faulahill freely constituted and ordained Margaret Houme his wife lawful assignee, as is contained fully in a letter made thereon and sealed, in and to all the place commonly called Louinshoup together with pertinents, lying in the ward of the forest of Ettric within the sheriffdom of Selkirk which the same James holds in tack of our most excellent lady Queen. Margaret asked this instrument before sir John Michilhill, James Craik, Adam Vaych, Adam Dalgless, Cuthbert McLauchlin.

Therefore the said Margaret shall be in peaceful possession from my heirs after my death for graces and favours to me and my children paying yearly from the said place according to law and custom. Margaret asked instrument before witnesses sir James Craik, John Fairbarne, Adam Vaiche, Adam Dougless, Cuthbert McLauchlyn and others.

66. **Elesabeth Dunhoup** 16 July 1528 Robert Brydin bailie came to the tenement of the deceased William Dunhoup burgess of the burgh of Selkirk with pertinents lying on the north side of the Volgat between a tenement of land of our Blessed Virgin Mary on the east and the tenement of Thomas Ellot on the west and there on the ground of the same the bailie gave sasine to Elizabeth Dunhoup heir of William Dunhoup following an old infeftment of the said William. Done on the ground of the same around 4 pm before witnesses master James Jonson, sir William Brydin, David Scot vicar, John Maxwell, John Chepman, John Mithag, Robert Chepman, Thomas Ker, James Hoppringill.

67. **James Hoppringill** Same day Robert Brydin bailie came at the request of Elizabeth Dunhoup to the main dwellinghouse and the same place lying as above and there on the ground of the same tenement with the consent of William Hogart her spouse resigned the ten-

ement of land in hands of the bailie who gave sasine to James
Hoppringill his heirs and assignees forever. Before witnesses above.

68. **_Jamsone_** Same day Robert Brydin one of the bailies of Selkirk came
at the request and special command of James Hoppringill to his tenement as above and there on the ground of the same resigned the said
tenement in hands of the bailie who gave sasine of the tenement to
George Jamsone forever paying an old annualrent and customary
burgh ferme. Before witnesses in previous instrument.

69. **_John Wod_** 25 Aug 1528 Robert Brydin one of the bailies of Selkirk at
the request of John Vycthman came to his tenement lying in the said
burgh between the tenement of Robert Chesholme on the south, the
tenement of William Trumbull on the west, the king's street leading to
the Fulbrig on the east, and there on the ground of the same John
Vycthman resigned the tenement in hands of the bailie who gave
sasine to John Wod so long always as the said John Vychtman and his
heirs pay £6 scots to John Wod his heirs and assignees as is specially
contained in a certain letter made thereon. John Wod asked instrument before witnesses James Jonsone, Thomas Jonsone, William Ellot,
Thomas Ellot, John Scot, Thomas Ker, David Toddryk.

70. **_Margaret Houme_** 2 June 1528 James Murray lord of Fallowhill...
makes, constitutes and ordains after his death Margaret Houme his
lawful assignee in and to his place of Levinshoup with pertinents lying
in the ward of Ettrick Forest and the sheriffdom of Selkirk for the
favour and affection she bears him and for her sustentation of their
children, the which place of Levinshoup the said James holds in tack
of our supreme Queen of Scots as is fully contained in a letter on
paper to the said Margaret from James sealed with his own seal.
Margaret asked instrument [before] witnesses sir John Michilhill, James
Craik, John Fairbair priests, Adam Vaich, Adam Dalgless, Cuthbert
McClauchlyn.

71. **_John Davidson attorney and Janet Scot_** 26 Sept 1528 John
Davidson attorney for John Crenstoun of that ilk and his spouse Janet
Scot came to the principal messuage of 20 poundlands with pertinents
lying in the town and bounds of Smalhame on the east side of the
town within the sheriffdom of Roxburgh and there on the ground of
the same the said John Davidsone presented a certain precept of
sasine of our lord king under testimony of the great seal written on
parchment with no erasures or cancellations...in hands of William
Hendersone sheriff in that part who...handed it to the notary to read
out as follows: James by the grace of God King of Scots to his sheriff
and bailies of Roxburgh and to William Hendersone, John Davidson
and John Stoddart our sheriffs of Roxburgh in that part greeting.
Because we have given and granted to John Crenstoun of that ilk and
his spouse Janet Scot 20 poundlands of Smailhame with pertinents

lying [as above] and 20 merklands of Sprostoun in the town and bounds of Sprostoun on the west of the same which lands with pertinents [belonged] heritably to the said John and which by staff and baton he resigns as contained fully in our charter to him made thereon now we command you to give sasine of the said lands without delay to the said John and Janet [and] whichever lives longer in conjunct fee, dated under testimony of the great seal 15 June 1523 at Edinburgh. After reading out which the said William Hendersone gave sasine of the said lands to John Davidsone attorney for John Crenstoun and his spouse Janet Scot according to the tenor of the charter they have of our lord king. John Davidsone asked instrument. Done on the ground of the said lands around 9 am, before witnesses sir William Lydderdall, William Crenstoun, Andrew Davidsone

72. 26 Sept 1528 John Davidsone attorney for John Crenstoun and his spouse Janet Scot, came to a principal messuage of 20 merklands lying on the west of the town and bounds of Sprostoun and there presented a precept of sasine of our lord king under the great seal written on parchment with no erasures or cancellations and there on the ground of the same John Davidsone attorney for John Crenstoun and Janet Scot [gave it] to William Hendersone sheriff in that part requiring him to execute it and he received it and handed it to the notary who read it out in the form of words as noted in the minute above. After which the said William gave sasine in conjunct fee to John Davidsone attorney for John Crenstoun and Janet Scot his spouse.

73. *Ker* 22 Oct 1528 William Ker in Schaw came to his own principal messuage and tower of Schaw and also to the principal place of the husbandlands of Gerssland and Caponland with pertinents lying in the town of Selkirk and there on the ground of same the said William declared that James Murray bore a false sasine which was now held for breaking, witness John Lumisden.

74. *Curror* 12 Dec 1528 James Scot one of the bailies of Selkirk at the request of John Cadzou came to the tenement of land with pertinents of the said John Cadzou lying within the burgh of Selkirk commonly called "Cauldshellis" near the Pelgat on the north side of the town between the tenement of James Helme on the east and the king's street on the south and the tenement of Thomas Morlaw on the west and the lands of James Murray on the north and there on the ground of the same John Cadzou resigned the tenement of land with pertinents in hands of the bailie who gave sasine to Walter Curror burgess of Selkirk, the said Walter his heirs and assignees paying annualrent and burgh ferme. Walter asked instrument before witnesses John Bryden, William Lermont, Thomas Morlaw, Willam Layng, John Curror.

75. *John Farle, younger* Same day James [Scot] bailie at the request of Simon Farle and his spouse came to their tenement lying in the said

burgh in the street called "Halliwells Hyll" between the tenement of
Stephen Loremer on the east, the tenement of Robert Toddryk on the
west, the bog on the south and the king's street on the north and
there on the ground of the same the said Simon with the consent of
his spouse Janet Fairle resigned the tenement in hands of the bailie
who gave sasine to John younger, his second son for filial love and to
his heirs and assignees after the death of his parents, paying annualrent and burgh ferme. John, younger asked instrument before witnesses Walter Scot in Haining, Robert Trumbull, Thomas Ker, Janet
Lermont, Alexander Scot, Walter Scot, John (illegible), Walter
Lermonte.

* Sir William 20 May Wednesday John Janet J (illegible) one of the
heirs of Glenraich resigns all the annualrents to the lord of the lordship (of Grenheid – scored out) 25 May in (illegible) James Scot.

* This note follows no. **75** but does not seem to relate to it or to the
next entry.

76. ***John Smail*** 15 Aug 1527 John Jonsone bailie at the request of sir John
Brydin chaplain living in Glasgow, came to one part of his tenement
that is to say the back house and the boundary part of a adjoining
close lying in the east and also the abutting part of all of a yard to the
west side of the said house, the boundary of which yard is 31 ells in
length and thirteen and [a] quarter of an ell in width, truly 13 and a
quarter ells and there the said sir John resigned the said back house
and boundary parts of the close and garden in hands of the bailie
who gave sasine to John Smail, his wife's brother and Janet Brydin [his
spouse] whichever lives longer and their heirs and assignees according to the tenor of their charter made thereon. John and Janet asked
instrument. Done around 2 pm before witnesses James Murray,
Thomas Ker, Alexander (p/t), Andrew Bradfut, Robert Chepman.

77. ***Andrew Ker*** 20 March 1527/28 Andrew Ker of Grenheid and Marion
Hoppringill his wife had a precept of sasine written on parchment and
sealed under red and white seals of the noble and potent lord, Robert
Lord Maxwell...and they gave it to the worthy man Nicholas Ainslie
who handed it to the notary public who read it out as follows: Robert
Lord Maxwell to Nicolas Ainslee, William Lauder, Mungo Robson and
Thomas Ker in Selkirk jointly and severally my bailies in that part
greetings. Because I have given and granted to Andrew Ker of
Grenheid and Marion Hoppringill his wife and whichever of them
lives longer...in heritable conjunct fee and to all their heirs lawfully
procreated, all the lands of "Maxwell Heuch" and half of the hauch
called "Maxwell Hauch" with half of the mill with pertinents lying in
the lordship of "Maxwell Fields" and sheriffdom of Roxburgh the
which lands pertained heritably to Andrew Ker and which he resigned
by staff and baton in my hands as superior lord according to my char-

ter to the said Andrew and Marion. Therefore I order and command
you to give sasine of the said lands "Maxwell heucht" and half of "le
haucht" called "Maxwellhauch" and half the mill of the same with pertinents in conjunct fee to Andrew Ker and Marion Hoppringill his
spouse whichever lives the longer or to their lawful attorney according to the tenor of their charter...without delay. In testimony of which
I append my seal and sign manual at Edinburgh 31 January 1527.

The precept being read out the bailie gave sasine of the said lands to
Andrew Ker of Grenheid and Marion Hoppringill his spouse and to
whichever lives longer in conjunct fee, personally present. Andrew
and Marion asked instrument. Done at the appointed place between
10 am and noon before witnesses sir William Penman, John Rankyne
priest, Robert Tait, William Ker, James Ker of Auldroxburgh.

78. *John Ker* 31 Dec 1528 Adam Ker of Schaw, son and heir of William
Ker, came to the ground of six "le daillis" of husbandlands of
Gerssland and Caponland with pertinents lying on the west side of the
burgh liberties viz. "le est burn" which one lies over "le hycht of the
flurris" and one of the rigs over "mylschot" and one rig over "le crukit
landis" and one rig over " Know" and there over "flurris", the said
Adam with consent of his father of his own free will by reason of his
lordship of the same gave sasine of the said six rigs with pertinents to
John Scot personally present and accepting...provided always that the
said Adam Ker and William his father and his heirs and assignees pay
between the rising and setting of the sun the sum of £10 scots to John
Scot his heirs and assignees or before the altar of St Ninian in the
parish kirk of [Selkirk] on premonition. Also that the said John his
heirs and assignees [note above text "described on the sixth day of
November"] so warned were not (*sic*) absent from receiving the said
sum of money that if it was done fraudulently it would be lawful to
return the said lands to Adam and William and put the said £10 for
safekeeping in hands of the bailies of Selkirk. And after redemption
the said John and his heirs will have the 6 rigs in tack for 2 years following paying yearly 12 shillings scots at two terms viz. Whitsunday
and Martinmas all fraud and guile excluded. [Done] before John Scot
bailie, William Ellot, Thomas Ellot, Robert Chepmen, Mathew Notman,
Thomas Jonson younger, John Jonson.

Moreover and [under a clause of warrandice?] the said Adam came to
the tenements of Robert Chepman, John Vod, William Trumbull and
another portion of land lying alongside and Stephen Loremer and on
the ground of the same the said Adam resigned certain annualrents in
hands of the bailie viz. from the tenement of Robert Chesholme 2s,
from the tenement of John Vod 4s, from the tenement of William
Trumbill 17d, from the (illegible) landis 17d, from the tenement of
Robert Chepman 18d, from the tenement of Stephen Lorimer [10d?]
uplifted from the said tenements yearly at two terms by pennies and

the said bailie gave sasine of the said annualrents to John Scot in warrandice for the said rigs by delivery of pennies.

79. 11 Oct 1528 Walter Lauder, brother-german and heir to the deceased
Cuthbert Lauder of Todderyk made, constituted, created and solemnly
ordained and by the tenor of this instrument makes, constitutes, creates and ordains James Lauder his brother his true, lawful, undoubted
and irrevocable procurator, actor, factor, administrator of all his affairs
underwritten and his special and general messenger, the principal
constituting him giving and granting to his procurator aforesaid his
plain, pure, free and utmost power and special and general mandate
for him and in his name to the viewing, disponing, discharging and
quitclaiming of letters of reversion made to the heirs of the deceased
Cuthbert made on redemption of the said lands of S with pertinents
lying in the sheriffdom of Selkirk and in renouncing his right, title and
interest therein in favour of V L burgess of the burgh of Edinburgh or
his heirs or to anyone else with whom he could better agree for certain sums of money or profits to the advantage and benefit of the said
principal And also for suing for, exacting and taking the said letters of
reversion from any holders of them and handing over and delivering
the foresaid [letters] Villiam (scored out) ...and to his heirs or anyone
else with whom he could better agree, giving and transferring his right
in them against them and if necessary against the holders of these letters of reversion as far as recovering the same by summoning them
before any (p/t) spiritual or temporal judges on any competent and
suitable days and places and raising action, making litiscontestation or
litiscontestations and seeing litiscontestation made, producing possessions and articles, giving to anyone asking them an oath of calumny
or verity and any other lawful oath on the soul of the principal and
seeing them given in return, producing witnesses, letters and instruments and any other kinds of proof for or against, making exceptions,
duplies, replies to duplies and if necessary quadruplies, making
protestations, raising instruments, making conclusions and asking for
conclusions, asking for acts, decreets and judgments, both interlocutory and final, to be made and heard and if necessary making objection to and appealing from them and any of them and pursuing the
appeals made, calling on the judge to exercise his office, with the
aforesaid full (p/t) of appointing substitutes And generally doing, per-
forming, saying and exacting all and singular that which [is established
as?] pertaining to the office of procurators in the premises according to
the law or custom of the realm, knowing if they require a more particular mandate than is expressed in these presents [that it will be given?]
and whatever the principal appointing them would or could do if personally present. Moreover the aforesaid principal promised to me
notary public subscribing, putting the question and receiving his reply,
by ostention of his right hand (illegible) touching the holy evangels,
that he ratified and would ratify (p/t) firm and enduring all and what-

soever (p/t) the said James or his substitutes or substitute or of them (p/t) anyone jointly or severally should in his name give (p/t) said in any promise or promises (p/t) should do under the legal penalty, hypothec and obligation of all his moveable or immoveable goods present and future. The principal and James his procurator asked instruments. Done in the parish church of Auldroxburgh around 1 pm before witnesses sir [text ends here].

80.   *Trumbull* 20 Jan 1528/29 Robert Trumbull of Howdene publicly declared in plain sheriff court that it is known that a suitable inquest is to give a determination of the cases brought in the same on the ground of absence of worthy men and barons from the four quarters. Robert asked instrument before the lord of Grenheid alderman, sir William Brydin vicar of Selkirk, Thomas Jonsone.

81.   *John Crenstoun of that Ilk* 20 Feb 1528/29 Robert Lauder of that ilk gave all right and claim of two husbandlands called "le Chykinlandis" and "Coitland" with pertinents lying in the lordship of Smailham within the sheriffdom of Roxburgh which lands the deceased Oliver Lauder possessed with all freedoms thereof as is contained fully in the charter made thereon to John Crenstoun of that ilk for the sum of £40 paid to the said Robert and extended by non-entries to the sum of £100 and if it happens that the said Robert produce instruments or records contrary to the said bond and gift of the said lands called "le chykinlandis" and "coitland" the said Robert binds himself and his heirs to refund the said John Crenstoun and his heirs and assignees £40 within 40 days of the said instruments or records being shown under the extreme penalty that the said Robert will freely renounce his own jurisdiction submitting himself to our jurisdiction. John Crenstoun asked instrument before William Crenstoun of Lauder Wodheid, William Hendersone.

82.   *Alexander Scot* 23 March 1529 Elizabeth Leychman, heir to the deceased George Kyll protested that James Scot bailie entered on her tenement lying in the burgh of Selkirk between the tenements of John Jonson on the east, the tenement of the heirs of Thomas Jonsone on the west, the tenement of William Lermont on the north and the king's street which leads to Hallevolhyll on the south, and there on the ground of the same resigns it in hands of the bailie who gave sasine of the same to Alexander Scot. Alexander asked instrument before Thomas Crukschankis, James Cant, James [Cadzow?], David Jonsone, Thomas Ker and Walter Scot.

83.   [This item was a loose page which has been repaired and encapsulated separately]

...personally compeared the honest woman Isabel Murray daughter and sole heir of the deceased James Murray of Bowhill who died under the banner of our deceased supreme lord king James IV and there of her own free will...the same being of mature age...for her own convenience...has given, sold, conferred and granted all right and claim forever to the estate and possession that she, Isabel has, had or will have to the south part of the lands of Bowhill lying in the lordship of Etrikforest within the sheriffdom of Selkirk, that the said deceased James Murray father of the said Isbelle had in heritable feu ferme of our supreme lord king as in the rental to the honourable man master Michael Scot of Aikwod, her uncle and to William Scot his firstborn son and heir apparent and this for a certain sum of money to be received as dowry at her marriage [in consideration of] many good deeds and acts done for her...the said Isabel transfers all right and claim to master Michael Scot and William his son without revocation and binds herself to give peaceful possession forever, before witnesses Robert Brydin, James Bradfut, George Michill(hill?) and Thomas Scot in Aikwod.

> George Harde 13 shillings f.
>
> Thomas Bruss 7 shillings f. of maill
>
> Ps   28[shillings?] 10 pence
>
> And And Andresone.

"In dei nomine Amen".

84. **Murray** 28 May 1529 master Michael Scot binds himself and his heirs and assignees according to the tenor of these present instruments: he binds himself faithfully to give and confirm the well known young woman Isabel Murray his cousin and niece without any demand or obstacle in and to all her west side of Kershoup and unhesitatingly to give the said Isabel in counted money the sum of 60 merks lawfully for her marriage contract. Before witnesses sir John Michilhill, Thomas Scot in aikwod, James Bradfut, George Michilhill.

85. **Maister Michaell Scott** 28 May 1529 The young woman Isabel Murray, only daughter and heir of the deceased James Murray in Bouhyll who died under the banner of our lord king at Flouden, freely alienated all right and claim which she has had or will have in the south part of Bohyll which her father the deceased James Murray held heritably in rental and feu of our supreme lord king, to master Michael Scot her uncle for a certain sum of money to be received on her marriage settlement and for the many graces, done or to be done as is fully contained in his instrument of obligation to Isabel made thereon. Before witnesses Thomas Scot, sir John Michilhill, James Bradfut, George Michilhill.

86. The following list and memorandum was inserted between the pages on a loose sheet. It has been repaired as a separate sheet. [The first part of the list is illegible.]

Side 1

Jhone Hayte

Mychell Ranaldsone

James Leycham Dand Ba( )

Volle Stevinson iurates

Removit

Dande Vilsone 3 a Rig on harkas carn

Thome Lille 3 ane R ri[g?]

Pait Roull 3 a R[ig] on haikas

Jame Leycham a but one the brery bank

David Hog a Rig one bank

Vol Halliwell a croft on the (?) flat

Jame Bauld at est end of the toun, ane coit croft

(this item scored out)

Jame Leycham a croft of the baillie barn

Thome Hervy a croft of baillie berne

Robert Hog a croft of belle cross

Voll Hallewell a croft of end [?raw] (scored out)

Jhone Haiste a croft of belle croft

John Roull a croft of over raw

James Leycam a croft of belle bern

George Vatsone a croft of b (scored out)

Martyne of Bonnatoun a crooft one the au[ld] raw croft

Voll Hountar a croft of the end raw

James Hog a croft of the but croft

Stevin Bonnatoun a but croft

Memorandum.

Nyche Ranaldsone a 2 of orfla (scored out)

David Hog ane braid Rig of orfland (scored out)

(illegible) vels bigang 3 a R of viffland

Med (?)

Michell Ranaldsone croft under the toun of husbandland

(scored out).

Side 2

James Hog a croft rig under the toun

Velle Bonntoun a croft rig under the (illegible)

Jhon Clanat a croft rig under the toun

Stevin Bonetoun a rig under the toun

Voll Stevinston a croft rig under aittes

Pait of Roull a croft (scored out)

Ysabel Jak a croft rig under the toun

David Hog a croft rig

Martyne Bonnetoun a rig of ry under toun

Jok Millar a rig of quheit under toun

Voll Mychelsone a croft rig of a[ittis?] under the toun

Pate Roull a croft rig of b under toun

Matho (scored out) Andro Swanston croft of R

under the toun

Pait Roull a but at (illegible) of toun

Georde Vatson 2 crofts at est end of [the town?]

calit Kilspett

Andro Swanston 3 a croft in the Kylpett

James Lycheam a butt under the bankes

Item Volle Millar a croft in the C(illegible)

Andro Swanston(?) a croft in the f/sost croft.

David Newbigin a 3 croft frs C

Mychel Ranaldsone a croft in fost (scored out)

Robert Hog a rig in the luleess

David/Dand Bonetoun...

Side 3

...Ysabel Jak of rig end of Thowlesbern

Marytne of Leycham a croft rig of quhitreig

(scored out)

Watte Elwand a rig q/g of quhitreig

Voll Nycholsone a rig of q aittes

David Hog a 31 rig of gres aittes (scored out)

Jhone Haiste 1 rig of q aittes

Nycholl Ranaldsone 1 rig of qrig aittes (scored out)

Dand Hog 3 (?) of aittes quhitrig (scored out)

Voll Millar a quarter rig of (?)

Vell Vilsone a quarter croft of nov(?) of bere

Jame Hog a quarter rig aittes

Stevin of Bonatoun 1 quarter rig (?) bere

Robert Hog 3 a rig one the (?)

James Roul a croft one the grene syd of aittes

Voll Stevinsone a croft above the grene syd aittes

Joke Millar above the grene sid, a croft of aittes

Martyne Bonnatoun 1 croft aittes in todho[ll?]

Jok of Lycham 31 rig of tod holl aittes (scored out)

Voll Millar 31 rig under the tod hoit (scored out)

Ysabell Jak a rig of aittes tod hot

Robert Hog, Andro Hog for a coit/cot lands in the briglands aittes (scored out)

Jame Millar a coitlands lyand in the crulzes beir (scored out)

Side 4

( )yne Bonaton

Philes Roull

Vol or Nycholl Ranaldsone

Joke Mathesone

Helyne Vilsone

Kaitte Drouchquhen

Kaite Snyp (?)

Ane tenement of Martyne Leicham ane merchand Cristeanne

Newbiging tenand to Hob Robesone

Voll Brig (scored out)

Corne Suborand to him to Voll Brig

Ysabell Ormston

Watte Elw(and?)

Jhone Lowe (illegible)

Woll Stevinsone.

* "Memorandum the coumpt of the skynnes deliverit be Jhone Vilsone to the lady that comes fra James the greiff of the berues.

Item X rouch skynnes and fyv clippit skynnes.

Item VI skynnes that the lady sent out of Roxburgh by the first coumpt".

87. *John Chesholme* 10 June 1529 James Scot bailie of Selkirk at request of Robert Chesholm came to his tenement lying in the street commonly called "Fulbrig Myr" between the tenement of Simon Fairle on the south, the tenement of John Vychtman on the north, the yard of Simon Fairle on the west and the king's street on the east, and there on the ground of the said tenement resigned the tenement in hands of the bailie who gave sasine to John Chesholm first born son of Robert personally present and accepting and to his heirs and assignees, the said John paying yearly 6 shillings after the death of his father to Adam Ker of Shaw his heirs and assignees and 3 halfpennies in burgh ferme observing all articles and clauses after written viz. the said John gives his parents £8 for favour [done] to him and the said John gives £7 for the purchase of the tenement and if the said Robert or his wife are impoverished, the said son will pay as much for the said tenements as they might have had from others. John Chesholm asked instrument before witnesses John Chesholm in Pelgait, Thomas Jonsone, John Vychtman, David Jonsone.

88. **John Scot** 8 May 1529 John Scot bailie of Selkirk at the request of the young man William Lermont son and heir of the late William Lermont burgess of Selkirk came to his tenement lying in "le Halleuolhill" between the tenement of Thomas Jonsone and Alexander Scot on the south, the king's street leading to the kirk on the west, the tenement of Thomas Melross son of the deceased [?John] Melross on the north and the yard of John Jonsone son and heir of the deceased John Jonsone burgess of the said burgh on the east and there on the ground of the same William Lermont resigned all the tenement with a croft of arable land and pertinents lying within the liberties and bounds of the said burgh between the lands of William Keyn and (blank) in hands of the bailie who gave sasine of the said tenement and croft with pertinents to John Scot burgess and Elesabeth Chepman his spouse and to whichever lives longer.

89. **Margaret Hoppringill** 17 July 1529 David Hoppringill in Galloschellis and lord of the lands of Smailham Crag, made his testament and made his executors, Margaret Lundy his spouse and James Hoppringill his first born son, procreated with the lady Margaret, and the said David Hoppringill appoints as advisers ["adiutores"] his superiors, master Andrew Dure lord abbot of Melrose and master Andrew Houme rector of the church in Lauder in all and singular causes affecting or seeking to affect these executors and the said David...of his own free will leaves all his moveable goods, grain, utensils and household [goods] to his four daughters viz. Agnes, Christian, Janet and Margaret Hoppringill on his decease to be shared between them. Margaret asked instrument before witnesses Elizabeth Hoppringill lady of Polvort, master Robert Hoppringill rector of Morham, James Hoppringill of Tynnes brother-german of the same, Bartholomew Houme, Agnes Cogburn, sir George Ellot and David Gray.

90. **John Haw** 6 Aug 1529 On which day John Mithag renounced forever his interest which he and his brothers and sisters have against John Haw in all the goods of the deceased Katherine Mithag spouse of the said John and quitclaimed them forever. The said John asked instru-

ment before witnesses master James Jonsone and Robert Chepman with the proviso that the said John Mithag requested all his mother's clothing to be given to his three sisters with [?], one bed covering, a patchwork cloth and small linen cloths ["lenthaminibus"] new and of the best and all these specified things the said John Haw gives kindly at the request of the said John.

91. *Alan Keyne* 16 Oct 1529 Alan Keyne came at the request of the venerable man sir John Keyne, chaplain in Glasgow, to the principal tenement of Alan Keyne brother-german of the said sir John Keyne, lying in the burgh of Selkirk on the north of the town between the tenement of Adam Vilkesone on the west and the tenement of Elesabeth Strang widow on the east and the king's street on the south and the croft of the heirs of the deceased John Smyth on the north and there on the ground of the same Alan Keine brother of the said sir John Keyne presented a precept of sasine sealed and written on paper and put it in hands of Robert Portuis bailie requiring him to execute the said precept and he received it and handed it to the notary to make it public as follows: John Keyne chaplain to James Brydine, Robert Portuis and James Keyne bailies in that part, greetings. Because I have given and delivered to Alan Keyn burgess of the burgh of Selkyrk all those lands with pertinents belonging to the said Alan lying in the said burgh I order and command you to give sasine of the said lands to Alan according to the above without delay and without omission. In testimony of which I append my own seal at Glasgow (p/t) 1529 before (p/t) James Farbarin and others.

92. *Simon Fairle* 26 Oct 1529 Robert Chepman bailie came at request of Alan Keyne burgess of Selkirk to his two crofts viz. a lower and an upper of which the lower is between the lands of the lord vicar viz. "the gled" [the glebe?] on the west and the lands of James Murray on the east and on the north the common loaning and the croft of the heirs of Robert Scot on the south and there on the ground of the same the said Alan freely resigned the two crofts in hands of Robert Chepman bailie who...gave sasine of the said crofts to Simon Fairle burgess personally present and accepting by delivery of a penny and also delivered 40 shillings uplifted yearly at two terms, Whitsunday and Martinmas, provided always that the said Alan, his heirs and assignee pay Simon Fairle his heirs and assignees £32 scots. Simon Fairle asked instrument. Done on the ground of the said crofts around 8 am before William Portis, John Bradfut, John Stenson.

93. *Master Robert Hoppringill, James Hoppringill* 15 Nov 1529 master Robert Hoppringill and John Hoppringill in Tennes interlocutors, procurators and factors for David Hoppringill [in Galo]schellis came to a general council of all the whole of the convent and abbey of Melross where (illegible) Robert Hoppringill and John Hoppringill publicly showed to the said master that the said field ["glebella"] called

(blank) which lies near (illegible possibly Moshouse) and all the lands of the moss of Langshaw specified in our tack contained in the rental book of the said monastery where it says "with its pertinents" by reason of which the said field is in our pertinents of Langshaw as we have faithfully proven through indwellers and neighbours on the ground of the same. Master Robert and James asked instrument before witnesses dean Alexander Bellendene, John Maxwell, Patrick Vychtman.

94. **Dene** Same day, place and hour. The dean, interlocutor for the whole convent of the monastery of Melross, publicly and in a loud voice showed in presence of witnesses underwritten that David Hoppringill in Galscheillis, his men, accomplices and tenants has witheld or sought to withhold our portion or field of the said land (blank) which is part of the pertinents of our place of Moshouss held by force and strength, oppressed by strong men and his [young men?] put to flight and with no little hurt and [destruction?] to us and ours, our profit despoiled, by reason of which the said assedation of Langshaw given to David and his heirs is made null and void.

95. **John Hoppringill** 6 Dec 1529 John Ruderfurd, Lord of Honthill and Christian Hoppringill laymen, desirous of a marriage contract between themselves first read the banns three times in their parish churches viz. Lyndene and Jedburgh...before Master Adam Mostrope curate in Jed and sir George Ellot curate in Lyndene and then on the same day Adam Rudirfurd, burgess of the burgh of Jedburgh declared in the chapel of Galloschellis to all having an interest that the said John Ruderfurd and Christian Hoppringill were barred from marriage by reason of being within the prohibited bounds of the third and fourth degrees of consanguinity so that they might not be joined in marriage and John Hoppringill showed a dispensation from the apostolic see [i.e. Rome] procured by the venerable man sir John Dingwell, chancellor of Aberdeen and [provost] of [the college] of the Holy Trinity near the burgh of Edinburgh in the diocese of St Andrews, signed and sealed with an oblong seal of red wax stamped on white in a certain iron box with cord of grey colour hanging [therefrom] whole and not erased but sound and not spoiled, not in any way cancelled or suspect but lacking all blemish and suspicion of blemish along with the following instrument and under the subscription of master William Meldrom notary public containing the said bull and the said dispensation whose opening is phrased "Laurence by the mercy of God, bishop of Praeneste etc..." and this was put in the hands of the curate of Lyndene sir George and after the dispensation was made public and truly understood the said curate solemnized the marriage of the said John and Christian in face of the said chapel before witnesses underwritten. John Hoppringill in the name of the said John and Christian his sister asked instrument. Done around ten am in the oratory ["oritorum"] or chapel of Galloshellis before witnesses master

John Doby official of Teviotdale, Robert Hoppringill, sir John Ruderfurd, George Davidsone and David Gray priests, [Robert?] Hoppringill, George Hoppringill, Duthac Ruderfurd, John Ruderfurd, Robert Ruderfurd, Patrick Ruderfurd.

96. ***Alexander Scot*** 22 March 1528(*sic*) Thomas Crukshank and his mother [Violet?] Leychman bind themselves faithfully to give sasine of all a tenement to the said Alexander (illegible)] with an annualrent of 6 shillings in hands of John Mithag and of certain rigs of field land in the lordship of Selkirk and on the same day he acknowledged he was given a chest viz. "ane kyst, foir treis of ane wovin [i.e. weaving] loum and the maill that Thome Scot tuk vrangusly that yeir by past". Before witnesses John Jonsone, William Diksone, Thomas Ker.

97. (This entry is scored out as far as *)

Thomas Morolawe 23 Dec [1530] (7th year of Pope Clement). James Scot one of the bailies of the burgh of Selkirk, at the request of Thomas Prechour and Janet Lermont his spouse came to a rig or portion of land lying near the town on the west side between the loch and the boundary of the town and a portion of land of Walter Curror on the (illegible) part and another portion of Andrew Schortreid's on (blank)* and there on the ground of the same the said Thomas and Janet resigned the said portion of land in hands of the bailie who... gave sasine of the same to Thomas Morolawe. Before witnesses Walter Curror, John Scot, William Lermont.

98. ***Crukschankis*** 10 Jan 1529/30 Robert Chepman bailie at the request of Christian Crukschankis relict of the deceased Alexander Crukschankis came to the store room and back chamber over the tenement of the said Christian, lying in the burgh of Selkirk between the tenement of the deceased David Brown on the east, the tenement of Walter Ker on the west and the yard of George Jamesone on the south and the king's street on the north and there on the ground of the said chamber the said Christian resigned the same in hands of the bailie who gave sasine of all the back part of the tenement, the boundaries of which are upper and lower to the "propell vallis" [i.e. boundary walls], to Thomas Crukschankis, first-born son to Christian, burgess of Selkirk. Thomas asked witness instrument before witnesses Lance Ker, Alan Keyne serjeant, Henry Young, John Vylsone .

99. Same day, same place. Robert Chepman bailie came at request of Christian Crukschankis and Thomas Crukschankis, heir of the deceased Alexander Crukschankes to a storehouse and back chamber with inner wall of the same tenement of the said Christian and Thomas lying in the burgh of Selkirk [same boundaries as no. 98] and there on the ground of the said storehouse Christian and Thomas resigned the storehouse and back chamber measuring in length four and a half ells and the same in breadth in hands of the bailie who gave sasine to Lance Ker personally present and accepting. Lance Ker asked instrument before Alan Keyne, Henry Yoing, John Vic, David Jonsone.

100. **George Ker of Lyntoun** 3 Feb 1529/30 Archibald Ellot, Gavin Ellot brothers-german, Simon Armistrang Lord of Quhithauch, Ninian Armistrang from their certain knowledge and in the name of Robert Ellot alias Flaskvod for repledging and bringing of the said Robert sound and whole on the 7th March 1529 within the iron and wooden gates of the manor of Fairnele in safe keeping with lawful delivery to George Ker of Lynton, his heirs and assignees and remaining there until he was lawfully delivered to the said George his heirs and assignees all fraud or guile excluded, failing which we moreover Archebald Ellot, Gavin Ellot, Simon Armistrang, Ninian Armistrang foresaid bind ourselves to the said George Ker, his heirs and assignees, jointly and severally to be content to pay the sum of 300 of the english "le angell nobillis" of gold within 40 days after and immediately following for the attacks, armed raids, losses and diverse troublesome actions of plunderers and evil deeds by the said Robert Ellot and his accomplices perpetrated openly and in secret against the said George Ker... in corroboration of which faithful promise the said Archebald Ellot, Gavin Ellot, Simon Armistrang and Ninian Armistrang hold up their hands in a sign of a faithful promise. George [Ker] asked instrument before witnesses Martin Ker in Lytilden, George Ker in Fausyd, Andrew Ker in Grenheid, Philip Scot in Edschaw, Walter Scot in Synton, John Riddail.

101. **Hoppringill** 3 Feb 1529/30. James Hoppringill in Tennes and Sibella Carmichell his spouse presented a precept of sasine written on parchment with parchment tag sealed with stamped white wax of our noble lord king James without erasures or cancellations, not spoiled or suspect, to Gilbert Chesholme and he received it and handed it to the notary to be read out as follows: James by the grace of God king of Scots to the sheriffs and bailies of Selkirk also George Chesholme, Thomas Patersone our sheriffs in that part greetings. With the advice and kind consent of the lady queen liferentrix of the lands and lordship of Etrik forest and of our comptrollers of the rolls, we have given and granted in feu ferme and demitted heritably to James Hoppringill and Sibella Carmichell, lady of Caldervod his spouse and to whichever lives longer in conjunct fee and to their heirs, all our lands of Tennis with tower, manor, woods thereto and pertinents lying in our lordship of Ettrik forest and sheriffdom of Selkirk extending yearly in our old rental to the sum of £9 as contained fully in our charter made thereon. We command you and order you to give sasine of the said lands to James and Sibella or their lawful attornies without delay according to the tenor of our said charter. Dated under testimony of the great seal at Edinburgh 19 Oct in the 17th year of our reign.

After the precept was read out the said Gilbert gave sasine of the lands of Tennis with tower, manor and woods thereof to the said John and Sibella and their heirs and to whichever lives longer in conjunct fee by delivery of stones and wood as is the custom according to the tenor of their charter. James and Sibella asked instrument or instruments done around 1 pm before witnesses sir George Andersone chaplain, David Maxwell, William Thomsone.

102. ***Brydin*** 22 March 1529/30. Robert Chepman bailie of the burgh of Selkirk at the request of Andrew Dounaldsone burgess came to two rigs lying between the lands of Patrick Murray and there on the ground of the same the said Andrew resigned the 2 rigs in hands of the bailie who gave sasine to John Brydin burgess of Selkirk, and to his heirs. John asked instrument before William Ker lord of Schaw, John Lumisdene, George Bayne.

103. ***Philip Scot on the part of Thomas Forest*** 13 April [1530] Robert Trumbull superior of Phillophauch, declared he is content to set in tack that half of the lands called Ladylands specified in his charter to Thomas Forest and his heirs and assignees for the sum of £5 scots paid to the said Robert by Thomas and that the said Thomas his heirs and assignees shall possess and enjoy the said lands one year after relaxation and payment of the said sum. Also the said Robert chooses the said Thomas and his heirs faithful tenants to him and his heirs. Also that the said Thomas and his heirs are satisfied thankfully as much as any others would wish to be. Philip Scot in the name of Thomas Forest asked instrument before Walter Scot in Synton, master Michael Scot in Aikvod, sir John Michilhill, James Scot, Alexander Bradstanes, Walter Scot in Haining and others.

104. ***William Scot in Harden*** 10 April 1530. On which day the underwritten worthy men swore in the presence of notary and William Brydin vicar of Selkirk and in the presence of Margaret Lauder spouse of the deceased Stephen Lauder by touching the Evangel [saying] in the vernacular: "Item first, Woll Scot of Harden sweir that he was awud na mair bot ane merc to the gud man Stevin of Lauder fulfilland all condicionis by past and rychtsua Andro Schortreid, Vol Scot in Toddryg, John Hovatsone, Thomas Michell, Thomas of Chesholme, John of Chesholme sweir all [quhost but?] upone the holy evangell of God the said William Scot in Toddryk was awud na mair but ane merc to Stevin Lauder his ayris and assignas". William Scot asked instrument before witnesses above written.

105. 5 Aug 1530. Mark Ker, Walter Scot in Hanyng, James Ker in Grenheid, Thomas Ker in Selkirk, Robert Ker, John Scot in Aikwod, Thomas Scot younger there, Roger Murray, William Lauder in the presence of notary and witnesses publicly declared in the vernacular that: "We the efforsaid Mark Ker etc tuk horss, meill and men and uther diverss geiris fra travelouris quhilke var don us to understand that thai ar of Annandaill and supportit tratouris and theiffis rebaldis of the kingis graice and now by thairis greit aychtis and utheris fathful informationes, we understand that thai ar trew travelouris in Moffat toune, we haf geffin all thairis geiris that we intrometit unto thaim agane. In vytness heirof be for our bailye Simon Fairle, Robert Trumbull, William Brydin, William Chepman, sir John Brydin and others".

106. *James Ker* 7 Aug 1530. Margaret Hountar relict of the deceased Robert Ker in Sonderlandhall ordains and appoints by the tenor of this instrument James Ker her second son her true and lawfull assignee for favours and good deeds done and to be done in and to all her lands of Brigheucht and Lynden, the grain, oxen, cows, plough, teinds, fines, fermes and profits pertaining to the same and all moveable and immoveable goods belonging to the said place or held to belong as specified in other evidents and the said Margaret renounces all right and claim, possession, ownership, assedation from herself and her heirs and all right or title in future to the said place with pertinents in favour of the said James forever. James asked instrument before witnesses William Carncross, master Michael Scot, sir William Bryden, Robert (illegible).

107. *Chepman* 16 Aug 1530 Simon Fairle one of the bailies of the burgh of Selkirk at request of sir John Chepman chaplain in Fairnele came to his tenement lying in the burgh of Selkirk between the tenements of master John Chepman on the north and west, the tenement of sir John Brydin, chaplain in Glasgow on the south and the king's street leading to the loch in the east and there on the ground of the same sir John resigned the tenement in hands of the bailie who gave sasine to the young man James Chepman brother-german of sir John for brotherly favours and kindness. James asked instrument. Done on the ground of the same around the hours of 3 and 4 pm before witnesses sirs William Chepman, Thomas Skune, Laurence Jonson priests, James Murray, William Chepman, William Trumbull.

108. *Robert Chepman one of the bailies* 29 Sept 1530.

[No details given.]

109. *Chepman* 3 Oct 1530 sir William Brydin vicar pensioner of the parish church of the burgh of Selkirk, came to a tenement of land of master John Chepman burgess of Edinburgh lying within the said burgh on the west of the mercat cross, between the tenement of land of the deceased Stephen Lauder on the south and the tenement of land of the deceased Robert Brydin on the north and there sir William resigned forever an annualrent of 4 shillings scots sold and alienated to him by Christian Inglis with consent and assent of her spouse Thomas Geddess which annualrent was uplifted at two terms in the year viz. Whitsunday and Martinmas in equal parts, from the tenement

belonging to the said master John in hands of the bailie by delivery of one penny and the bailie gave sasine of the annualrent of 4s to master John Chepman according to the tenor of the charter to him from sir William Brydin. Master John asked instrument before witnesses sirs John Keyne, John Chepman chaplain, James Keyne, William Chepman, John Craw, William Trumbull burgess, Thomas Mab[one], "Murray in the sheriff court of Selkirk".

110. **Lauder** 29 Oct 1530 Patrick Murray of Faulawhill and lord of the husbandlands of Selkirk, of his own free will came to a tenement of land of the deceased John Keyne burgess of the burgh of Selkirk, lying in the east of the burgh between the lands of Robert Chepman on the east, the lands of the deceased Cuthbert Trumbull on the south, a tenement of land of Alexander Haw on the west and the king's street on the north, and there on the ground of the same Patrick Murray of his own free will gave sasine to William Lauder burgess of the burgh of Edinburgh and his heirs and assignees according to the tenor of his charter from Patrick Murray made thereon. William asked instrument. Done on the ground of the same around 3 pm before witnesses sir John Michilhill chaplain, Thomas Jonsone, Thomas Murray, James Scot bailie, John Brydin.

111. **Dounaldsone** 5 Nov 1530. James Scot bailie came at request and special command of an inquest to the tenement of the deceased Ninian Dounaldsone elder lying in Selkirk between a tenement of land of John Lumisdene on the east, a tenement of land of William Ker on the west, a tenement of land of Thomas Mynto on the north and the king's street leading to the well on the south and there on the ground of the said tenement the bailie gave sasine to John Dounaldson lawful heir of Ninian Dounaldsone of all the said tenement with pertinents, paying yearly to Adam Ker of Schaw the customary annualrent. John asked instrument before witnesses William Portuus serjeant, John Lumisdene, John Cruk, John Achesone, Andrew Dounaldsone and Ker of Schaw.

The same day, place etc, William Ker of Schaw broke the said sasine before the above witnesses.

112. **Howatsone** 17 Nov 1530 John Mithag bailie of Selkirk at the instance of John Achesone burgess of Selkirk came to a tenement of land of the said John Achesone lying within the burgh in a vennel called "Voll Gait" between a tenement of land of John Lumisden on the east, a tenement of land of William Ker in Schaw on the west, the lands of Patrick Murray on the south and the king's street leading to the well on the north and there on the ground of the same the said John Achesone of his own free will resigned an annualrent of 10 shillings in hands of the bailie who gave sasine of the annualrent to John Howatsone, his heirs and assignees, provided always that John

Achesone and his heirs pay the sum of £8 scots to John Howatsone and his heirs and assignees. John Howatsone asked instrument before witnesses James Viss, Robert Hog, David Jonsone.

113. **Walter Scot, knight** 26 Jan 1530/31 Andrew abbot of the monastery of Melrose of the Cistercian Order in his head court held at the said monastery on the said day, gave and granted apostolic letters of the heritable office of bailie of the said monastery to the honourable man, Walter Scot of Branxhame, knight to administer the same according to the tenor of letters of obligation made by the said Sir Walter to the abbot and convent. Walter asked instrument. Done in the face of the said court between 11 and 12 am before witnesses Mark Ker of Dolphynstoun, John Houme of Coldenknovis, Andrew Ker of Prumsyd, George Hoppringill of the Chapel of St John, George Ker of Lyntoun with many others Patric Craufurd, sir William Brydin, sir John Scot, Ninian Brydin notary public.

114. **Venerable Father Andrew Dury Abbot of Melross** Same day the venerable father Andrew in the same court after he had given the said apostolic letters of the heritable office of bailie of the said monastery to Walter Scot of Branxham, knight, said that the said office of bailie was not to be given to the said Walter unless under the condition that he observe and firmly guard all the bounds and keep all promises of his letters of obligation under sign manual subscription and seal of the abbot and his monks and the said Walter Scot faithfully binds himself to the abbot and his convent and the abbot handed over the same letters of obligation in face of the court. Abbot Andrew asked instrument before witnesses underwritten. [As no. **113**]

115. **Davidsone** 9 Feb 1530/31 Agnes Davidsone relict of the deceased Adam Grymislaw and Elizabeth his heir declare that they have of their own free will received the sum of £40 scots in pennies and penny-worths from their cousin Ralf Davidsone in Chames and that for a certain sum of money, Agnes Davidsone and Elizabeth Grymislaw heirs of Adam Grymislaw have set in tack and wadset their third portion of Chames with pertinents within the bounds of all the tack of Chames in the lordship of Myntou in the sheriffdom of Roxburgh provided always that the women their heirs and assignees pay £40 to Ralph Ker on one day between sun rise and set at the altar of St Mary the Virgin at the parish church of Mynto and also we wish that the said Ralf member of our household shall peacefully enjoy our said third part of Chames for nineteen years after the relaxation and paying yearly the said sum of two and a half merks from the said Ralf, his heirs and assignees to the women as is contained in a letter of assedation sealed with the appointed seal of the venerable man sir William Brydin vicar of Selkirk. Concerning which we Agnes Davidsone and Elizabeth Grymslaw jointly and severally in the strict form of an obligation faithfully and by touching the Holy Evangel bind ourselves to the said Ralf

purely and simply to observe all articles and points contained in the said letter of assedation and wadset made to the said Ralf, his heirs and assignees all cavil, fraud and guile excluded failing which should the said Ralf his heirs and assignees be in any way disturbed, vexed and troubled in his peaceful possession of the third part of Chames, we are bound as above in all our goods moveable and immoveable and places [that we] have and will have and of our livings under penalty of the sum of double £40. Ralf asked instrument before witnesses Mark Ker burgess in Selkirk, William burgess in Edinburgh, John Hawe, Stephen Hendisone, David Jonsone.

116. *Andrew Ker* 30 Jan 1530/31 Helen Fallaw, one of the ladies of the lordship of Softlaw...of her own free will...as is fitting has wadset and alienated all right and claim, ownership and possession which she has or will have in and to her half of all the lordship of Softlaw with pertinents lying in the sheriffdom of Roxburgh to Andrew Ker of Prumsyd loucht his heirs and assignees for the sum of £160 scots thankfully paid to the said Helen also I will for more security seal a precept of sasine and according to the tenor of the same [give] sasine to the said Andrew Ker his heirs and assignees of all my half viz. (illegible) of the lordship of Softlaw. On the same day Andrew Ker of Prumsyd binds himself faithfully by touching the holy Evangell to seal with his own [seal] a reversion of Helen Fallaw in which reversion was plainly laid out that the said Helen and her heirs shall peacefully enjoy two husbandlands of the lordship of Softlaw which failing the said husbandlands with pertinents shall revert to the said Andrew and his heirs and furthermore the said Helen and her heirs on one day between sun rise and set to [pay] at the altar of St Katrin in the monastery of Calco [Kelso] the sum of £160. Andrew and Helen asked instrument before witnesses Gavin Ellot, sir John Rankyne, James Ker, Andrew Louch, Henry Yong, John Richirtstone.

117. *Murray* 14 Feb 1530/31 James Scot bailie of the burgh of Selkirk came at the request of Roger Murray burgess of the burgh of Selkirk, to the lower part of his tenement lying in the east of the burgh commonly called Kyrk Wynd between the tenement of John Chepman on the north, the rest of the upper part of the said tenement on the south, the king's street on the west and the yard of George Jamisone on the east containing in length [blank] with barn behind and with part of a yard containing the width of the said barn...and there on the ground of the tenement Roger Murray freely resigned the tenement in hands of the bailie who gave sasine to James Murray second son of Roger Murray for the kind affection which the said Roger bears him. Before witnesses John Mithag bailie for the time, Alexander Collen, William Keyne, Thomas Curror, sir John Brydin, Stephen Loremur.

118. *Fairle* 21 Feb 1530/31 James Scot bailie, came at the request of Alan Keyne burgess of the burgh of Selkirk to all the upper part of the

lower croft lying in the lordship of Selkirk between the lands of the
deceased Earl of Angus now in hands of Patrick Murray, the croft of
Mark Ker on the east, the croft of Alexander Scot on the west, the
common loaning near Hadirle on the north and the croft of the heirs
of the deceased Robert Scot on the south and there on the ground of
the same the said Alan freely resigned half of his lower croft in hands
of the bailie who gave sasine to Simon Fairle burgess before witnesses
William Watsone, Patrick Ker, David Jonsone.

119. *Lady McDuell* 17 March 1530/31

[Note: This is the first of a series of documents recording a dispute
between Christian McDuell and Janet Hountar over the title of prioress
of the convent of Eccles, Berwickshire.]

On the which day the venerable prioress ["priorissa"] of Ekylls came to
the chapter with all her nuns in presence of witnesses underwritten
and publicly declared that she was lawfully admitted and placed in
the said monastery of Ekylls by power of our king James with his
great seal and with the seal of our most revered archbishop James of
the diocese of St Andrews and she had governed the said monastery
lawfully according to the form and custom of other prioresses for four
years past, then through John Houme our bailie, it was revealed to me
that the notorious woman Janet Hountar, sister of the same order,
acquired letters apostolic and royal bulls and also episcopal letters
presenting injurious statements and without reasonable cause depriv-
ing [me] of it. Which done, the said prioress in the said chapter
declared in a loud voice and it was noted by all having an interest that
I irrevocably appeal against all the sentences put forth and to be put
forth for the said noted sister Janet Hountar. The said prioress asked
instrument. Done around 8 am in the general chapter before all the
nuns and these circumspect men sirs David Brounfalld, Mark Dalgless
priests, Robert Dikeson, Alexander McDuell, Robert McDuell.

120. *Dikesone* Same day and place [the honest man Robert Dikesone –
scored out] personally compeared Dame Christian McDowell prioress
of the monastery of Eklis and convent thereof congregated in chapter
with unanimous consent and with mature deliberation declared that
Robert Dikesone in Assendayne Mains their servant would make an
account to the satisfaction of all...of all the victuals, chattels and live
animals...and all goods, gear and sums of money administered by
him...pertaining to the said monastery in any way (p/t) in whatever
way he could find out or demand...up to the date of this present
instrument. Robert asked instrument. Done at the said monastery of
Ekliss in the chapter of the same at the hour of 10 am before the witnesses in previous instrument.

121. *Chepman* 15 March 1530/31 the young man Adam Ker of Schaw with
the consent of his father William Ker, came to the two rigs of hus-

bandland called Caponland lying in the lordship of Selkirk between
the lands of Patrick Murray of Fallawhill over "le Knowe" on the east
of the town between the rigs of John Scot serjeant on the south,
another rig of the said husbandland now in hands of John Haw on the
west, and third rig on the east side in hands of Thomas Jonsone and
the Etrec haugh on the north and the other rig or portion of husbandland near "Bawethorn" between the lands of Robert Portus on the
south, another rig of land in the hands of George Chepman in the
north, a croft of George Lydderdaill on the west and "Gossoladaillis"
on the east, and there on the rig of land lying over "le Knowe" he
gave sasine of both rigs with pertinents to George Chepman his heirs
and assignees, the said Adam paying the said George £5 on one day
between sun rise and set at the altar of St Ninian in the parish kirk of
Selkirk moreover that after relaxation of the said rigs and payment of
the said sum the said George shall enjoy peaceably both rigs for all
year. George asked instrument before witnesses John Haw, John
Trumbull of Philophauch, John Brydin, John Haills, John Mithag.

122.

[Loose sheet which is encapsulated separately.]

"Debts which are owed to him:

> Item Johnnnis Haitly of Mellestanes owes to him vxx of pounds
> [?£25]
>
> Item of this resat ae horss the pur[chis?] x pounds
>
> Item viii bolls of aittes [oats]
>
> Item 1 resat fra h[im] x crownes of sonne
>
> Item Sanders Howme of Huton, air to John Howme, is awud to
> me xxxii crownes of the quhilke I haif his hand writt hereof for
> sic payment.
>
> Item the said Sanders is awund to me for our part of d[?] ane
> howndrethe merkes.
>
> Item Robert Roull and his vyf and bairnes executors is awud to
> me xx pounds for the p[urchase?] of twa horsses.

[This sheet is in the hand of Ninian Brydin although it is not clear if
these are debts owed to him. No date.]

123. *Ker* 17 March 1530/31 Andrew Ker of Prumsydloucht presented a precept of sasine written on parchment with parchment tag with a seal
impressed in red and white wax of Helen Fallaw, one of the ladies of
Softlaw for half of the lordship of Softlaw with no erasures or cancellations and not suspect in any way to Nicholas Ainslie who received it
and handed it to me notary public for reading and copying and rendering in public form as follows: Helen Fallaw one of the ladies of the
lands of Softlaw to Nicholas Ainslie, John Murray in [Kershoup],

Andrew Ker in Aldroxburgh my bailies in that part specially constituted, greetings. Because I have given, granted and sold to Andrew Ker of Prumsydloucht all my nine husbandlands viz. (illegible) half the lordship of Softlaw with pertinents lying in the sheriffdom of Roxburgh as contained fully in my charter made thereon, therefore I order and command you without delay to give sasine of the said nine husbandlands viz. one half of the lordship of Softlaw to the said Andrew Ker or his lawful attorney according to the tenor of the said charter. Which precept being read out Nicholas Ainslie gave sasine of the said husbandlands to Andrew Ker personally present and accepting by delivery of earth and stones. Andrew Ker asked instrument. Done around 10 am on the appointed year, day and place before witnesses Gavin Ellot, James Ker of Auldroxburgh, John Franch, Andrew Louch, William Trumbull, Patrick Gressone, Patrick Banantyne and others.

124. **Jamsone** 24 March 1530/31 Thomas Ker in Yair came to his place commonly known as Battis with pertinents in the lordship of Haderle within the sheriffdom of Selkirk between the lands of the venerable father Thomas Ker abbot of Kelso and convent of the same and the common loaning of Lyndene on the east, the "Millar's Aikers" of the said abbey on the north and the "king's fields" of the lands of Patrick Murray and the "Croft Buttis" on the west and south and there on the ground of "Battis", Thomas Ker resigned and gave sasine of all the place of the "Battis" with pertinents to George Jamsone. George asked instrument before witnesses William Ker of Schaw, Simon Jamsone, William Wod, James Thirbrand and others and it was plainly shown by the said Thomas that said George shall peaceably enjoy the same place for 3 years after relaxation paying £40 old ferme and 40s annualrent.

125. **Morlawe** 30 March 1531 James Scot bailie came at request of John Mithag and Christian Fairle his spouse to their tenement lying in Pelgait between the tenement of James Mithag on the west, the tenement of Alexander Scot on the east, the bog on the south and the king's street leading to the loch or Pelhyll on the north and there on the ground of the same with the consent of her spouse, Christian resigned all the said land in hands of the bailie who gave sasine of the said tenement to Thomas Morlaw. Thomas asked instrument before witnesses Walter Curror, Alan Mithag, James Layng, George Smyth, David Jonsone and others.

126. **Christian Fairle** Same place day and hour James Scot at request of Christian Fairle came to her tenement lying in the Pelgait within the bounds of Selkirk with the tenement of John Portus on the east, the tenement of the said John on the west, the croft of land presently in the hands of Janet Scot of the lands of Partick Murray on the north and the king's street which leads to the loch of the "louch" on the

south and there on the ground of the same John Mithag resigned the said tenement in hands of the bailie who...gave sasine in liferent and conjunct fee to Christian Fairle his spouse and others for familial kindness. Christian asked instrument before abovewritten witnesses and Simon Fairle, James Neuton.

127. *Lumisdene* 19 April 1531 William Ker in Shaw and Adam Ker his apparent heir faithfully bind themselves and their heirs to invest and give heritable sasine to John Lumisdene and his heirs and assignees of a tenement lying with pertinents in the burgh of Selkirk between the tenement of John Dounaldsone on the west, the king's street on the east and south and the tenement of Thomas Mynto on the north, failing which we bind ourselves irrevocably to pay all the expenses of building and constructing the said tenement under penalty of double the sum. John Lumisdene asked instrument before James Brydin, George Chepman, Andrew Dounaldsone, John Cruik, John Achesone, John Paitroo.

128. *Caverhyll* 29 April 1531 sir Stephen Wilkeson chaplain resigns all the underwritten goods in favour of Elizabeth Wilkesone and Margaret Caverhyll in safe keeping for the use and motherly care of the said my daughter and for all the graces, deeds and favours done for me thankfully by the said Margaret, as is writtten in the vernacular:

"Item first ane meit almery worth 28 shillings, item ane meit burde with crestis and formes worth 10 shillings, item ane cruk, item ane pot of five pynttes, item ane panne of three chopynnes, item ane maskynne fat, item ane troncher to vort, item gilfat, item three uther stands pertyening thereto, item eleiven pychers,

item ane stande bed furnest with ane covering, beds blankat, schet, bouster and code, item twa bolls of malt and ane half in soume keipinge of James Chepmen, item George Hountar's fyv bolls of beir and ane furlat with cherite and uther gudes the said Sir Stephen geffes frely in ferme keiping to Margaret Caverhyll to veill behouff and proffet of his douchter Elesabeycht Vilkesone" before witnesses John Mithag bailie, Alan Mithag, Alexander Gledstanes and others.

129. *Robert McDuell, procurator in the name and authority of Dame Christian McDuell* 1 May 1531 I notary public underwritten came to the monastery of nuns of Eklis of the diocese of St Andrews and there in the church of the same at the time of high mass intimated and notified the withinwritten appeal to Dame Janet Hountar personally apprehended before nuns [and] a great gathering of parishioners and witnesses underwritten and the petition given to me seeking in the final clause that Dame Janet should publicly compear according to the tenor of the summons in our previous appeal to be summoned in person or by her procurator on the day and place withinwritten which said notice and copy I fixed on the door of the said monastery and

afterwards delivered to the said Dame Janet Huntar. Robert McDuell asked instrument or instruments. Done in the choir of the monastery of Eklis around 11 am before the priests sirs Alexander Furd, David Brounfeld, James Neuton chaplain, William Jakson, Thomas Moffat, Robert Davscheill, Patrick Thomsone.

130. **Mayne** 2 May 1531 James Scot one of the bailies of Selkirk came to the tenement of the deceased William Mayne burgess of Selkirk, lying within the burgh between the tenement of John Curll on the east, the croft of master John Chepman on the south, the tenement of the heirs of the deceased William Ker on the west and the king's street leading to Pelhyll on the north [The text here is all scored out. It says to summarise that Margaret Mayne had resigned the tenement] and there on the ground of the same the said bailie gave sasine of all the tenement, paying yearly annualrent and burgh ferme, to Margaret Mayne daughter and heir of the deceased William Mayne notary. Margaret asked instrument before witnesses William Ker in Schaw, John Curll, William Notman, Thomas Ker, David Jonsone, Alexander Ailmuir and others.

Same day and place James Scot at the instance of Margaret Mayne came to the said tenement with pertinents specified before and resigned it in hands of the bailie who gave sasine to James Crawfurd his heirs and assignees the said James paying yearly an annualrent and customary burgh ferme. James asked instrument before witnesses above written.

131. **Bradfut** 16 May 1531 James Bradfut burgess of Selkirk declared that his fellow burgess John Smaill burgess of Selkirk declared the defence false in plain court before alderman and bailies and underwritten witnesses saying in the vernacular: "It is ane falss tail ye tell and nocht trew and ye leid". About which words the said James asked this instrument before witnesses underwritten. The same day in plain court, in defence John Smail denied that he had spoken wrongfully any wrongful or odious words and if he had so spoken, he was ignorant of it and protests it should not turn to my prejudice afterwards. [John] asked instrument before witnesses alderman Andrew Ker and James Scot, John Mithag bailies and all the inquest.

132. **Dame Janet Hountar** 1 May 1531 dame Janet Hountar prioress of Ekkylis in the diocese of St Andrews compeared and requested me notary public by command of or as procurator of Dame Christian McDuell or whomsoever else in her name to take note of and present a certain appeal made by the same. Dame [Janet] asked instrument before witnesses, the priests sirs Alexander Furd, David Brounfeild, James Neuton chaplain, Robert Danscheill, Patrick Thomsone.

133. **Maister Michaell Scot** 5 May 1531 [Title and date only.]

134. *Ker* 7 May 1531 John Achesone by his own confession, binds himself before witnesses underwritten as is set out in the vernacular: "I Jhone Achesone tuk 10 merkes of usuell mony of Schotland that day of this presentis and sone efter be tenor of this vrit I obliss me my ayris to pay the said 10 markes 6 dayes or martinmas next efter to William Ker and his ayris in Schaw and failyeing hereof I prey remitte and geffes oure all clag, clame, properte, possession that I haif or may haif fra me my ayris to the said William Ker his ayris all and haill my croft callit Blakes Croft with the pertinenchis so for ever my ayres happen to me. I ordande sir Ninian Brydin to geif William Ker or his heirs my chartoirs quhilk are in his keping". Before John Bryden, John Lumisden, John Trumbull.

135. *Trumbull* 2 June 1531 Mark Ker burgess of Selkirk not persuaded or compelled but of his own free will after the last day stated in a letter of assedation from Robert Trumbull tutor of Philophauch acknowledged he gave up all right and claim of possession which he has in and to the lands of Philophauch without due permission or consent of the heirs. Robert asked instrument before John Chepman, John Ker, James Bradfut, Mark Trumbull and others.

136. *Ker* 2 June 1531 Mark Ker burgess of the burgh of Selkirk, presented a precept of sasine written on parchment with parchment tag sealed in red and white impressed in wax with his own seal of Patrick Murray of Fallawhill lord of the husbandlands of Selkirk to John Chepman who gave it to me notary public to read out as follows: Patrick Murray lord of Fallauhill and of the husbandlands of Selkirk to James Scot, James Bradfut, John Chepman, Roger Murray my bailies in that part, greeting. Because I have given, granted and sold to Mark Ker burgess of Selkirk all my husbandlands with pertinents in hands of the said Mark now being in the bounds of Selkirk as contained fully in my charter made thereon, we now order and command you without delay to give sasine of the said husbandlands to the said Mark according to his charter he has of me...and in testimony of which I set my seal at Selkirk 26 May 1531 before...sir John Michilhill, William Brydin vicar, John Bryden chaplain, Adam Scot of Fausyd, Patrick Murray of Gle[?], David Stensone.

Which precept being read out, John Chepman bailie in that part...gave sasine of the said husbandlands with pertinents lying within the bounds of the burgh of Selkirk in ryndial and the principal tenement with croft of the husbandlands lying on the north of the king's street leading down to "le loninge gait" called Haderle between the tenement and lands of Jonet Couper relict of the deceased Andra Strang and Alane Keyne on the west, the lands occupied by Adam Vilkensone on the east, the said king's street on the south and "le common" called Hadirle on the north to Mark Ker burgess. Mark asked instrument. Done around 10 am before witnesses James

Bradfut, Alan Keyne, David Mynto, John Thomsone, sirs John Brydin, John Rankyn priests and others.

137. **Scot of Haning** 10 June 1531 John Scot of Myrris solemnly ordains by the tenor of this present instrument constitutes, creates, nominates and solemnly appoints Walter Scot tutor of Haning his dear cousin for favours deeds and acts his true lawful and undoubted assignee in and to all his lands of Myris in the barony of Lelescleiff within the sheriff-dom of Roxburgh which the said John holds from our reverend arch-bishop Gavin in his rental. Also if it befalls to sell, alienate or set in tack to any other then the said sale, alienation and tack to be broken and null and without any strength before whatever justices and I confirm before witnesses underwritten that my cousin Walter will give to me as much money as any other would want. Walter Scot asked instrument before witnesses James Scot bailie of Selkirk, Robert Trumbull of Houdene, David Jonstoune, William Scot younger, David Elphinstone and others.

138. **William Scot of Ormiston** 3 Aug 1531 Philip Scot of Edschaw makes, constitutes, creates, nominates and solemnly ordains his beloved second son Robert Scot of Edschaw for his good deeds and acts for all his relations his true lawful and irrevocable assignee to his place com-monly called Hartvodburn after his decease, the which place Philip Scot holds in tack of our lady Margaret queen of Scots lying in Ettrik Forest in the sheriffdom of Selkirk between the kirk lands of the most reverend archbishop of the diocese Glasgow viz. Synton and Edschaw on the south and west, le Myddilsteid on the west, Haning on the north and Selkirk Common on the east, and the said Philip renounces all rights claims, possessions, ownerships, tacks and whatever title to the same on his decease from his heirs to the said Robert forever. William Scot uncle of the said Robert Scot asked instrument around 1 pm before Mark Ker, George Gledstanes, George Scot in Blyndhauch, Walter Scot in Askyrk, sir William Brydin vicar in Selkirk, John Anguss.

[Note: Items **139** and **140** have probably been bound out of order.]

139. **Scot of Bukcleuch** 27 Jan 1531/2 in presence of the venerable Andrew Dwre abbot of the monastery of Melross with consent of the monks in the chapter court held in the said monastery in face of the court and with many of the people assembled, the office of bailie of the said monastery of Melross was given to Walter Scot of Branxham, knight by delivery of a rod and according to the tenor of apostolic let-ters and he with his heirs and successors forever was inducted to the office. Walter Scot asked instrument. Done in the court in the said monastery around 11 am before witnesses Mark Ker of Dolphinstoun, Andrew Ker of Grenheid, John Houme of Cowdenknovis, James Ker of Fairnile, George Ker of Lynton, sir Patrick Craufurd, John Scot, William Brydin notary and priest, and others.

140. *Dame McDuell* 16 March 1530 dame Christian McDuell prioress of the
priory or monastery of the Blessed Mary of Ekkylls of the Cistercian
Order in the diocese of St Andrews showed and declared on her faith
to me notary public underwritten that within the past two days it had
come to her ears that a certain pretended final decision was made in
the Roman Curia by the venerable man John, clerk and doctor of both
laws [i.e. Roman and Canon law], auditor of causes at the sacred apostolic seat, decerning that dame Janet Hountar nun of the said
monastery had full right to the office of abbess or prioress and that no
right to the same was competent to dame Christian, on the basis of
which, believing that she was injured, wronged and oppressed, she
therefore with general effect appealed and made objection ["preno-
tavit"] according to the tenor of a document handed to me, notary
public, which reads as follows: As the remedy of appeal or objection
was soundly introduced by both laws so that those injured, wronged
and oppressed, and fearing that they might falsely be injured,
wronged and oppressed in the future, might be duly assisted, for this
reason I dame Christian McDuell prioress of the monastery of the
Blessed Mary the virgin of Eklis of the Cistercian Order in the diocese
of St Andrews believing myself to be injured, wronged and oppressed
and fearing that I may be further injured, wronged and oppressed in
time to come by you, the venerable man John, clerk, doctor of both
laws, auditor of causes at the sacred apostolic seat and by your pretended final decision that dame Janet Hountar nun of the said
monastery has full right to the office of abbess or prioress and I have
no right to the same, inasmuch as I was nominated to the said office
by our most illustrious prince James V, king of Scots, by virtue of his
indulgence and privilege inviolably observed up to now and was
admitted by the convent of the said monastery with ordinary
confirmation thereof obtained in due time and there being no
sufficient confirmation of the pretended election of the said dame
Janet, wherefore full right to the said office is known to belong to me
and no right to the same can be competent to the said dame Janet and
in decerning in the matter as aforesaid no little injury and wrong has
been done against the law and the dictates of reason, saving your reverence in the foregoing as is fitting. Therefore, on account of the foresaid wrong done to the said dame Christian and which may be done
in future by you in spirit and intention, that this cause and affair along
with the principal affair and all and singular matters arising and con-
nected contrary to and against the said dame Janet and all and singular those having common or separate interest or believing that they
have such with her should be wholly devolved to the Roman Curia
from you the said venerable John, clerk [etc.] and from all and singular those believing they have a common or separate interest and also
from your or anyone of yours' warnings, sequestrations, reasons, cita-
tions, suspensions, and from excommunication, expulsion(?), aggravation, reaggravation, interdict and any other ecclesiastical censures and

penalties and from your molestations, disturbances and other impedi-
ments and all the other wrongs foresaid which have been inflicted on
the said dame Christian and in future may in any way be inflicted,
have been or may be threatened, have been or may be fulminated, in
these writings I appeal and make objection to the said holy father in
Christ Pope Clement by divine providence VII and to his sacred apostolic seat and I appeal urgently, more urgently and most urgently by
1st, 2nd, 3rd and 4th appeals that this be given (illegible) and con-
ceded to me [and] I ask at least testimonials if there be anyone here
who can give them to me and I summon you the said dame Janet
Huntar and all others [having interest etc. as above] peremptorily on
the hundredth day next to come after the notification above and withinwritten canonically given and if that day should [not] be lawful then
on the next lawful day immediately following that you or your suitable procurators, sufficiently instructed for this cause, compear at the
Roman Curia wherever it is sitting with all and singular your relevant
acts, articles, letters, writings, laws and muniments which may assist
you and this cause and affair, to proceed in this cause and affair to all
and singular judicial acts and terms step by step and in succession as
far as and including final decree and in all other things which may be
acted, said, alleged and done as required by law and reason And I
assign and intimate the said next hundredth day in the premises to
you and all and singular the others aforesaid so far as I validly can by
law with intimation and certification foresaid, that whether you compear at the said term or not I or my lawful procurators in that part
nevertheless will proceed in all and singular the aforesaid as far as
obtaining final victory in the cause and I will procure through justice
by means of the hearing of letters of contradiction of our lord pope
and others according to the style and custom of the said Roman Curia
that you have no further appeal or citation or other calling, placing
my lands, goods, fruits, emoluments and possessions and all pertaining to me in that respect or [which] I wish to pertain, goods and
benefits whatsoever, in the safekeeping, defence and all protection(?)
of the said our most holy lord pope and his said sacred apostolic seat,
protesting solemnly with regard to amending, diminishing, extending
and correcting this my appeal as often as need requires or as is
allowed by law, with the other necessary and best clauses, on all
which etc.

141. **Broun** 10 Oct 1531 James Brydin one of the bailies of Selkirk at
request of Janet Broun wife of the deceased David Broun came to his
principal tenement lying in the burgh of Selkirk between the tenement
of James Brydin on the east, a tenement of the virgin on the south, the
tenement of Thomas Crukschankes on the west and the king's street
near the mercat on the north* and there on the ground of the same
surrendered and purely and simply resigned the bailie gave sasine of
the said tenement fore and back to William Broun son and heir of the

said deceased David Broun paying customary annualrent and burgh fermes by delivery of earth and stones. William asked instrument before witnesses James Scot, John Craw, James Portus, John Angus, Thomas Crukschanks around the hour of 8.

William Broun resigns it in hands of the bailie who gives Janet Broun his mother sasine of the same for her lifetime.

[* A note in Latin appears here at the top of the page "In te Jhesu spes mea recumbit" in you Jesus my hope resides]

142. ***Scot Vaych opposing parties*** 3 Sept 1531 Walter Scot, Walter Vaich and his heirs and his brother-in-law? Adam Scot on the one part and John Vaych, William Vaych and their brothers-german on the other part adversaries, have finally admitted and made compromise to stand by a decreet of the worthy arbiters Andrew Ker of Prumsydloch and John Riddaill of that ilk on the part of Walter Scot, Walter Vaych heir of the deceased George Vaych and Adam Scot, and George Ker of Lynton and Thomas Ker in Yair on the part of John Vaych and William Vaych as is fully specified in the compromise underwritten to decide about the heritage of North Synton and "le kyndness of Corsle" as follows: "The third day of September in the yeir of God ane thousand 531 yeirs, it is contrakit, compromittit, appointit and irrevocabilly aggreit betwix honorabyl men Walter Scot in Synton, Walter Vaych ye said Vat Scot doughters sone and ayr to umquhill George Vaych of Norcht Synton and Ad Scot Vattes mauch in to ane pairt and Thome Vaych, Villiem Vaych the bredder pleand gadersaids for tutory of North Synton and kyndness of the steid callit Corsle in forme in manner and effec as efter follows, that is to say ayther of the partes forsaid ar oblyst and boundyne and deuly thereto sworn be ostentioun of his handis to the haly evangill to byd under[lie] stand stedfastlie without revocation to the (illegible) diecreit of their four unsuspekit arbytouris undervrittin thereto deuly sworn be faith and trouth in their bodeis and tweychin the haly evangill viz. Andrew Ker of Prumsyd loch, Jhonne of Ryddail of that ilkane, Valter Scot, Vatte Vaych his doughter sone and air of umquill George Vaych and Ade Scot in ane part, George Ker in Lyntoun and Thomas Ker in Yair for Thomas Vaych Villiam Vaych the breders in the tother part that the saidis arbytouris sal decreit deliver lelely and treuly without fraud or gyll betwixt this and allhallowes next for to cum and gef the saidis arbitouris can not aiggre in the said mater movit than with all thair avys thai sal chess ane discret full ourma[n?] haiffand god before his ey ripply advyssit in the said mater quhilk sall intromet decyd decreit and deliver fathfully without fraud or gyll in the saidis mater and for the mayr securite ayther of the partes admissar tuk the instrument and subscribit this present [memorandum?] with thair handis at the pen and rychtsua the forsaidis arbitouris unsuspekit tuk instrumentis that the said partes admissairs suld not revok nor nan vay agane call the

decreit deuly deliverit be thaim" before witnesses George Reddaill,
George Scot in Blyndhauch, James Ker, Andrew Shortrede, sir Simont,
sir Shortreide, Mark Ker, sir N[inian] Brydin notar and others.

143. (**Vaych** – scored out) **Scot** 3 Sept 1531 Walter Scot in Syntoun and
Adam Scot his brother-in-law in name of Walter Vaych son and heir of
the deceased George Vaych make note that Andrew Ker in
Prumsydloucht and John Reddaill of that ilk arbiters for Walter Scot,
Adam Scot and Walter Vaych and George Ker in Lyntoun and Thomas
Ker in Yair arbiters for John Vaych and William Vaych will make an
unanimous agreement between now and All Hallows concerning the
kindness of Corsle and North Synton. Also Walter and Adam Scot his
uncle and their heirs bind themselves to keep to the contract and give
Walter Vaych everything due to him as contained in the decreet.
Before witnesses Philip Scot in Edschaw, George Scot in Blyndhauch,
Andra Schortreid, James Ker, James Scot in Selkirk, Walter Scot in
Askyrk.

144. **Vaych** Same day place and hour. John Vaych and William Vaych make
note that the said arbiters should come to some agreement regarding
North Synton and the kindness of Corsle between now and All
Hallows and if it happens that the said arbiters cannot decide lawfully
between this and the [said] feast we declare that our royal letter has or
shall have tail [i.e. be sealed?] completing the said agreements. John
asked instrument before witnesses William Ker in Quhitmureha, sir
William Brydin vicar, Mark Ker in Selkirk, James Ker in Quhitmure.

145. **Scot** Same day place and hour. Walter Scot in Syntone, Adam Scot his
brother-in-law in the name of Walter Vaych son and heir of the
deceased George Vaych choose the discreet men their arbiters viz.
Andrew Ker of Prumsydlouch and John Reddaill of that ilk and John
Vaych and William Vaych choose their two arbiters viz. George Ker of
Lyntoun and Thomas Ker in Yair...to make judgement regarding North
Synton and le kyndness of the said place [i.e. Corslie] between now
and the feast of All Hallows next following according to the tenor of
the compromise between the opposing parties. Also Walter Scot and
Adam Scot his brother-in-law bind themselves faithfully to discharge
all that is contained in the decreet concerning Walter son of the
deceased George Vaych. Before witnesses abovewritten .

146. **Scot** 10 Dec 1531 John Scot serjeant and sheriff in that part came to
the mercat cross in the burgh of Selkirk and there in a loud voice proclaimed royal letters and according to the tenor of the same delivered
the rod of peace to Adam Scot personally present and accepting and
the letters were as follows: "James be the graice of God, king of
Scottis, to our lovittis Jhone Scot schirjiand and schireff messinger in
that part coniunctlie and severallie specially constitut, greting.
Forsameikyll as it is humele menit and schawn to ws be our lovit

Adam Scot in Synton that quhair he vas [denuncit?] oure reball and put to our horne be ouris utheris lettres purchest at the instanche of William Vaych in the Yair for not delivering to him as tutor to Walter Vaych his bruder sone and now the said Adam hes obtemperit the charge of our utheris said letters and hes deliverit to the said William the house of Norcht Synton and plessit hyme at all pountis efter the tenor of oure utheris lettres as is allegit. Oure vyll is therfor and we chargis yow straitlie and commandis that incontinent ther our letters sene ye seand and understandand perfitlie that the said Adam hes obeit the charge of our utheris letters quharby he vas put to our horn and has plessat the said William purchusar therof eftir the tenor of the samyn that ye in oure nayme and autorite relesche the said Adam fra the said process of our horne led upone him in the said mater resave hime to our peace and deliver to hyme the vand thereof simpliciter because the said William confessit the samyn in presence of our lordis of our counsel the quhilk to do we commit to yow coniunctlie and severlie our full pouer be thir our lettres delivering thaim be yow deuly execut and indorsat agane to the berar, gevin under our signet at Edinburgh the vi day of December and of oure regne the xix yeir". "Ex deliberatione dominorum consilii Gud...scriba".

147. Davidsone 10 Dec 1531 William Turnbull of Mynto and his son William Turnbull lawful heir and in fee (illegible)...of his own free will resigned, sold and alienated a non-entry of a portion of land called "Nukland" lying in the lordship of Mynto within the sheriffdom of Tevidale from himself, his heirs and assignees paying yearly 9 shillings to his brother-in-law Ralf Davidsone and his heirs and assignees provided that the true heirs of the said land have freedom of entry to the same from their superior lord. Also the same day William Turnbull resigned all right and claim which he has or will have in a non-entry of 10 merklands in Chames, occupied by the deceased James Grymslaw and the true and nearest heirs shall have lawful entry with the assent and consent of his superior lord. Ralph asked instrument. Done at 1 pm before witnesses Mark Ker bailie for the time in Selkirk, John Ker burgess of the said burgh, Robert Tait, Stephen Hendirsone, David Jonson.

148. Morlawe 10 Jan 1530/31 William Ker in Schaw and Adam Ker his only son and heir came to certain of his rigs in the open fields of "Gersland" and "Caponland" in the lordship of Schaw lying in ryndaill between the lands of Patrick Murray of Fallaahyll, the first rig lying over "le Taittis Hyll" between the lands of John Scot on the south, the rig of John Haw on the north; the second rig lying over "le Fluris" between the lands of Patrik Murray now in the hands of Alexander Scot in the south and the lands of Robert Portuus on the north; the 3rd rig over "le Vester Lais" between the lands of Alexander Scot on the north and the lands of master John Chepman on the south; the 4th rig lying over "le Gouslodaillis" between the lands of master John

Chepman on the north and the lands of Thomas Ker on the south; the 5th rig lying over " le crukitlandis" between the lands of Jonet Scot relict of the deceased George Scot on the south and the lands of William Bennat on the north; 6th rig over " le mulschot" [i.e. Milnshot] between the lands of master John Chepman on the north and the lands of Thomas Mynto on the south; the 7th rig lying over "Donsedaillis" between the lands now in the hands of James Brydin on the south and lands of George Chepman on the north; 8th rig over "Le Donsdaillis" between the lands of John Brydin on the south and John Chepman of "Kyrkstille" on the north and there on the ground of the same the said William Ker and Adam Ker and their heirs gave sasine of all the rigs to John Morlaw personally present and accepting. Also the said John binds himself to seal a reversion in sum of £20 to the said William and Adam and if it should happen the said William, Adam and their heirs pay the said sum on one day between sun rise and sun set and the said John and his heirs fraudulently absent themselves from receiving it on the altar of St Ninian, we will that it be placed with the bailies for that time of the burgh. Also we grant that the said John Morlaw his heirs and assignees shall peacefully possess the said 8 rigs for 3 years following and if it happens that the said John be disturbed in his peaceful possession we of our own and spontaneous wills assign by a clause of warrandice an annualrent of 10 shillings uplifted yearly from the tenements of John Vod and Robert Chesholme lying in Pelhyll between the tenements etc. John Morlaw asked instrument before James Brydin bailie for the time being, John Lumisden, Alan Mithag, John Haw burgess, Thomas Morlaw, David Jonsone, James Lumisden.

149. *Brydin* 16 Jan 1531/32 sir William Brydin in the name of Jonet Brydin and Elizabeth Scot asked instrument in plain court.

150. *Alison Hendersone* 17 Jan 1531/32 Mark Ker bailie, at request of James Brydin son and heir of Alan Brydin burgess of the said burgh came to his tenement lying in Selkirk between the tenement of William Brydin on the west, the yard of master John Chepman on the east, the yard of sir John Chepman chaplain on the north and the king's street leading to the well on the south and there on the ground of the same James Brydin resigned the tenement in hands of the bailie who gave sasine to Nicholas Hendersone and Alison Hendersone his spouse and whichever lives longer, their heirs and assignees. Nicholas asked instrument before witnesses William Portuus serjeant, William Brydin, Adam Ker of Schaw, Walter Dunhoup.

Note that Nicholas and his spouse shall enjoy peaceful possession of the same provided that James Brydin and his heirs pay £8 on one day between sun rise and sun set at the altar of St Ninian. Also Alison lent James £3 of money a long time before making these presents; I did not hear the said James and they are granted on the report of worthy witnesses Thomas Andersone and his spouse.

151. *Wode* 25 Jan 1531/32 Helen Wychtman freely discharged all right and title in and to a tenement of the deceased John Wychtman and now in hands of his son and heir John Wychtman as is specified in a subsequent minute. Before witnesses underwritten.

152. *Wod* Same day place and hour. James Brydin bailie at the instance of the young man John Vychtman came to his tenement lying in the burgh of Selkirk between the tenement of William Turnbull on the north, the yard of Stephen Loremur on the west, the tenement of Robert Chesholm on the south and the king's street leading to the "Fulbrigmyre" on the east and there on the ground of the same the said John freely resigned his tenement in hands of the bailie who gave sasine to John Vod personally present and accepting and paying yearly an annualrent of 5 shillings to the lord of Schaw his heirs and assignees over and above the burgh ferme. John asked instrument before witnesses John Chepman, Thomas Jonsone, John Broun, William Chepman, Thomas Jonsone younger and others.

153. *Joneta Vod* Same day and place. John Vod resigned the above tenement in hands of the bailie who gave sasine for her lifetime to Janet Vod his wife paying annualrent and ferme as above before witnesses abovewritten.

154. *Fairle* 21 Feb 1531/32 Alan Keyne burgess of Selkirk has confessed that he owes Simon Fairle burgess of Selkirk £21 scots. On the same day, Alan Keyne leased 2 rigs of his lands for a ferme paid thankfully from his hands, one of which lies over "le Taittis Hyll" and the other over "le Bawethiorne" for the space of 12 years next after the final dates to John Best baxter. Before witnesses William Flecher, William Craw, James Flecher, Patrick Jonsone and others.

155. *Howatsone* 6 March 1531/32 John Brydin bailie at request of John Achesone came to his tenement lying in a vennel called "Volgait" between the tenements of John Lumisdene on the east, a croft of arable land of master John Chepman on the south and William Ker of Schaw on the west and the king's street on the north and there on the ground of the same John Achesone of his own free will resigns all right and claim in and to his tenement of land with houses, yard and rig thereto in hands of the bailie who gave sasine of the tenement, yard and rig to John Howatsone. John asked instrument before witnesses John Mithag, John Ker, John Lumisden, John Cruk, John Paike,John Brydin and others.

156. *Ker in Greinheid and Ellot their agreement* "Thir contrak maid at the Grenheid, the nynt day of Februar in the yeir of God, ane thousand v hundred xxviii yeiris betweix honorabyll men that is to say

Andreu Ker in Prumsyd upone the tane pert and Gawin Ellot in the tother pert, propones contenis and beires leill vytness that it is fullely and unrevocabelly aggreit accordit betweix the foresaidis persones in maner forme and effec as efter follovis that is to say the said Gawin sal, God vylland, contrak mary and have to vyf Margaret Mackduell, douchter to Andreu Mcduell in Mccarstone in all gudlie haist that the saidis partes may be reddy thereto for the treitting and completting of the quhilk mariage to be contretit and completit in the faice of holy kirk. The said Andreu Ker sall eislie content and pay to the said Gawin, the sowme of twa hundrecht merks in penny and penny-worchtis and in gud and usuell mony of Scotland, in this maner the said Margaret hess of hir awin propir guddis quhilk sal be thankfully pait within six oukis eftir the treiting of samyn and the remayne of the said sowme to be pait at the voll of the forsaidis Gawyne Ellot. Alswa it is accordit betweix the saidis partes that the said Gawin [inconti-nent?] efter the completing and solempnizeing of the said marriage sall invest and seiss the said Margaret in coniunct fee for all the dais of hir lyf in all xvi oxingait of lands callit "Toftlawe" and "Boucherflat" with the pertinenchis lyand within the barony of Hasyndene within the schireffdom of Roxburgh be chartour, seissing and evidenss in dow forme as effeiris the said Gawin makand resignatione or be his procu-ratouris of all and haill the foresaidis landis of "Toftlawe" and "Boucherflat" in the our lordis handis of the samyn and the saidis Andreu to do his diligens for neu infeftment of the saidis landis con-tenit and gottin fra the said our lord to the saidis Gawin and Margaret in to hir coniunc fee and to the langar levar of thaim heretablylly to thir ayris procurit and for to be procurit betweix thaim and mair attour gef sa happiness that the said Margaret be chanss of deid and permis-sione of God to be lady heretabyll of the lordship of McCarstoune or in ony partes of the samyn that the said Andreu sall haive brouk and joiss be vertue of tak and assedatione all the samyn be ane conpatand priss and better chepe yeirlie for ferme and maill than ony other vyll gef for thaim or ony part of thaim forfulfylling, obschirving and keip-ing of all and syndry the condiciones and appountmenttis above vryt-tin baith thir saidis partes ar boundynne oblist thereto and sworne be fath and treucht in thir bodeis and for the mair securite hess twechit the haly evangill be ostencionne of thir hands to sell [i.e. seal] this for-said compromit and attour ayther of the partes tuk instrumentis upone the foresaidis vordis" as this present note before witnesses Thomas Ker in Yair, William Lauder, John Rychertsone, sir John Rankin.

The following note appears in the margin of the above deed. "Same day, the said James Brydin bailie by virtue of his office after the delib-eration of an inquest written in the burgh book, invested John Achesone in all his tenement by rod and baton as the true heir of Ninian Achesone his brother-german before witnesses within written".

157. *Doune* 15 Feb 1531/32 James Brydin one of the bailies after an inquest of worthy men came to the tenement of the deceased George Down lying in a vennel called "Gousslynraw" between the tenement of sir John Michilhill on the west, the house of John Bennat on the west (*sic*), the tenement of William Bennat and William Wynterhoup on the south and the king's street on the east near the mercat cross and there on the ground of the same the bailie gave sasine to Robert Dwne son and heir of the deceased George Dwnne paying yearly burgh customs and ferme as is specified in his charter. Robert asked instrument before witnesses Alan Keyne, William Portius serjeant, Nicholas Ker, David Jonson, Thomas Dwnne and others.

158. *Gottarsonne* 22 Feb 1531/32 Thomas Gotrasone in Melrose lent £6 scots to Elizabeth Davidsone and Nicholas Forret her son and heir apparent for two acres of arable land held in tack lying under the wall of the monastery of Melrose which was held of the reverend father in Christ, lord abbot Andrew and the monks of Melrose, about which Elizabeth and John Forret bind themselves as follows in the vernacular: "That the foresaid Thomas Gottrasone hes lent instantlie befor thir vytness under vryttin to ane honest discretful voman, Elesabecht Davidsone and Nychoil Forret hir son and ayr apperand, the sowme of £6 of gud usuell mony of scotland in pur and clen layne actualy laid down in reall paiment and for sou[er]te of detfull paiment of the said sowme the said Elesabecth and Nycholl Forret obliss thaim self in the straitest forme of obligation that can be devissit and thir ayris executoris in this present forme of instrument to lay in wod twa aikrs of landis of thairis mailings under the abbey vall of Melrose the quhilkis twa aykeris the foresaid Thomas Gottrasone his ayris executoris and assignais sal joiss and brouk all and haill the forsaid twa aykers payand to the abbay twa bollis of vyttaill ay and quhill the forsaidis Elesabecth and Nichol thair ayris executoris and assignais sall refund and pay thankfully to the said Thomas Gottrasone his ayris, executoris and assignais the forsaid sowm of £6 upone ane day betweix the sonne rysing up and passing down of the saymn alsua gef it happenes the forsaidis Elesabeth or Nycholl to sell vodsit bartour or [saw] into menes ouchter all or ane part of all the remaynent of thair maillings forsaid under the vall of Melross, the foresaid Thomas sal be first chargit thairto and sall haif the first lof of it owther in part or in all and sal say nay therewith or ony vtheris be chargit therewith the said Thomas gevand alss meikyll to thaim for thair kyndness as ony vther in the countrie vyll gef for it mair attour it sall nocht be lefull to the said Elesabet and Nycholl hir son and thair ayris, executoris and assignais to sel thair kyndness of the forsaid twa aykers to nane vtheris for to mak paiment to the said Thomas of the said sowm of £6 in redemying of the forsaid twa aykers fra the forsaid Thomas bot gef thai happen to redeme thaim with thairis awin propir vyne gowdes nowder to get the mony nor tak it at nayne vtheris handes without fraud or gyll and for mair securite bath Elesabecht and Nicholl hes commandit to subscryb this present instrument with thairis hands". Thomas Gotrasone asked instrument. Done in Hontlie Wod around the hour of 1 pm before Richard Davidsone.

159. ***Brydin procurator in the name of Janet Portuus and Elesabeth Portuus*** 26 Feb 1531/32 sir William Brydin vicar of Selkirk procurator in the name of Janet Brydin alias Portuus and Elizabeth Portuus daughters and heirs of the deceased William Portuus declared to the sheriff and inquest for serving a writ of the said women that he had heard nothing to impede or contradict by means of an objection. sir William asked instrument before sir John Michelhyll, John Brydin notary and Mark Ker, Adam Ker, John Ker and all the inquest.

160. ***Mark Robesone*** 29 Feb 1532/3 Mark Robesone of his own free will asserts in the vernacular that: "Johne Robesone his belovit sone sall haif twa lwmyss viz. ane wollon and ane lynning lwyme with thir pertinenchis to pay William Ker in the Schaw 40 shillings and utheris dettis awud to diverss with thir condiciones that the saidis Thomas Robesone sal haif his leffin and sustentatione for his lyf time alss veill as the said Jhone may furness with cherite Item the said Thomas sall haif na pouer to sell and dispon na geir without consent of his sone Jhone nor the said Jhone without consent of his fader Thomas and in the tenor of these present instrumentis". The said John intromitter with all these goods made these conditions faithfully. John asked instrument before William Ker, John Lumisden, John Patro.

161. ***Melrose and Smyth*** 19 March 1531(*sic*) James Brydin bailie after deliberation of an inquest of worthy burgesses came to the tenement of the deceased John Melross lying in the said burgh between the tenement of John Scot on the south, the tenement of John Mithag on the north, the tenement or yard of George Jamesone on the east and the king's street called "le Kyrk Vynd" on the west and there on the ground of the same the bailie gave sasine to the young man Thomas Melross heir of the deceased John Melross his brother.

John Smyth The same day Thomas Melross freely resigned the said tenement with pertinents in hands of the bailie who gave sasine of the same to John Smyth, the said John Smyth and his heirs paying yearly 20 shillings and burgh ferme. John Smyth asked instrument before witnesses sir William Brydin, John Brydin chaplain, Robert Chepman, John Mithag, Robert Turnbull, William Brydin and others done around 10 am.

162. ***Ker*** 15 April 1532 James Brydin bailie at the request of the young man Robert Downe son and heir of the deceased George Downe came to his tenement lying in a vennel called "Goslynrawe" between the tenement of sir John Michilhill on the [north east? – "borientali"], the tenement of William Bennat on the south, the king's street near

the cross on the east and the house of John Bennat within the close on the west and there on the ground of the same Robert Downe resigned the tenement with pertinents in hands of the bailie who gave sasine of the same to Andrew Ker of Prumsydloucht his heirs and assignees, the said Andrew and his heirs paying an annualrent and burgh ferme. Andrew asked instrument. Done at 1 pm before witnesses George Ker of Lynton, Mark Ker bailie for the time being, sir William Brydin, Ralph Ellot, John Brydin chaplain, James Ker, John Mithag, James Scot.

163. *Down* Same day Thomas Downe burgess humbly asks and protests to the honourable man Andrew Ker in Grenheid that he should keep the rest of a sum [of money] in his own hands provided always that he will put Robert Dwne to the noble craft by presentation to the craft with consent of his parent. Therefore I discharge the rest of the said sum in your hands that was not given to Jonet Dwn or Gray his mother by him who wished to [take?] all she has. Thomas asked instrument before abovewritten witnesses.

164. *Wynterhoup* 26 April 1532 James Brydin bailie after the deliberation of an inquest of worthy burgesses came to the tenement of the deceased ["Andrew" scored out] George Vynterhoup in Selkirk between the tenement of James Chepman on the east, the tenement of sir John Chepman on the east (*sic*), the yard of the said James Chepman on the north and the king's street called "Pelgait" on the south and there on the ground of the same the bailie gave sasine of the same to the young man William Vynterhoup true and undoubted heir of the deceased Andrew Vynterhoup his uncle. William asked instrument before James Champerna, William Trumbull, James Haw, James Bradfut.

165. *Ker of Prumsydloucht* 27 April 1532 Robert Scot tutor of Houpaslot and George Scot of Blyndhauch bind themselves their heirs and executors to pay a certain sum of money viz. 100 merks scots for their great arrears to Andrew Ker of Prumsydloucht and his heirs and assignees at the feast of Whitsunday viz. the year 1533, 50 merks scots and 50 merks at the feast of Martinmas irrevocably for his favour and lack of obstruction concerning the marriage between Thomas McDuell lord of McCarston and Janet Scot of Houpaslot as is specially noted in a letter of obligation made between the said parties through the venerable man sir William Brydin vicar of Selkirk. Andrew asked instrument. Done around 3 pm before witnesses George Ker, Laird of Lyntoun, James Ker of Fairnele, James Ker of Auldroxburgh.

166. *Scot* Same day and place. Robert Scot tutor of Houpaslot binds himself, his heirs etc to warrant and alienate his moveable and immoveable goods for his beloved friend George Scot of Blyndhaugh against payment of the above sum before witnesses above.

167. *Ker of Gattshawe* 6 June 1532 James Brydin bailie, at the request of Christian Crukschankis with consent of her son Thomas Crukschankis her true heir, came to a certain portion of a house viz. from the door of the hall to the gable viz. "the gavyll that Lanselot Ker bigit" on the fore side and the hall inhabited by Christian and Thomas the upper part of which portion contains (blank) in length and (blank) in width and there on the ground of the same the said Christian and Thomas resign the portion in hands of the bailie who gave sasine of the same to Lancelot Ker personally present and accepting. Lancelot asked instrument before witnesses Alan Keyne serjeant, Robert Toddryk, John Yong, Henry Yong, Adam Vilkesone burgesses.

168. *Lauder* 7 June 1532 James Brydin bailie came to the principal tenement of the deceased Stephen Lauder lying in Selkirk between the tenement of master John Chepman on the north, the tenement of John Mithag on the west, the kirkyard of the parish kirk on the south and the king's street on the east and there on the ground of the same the bailie gave sasine of all the tenement with pertinents to William Lauder true and lawful heir of Stephen Lauder his father paying yearly according to the charter made thereon. William asked instrument before witnesses John Chepman, William Ker of Schaw, James Bradfut, James Cant and there received sasine as heir.

169. *Nicholas Ker* in the year 1532 James Brydin bailie came at the request of William Lauder burgess of Edinburgh to the upper half of his tenement in Kyrk Vynd between the tenement of master John Chepman on the south, the storehouse of the said master John Chepman on the west of the yard of the said half tenement, the rest of the tenement inhabited by James Cant on the north and the king's street commonly called Kyrk Vynd on the east and there on the ground of the same William Lauder of his own free will resigned all the upper part of his tenement with yard near the yard of Robert Chepman on the north reserving a portion of the yard of my principal messuage occupied by his own parents in hands of the bailie who. gave sasine of the said half tenement excepting the said portion to Nicholas Ker and Marion Brydin his wife and to whichever lives longer paying the said William and his heirs 20s scots of annualrent. The said tenement of land to be divided between the heirs or assignees of the said Nicholas and Marion by bailies and two burgesss of the burgh according to their charter. Nicholas and Marion asked instrument before witnesses William Ker of Schaw, James Bradfut, John Chepman, Robert Chepman, John Smyth. Therefore after the death of Marion her half goes to David Jonsone and after his decease to Mungo Jonsone or Janet Jonsone their heirs.

170. *Morlawe* 22 July 1532 William Valker of Hawyk nephew and lawful heir of the deceased John Valker judicially brought before an inquest of the burgh of Hawyk, binds himself for his heirs by the ostention of his hands…to invest and give sasine to John Morlawe of Todschawe in a certain croft in the bounds of the lordship of Hawyk and a tenement in the town of Hawyk on the north side of the king's street between the tenement of Alexander Paslaw on the east, the Slytryk water on the west and north and the said king's street on the south and the croft lies on the east side of the Slytryk water with the Teviot water on the north and the tenement of James Blair on the west and if it happens that the said John must build or rebuild the said tenement in a better form than it now is, then the said William Valker shall compensate the said John 40 shillings scots against his labours on the one day between the sun rise [and sun set]. John asked instrument before witnesses John Mairgerobankis burgess of Edinburgh, Alexander Hawdene, William Wynterhoup, John Haw and others.

171. **Scot** 24 July 1532 Walter Scot in Edschawe in the porch of the parish church of Selkirk publicly and in a loud voice declared that he personally presented John Reddaill of that ilk and William Scot of Harden his true arbiters on the due day and place determined and laid down in the case moved between him and Elizabeth Murray his adversary and the said [Elizabeth] did not produce her arbiters before witnesses sirs Ralph Ellot, Simon Schortreid priests, Walter Scot of Askirk, Robert Melross, Andrew Shortreid and above arbiters.

172. *A form of appeal* 29 July 1532 by this present public instrument be it plainly evident and known that before us notaries public and witnesses withinwritten personally constituted the noble man Walter Scot knight and the discreet man Robert Scot having and holding in their hands a certain document on paper in the form of an appeal or notice of objection which they handed to us the withinwritten notaries to read out, by virtue of which document they duly and effectively make objection and appeal as follows: As appeal or notice of objection was introduced by both laws sensibly and soundly so that not only those injured, wronged and oppressed but also [those fearing that they could] falsely [be further injured, wronged and oppressed] might be duly assisted, it has come anew to our or to your(?) notice that the venerable and notable men, masters Adam Colquhoun, canon of Glasgow and official general of the same and John Sprevyll, vicar of Dundownald and commissary of the said lord official wronged, injured and oppressed us the abovewritten appellants and fearing that we may be injured, wronged and oppressed in the future by the same official and commissary in a certain cause moved between us the appellants on the one [part] and master John Hepburne pretended rector of Hawyk on the other part:

First because when the said master John produced a certain false and inept writ unworthy of response before the said official and commissary regarding certain teind sheaves sued for from us by the said master John and at the term assigned to us in the said writ we produced certain lawful exceptions and laws against this false writ relevant in law and fact to show why we were not bound to answer to the said writ and we demanded that a term be assigned to us for discussing the exceptions by our procurator lawfully constituted but the same masters Adam official and John commissary proceeding in this matter both improperly and unjustly by a pretended interlocutory decree in favour of his [claims] required us to reply to this pretended and false writ notwithstanding our lawful exceptions produced to the contrary and relevant in law as this false writ and the lawful exceptions against it show.

Secondly, the said masters John and Adam on another head and ground wronged and injured us, proceeding in this both improperly and unjustly, in that against law and order of law they fulminated their letters of excommunication against us at the instance of the said master John on account of our not returning the citation to the said false writ proceeding against us against all provisions of law as has lately come to our knowledge.

Because of these wrongs and others perhaps more serious, at a suitable and opportune place and time, in these writings we make objection and appeal from you master Adam official and John commissary and your substitutes or those who may be substituted and your penalties of suspension, excommunication, aggravation and reaggravation and interdict or other censures and processes whatsoever, imposed or to be imposed, promulgated or to be promulgated, to the most holy our father in Christ, lord Clement by divine providence Pope for this time and his sacred apostolic seat and we ask appeals urgently, more urgently and most urgently and if you should deny us we again on this ground make objection, appeal and ask appeals repeating the instance in turn and subjecting ourselves, all and singular (p/t) pertaining to us or wishing to pertain in this part (illegible) our and their moveable and immoveable goods present and future to the safekeeping and defence of our said most holy Pope and his apostolic seat, making objection and protesting with regard to additions to and changes in this our appeal as often as there is need and is allowed by law etc. and so these appeals [are] and [were made] by such a document...The said appellants asked instrument. Done near S[elkirk] on year, day, month and pontificate and indiction as aforesaid."

173. *Ker of Sunderland Hall* [Date – 1 Aug 1532 – scored out.] Nov 1536 [Master Thomas Ker of Sunderland Hall – scored out] in the name of Walter Scot his brother-german came to the mercat cross of Selkirk between the hours of 8 and 9 in the morning and in a loud and clear voice requested due entry by Andrew Shortreid on behalf of Adam Gledstanes because he had faithfully promised to produce the same Adam [sound and safe?] at the said hour of 8 am and the said Andrew and Adam had not compeared and had fraudulently absented themselves. Master Thomas asked instrument before witnesses Mark Ker, David Ker, David Downe, James Borthwick, sir William Brydin vicar pensioner of Selkirk, James Melrose, James Brydin bailie, William Brydin.

174. **Shortreid** 2 August [1536?] Andrew Shortreid in the name of Adam Gledstanes publicly declared in the presence of witnesses underwritten that the said Adam today faithfully kept the day of his promise of entry made to Walter Ker of Sonderlandhall viz. he had [compeared?] on the first day of August and in the place and town I had appointed for him from sun rise to sun set and remained until 4 pm the following day and before Walter Scot of Edschaw, Walter Scot of Askirk, sir Simon Shortrede, Ralph Ellot priest, Thomas Crukschankes, John Bauld, William Portuus.

175. **Marion Down** 28 Sept 1532 James Brydin bailie of Selkirk came at the request of John Portuus [instrument ends here].

176. **Simon Fairle** 8 Oct 1532 Simon Fairle and James Vatsone bind themselves by oath in the presence of Mark Ker bailie to stand faithfully without revocation to the decreet of Thomas Crukschankes ["for the debt of his brother" in the margin]. On which day the said Thomas came to the wall in question and decreed...that the said wall [belonged to] Simon Fairle even the posts holding up the wall. Simon asked instrument before John Mithag, Robert Melrose, James Helme, Nicholas Ker, William Swan.

177. **Watsonne** Same day and place. James Vatss[on] renounced the said promise made between me and Simon...because I do not wish to abandon the force of my charter made thereupon sealed by the said Thomas. James asked instrument before the same witnesses.

178. **James Keyne** 29 Aug 1532 Mark Ker bailie of the burgh of Selkirk came to the tenement of land of John Haw son of the deceased Thomas Haw elder burgess of Selkirk, lying within the said burgh between the tenement of land of Thomas Jonss[on] on the west and north and the public road "le Fulbreg" called "Fulbreig Myre" and the other common lands of the burgh on the south and there John Haw resigned all right and claim to the said tenement of land with houses and yard and with pertinents forever in hands of the bailie who gave sasine of the same to James Keyne uncle of the said John Hawe personally present and accepting according to the charter of the said John to James made thereon. James asked instrument. Done at the ground of the lands around 11 am before witnesses James Dowby, John Thomsone, James Keyne younger, James Mcduell.

179. **Andrew Ker of Prumsyd** 8 Oct 1532 [Note: The instrument has been scored out.] Andrew Ker of Prumsyd presented and showed a precept of sasine with the seal of Robert Scot of Howpaslot and lord of the

lands of Birkinsyd which appeared to me notary public not spoiled or
suspect in any way to James Ker of Auldroxburgh... as follows: I
Robert Scot of Howpaslot and lord of the lands of Birkinsyd to
Thomas Feregreff, James Ker special bailies in that part, greeting.
Because I have given, granted, sold and alienated to Andrew Ker of
Prumsyd all of my 10 merklands with pertinents lying in the bounds
of Byrkinsyd and within the sheriffdom of Berwick as contained in my
charter made thereon. Therefore I order you and command you to
give sasine of the said 10 merklands to the said Andrew Ker or his
lawful attorney without delay. In testimony of which I affix my own
seal at Grenheid on 8 Oct 1532 before witnesses James Ker of
Auldroxburgh, Thomas Fergreff, David Dalgless, Andrew Louch, sir
Ninian Brydin notary public and Patrick Flecher. After which James
Ker bailie gave sasine of the 10 merklands of Byrkinsyd with perti-
nents to the said Andrew Ker personally present and accepting.
Andrew asked instrument. Done at 10 am at Birkinsyd before James
Ker, Thomas Fergreff, Ralph Davisone, William Turnbull, Thomas
Gibsone younger and Thomas Gibsone elder.

180. **Curror** 5 Nov 1532 Robert Chepman bailie came at request of
Alexander Scot to his tenement lying in the town and bounds of
Selkirk with the tenement of Thomas Jonsone younger on the east, the
other tenement of Thomas Jonsone elder on the west, the tenement of
John Scot on the north and the king's street leading to "Hallevolhill"
on the south and there on the ground of the same Alexander Scot
resigned the tenement and two rigs in the open fields belonging to it,
one of which lies in "Le Delff" and the other over "le Myrscawis"
between the lands of (blank) in hands of the bailie who gave sasine
of the tenement and rigs to Thomas Curror burgess of Selkirk, paying
18 shillings in annualrent to Walter Scot tutor of Hayning and 2
shillings to Alexander Scot and burgh ferme. Thomas asked instrument. Done around 9 am before George Michilhill serjeant, William
Cadzow, James Cadzow, Thomas Crukschankis, Thomas Jonsone,
Matthew Dristair.

181. **Scot of Paless** Same day and place. Robert Chepman bailie came to
the tenement of the deceased sir David Scot lying in the burgh of
Selkirk over "le Pelgait" between the tenement of William Mithag on
east, the tenement of Thomas Morlaw on the west, the bog on the
south and the king's street leading to the loch on the north and there
on the ground of the same the bailie gave sasine of the said tenement
to Alexander Scot lawful heir of sir David Scot vicar of Ashkirk paying
yearly 30 pence in name of annualrent to Thomas Jonsone and burgh
ferme. Alexander asked instrument before witnesses as above [no.
180].

182. *[Mynto younger* – scored out] **Dounaldsone** 10 Nov 1532 Robert
Chepman bailie at the request of the young man, John Dounaldsone

heir of the deceased Ninian Dounaldsone burgess, came to a rig of
arable land lying over "le Voster Layis" between the lands of Patrick
Murray now in the hands of William Keyne elder on the north and the
lands of William Keyne younger on the south near "Symer Furd" and
there on the ground of the same the bailie gave sasine of the said rig
to the said John Dounaldsone. Before John Lumisden, Thomas Mynto
elder, John Cruik, Robert Thomsone, John Freir done on the ground of
the same around 2 pm.

183. *Mynto, younger* Same day and place. Robert Chepman bailie came at
the request of John Dounaldsone to the said rig lying as above and
there on the ground of the same the said John resigned it in hands of
the bailie who gave sasine to Thomas Mynto younger. Thomas asked
instrument before witnesses abovewritten.

184. *Marion Wilkesone* Same day. Robert Chepman bailie at request of
George Michilhill burgess of Selkirk came to a certain part or portion
of his tenement viz. a forehouse, back hall and bakehouse with free
exit and entry to the close lying within the burgh of Selkirk between
the tenement of Andrew Ker of Prumsydlouch on the east, the tenement of Helen Lydderdaill on the west, the king's street leading to
Moresonhyll on the north and the tenement of John Bennat on the
south, and there on the ground of the same George Michilhill resigned
the said land to his wife Marion Wilkesone in liferent and the bailie
gave sasine of all the said portion of tenement of land for her lifetime
with the condition that if the said George dies before the said Marion
the sasine be null and void if she contract marriage and she shall
manage ["gubernet"] the said tenement to sustain her children. Marion
asked instrument before witnesses Martin Pot, William Mathesone,
David Jonsone.

185. *Andrew Ker of Prumsyd* 13 Jan 1532/33 Mark Ker bailie came at the
instance of William Vynterhoup son and heir of the deceased Andrew
Vynterhoup to the tenement of Andrew Ker of Prumsyd lying in a
vennel called "Gossynlynraw" between the tenement of William
Bennat on the south of the fore side, the barn within the bounds of
the close on the west, the tenement of George Michilhill on the north
and the king's street near the cross on the east and on the ground of
the same William freely resigned an annualrent of 10 shillings scots in
hands of Mark Ker bailie who gave sasine of the annualrent by delivery of a penny to Andrew Ker of Prumsyd personally present and
accepting according to the tenor of my charter made thereon. Andrew
Ker asked instrument before James Ker of Auldroxburgh, Thomas
Feirgreff, sir William Brydin vicar of Selkirk, John Brydin, John
Michilhill chaplain, James Brydin, James Scot, William Scot, William
Brydin.

186. ***Brydin resigned in the hands of sir Richard*** 28 Jan 1532/33
Robert Chepman bailie at the request of James Brydin came to a tenement, with pertinents, of the said James lying in Selkirk near the court
house between the tenement of sir John Chepman on the east, the
yard of William Brydin on the south, the tenement of the deceased
David Brown on the west and the king's street leading to the mercat
cross on the north and there on the ground of the same the said
James freely resigned all right and claim from himself and after death
from his heirs and assignees which he has or will have in and to the
said tenement viz. "Quhittis Croft" in hands of the bailie who...after
the death of the said James gave sasine of "le quhittis croft" to his
second son David Brydin and his heirs and assignees forever paying
yearly the burgh ferme and an annualrent. David asked instrument
before witnesses sir William Brydin vicar of Selkirk, James Scot, Adam
Scot, Thomas Douguell, William Portius, Martin Pot, David Jonson.

187. ***Thomsone*** 7 Feb 1532/33 John Achesone freely confessed he has
received the sum of £5 scots from his brother-in-law Robert
Thomsone for a rig lying over "le Goslodaillis" between the lands of
Patrick Murray of Fowlahill as is specified in an instrument thus: that
the said Robert shall peacefully [enjoy] the said rig provided the said
John Achesone his heirs and assignees pay Robert Thomsone his heirs
and assignees £5 on one day between sun rise and sun set from his
own goods and no others. Robert asked instrument before witnesses
Walter Haw at Evart, Thomas Mynto, David Jonsone, John Craige.

188. ***Cravfurd*** 12 Feb 1532/33 Robert Chepman bailie at the request of
Robert Turnbull came to a certain part or portion called "le Ladyland"
inhabited by Thomas Mynto and belonging to Robert Trumbull the
superior lord lying between the lands of Patrick Murray of Faulauhill
and Thomas Ker called "Kyncroft" now in the hands of Andrew Ker
and there on the ground of the same he freely resigned half the said
arable land called "Ladyland" in hands of the bailie who gave sasine
of the same to James Craufurd and Christian Turnbull his spouse and
to whichever lives longer, their heirs and assignees paying yearly at
the altar of our Saviour 10 shillings scots at two terms of the year viz.
Whitsunday and Martinmas. James and Christian asked instrument
before witnesses Robert Chepman, George Lauder, Alexander Almur,
Thomas Mynto burgesses, John Craig layman. Also it was agreed that
the said James and Christian shall peacefully possess the said half the
arable land called "Ladyland" paying said annualrent at the said altar
provided Robert Turnbull his heirs and assignees pay £6 to the said
James and Christian, their heirs and assignees.

189. ***John Morlaw*** 28 Feb 1532/33 Robert Chepman bailie at the request
of Elizabeth Portuiss one of the heirs of William Portuiss burgess came
to 2 rigs of his arable land lying in the town of Selkirk in his croft
between other rigs of Jonet Portuiss his sister on the east, other rigs of

Elizabeth on the west, the Atrik water on the north, the king's street on the south, and there on the ground of the same the said Elizabeth with her spouse John Scot freely resigned forever the two rigs of arable land fore and back, over and under descending from the king's street to the Etrik Water with free ish and entry and with pertinents in hands of the bailie who gave sasine of the same to John Morlaw. John asked instrument before John Smyth burgess, John Smyth shepherd, John Couper, John Scot, John Craig layman provided that the said Elizabeth pays £5 in gold and silver before the altar of St Ninian in the parish church of Selkirk on one day between sun rise and set to John Morlaw his heirs and assignees. And if the said John fraudulently absent himself from receiving the said sum I will that it be placed in the hands of the bailie for the time being. Also I will that after payment of the said sum the said John and his heirs shall enjoy peaceful possession of the 2 rigs for two years or "twa cropis" immediately following.

190. This rhyme is scribbled at the bottom of the page:

> "that brydin keipveil and [fle savin/ sevin?]
> and sa you sal cum to the blyss of hevin"

191. *Mithag Elder Alexander Scot* 7 March 1532/33 Robert Chepman bailie came at the request of Alexander Scot of Paliss to an annualrent of 6 shillings uplifted from a tenement of John Mithag and there on the ground of the same the said Alexander freely resigned the said annualrent in hands of the bailie who gave sasine of the said annualrent to John Mithag. John Mithag asked instrument before Simon Fairle, John Curror, Robert Toddryk, John Fairle, David Mithag and others. Also it was agreed that John Mithag shall peacefully enjoy the said annualrent provided Alexander Scot, his heirs and assignees pay 40s to the said John, his heirs and assignees so that after payment of the said sum John will have a final remittance to him of 3 shillings.

192. *Ker de Luco* 10 March 1532/33 William Ker of Schaw in the presence of bailies and inquest...[text ends here.]

193. *Scot in the name and part of John Howatsone of Langhoup* Same place and day master Michaell Scot in the name and part of John Howatsone...[text ends here.]

194. *Brydin of the Well* 27 March 1533 William Ker and Adam Ker his son and lawful heir came to their tenement in the burgh of Selkirk lying between the tenement of the said William and Adam on the east, the lands of master John Chepman on the south, the yard of George Chepman on the west and the tenement of James Brydin on the north and there on the ground of the same the said William gave sasine of all the said tenement with a portion of land extending from above and another portion of land lying between the lands of master John

Chepman on the east, the lands of the said William and Adam on the
south, the lands of George Chepman on the west and the lands of
master John on the north to John John (*sic*) Brydin. William and Adam
asked instrument before Robert Chepman bailie, Stephen Loremur,
Robert Smyth, William Turnbull, John Ker, John Couper.

Turnbul Same day. James Brydin came to the principal house "viz. all
betvex the gavells of the foir house and the beir loft in the east part"
and there on the ground of the same the said James freely resigned
the said forehouse near the well in hands of the bailie Robert
Chepman who gave sasine of the said forehouse viz. within the
bounds of the ground and under the wall on the east of the main
dwelling house and the lower chamber near the orchard to Janet
Turnbull spouse of the same James in conjunct fee after the decease
of her spouse. Janet asked instrument before witnesses abovewritten.

[Note at bottom of page that on the same day James Brydin resigned
the said tenement and [house?] and gave charter to John Brydin son of
James and his wife Janet Turnbull.

195. *Lumisden* Same day. William and Adam Ker his only son and lawful
heir came to their tenement lying in the burgh of Selkirk called
"Caponland" and with the common "Lonyng" and "Ponfaulds" on the
east, the tenement of John Dounaldsone on the west, the king's street
on the south and the yard of Thomas Mynto on the north and there
on the ground of the same they resigned and gave sasine of the said
tenement to John Lumisden. John asked instrument.

196. *Marion Haw* Same day. The said John resigned the said tenement
(i.e. as in no. 195) in hands of the superior lords and the said William
and Adam gave sasine to Marion Haw spouse of John Lumisden in
conjunct fee for her lifetime before witnesses abovewritten.

197. *Murray of Kershop* 28 March 1533 William Scot son of the deceased
Adam Scot, native of Kershoup has made, constituted and solemnly
ordained and by tenor of this present instrument makes constitutes
and ordains John Murray of Kershoup on account of the singular
favour and kindness which he bears him his true and undoubted
assignee in seeking out, enacting, retrieving and recovering all the
moveable and immoveable goods violently stolen from Kershoup by
Robert Scot of Howpaslot and Philip Scot [in] Dryhoup belonging to
William Scot and the said William renounces all right and claim to title
of the moveable and immoveable goods in favour of John Murray his
true and lawful assignee. John asked instrument. Done around 9 am
in the parish kirk of Selkirk before sir John Michilhill notary, Robert
Scot, Thomas Ker, James Wilkeson, David Jonsone.

198. *Ker of Luco* 29 April 1533 William Ker of Schaw declared in plain
court that Mark Ker and Robert Chepman bailies promised that they

would see to bringing back all the wood and boards taken away by David Brydin and kept in a tenement inhabited by John Achesone on the afternoon of the said day and they had not fulfilled this. William asked instrument before witnesses William Ker, Thomas Vatsone, George Michilhill, William Michilhill.

199. **Scot of Bukcleuch** 4 July 1533 Walter Scot of Branxhelm, knight, declared in the vernacular: "Quhilk is to say that day was ane precept of the Qwenes Graice shawin be Alexander Carmag pursevand the quhilk precept suld haif varned the forsaid Valter Scot knycht to remoiff fra the landis and steydingis contenit in the forsaid precept 40 dais afor this instant terme of vytsonday, the quhilk precept had na officiar nemmit in to it nor indorsing as the copy of that ilk purports quhilk was of na strencht norcht valour. Attour Alex Carmag allegit that he had utheris preceptis for intimacione and removing of the forsaidis landes and steddinges upon this saidis allegeans the forsaid Valter Scot knyt".

200. **Blair Wife** 20 July 1533 Gilbert Blair discharges all right and claim after his decease in and to "ane almery, ane bed with the pertinenchis". [No further details.]

201. **Stewart** 23 May 1533 The young man William Turnbull son and apparent heir of the deceased John Turnbull his father, chooses Robert Stewart as his master all men excluded except our most serene king and his successors on which Robert asked instrument. On the same day, Robert Stewart receives William Turnbull in kindly service to him to him and will firmly defend the said William in all legal negotiations. William Turnbull asked instrument before sir William Brydin, William Lyderdaill chaplain, Ralph Davesone, William Turnbull of Mynto.

On the same day, Robert Stewart promised faithfully under a penalty of £100 to bring back and deliver an old reversion which he has of Thomas Turnbull in Rauflat and put the same in the safe keeping of sir William Brydin as by tenor of the same, the said Robert or his heirs can exhort the said Thomas and his heirs to receive the sum contained in the reversion. On which William Turnbull asked instrument.

On the same day and place: "that day Robert Stewart oblisses hyme selff to resaif Villiem Turnbull elder, to his tenent at the martynmess next efter the dait of thir presentis in and to twa husbandlandis quhilk ar now inhabeit be [Jok?] Turnbull and Wolle Sinklar for all the dais and termes of fyv yeiris next efter payand maillis and dewitees as uss is bot he sal pay na gersummes". The said William asked instrument before above witnesses.

202. **Stewart** On which day he took instrument that William Turnbull confessed of his own free will that he will alienate all right and claim to

his 2 husbandlands after the end of the term of 5 years. Robert asked
instrument before witnesses abovewritten.

203. **William Turnbull** 20 July 1533 Robert Stewart lord of Mynto, declared
in presence of witnesses underwritten that I and my heirs have not
relaxed after due intimation as noted in a reversion of all my lands
before Martinmas from Thomas Turnbull of Rauflat. At the instant I
receive or we will receive the sum from William Turnbull heir of John
Turnbull we will without delay relax the said lands to William
Turnbull and failing that to his brothers-german. William Turnbull of
Mynto asked instrument before sir William Brydin vicar and notary,
David Turnbull, David Jonson, Ralph Davidsone. "quod brydine n b".

204. **Ker of Gaitschawe** 30 July 1533 Robert Chepman bailie came to the
tenement of Christian Bradfut, relict of the deceased Alexander
Crukschankis, and Thomas Crukschankis her son and heir apparent,
lying in the burgh of Selkirk between the tenement of land of the
heirs of the deceased David Broun on the east, the tenement of the
heirs of the deceased William Ker on the west, the yard of George
Jameson on the south and the king's street towards the court house
on the north and there on the ground of the same Christian and
Thomas resigned the tenement with house yard and pertinents forever
in hands of the bailie who gave sasine of the said tenement to
Lancelot Ker personally present and accepting according to the tenor
of his charter. Lancelot asked instrument. Done at around 1 pm before
sir William Brydin vicar, John Michilhill chaplain, William Portuus serjeant, Adam Wilkesone, James Wilkesone, John Broun, master Patrick
Wrycht.

205. **Dougless** 10 July 1533 Janet Ker, daughter of Andrew Ker of
Prumsydloucht, has made, constituted, created, nominated and
ordained and by the tenor of this instrument makes constitutes and
ordains John Dougless, burgess in Edinburgh her lawful and
undoubted procurator in all causes touching her and especially to
fulfil all articles and appointments contained in our dispensation
before our reverend father sir Gavin archbishop of Glasgow or his
officials or deputes. John Dougless procurator asked instrument before
master Robert Dougless, James Ker of Auldroxburgh, Thomas Fergreff,
Thomas McDuell.

206. **Ker of Prumsyd** 16 Aug 1533 [Text ends here.]

207. **Scot of Kyrkhoup** 20 Aug 1533 Robert Chepman bailie came to [text
ends here.]

208. **Wilsone Howatsone to a mutual agreement** 21 Aug 1533 "The 21
day of August in the yeir of our Lord 1533 yeirs, it is finelie contrakit
finelie compromittit and irrevocabylly aggreit betueix honest person-
nes in presens of thir witnesses under vryttng that is to say Jhone

Vylsone in Sondhoup for slauchter of his [fader] Thome and his frendis kynes and allya alss veill nocht nemmyt as nemmit for ane part and Jhone Howatsone his frendis, kyne and alya in ane uthir part, that is to say, the forsaid Jhone Howatsone for slauchtter of Thome Vylsone sall content and thankfully pay to Jhone Vylsone, Thomas sone, the sowme of 20 merks in penny and pennyvorchts, the first 10 merkes at Martinmess next efter the date of thir presentis, the tother 10 merkes at Vytsonday next efter and ourepruffit at the Fest of the Assumcione of Our Lady, and instantlie in the presence of thir vytness Jhone Vylsone of his fre vyll with consent of kyne, frendis and allya, hes hartlie forgeffin the slauchter of his fader and all uther fed [i.e. feud], invy, maless or discorde that he or ony of his [frendis] may lend in tyme to cum to his nychtbour Jhone Howatsone and for veryficacioune, Jhone Vylsone hes tane hyme and his frendis of thair kneis in the paroche kyrk of Selkirk and failyng detfull paiment of the foresaid sowme al feid slauchter to stand in effec as [it] did at the makin of compromit and [as] bath the parties hes sworne [the aitht] be ostentionne of the handis to the haly evangeill that party breikis ther promise abone vryttin sall pay within 40 dais ther efter to the party bydands stidfastlie without revocatione, the sowme £40 usuell mony of Scotland". John Howatsone and John Vylsone asked instrument before witnesses William Scot in Sondhoup, David Armstrang in Elreg, William Scot in Toddryk, John Scot there, John in Kyrkhoup, Adam Howatsone, George Smyth, John Coutart, John Blaike.

209. *Lauder on part of Brydin* 7 Feb 1533/34 William Ker of Schaw of his own free will has allowed all the inhabitants of the lands called "Kylcroft, Gersland and Caponland" to remove all stones and wood brought in by them to the said land which remains held by me without claim from any other. Stephen Lauder burgess of Edinburgh asked instrument around 8 pm in his house on the part of the inhabitants before men and priests sir William Bradfut, Bartholomew Robesone, Stephen Bell, Alexander Lauder and others servants of the family.

210. *Chepman* 18 Feb 1533/34 John Mithag bailie came to the tenement of the deceased John Chepman burgess in the burgh on south part of the king's street between the tenement once held by William Loremer and now Robert Thomson on the east, the tenement of the deceased John Lauder now James Keyne on the west, the king's street on the north and the land of William Ker's on the south and there on the ground of the same the said John Mithag...entered and invested George Chepman, son and heir of the deceased John Chepman in and to the whole tenement with house, yard and pertinents by staff and baton as is customary. George Chepman asked instrument. Done on the ground of the said tenement around 7 am before John Best, John Brydin, John Freir, John Lumisden, William Birne, William Haw.

211. *Brydin* Same day and place. John Mithag bailie of Selkirk came to the tenement of the deceased John Brydin burgess of Selkirk lying within the burgh between the tenements of John Best on the east, the lands of master John Chepman on the south, the tenement of David Brydin on the west and the king's street leading to Pelhyll on the north, and there on the ground of the same the bailie entered and invested the young man, John Brydin, son and heir of the deceased John Brydin in and to the said tenement with house and pertinents by staff and baton as is the custom in the burgh. John asked instrument before witnesses abovewritten.

212. *Haudene* On the same day as above. John Mithag bailie gave sasine to Elizabeth Haudene of all the tenement of her father George Hawdene lying between the tenements of Andrew Ker of Prumsydlouch on the east, the lands of master John Chepman on the south, the tenement of David Brydin on the west and the king's street on the north by staff [text ends here].

213. *Turnbull* 14 March 1534 John Turnbull son and heir of the deceased George Turnbull of Hassyndenbank declared that he had lawfully intimated to Andrew Davidsone son and heir of the deceased James Davidsone to compear and receive the sum of £12 scots for [the redemption] of a tenement with pertinents lying in the burgh of Selkirk on the west side between the tenement of Thomas Hendersone on the east, the house of William Brydin on the south, the tenement of John Mithag on the west and the king's street leading to Moresone Hill on the north with an acre of arable land lying under the Pelhyll between the lands of sir John Michilhill on the east and the lands of the blessed Virgin Mary on the west, "this lawfull varning beand doun comperit David Davidsone ane with his procurators in the borrow court of Selkyrk before alderman and bailyes of the sammyn and producit the evidenss of the said George Turnbull alienatione of the said tenemont and aiker of land maid to the said James Davidsone contenand purportend in the said evidenss the tenor of ane reversione extendand to ane sowme of £12 and the said Jhone Turnbull beand present offerit the said sowm of £12 to David air to James Davidsone for the redemyng of the said tenemont and ane aiker of land, the quhilk sowme he refusit and immediatlie the said John put the said sowm in souer kepying in the hands of ane vorchty man James Bradfut burgess of Selkyrk and hes bene this 5 yeirs in the saidis handis by past and salbe keipit to the utilite and proffeit of the said David Davisone his ayris executoris and assignais. And attour this the said Jhone Turnbull consideiris his greit skaytht be spulze of his house and the aiker of land lyand vaist and his mony in souer keiping in hands of the foresaid burgess be the spaice of fyv yers considering the evidenss shawin in plane court beiris and purportis the tenor of the reversione now I vyll despone me to intromet with my tenemont and aiker of land". John asked instrument. Done around 1 pm before witnesses sir William Brydin, John Michilhill chaplain, Robert Chepman, William Brydin, Thomas Crukschankis, James Scot bailie.

214. *Curror* 20 April 1534 James Scot, bailie came to the tenement of the deceased Walter Curror within the burgh of Selkirk at Peilgait between the tenement of Alan Mithag on the east and the Common viz. "le Bog" on the south, the tenement of Thomas Prechour on the west and the king's street leading to the loch on the north, and there on the ground of the same gave sasine of the whole tenement with house, yard and rigs of arable land and pertinents to John Curror son and heir of the deceased Walter Curror and invested him in the same. John asked instrument.

Same day James Scot bailie after viewing evidents came to the tenement now inhabited by James Cadzow lying in Cauldshellis between the tenement of James Helme on the east, the land of Patrick Murray inhabited by Janet Scot on the north, the tenement of Thomas Morlawe on the west and the king's street leading to the Peel on the south and there on the ground of the same gave sasine of all the tenement with house and yard to John Curror and entered him as heir to the deceased Walter Curror by staff and baton. John asked instrument.

Same day. James Scot bailie at the request of John Curror came to his tenement lying in Peilgait between the tenement of James Helme on the east, the lands of Patrick Murray on the north, the tenement of Thomas Morlawe on the west and the king's street on the south and there on the ground of the same of his own free will, John Curror resigned all right and claim, ownership and possession which he has or will have to the tenement* in hands of the bailie who gave sasine to James Curror. James asked instrument. Done around 2 pm before John Mithag, bailie, sir John Brydin, William Portuiss serjeant, Cuthbert Curror, John Craw, Alan Mithag.

* Note here referring to next item **215**. "Leychman xx day of the month of April year xxxiiii".

215. *Leychman wife with consent of sister* 23 April 1534 "In the presence of Jhone Mithag our bailie of Selkyrk and vytnesses undervryting comperit ane vorcthy voman Elesabetht Lychtman with consent and assent command of hir saster Jenot Lychman lawful ayris of umquhill George Kyll, burgess of Selkirk efter the tenor of thairis infeftment and lauful resignatioune of the sammyne in the bailyeis handis of forsaid burgh gaif and grantit full pouer to Jhone Mithag bailye effor saidis to by ae seill for hir, ane uther for hir saster and seill ther chartouris with in our absenss becauss we ar fer of and may evyll traveill and deliver the sammyn to Sande Scot in Palyss". Alexander asked instrument before Robert Chepman, John Scot, John Scot, John Smyth, Alexander Collen, John Lauder, William Turnbull, James Tait, Thomas Nychoill.

216. ***Doune*** 23 April 1534 William Ker and Adam Ker of Sanct Helyne Schaw came to the east of half of their tenement which was once inhabited by Andrew Sandersone lying within the burgh of Selkirk between the tenement of John Dounaldsone on the east, the king's street on the south, the rest of the said tenement on the west and the yard of George Chepman on the north and there on the ground of the same the said William and Adam freely resigned and gave sasine of the said tenement in favour of John Dounne. John asked instrument.

On the same day William Ker and Adam Ker his son and heir came to the west side of the tenement the "lang haw" with its pertinents and there on the ground of the same resigned the upper part of the tenement and gave sasine to John Dounne, burgess, provided that the said William and Adam, their heirs and assignees pay on one day between sun rise and set at St Ninian's Altar in the parish church of Selkirk, the sum of £10 scots to John Dounne and his heirs. We will also that the said John Doune his heirs and assignees shall enjoy peacefully the said upper tenement for one year after relaxation and payment of the said sum for his expenses and lawful labour. John Doune asked instrument before witnesses Adam Ker clerk, John Lumisden, Thomas Lumisden, John Pato, John Doungall, Thomas Vatson, Thomas Mynto.

217. ***Ker of Prumsydloucht*** 24 April 1534 The greater part of the community of the burgh of Selkirk resigned all right and claim, ownership and possession which they have to the mill of Bulliheuch. The said Andrew Ker asked instrument from me notary public, before James Scot, John Mithag bailies.

218. ***Jonsone*** 20 May 1534 James Scot bailie at request of Thomas Jonsone elder, burgess of the burgh of Selkirk came to one of his crofts of arable land between the lands of John Curror and our common viz. "the Bog" on the south, the loch of Hayning on the west and a portion of our common land on the north and there on the ground of the same Thomas Jonsone elder, resigned his croft in hands of the bailie who gave sasine to the young man Thomas Jonsone heir of the said Thomas Jonsone elder, and to his heirs and assignees the said Thomas paying yearly 6s 8d annualrent to the venerable father curate of Selkirk, sir William Brydin and his successors forever to celebrate devoutly a soul mass yearly for the souls of the aforesaid Thomas Jonsone and Katherine Scheill, his spouse and their children present and to come. Thomas Jonsone younger asked instrument. Done around 10 am before witnesses sir William Brydin, John Brydin chaplain, William Portuis, Robert Chepman, Alan Mithag, Robert Todryk, David Todryk, John Curror.

Chepman Same day and place. James Scot bailie came at request of Thomas Jonsone to the tenements of John Scot, William Mithag, John Bradfut, Alexander Scot lying in the burgh of Selkirk between the tenements of Robert Todryk on the east and Thomas Morlawe on the west, the common viz. "the bog" on the south and the king's street on the north on the one part and the other tenement of John Bradfut on the north of the king's street between the tenement of John Mithag on the east, the tenement of James Helme on the west, the king's street on the south and the lands of Janet Scot on the north and there on the ground of the same Thomas Jonsone resigned an annualrent of 15 shillings scots viz. 5 shillings on the tenement of John Scot, 5 shillings on the tenement of Alex Scot, 5 shillings on the tenement of John Bradfut, payable at Whitsunday and Martinmas in equal portions and the bailie gave sasine of the annualrent to Elizabeth Chepman alias Jonsone personally present and accepting. Elizabeth asked instrument. Done on the ground of the same around 10 am before witnesses abovewritten.

219. *NB [Ninian Bryden] on the part of David Jonsone and Mungo Jonsone, Janet Jonsone* Same day place etc. Thomas Jonsone, burgess came to his tenement now in the hands of John Broun, once of John Jonsone, lying in the burgh of Selkirk between the tenement of Thomas Ellot on the east, the tenement of Thomas Curror on the west, the king's street leading to Peilhill on the south and the yard of the heirs of Thomas Jonsone on the north and there on the ground of the same Thomas Jonsone resigned an annualrent of 18 shillings uplifted from the tenement in the hands of the bailie who gave sasine of the 18s to Ninian Brydin procurator of the said David [Jonsone], Mungo Jonsone, Janet Jonsone. Ninian Brydin, Mungo Jonsone and Janet Jonsone asked instrument before the witnesses abovewritten.

220. *Haudene* 22 May 1534 Robert Haudene on the one part and Marion Mar on the other, as is clearly shown, in the vernacular: "The forsaidis Robert and Mairyone executoris and intromettoiris of the gudis of umquhill Alexander Haudene and his barnes viz. Georde, Robert and Margaret and in presens of thir vytness undervrytting the said Robert Haudene byndis hyme and obliseis hyme under pane of all his gudis present and to cum that he sall be benevolus efter his pover to the debact [*sic*] of his broder barnes forsaidis in all necessairis and maist specially to the tak and stedinge of Boldsyd quhilkis thairis faderis had of David Hoppringill. And attour the said Robert sall tak the barnes part of gudis of George Haudene and Robert Haudene forsaidis in souer keipinge quhill Beltein next to cum efter the dait of thir presentis payand thankfully xl shillings [40 shillings] to his gud sister Mairyon Mar in part of paiment and the barnes sustentacione, feiding and cleything, the tane quarter paiment of xx shillings [20 shillings] at the fest of Sanct Martyne next to cum, the tother quarter paiment of xx shillings at Beltene next efter. And the forsaid Mairyone Mar byndis hir be the fath and troucht in hir body that scho sall do hir uter deligenss in cleythinge and feidinge hir barnes viz. George, Robert and Mege in hir awin handis as use is in the countre. And the forsaid Mairyone

obliseiss under the pane of inhabilite and all repruff and pane may follow heirefter that quhat tyme and how sone scho cheissis and cleythis hir with ane housband or ony uthir opinlie that ilk tyme instantlie without fraud or gyll sall deuvyd fra hir the tak and steidinge and do hir uter deligenss to put hir barnes in the samyne all fraud gyll cavillation secludit". Before witnesses John Dunlop, Matthew Mar, William Scheill, Robert Scheill and others.

221. *Brydin* 22 May 1534 Adam Ker in Sanct Helyne Schawe came to the tenement of James Brydin lying in the burgh of Selkirk between the tenement of the said Adam on the east, the lands of George Chepman on the west, the king's street leading to "Sanct Marie Voll" [St Mary's Well] on the north and the lands of John Chepman on the south and there on the ground of the same Adam freely resigned an annualrent of 13s 4d in hands of John Mithag, bailie, who gave sasine of the said annualrent to James Brydin and John Brydin his son and heir provided that the said Adam his heirs and assignees pay James or John 10 merks scots. James asked instrument before William Ker of Whitmuirhall, Thomas Mynto, John Lumisden, John Cruik, Thomas Lumisden, John Freir, Thomas Vatson.

222. *Katherine Scheill* 24 May 1534 Thomas Jonsone burgess of the burgh of Selkirk resigned his tenement lying in the said burgh between the tenement of James Jonsone on the north, the king's street on the east, the tenement of Mungo Jonsone on the south and the tenement of Simon Fairle on the west in hands of the bailie John Mithag who gave sasine to Katherine Scheill, spouse of Thomas Jonsone, in liferent. Katherine asked instrument before sir William Brydin vicar, John Michilhill, John Chepman chaplain, Robert Chepman, George Paterson, James Keyne.

223. *Jonsone younger* Same day and place. Thomas and Katherine resign the said tenement with houses and yard thereof and with pertinents in form and effect as is [presented?] in time of making with (illegible) to him after the decease of the same [note in margin: "cassato" broken] in hands of John Mithag bailie who infefted and entered the young man Thomas Jonsone younger as true and lawful heir of the said Thomas Jonsone elder, as was written above after the death of Thomas and Katherine.

Also the said Thomas Jonsone elder...promises Thomas younger if he weakens in strength he shall have straightway all the backhouses to support them in their need. Thomas younger asked instrument.

On the same day Thomas Jonsone weak in body but sound in mind appoints his cousin John Haw to act as procurator at the infeftment of Thomas Jonsone younger in 6 rigs over "the Flures" between the open field lands of Patrick Murray, and also as his procurator to give sasine to Elizabeth Chepman of one rig lying under "le Know" as follows:

"Be it kend till all men be thir presentis lettres, me Thomas Jonsone burgess in Selkyrk to haif maid constitut and ordinet and be this presentis lettres makes constitutis and ordines my veilbelovit frendis Jhone Chepman, Jhone Haw coniunctlie and seuerlie my verray lawfull and undoutit procuratoris auctouris factouris and speciall messingearis gevand and committand to the samyne and ilk ane of thaim myne foull povir for me in my nayme and in my behalff to resign and upgeif in the handis of ane vorchty man Jhone Mithag ane of the bailyeis of the burgh of Selkyrk all my sex rigis of land within the fredome of the samyne burgh lyand in ryndaill as it is at mair lenchte specifeit in chartouris maid thereupone fra me myne ayris and assignais to my veilbelovit Thomas Jonesone nerest and laufull ayre, his ayris and assignais and alswa ane rig of land lyand under the know in the est part of the toune to my veilbelovit douchter Elesabecht Jonsone, hiris ayris, executouris and assignais fra me myne ayris and assignais. And generalie all utheris thingis to do hant and uss as to the office of procuratory is knawin to pertene or that I mycht doo my selff and I var put in propir ferme and stabyll hauld and for to hauld all and quhatsumever thing the said procuratouris or ony ane of thaim in my nayme in the premissis leidis to be done and I sall releif thaim of all chairgis thair throu in tyme to cum under the ypoteik and obligationne of all my gudis present and to cum. In vytness of the quhilk thing to this present procuratoury I haf set to my propir seil vith my awin hand and hess subscrixit thatt ilk vith my hand at the pen befor thir vytnesses sir Jhone Michilhill, sir Ninian Brydine notairis, Robert Chepman, Thomas Hawe, Jhone Chepman, James Doby, Jhone Mithag bailie the last day of may in the yeir of god 1534".

224. *Jonsone younger* 31 [May 1534] John Haw with letter of proxy of Thomas Jonsone elder the tenor of which is abovewritten and sealed with his own seal on paper, came...to six rigs of arable land lying over "le Fluris" in ryndaill between the lands of Patrick Murray (blank) resigns the said [rigs] in hands of the bailie John Mithag who gave sasine of all the 6 rigs to Thomas Jonsone, lawful heir of Thomas Jonsone elder after his death. Thomas younger asked instrument before witnesses underwritten.

On the same day, the procurator came to a rig of arable land under "le Know" between the lands of (blank) and there on the ground of the same the procurator in the name of Thomas Jonsone elder resigned the said rig in hands of the bailie John Mithag who gave sasine to Elizabeth Jonsone. Elizabeth Jonsone asked instrument before witnesses John Brydin, John Hawe, Robert Chepman, Thomas Curror, John Brown.

225. *Scot, Ker of Prumsydloucht ask instrument* 31 May 1534 Andrew Ker of Prumsydloucht leased his mill commonly called "Bullisheuch

Myll" to Janet Scot relict of the deceased George Scot burgess of
Selkirk and her son James for the term of 5 years immediately following paying yearly from the said Janet and James their heirs and
assignees to me, my heirs and assignees £20 scots at two terms i.e.
Whitsunday and Martinmas in equal portions. Also Janet and James
bind themselves to hand over and demit the said mill in a better state
than they received it before witnesses underwritten. Also they bind
themselves to take to the mill all the grain pertaining to the place of
Grenheid viz. corn and malt or any other (illegible) and payment
whatsoever. And the said Janet and James shall repay the noble men
James Bradfut and Simon Fairle for debts paid of the said sum to
Andrew Ker his heirs and assignees. Also the said Andrew Ker faithfully promises to give all his own grain and also that of his tenants viz.
Grenheid, Quhitmur, Myddilsteid and Blakmeddinges and to repair
and build "viz. the caull [i.e. cauld] with horss and men". Andrew
asked instrument before witnesses Gavin Ellot, James Keir, Ralph
Davidson, Simon Fairle, James Bradfut.

226. **Mathosone** 31 May [1534] James [Scot] bailie at the request of William
Lauder burgess of the burgh of Selkirk came to his tenement lying in
the vennel called "Vol Gait" between the tenements of James Melross
on the east, the tenement and yard of Helen Keyne on the south, the
tenement of James Cadzow on the west and the king's street leading
to Peilhill on the north and there on the ground of the same the said
William freely resigned the said house or tenement with small yard in
hands of the bailie James Scot who gave sasine to William Mathosone,
the said William paying 14 shillings scots yearly at two terms [i.e. at
Whitsunday and Martinmas]. William asked instrument before William
Cadzow, James Bradfut, Thomas Curror, John Brown burgesses, James
Cant.

227. **Murray Michilhill** 31 May 1534 Robert Turnbull leases and demits
his place of Howdene lying within the sheriffdom of Selkirk between
the lands of Walter Scot tutor of Hanyng on the east, the lands of
master Michael Scot of Aikvod on the west, the lands of Blakmedinges
on the south and the Atrick Water on the north for the term of 2 years
immediately following and the entry of the above George and John
[Murray] should be at the feast of holy Whitsunday next, paying yearly
£7 annualrent in two equal portions at Whitsunday and Martinmas,
and the said Robert assures the said George and John their heirs and
executors that they will be free from all damage and molestation
whatsoever at the end of the term. George and John Murray asked
instrument before sir John Michilhill notary, John Doune, Thomas
Lame, James Murray, John Michilhill, Robert Doune, Robert Turnbull
have underwritten the deed.

228. **Morlawe** 7 July 1534 William Ker and Adam Ker his son and lawful
heir, came of their own free wills to their rigs of open field of

"Gersland" and "Caponland" of which the first lies over "le Know" on the east side of the town between the lands of George Chepman on the east, the lands of Elizabeth Scot or Portuiss relict of the deceased John Scot on the west, the king's street leading to the burgh of Selkirk on the south and the Etryk water on the north; the second rig lies over "le Thurbrandcorss" with the lands of George Chepman on the north and Patrick Murray on the south; the third rig lies over "Dounsdaillis" with the lands of master John Chepman on the south and James Brydin on the north; the 4th rig lies over "Raton Taillis" [Rat's Tails] between the lands of master John Chepman on the north and Patrick Murray on the south; the 5th rig lies over "le Goslodaillis" between the lands of George Chepman on the north and Cuthbert Turnbull on the south; the 6th rig lies over "le Fluris" between the lands of George Chepman on the north and Patrick Murray on the south; the 7th rig lies over "le Flures heids" between the lands of George Chepman on the south and Patrick Murray on the north; the 8th rig lies over "Tattis Hill" between John Morlaw on the north and George Chepman on the south. And there on the ground of the same William and Adam gave sasine of the said rigs to John Morlaw. John asked instrument before witnesses Adam Ker younger, John Mithag bailie, John Haw, William Portuis.

Also John Morlawe promises to seal a reversion to William and Adam if the said William and Adam pay instantly the sum of 20 [pounds] on a day at the altar of St Ninian in the parish kirk of Selkirk. Also that a premonition 40 days beforehand ought to be made in presence of notary and witnesses as is the custom. If it happens that the said John fraudulently absent himself from receiving the said sum we will that it be put in safe keeping of the bailies of the burgh for the time being. Also the said William and Adam bind themselves and their heirs that the said John shall peacefully enjoy the said rigs for 3 years immediately after relaxation, paying the sum of 12 shillings at two terms.

229. _Mithag_ Same day John Mithag bailie at the request of John Haw came to 2 rigs lying in Selkirk of which the first is in "Gosloodaillis" with the lands of Margaret Howdene on the north and of James Yong on the south and the other lies over "le Fluris" between the lands of Thomas Jonsone on the south and Thomas Mynto on the north and there on the ground of the same John Haw resigned the said rigs in hands of the bailie who gave sasine of the rigs to the young man James Mithag. [James] asked instrument before witnesses Robert Chepman, James Chepman, William Chepman and others.

230. _sir William Brydin_ 15 July 1534 James Scot bailie came at the instance of Thomas Hendersone burgess and Katherine Burne his spouse to the upper part of his yard in Selkirk between the yard of Helen Lydderdaill on the east, the tenement of sir William Brydin on the south, the yard of Andrew Davidsone on the west and the said

yard of Thomas and Katherine on the north, and there on the ground
of the same Thomas freely resigned the upper part of his yard containing the width of the house of sir William Brydin, in hands of the
bailie who gave sasine of the yard to sir William Brydin his heirs and
assignees paying yearly 12 pence to the said Thomas and Katherine
and thereafter to the superior lord as above if he so pleases. Sir
William asked instrument before Alan Keyne, Alexander Hawe,
Thomas Doungaill, James Edmonte, Henry Pattersone, George Clerk.

231. *Loucht* 17 July 1534 John Dounaldsone, son and heir of Ninian
Dounaldsone of his own free will came to his tenement in the burgh
of Selkirk between the tenement of John Brydin on the east, the lands
of James Wilkesone on the west, the king's street leading to the cross
on the south, the Etreke water on the north, the which tenement the
said John holds from the reverend father in Christ, sir Andrew Betone
[*sic* – Andrew Durie in no. **238**], Abbot of Melross and his monks, and
John resigns all right and claim that he has or will have in the said
tenement in favour of Andrew Loucht his heirs and assignees forever.
[Andrew] asked instrument before Andrew Dounaldsone, John Paico,
Henry Yong, John Lumisdene, Thomas Vatsoun.

232. *Ellot procurator of Gavin Ellot* 24 July 1534 Thomas Ellot procurator in the name of Gavin Ellot, came to the church of Hassyndene
according to the tenor of a letter of premonition made by William Scot
of Hassyndene to receive a certain sum of money and other things
contained in a letter of reversion made by Gavin Ellot to the said
William Scot of 40 shillinglands of Neder Gallelawe and there the said
Thomas asked me notary public to read out the said reversion which
being done Thomas asked instrument as follows: "I, Thomas Ellot
procurator of ane vorchty man Gavin Ellot is heir present at the
prenoted day and plaice efter the tenor of the premunicioune made
be Villiem Scot and is reddy to resaif all things contenit in the reversioune and the said Thomas desiris the said Villiem to seill an letter of
tak of the 40 shillingland be tenor of the reversioune and if he vauld
not seill it vt his propir seill bot he offerit to subscrib it with his hand
at the pen and attour the said Thomas Ello[t] procurator desyris sic lyk
mony as the reversion purports viz. angellis nobyllis crownes of
veycht unycornes and 33 shillings of quhit money and the said Villiem
offerit ane certane [sum] of gouldis and quhit mony". Thomas Ellot
asked instrument before sir John Scot vicar of Hawyk, Thomas
Hountar, Adam Scot of Alanhauch, William Kynhard, John
Dounaldsone, John Swan, John Scot.

233. *Ker of Mersyntoune* 27 July 1534 James Ker of Mersyntoune offers
to fulfil or implement all appointed promises made before Andrew
Ker of Prumsydloucht and James Ker of Fairnole and also all the
promises, conditions, consents made in a letter of obligation between
himself and Janet Neuton, William Ker and Adam Ker of Sanct

Helynes Schaw, heir of William and spouse of Janet Neuton, and the said William Ker personally present in the said place of Grenheid humbly requests that Andrew Ker of Prumsydloucht, master William Ker, rector of Aldroxburgh and Thomas McDuell of Stedrig hear the obligations, conditions and all contracts between James Ker and Janet Neuton, William Ker and Adam Ker and the said William Ker now withdraws and does not appear in the presence of James for the hearing. James Ker of Mersyntoun asked instrument before Andrew Ker of P[rumsydloucht], master William Ker rector of Auldroxburgh, Thomas McDuell of Stedrig, Thomas McDuell Laird of McCarstoun, Andrew Loucht.

Same day. Thomas McDuell procurator for James Ker of Mersyntoun came to the tower of St Helyne Schaw where Janet Neuton, William Ker and his son and heir Adam Ker live and the said Thomas pounded the doors and they gave no reply and straightaway the said Thomas in a loud voice proclaimed and offered three times faithfully to implement all the appointed promises before Andrew Ker of Prumsydloucht, James Ker of Fairnele and also wrote it in a contract and a letter of obligation. Thomas McDuell procurator asked instrument before William Lauder, Richard Palmer, Patrick Dikesone and John Robesone.

234. *Jamesone* 7 Oct 1534 In plain head court, George Jamesone alleges that all the inhabitants of the burgh of Selkirk have insulted him and assert that he is a common oppressor and the said George protests that the same should be shown and proven. George asked instrument before the whole court.

235. *Jonsone* 16 Oct 1534 John Scot in Hawik renounces and quitclaims Thomas Jonsone from all the appointed promises made to him or made in these present instruments. Thomas asked instrument before William Brydin, John Scot, James Yonge vicar, John Haw, Robert Chepman, Thomas Scot.

236. *Jonsone* Same day. sir John Scot vicar of Hawik and Thomas Scot bailie of the same place bind themselves their heirs and assignees according to the form of this present instrument in the style of a contract in the name and on the part of John Scot of Hawik to pay to Thomas Jonsone son and heir of the deceased James Jonsone burgess in Selkirk, the sum of 80 merks scots without any favour for the marriage contract between the same Thomas Jonsone and Janet Scot, daughter of the same John Scot, £20 at the time of the contracting and the rest after the marriage and with the consent of her father John Scot. And one year after making the contract the said Thomas and Janet after their marriage shall be vested in the house of the said John, by his childrens' and kinsmens' wishes without any consideration until the end of the year...when they will pay 50 merks in pennies and

pennyworths by which payment the said Janet will receive sasine of the said house in conjunct fee. Thomas asked instrument. Done in the chamber of sir William Brydin at around 5 pm, before witnesses sir William Brydin, James Yong, Robert Chepman, John Hawe, John Couper.

237. **Scot** 16 Oct 1534 Robert Chepman came at request of Thomas Jonsone to the tenement of the deceased master James Jonsone lying in the burgh of Selkirk with the tenement of the deceased Thomas Jonsone on the south, the yard and tenement of Simon Fairle on the west and south and the king's street on the east and there on the ground of the same the said Thomas resigned it in hands of the bailie who gave sasine of the said chamber and tenement to Janet Scot in conjunct fee. Janet asked instrument before sir John Scot, James Yong, John Mithag, Thomas Scot, John Hawe.

238. **Brydin** 23 Oct 1534 The venerable priests Robert Liddaill and Thomas Mersair, lord and dean of Melross presented a certain precept of sasine written on paper and sealed with the signet of sir Andrew Dure, Abbot of Melross and which appeared to me notary public to have no erasures or corruptions or to be in any way suspect, to Robert Chepman bailie specially constituted also bailie of the burgh of Selkirk at that time who handed it to the same Robert who received the said precept and gave it to the notary to read out as follows: "Androo be the permissioun of God, abbat of the abbay of Melross tyl honorabyll men and our luffit frendis Robert Chepman burgess of Selkirk and balye of the samyn William Notman and Henry Symsone coniuntlie and severlie our bailyeis in that part, our express vyll is and we chairgis you and commandis you in our name ane or ma that incontinent after the seyng of thir our writtingis ye pass to ane tenement of landis lyand within the burgh of Selkyrk one the norcht syd of the toun togydder wt ane aiker of lands lyand at the taill of the samyn betveix the lands of David Haw one the vost part the lands of Patrick Murray one the est part the Kyngis common street one the soucht part and the vatter of Ettrik on the norcht part quhilk lands and tenements pertenes nou tyll us and our abbay as patromony thereoff and thair ye sall geif stait sasing heretabyl possession in our nayme of the samyne to Jhone Brydin burgess in Selkyrk conformein to all things to the use and consuetud of the said burgh and to our chairtour of few maid be us and our convent therupone and deliverit to hyme. The quhilk to do we commit to you coniunctlie and severally oure full express and plane pouer be the tenor of this precepe giffen under our signet and subscriptioune manuall at our abbay of Melross the xix day of October in the yeir of God ane thousand fyf handretht therty and four yeres" and here is the subscription of Andrew, Abbot of Melross.

The precept being read out the said Robert Chepman gave sasine of the tenement inhabited by the deceased David Brydin to John Brydin burgess of Selkirk. John asked instrument. Done on the ground of the same around 11 am before John Hoye in Cumlyhill, John Hawe, George Chepman, Thomas Mynto burgesses, James Vilkesone, John Scot, John Brydin, Andra Brydin, John Ranwyk of the forest [Ettrick Forest?].

239. **Hawe** Same day and place the venerable men Robert Lyddaill and Thomas Mersure deans of Melross presented a precept of sasine written on paper and sealed under signet of the reverend father Andrew Dure abbot of Melross and it appeared to me notary public to have no erasures or corruptions or to be suspect in any way and he received it and handed it to me to read out as follows: "Andro be permissioune of God abbot of the abby of Melross tyll honorabyll men and our luffit frendis Robert Chepmen burgess of Selkirk and bailye of the samyne William Notman and Hendry Symsone coniunctlie and severalie our bailyeis in that part Our express vyll [is] and ve chairge you and commandis you ane or ma incontenent efter the seyng of thir our vryttingis ye pass to ane tenement of lands lyand within the burgh of Selkyrk one the norcht syd of the toune to gidder with ane aiker of lands lyand at the taill of the samyne betueix the lands of James Vykesoune on the vost part and the land of Jhone Brydin one the est part and the kingis common streit one the soucht part and the vatter of Ettreik one the norcht part quhilk land and tenement pertenes nou to us and our abbay as patrimone thereof and thir ye shall geif stait and sessing heretabyll possessioune to David Haw son and appearand [heir] to Jhone Haw burgess of the said burgh of all the said tenement of land conforme in all thingis to the uss and consuetud of the said burgh and to our chairtour of few maid be us and our convent thairupone and deliverit to hyme. The quhilk to doo ve commit to you coniunctlie and severaly our full express and plane pouir be the tenor of this precept gevin under or signet and oure sebscriptioune manuel of oure said abbay of Melross the xix day of october the yeir of God ane thousand vc xxxiii yeiris [1534]". The subscription of the said abbot is "Andro, abbat of Melross".

240. The which precept being read out the said Robert Chepman gave sasine of the said tenement and croft to the young man David Haw. David Haw asked instrument before witnesses abovewritten.

241. **Haudene** 30 Dec 1534 John Brydin son and heir of the deceased John Brydin burgess of the burgh of Selkirk and Elizabeth Haudene relict of the same John Brydin and mother of the said John presents as follows an extract from the burgh book: "That the said Elesabetht sall haif the tenement of the north syd of the toune with the halff husbandland perteining to the samyn for all the dais of hir vedoheid payand the deuytess as effeiris and quhen it sal happen her to be cled with ane man than scho sal haif the tenement foresaid and the yaird allanerly payands therfore yeirlie 8 shillings or ellis the lytill houss inhabeit be

Done Coltert in the vost part of the tenemont at the setting of the said
Jhone his ayris or assignais part with the halff husbandland frely with
consent of the overlord. Thane I forsucht Jhone Brydin myne ayres
executoris and assignais be vertue of this compromet and strencht of
this instrument and vytness undervrytting that quhat tyme or howe
sone scho be inquiet of peciabill joyssing of the forsaid tenement and
yaird for the uphaldin of it nychtburlyk and 8 shillings payand as
saidis the quhilk inquietatioune beand opinly knawing that incontinent I my ayres or assignais sal gef hir to hir coniunt fee for the houss
inhabeit be Elesabetht Haw and roum to big ane houss in the yaird
thair to next adiacent with the overyaird to the nedderberne end roum
in the clois and oyss of the kyll nychtburlyk with fre usche and entray
to the sammyne throu the principaill clois to the fredome. In vytness
of the quhilk thing aye of the parteis are bound be faicht and troucht
of ther bodeis and for the mair securite thai haif subscribit ane compromet in the comon buk contenit with ther handis at the pen in the
presence of vytnesses thir under vryttinge sir William Brydin, sir
Ninian Brydin notairis, James Keyne bailye of Selkyrk for the time,
Robert Haudene, David Jonsone, Valter Stoddert".

242. **Keyne baillie** 26 Jan [1534/35] James Keyne one of the bailies of
Selkirk in a loud voice declared before witnesses that Patrick Murray
of Faulauhill sheriff forbids us to hold the burgh court in the first
place according to the tenor and customary right beyond human
memory. Now he intends to proclaim the sheriff court before the
burgh court. John Michilhill asked instrument before witnesses John
Michilhill, John Brydin chaplain, James Brydin, John Chepman, James.

243. **Murray** Same place and date. Patrick Murray sheriff publicly declared
he desires and ought, by law, to hold the sheriff court before the
burgh court and the said Patrick asked this instrument that he does
not make impediment out of contempt for the burgh but for the sake
of justice. Patrick asked instrument before witness as above.

244. **Jaksone of Ruderfurd** 1 Feb 1534/35 John Dougless in Cavers sheriff of Roxburgh in that part specially constituted and of our lord king
by his precept of sasine under testimony of the great seal came to
those husbandlands in the town of Rutherfurd, now inhabited by
William Jaksone and half a husbandland in the same town of
Rutherfurd inhabited by William Jaksone in Nuk and also to another
half of the said husbandland occupied by William Deiphoup, thence
to a husbandland in the same town occupied by William Dikman and
a half husbandland in the town occupied by Stephen Colterd, a half
husbandland inhabited by Thomas Feiche and a husbandland now
occupied by Ninian Brydin with pertinents lying within the sheriffdom
of Roxburgh...and at the ground of each singly the notary read out
the precept as follows: James by grace of God, King of Scots to...John
Dougless in Cavers, William Haw and Robert Jaksone and our sheriffs

in that part, greeting. Because we have given and granted heritably to William Jaksone all the lands with pertinents written below viz. a single husbandland of the town of Rutherfurd inhabited and occupied by William Jaksone, a half husbandland of the town of Rutherfurd inhabited by William Jaksone in [Nuk], a half husbandland occupied by William Dephoup, a single husbandland in Rutherfurd inhabited by William Dikman, a half husbandland in Rutherfurd inhabited by Stephen Colterd, a half husbandland occupied by Thomas Feiche and 12s 7d and threequarters of a husbandland in Rutherfurd now occupied by Ninian Bridin, lying in the sheriffdom of Roxburgh which were heritable [property] of Helen Rutherfurd of that ilk and with debts worth £88 4s above the same recovered from William Vatsone and the sum of £4 8s as the sheriff's fee for execution of his office in assessing the worth of the lands and moveable goods of the same Helen for the same sum distrainable according to the tenor of our act of parliament concerning debts made and our letters regarding sale and assignation as contained in our charter to the said William made before we therefore charge and command the said William or his lawful attorney...to [receive] sasine of the assessed lands worth with pertinents according to the charter he has from us and without delay from our sheriffs of Roxburgh in that part...dated under testimony of the great seal at Edinburgh 15 Jan 1534 and 22nd year of our reign. After which John Douglas, sheriff by virtue of his office, gave sasine of the said lands occupied by the above persons to William Jaksone. William Jaksone asked instrument. Done at the ground of the said lands one by one around 10 am before William Deiphoup, Thomas Symsone, William Wod, George Feiche, John Vylsone, William Jaksone younger, William Gressone, Stephen Colthird, John Couper and John Symsone.

Witnesses to the promise William Deiphoup, Thomas Symsone, William Wod, George Feych, John Vylsone, William Jaksone younger, William Gressone, Stephen Coltert, John Couper, John Symsone.

* "all suttis service and arrestments that I ame oblyst to the shireff and his deputis". George asked instrument before Robert Chepman and James Keyne bailies.

* This clause does not seem to relate to no. **244** or any of the instruments close by.

245. *John Scot, Peilgait* 4 Feb 1533 (*sic*) John Scot in Peilgait burgess of the burgh of Selkirk freely and for conjugal affection and sustentation of his children came to half a tenement of Le Est Hanying which [he] has in heritable fee of John Scot in Hanying and this under a reversion and there near "le Bogheidis" the same John Scot of Peilgait burgess from his own hands gave sasine in liferent to Margaret Scot his spouse of all the half tenement at "le Est Hanyng" provided always that the said land may be redeemed by the heirs and assignees of John Scot lord of Hanyng and also I will that after redemption the said sum contained in the reversion of the said late John Scot be returned to my heirs without revocation or any obstacle. And that the said Margaret my spouse shall find a trustworthy cautioner that neither she nor any other in her name shall quarrel or act in prejudice of my heirs after my death or the redemption of the said lands by fraudulently detaining the sum contained in the reversion, as a rule of law requires [of her]. Margaret asked instrument. Done on the ground of the same around 2 pm before witnesses sir Simon Shortreid vicar of Ashkirk, James Scot bailie of Selkirk, William Fleigar elder, David Todryk, Walter Scot.

246. *James Haw, smith* 20 Feb 1534/5 Robert Chepman bailie at the request of William Wynterhoup, came to his tenement in Peilgait between the tenement of James Chepman on the east, the king's street on the south, the tenement of sir John Brydin on the west and the yard of said James Chepman on the north and also concerning one yard pertaining to the tenement having an entry of 7 feet lying near the tenement of master John on the west and the workshop of Stephen Loremer and James Helme on the south and the tenement of sir John Brydin on the east and the yard of James Chepman on the north and there on the ground of the same the said William Wynterhoup resigned the tenement and yard in hands of the bailie who gave sasine to James Haw burgess in Selkirk paying yearly to sir John Brydin chaplain of Glasgow 24 shillings. James asked instrument before John Mithag, William Chepman, Robert Melrose, John Curror, David [Mithag?]

247. *John Hawe* 4 March 1534/5 John Haw burgess of Selkirk publicly declared in the presence of witnesses underwritten that by no means did he wish to pay beyond what he is accustomed to pay for past terms for the said term of Whitsunday immediately following. John asked instrument before witnesses John Lumisden, sir Richard Brydin chaplain, Andrew Bradfut, James Wilkesone, John Cruk.

248. *Morlawe* Same day. John Morlawe publicly declared that the honourable man William Ker of Sanct Helyne Schaw faithfully promised to pay two bolls of flour according to the use of the market of the burgh of Selkirk, from his 8 rigs of arable land at the feast of St Martin or St Andrew immediately following. Also that after payment of the said flour, neither the said William Ker nor anyone in his name will disturb the said John Morlawe in his peaceful possession of the said 8 rigs. John Morlawe asked instrument before witnesses abovewritten.

249. [Note: this item is interrupted by an inserted page as no. **251**.]

Jaksone 30 March 1535 William Jaksone of Ruderfurd came to certain of his tenants living in the town of Ruderfurd whose names are as fol-

lows William Deiphoup, Ninian Brydin, Stephen Coltert, William
Dikman, Thomas Feich, William Jaksone younger and the said William
present from door to door and lawfully discharged ["exoneravit"] the
possession of all the said tenants that they should be ejected and flit
from all the lands and tenements apportioned to him by the deliverance of the lords of council. William Jaksone asked instrument before
William Champlay of Langneuton, Thomas Jaksone, Andrew Lek,
James Jaksone, Thomas Symsone, George Feych, John Cant, Thomas
Vauch, Thomas Gressome.

250. **Hoppringill** 1 April 1535 The young man James Hoppringill, first
born son of James Hoppringill of Teness in name and on part of his
father discharged all and each of both sexes by name, door to door in
expectation of being ejected and flitting from his place of Bukhame at
the feast of Whitsunday immediately after. James in name of his father
asked instrument. Done in the presence of witnesses underwritten
Alexander Franch, George Turnnor, Thomas Blaik, Thomas Mude.

251. [Page inserted.] 30 March 1535 William Jaksone in Nuk now occupying
half a husbandland in the town of Rutherfurd, William Deiphoup
occupier of another half husbandland of the same William Dikman
inhabitant of a husbandland of the same town, Stephen Colthird occupier of [half] a husbandland of the same town, Thomas Feiche occupier of half a husbandland of the same town and Ninian Brydin
occupier of land in the said town with pertinents heritably belonging
to William Jaksone lying in the bounds of the said town and within
the sheriffdom of Roxburgh, personally apprehended to remove themselves and their servants and their goods from the husbandlands
singly and respectively by Whitsunday next to come [and] he lawfully
warned them intimating and signifying that if they occupied the said
lands after Whitsunday, they would be deemed to be in violent possession of the same. William Jaksone asked instrument. Done at the
dwelling houses of the underwritten persons around 10 am before
witnesses William Champlay in Langneuton, Thomas Jaksone, (p/t)
Feich, Thomas Vauch, Andrew Lek, James Jaksone,Thomas Symsone,
John Cant, Thomas Gressone.

252. **Spotssvod** Same day and place [as no. 250]. Marion Spotissvod relict
of the deceased James Ker of Bukehalm, declares that this strong
warning by James Hoppringill might not turn to her or her tenants'
prejudice for this reason that it never was the modern custom that a
chaste widow living in the lordship of Melrose was excluded from
lawful possession by any reason and James Hoppringill faithfully
promised before George Steill that the said Marion or her tenants
would be neither removed nor disturbed if she paid always her ferme
and fruits ["fructus"] to Andrew Dury lord Abbot of Melross. Marion
asked instrument before witnesses abovewritten.

253. *sir John Michilhill on the part of David Jonsone* 5 April 1535
Mungo Jonsonsone (*sic*) freely resigned all claim he has, had or will
have in and to to an annualrent of 6 shillings scots uplifted from a tenement of John Broun lying in Peilhill between the tenements of
Thomas Ellot on the east, Thomas Curror on the west, the yard of the
heirs of Thomas Jonsone on the north and the king's street on the
south. Also the said Mungo quitclaims to the said David all the sum
belonging to him after relaxation. David Jonsone asked instrument
before sir William Brydin vicar of Selkirk, David Scot vicar of Cavers,
John Brydin chaplain, Robert Chepman.

254. *Jonsone* 6 April 1535 Robert Chepman bailie came to the tenement of
the deceased master James Jonsone lying in the burgh of Selkirk
between the tenements of the deceased Thomas Jonsone on the
south, the king's street called "Fulbrig Vynd" on the east, the tenement
of Simon Fairle on the north and the yard of Simon Fairle on the west,
and there on the ground of the same the bailie gave sasine of the tenement with houses and yard and by staff and baton invested Thomas
Jonsone lawful heir of the deceased master James Jonsone his uncle.
Thomas asked instrument around 10 am before sir John Michilhill,
David Mithag, Mungo Jonsone, James Doby.

255. *John Brydin of the Malt Kiln* 9 April 1535 Robert Chepman bailie
came to certain rigs of open field of the deceased John Brydin burgess
lying in ryndaill between the lands of Patrick Murray two of which lie
in "Myl Croft" on the west of "Donsdailles", the lands of Patrick
Murray on the north in hands of Simon Jamsone, the millburn on the
west, the lands of John Chepman on the east and the croft of Mark
Ker now in the hands of Elizabeth Bayne, relict of the deceased
Robert Portuis [on the south]. A third rig lying in "Donsdaillis Balkis"
on the north part of "le ester struder" [i.e. easter pool] between the
lands of William Lauder now in the hands of William Keyne on the
south and east and the lands of Patrick Murray now in the hands of
(blank). And another 2 rigs lying on the south part of "Le ester
struder" with the lands of Patrick Murray on east, west and north, and
there on the ground of the same the bailie gave sasine of all the said
rigs with pertinents to John Brydin son and lawful heir of John Brydin
burgess. John asked instrument. Done around 10 am before witnesses
John Turnbull heir of Philophauch, Thomas Ker, heir of Mark Ker,
David Jonson, Thomas Lumisden, Walter Stoddart and Robert Ellot.

256. *Brydin 3rd* Same day and place. Robert Chepman bailie after reading
evidents of the deceased John Brydin burgess, came to two rigs of
arable land not the meadow lying under "le Reidheild" with the lands
of Robert Chepman on the east, the king's street on the west, a
meadow of William Ker of Sanct Elene Schaw viz. at
"Thurledenburne" on the west and the lands of Patrick Murray now in
the hands of Helen Lauder relict of Thomas Ker on the south and

there on the ground of the same the bailie gave sasine of the two rigs with meadow extending to "Thurlidenburn" to John Brydin, son and heir of the deceased John Brydin, his father. John asked instrument before witnesses abovewritten.

257. **Brydin** Same day. Robert Chepman bailie came to a further 2 rigs of arable land lying in the west part of "le Donsdaillis" with the Ettrek water on the north, the lands of Patrick Murray now in the hands of Simon Jamsone on the south, the lands of John Scot on the east, the burn called Millburn on the west and there on the ground of the same the bailie gave sasine to John Brydin true and lawful heir of his grandfather Thomas and his father John Brydin burgess. John Brydin asked instrument before witnesses abovewritten.

258. **Patersone, Andersone, Broun** 27 April [1535] Robert Patersone, Bartholomew Andersone and Archibald Broun asked instrument that Alexander Scot then called of Paliss near Ashkirk faithfully promised before witnesses underwritten to forgive all charges, debts or harmful words against him by the said Robert, Bartholomew and Archibald and afterwards never to repeat the same in law or outside the law. The said [men] asked instrument before witnesses Patrick Dobsone, William Frater, James Frater, Walter Stoddart, David Jonsone, Ninian Smyth, Robert Ellot layman.

259. **Lauder** 1 May 1535 William Lauder burgess of Edinburgh and lord of the lands of Toddryk came to his principal dwelling house assigned to William Scot tenant of the said place and straightway by casting away and placing outside of a stool at the front door as is the custom in such things, discharged the said William Scot and his friends to be ejected and removed from my place of Toddryk at Whitsunday next following and declared this publicly before witnesses William Hendersone, John Blaike, John Scot, Patrick Moffat, Patrick Harde.

260. **Reddaill younger** 5 May 1535 George Reddaill son and heir of the lord of Reddaill presented a certain precept of sasine under the seal of Michael Clerk lord of a third part of Purveshill to Thomas Hereot who received it and handed it to the notary to read out as follows: Michael Clerk to James Reddaill, John Reddaill, William Reddaill, Thomas Herrot my bailies in that part, greetings. Because I have sold, granted and alienated to George Reddaill, son and heir of John Reddaill of that ilk and Elizabeth Ker his spouse and to whichever lives longer in conjunct fee and to their heirs lawfully procreated failing which the nearest heirs of the said George all the third part of the lands of Purveshill with tenants and tenandry and pertinents lying in the sheriffdom of Peebles held from our lord king and his successors as contained in my charter to the said George and Elizabeth we charge and command you to give sasine of the said lands without delay...to George Reddail and Elizabeth Ker and to whichever lives longer in conjunct fee according

to the tenor of their charter… in testimony of which I append my seal
and sign manual at Jedburgh 29 April 1535 before sir George Marchaill
treasurer of Aberdeen, John Dougless burgess of Jedburgh, Ninian
Knox, Thomas Singlar notary public and Stephen Andersone. And I
Thomas Keyne notary public subscribe the present precept of sasine
by special command of the foresaid Michael Clerk who as he asserted
is unable to write with his hand at the pen witness my manual subscription. "Ita est T.K." The which precept being read out and made
public the said Thomas Hereot bailie in that part gave sasine of the
lands of the third part of Purvishill to George Reddaill. George asked
instrument. Done around 11 am before witnesses Hugh Dougless
burgess in Edinburgh, John Reddaill, John Braikreig, John Hesloip,
John Purvess, Thomas Hog.

261. *Smyth wife of John Mithag* 7 May 1535 The venerable father
William Lermont brother of the order of Saint Dominic in the place of
Sterlyng gave to me Janet Smyth for consanguineous love and favours
acts and deeds, all the ash trees ("fractinos") and willows now in his
yard lying in Peilhill between the tenements of John Curror on the
east, Andrew Shortreid on the west. Janet asked instrument at the
door of James Wilkeson around 1 pm before George Chepman, David
Jonsone, John Vrycht.

I, Vincent Strauchan notary by special command of Janet Wilsone subscribe this present charter with my own hand in the appointed chamber.

262. *Robert Chepman and James Keyne, bailies in name and on part
of the community of the burgh of Selkirk ask an instrument* 25
May 1535 the notary public, witnesses and all the inhabitants of the
burgh of Selkirk came to the north common viz. "the north syd of Yair
Common, raid the marchis distinklie be the devyss of our eldest and
vysset burgess and set up march stanes be tweix Carterhaucht and us,
and Philophauch, Hareheid and Fausyd at command of the haill com-
monite that var chossin landmaires [landmeasurers] to pass and rid the
boundis of the common viz. Thomas Mynto, James Bridin, Johne
Bridin elder, Jhone Haw, Andro McDuell, Symon Fairle, Ad Wilkesone,
Jhone Curle, James Mousse, Johne of Cadzow aigis est of the toun and
that ilk day, tuk doune twa schelles [sheilings] anent the Yair and
Thome Ker in the Yair promised to tak doune ane dyk neulie begit be
yonger Voll of Vod and als maister Thomas Ker in Sonderlandhall, ane
porcionne of ane dyk one Tweid syd and uther portioun over the
Yairsyd Pottis faithfully promist to put thaim doun with his awin servand ore thai raids agains and alss James Ker in Bregheuch vranguslie
manuris twa rigs sawin cornes lynelie descandand doune fra the diks
that cumes to the Kirkburn and evin doune to the foundament of ane
auld dyk one the Bregheuch and all contenit one the north syd quhill
it cum to the vater of Ettrik". Before sir Stephen Vylkesone, John

Brydin chaplain, Gilbert Ker, James Ker of Aldroxburgh, Thomas Ker of Yair, John Thomson and the whole community.

263. **Ruderfurd on the part of the lord of Hunthill** 8 June 1535 the venerable sir William Ruderfurd protested in plain court that the deliberation of the inquest should not turn to his prejudice from the fact that he openly produced an instrument of sasine of Blakhauch and all right and claim that the most excellent lady Queen or the lord of Maxham has, had or will have.

264. **James Keyne bailie "pro re publica"** 25 June 1535 James Keyne one of the bailies in the name and on the part of his office and the community of the burgh of Selkirk and by virtue of a letter given by the king in favour of the freedom of the burgh, discharged all without freedom of the burgh buying wool, skins and loads ["carga"] or any goods contrary to the interest ["rem publicam"] and freedom of our burgh before the appointed hour and especially Robert Hauden, Thomas Govan, William Vylson, John Vylson, William Vynterhoup, David Jonsone, Adam Vylsone, John Downlop, principally buying against the burgh's freedom and oppressing their fellow burgesses weekly secretly (?) and openly for a long time. James asked instrument before witnesses master Robert Ker vicar of Lyndene, sir William Brydin vicar of Selkirk, John Mithag, James Bradfut, John Brydin, Robert Chepman, Peter Moffat, James Scot and others.

265. **Keyne** 21 July 1535 James Keyne bailie of Selkirk in the name of the whole community made William Portuus proclaim royal letters concerning the customs and freedoms of the burgh of Selkirk near the cross around noon. Before witnesses William Hog in Prestoun, William Scot in Feldishoup, Walter Scot in Hanying.

266. **William Curror** 3 Sept 1535. William Ker and Adam Ker of St Elyne Schaw of their own free will came to the tenement of David Brydin lying in the burgh of Selkirk in the vennel called Volvynd with the tenement of John Brydin on the east, the tenement of John Lumisdene on the west, the lands of master John Chepman on the south and the king's street on the north and there on the ground of the same resigned an annualrent of 20 shillings scots from the said William, Adam their heirs and assignees uplifted yearly from the said tenement in favour of William Curror presonally present and accepting and invested the said William in the same provided that William and Adam pay £19 scots on one day to William Curror after and according to the tenor of a reversion to William Curror...pay £10 now and the other £9 at time of reversion and straightaway the said William [Curror] will renounce all right and claim and deliver all evidents to William, Adam their heirs and assignees. William Curror asked instrument before John Lumisden, John Paito, John Cruik, James Lumisden, John Dwnne, David Jonsone.

267. **John Hawe** 18 Sept 1535 John Haw burgess of Selkirk, declared in
the presence of witnesses and notary public that Andrew Louche,
William Ellot, Parsevell Ellot, Patrick Gourlaw [gap left blank for other
names] with whatever messengers or soldiers with their accomplices
with the strong hand, armed or without any precept from the bailie,
officer, messenger, serjeant or any one, stole or took away grain from
one rig of arable land lying under "le Schaw" heritably belonging to
the said John Haw as he alleges he has proven by faithful witness. All
asked instrument before witnesses Alexander Hawe, John Keyne
bailie, Alexander Hawe, John Keyne, James Vilkesone, James Keyne
younger.

268. **Louche** Same day Andrew Louche and his attorney Andrew Ker publicly declared that the said rig and grain was sown by them in the time
of sowing, belonged heritably to his master Andrew Ker and the said
Andrew alleges he discharged and lawfully cautioned the said John
Hawe from occupation of the said rigs by reason that the said Andrew
and his friends reap and take away their own grain from the said rigs.
Andrew and friends asked instrument.

269. **Haw** Same day John Hawe burgess publicly declared in the presence
of witnesses abovewritten that he sowed with his own corn the 2 rigs
lying over Goslowdaillis and he held them in assedation and possession because he was not lawfully discharged before Martinmas, and
immediately he asked and demanded that James Keyne bailie arrest
his grain in the name of the king because it was removed from the
said rigs and arrested with the authority of the office of bailie and
arrest the said Andrew and his accomplices that had reaped and led
away the said corn by arrestment. John asked instrument before witnesses abovewritten

270. **Bradfut** 12 Oct 1535 James Bradfut one of the burgesses of the burgh
of Selkirk in name and on the part of the whole community of Selkirk
before alderman, bailies and jurors in the face of plain court publicly
declared that William Vylsone, Thomas Goven, David Jonsone, Robert
Hauden, William Vynterhoup and their accomplices came on Thursday
to the mercat place with a view to waylaying both openly and secretly
the burgesses of the said burgh and they gave signals and used tricks
and devices to let men selling goods know that they should slip away
secretly with their goods for sale to inns so that all defrauded the customs and the weill of the burgh to the hindrance of all the indwellers
of the town and the said James proved the same. James asked instrument before all the inquest of alderman and bailies.

271. **Mithag** Same day. John Mithag burgess of the said burgh discharged
William Vynterhoup, Robert Haudene, David Jonsone, William
Vylsone, Thomas Govan also all in general and particular "that bies
and in specie within the schireffedom or in the burgh of gudis stapill

viz. hempe, lynte, ter, pyk, saip, irne, valx, irne, spir, vyne eftor the tenor of the Kingis lettres devyssat be the lordes of the counsaill". John Mithag asked instrument.

272. **Wrycht** Same day master Patrick Vrycht procurator for Thomas Goven, Robert Haudene, William Vynterhoup, David Jonsone in a loud voice declared in plain court that the reading of the same letter of the king did not turn to the prejudice of the said men in respect that it did not make mention of the market constituted in the burgh of Selkirk or why all Scots men should not have licence to buy and sell their goods. Master Patrick asked instrument.

273. **Brydin** Same day. sir William Brydin in the name and on the part of the whole community of Selkirk asked instrument that master Patrick Wrycht procurator for the above men alleges and contradicts and argues against the profit of the king and the general weill of the state of the said burgh and the decreet of the lords of council.

274. **Vrycht** Same day. master Patrick Wrycht asked instrument that sir William Brydin and John Chepman burgess in plain court acknowledged William Vylsone burgess disallowed from selling in the market ["extravenetratum"].

275. **Hoppringill** Same day George Hoppringill in Torwodle in face of plain court requested a copy of the expenses of the king's letter incurred by the burgesses and community of the burgh of Selkirk, and the same burgesses by no means wanted to give a copy until they had consulted with lawyers. George asked instrument.

276. **Turnbull** Same day Robert Turnbull declared in plain court that Ralph Turnbull was never given sasine of ten shillings of annualrent uplifted yearly from a tenement of William Turnbull and this he intends to prove. Robert asked instrument before Andrew Ker, James Scot, sir William Brydin, John Brydin chaplain.

277. **Burne** 12 Oct 1535 James Scot bailie at the request of Alexander Scot called of Paliss came to three rigs of arable land the first lying over "Fluris", the second over "Layes" and the third over "Briglandes" as is fully specified in the burgh book and there on the ground of the same the said Alexander...freely resigned the said rigs in hands of the bailie who gave sasine of the same to William Boirne and William asked instrument before witnesses underwritten. Also the said Alexander asked instrument that if he will have relaxed and paid £3 scots before the feast of St Luke the Evangelist next following, the said William will pay 3 firlots of barley and flour and if he does not pay the said sum on the appointed day, he will pay nothing for these 3 rigs and after relaxation of the same, the same William will peacefully enjoy the 3 rigs for 6 firlots of barley and flour. Before witnesses Alan Keyne,

George Chepman, William Portuus, Henry Young, Thomas Mynto elder.

278. **Keyne** 3 Nov 1535 James Scot bailie of the burgh of Selkirk after deliberation of an inquest and reading of evidents, came to the tenement of the deceased William Keyne, burgess of the said burgh lying near Fulbrig and the common street which leads to Selkyrkhill on the west, the lands of Patrick Murray on the south, the lands of (blank) on the east and the lands of George Chepman on the north, also a meadow with a portion of arable land lying at "Yperlaw Peich" between the common on the north and the lands of James Brydin called "Quhittis Croft" belonging to the said tenement and there on the ground of the tenement the bailie gave sasine of the tenement meadow and croft with pertinents to James Keyne son and heir of the deceased William Keyne according to the evidents shown. Done before bailie, inquest and witnesses James Brydin, James Craufurd, Thomas Jonsone burgesses, John Scot, George Michilhill serjeant, Patrick Keyne, John Thomsone.

279. **Fleicher** ("Curror" scored out) 15 Nov 1535 John Mithag bailie of the burgh of Selkirk at the request of the young man William Mithag came to the place of his tenement lying in Peilgait in the said burgh between the lands of the heirs of the deceased John Scot in Peilgait on the east, the common viz. "the bog" on the south, the tenement of Alexander Scot on the west, the king's street on the north and there on the ground of the same the said William resigned the tenement in hands of the bailie who gave sasine of all the tenement and yard to William Flecher burgess. William asked instrument. Done around 2 pm before witnesses John Mithag elder, James Melross, John Broun, Patrick Freir, James Curror.

280. **Vayche of Syntoun** 16 Nov 1535 John Vayche of Norcht Syntoun came before witnesses underwritten to William Portuus constituted sheriff of the community of the burgh of Selkirk and asked a copy of the royal letters for expenses under the penalty following thereon and the said William, sheriff in that part, declared that the said John Vayche and not any other in his name had asked a copy at the time of summons and immediately after summons the said William delivered these royal letters to James Keyne and Robert Chepman, bailies of the burgh of Selkirk. The said John asked instrument in the burgh mercat around 12 noon before witnesses David Damphoy, Walter Scot, William Turnbull of Mynto, Walter Scot of Askyrk, John Young, John Broun.

281. **John Morlaw** 3 Dec 1535 John Mithag bailie at the request of Alan Mithag his brother-german came to his tenement lying in Pelgait between the tenement of Thomas Morlaw on the east, "the bog" on the south, the tenement of John Curror on the west and the king's

street leading to the loch on the north and there on the ground of the same Alan Mithag resigned the tenement in hands of the bailie who gave sasine of all the tenement with yard to John Morlawe. John Morlawe asked instrument. Done around 3 pm before William Portuus serjeant, William Mithag, Thomas Melross, John Hawe.

282. *James Keyne on the part of William Hawe, burgess of Edinburgh* 12 Jan 1535/36 James Scot bailie of the burgh of Selkirk came to the principal dwelling house of that husbandland with pertinents belonging heritably to John Hawe lying on the east of the burgh on the north side of the king's street between the lands of Archebald Vatsone on the east and the lands of James Mynto on the west and there on the ground of the same he resigned the said husbandland with house, buildings, yards, crofts, tofts and rigs with pertinents in hands of the bailie who gave sasine of the same to James Keyne burgess of Selkirk and procurator for William Hawe burgess of Edinburgh brother-german of the same John according to the tenor of his charter. James Keyne asked instrument. Done on the ground of the said house around 2 pm before witnesses John Keyne, David Hawe, David Jonsone and William Hawe.

283. *Keyne* 15 Jan 1535/36 James Scot bailie came to the ground of 2 rigs of land belonging heritably to Thomas Ellot and Helen Ruderfurd of which one lies over "Know" on the east side of the burgh between the lands of sir Ninian Brydin chaplain on the east, the lands of Andrew Ker in Grenheid on the west, the king's street on the south and the Ettryk water on the north. The other rig lies over "le Fluris" between the lands of Andrew Ker on the south, the lands of Patrick Murray on the north, the lands called "Lady land" on the west and the lands of the said Patrick on the east and there on the ground of the same Thomas Elwand and Helen Ruderfurd his spouse resigned the two rigs in hands of the bailie who gave sasine of the two rigs with pertinents to John Keine son of the deceased Patrick Keine burgess of Selkirk on the ground of the above lands around 2 pm before James Keine, David Hawe, David Jonsone, William Hawe.

284. *Master Richard Rychersone* 15 Feb 1535/36 [Text ends here.]

285. *Brydin* 22 Feb 1535/36 John Mithag bailie came to certain rigs of land of Alan Keine the first lying over "Reidheildis" with the kirklands on the east, the lands of Andrew Ker called "Burgess Vallis" on the north and the lands of Patrick Murray on the south; the second rig lies over "Norland heid" with the lands of Patrick Murray on the east and the lands of David Brydin on the west and the lands of John Brydin on the (blank); the third rig lies over "Norchtlandis" extending to "Thurlidene Burne" on the west, the lands of Andrew Ker in the hands of John Young on the south and the lands of Patrick Murray in the hands of Thomas Jonsone on the north and there on the ground of

the same the said Alan resigned the rigs with pertinents in hands of the bailie who gave sasine to David Brydin son of the deceased John Brydin. David Brydin asked instrument. Done on the ground of the lands around 8 am before John Lumisden, John Caiyk, Andrew Brydin, John Turnbull.

Also another two rigs in "Myrscaur with Dikdaillis" in the east and "West Myrscares" on the west and the lands of the deceased William Keyne on the north and south giving sasine to the said David provided that Alan pays David and his heirs £6 scots so that David shall enjoy the said [rigs] for two years after relaxation.

286. *Jonsone* 16 March 1535/36 Thomas Jonsone bailie of the burgh of Selkirk presented a precept of sasine under the red and white seals of Patrick Murray of Fawlawhill and the lord of the husbandlands of Selkirk which appeared unspoiled in any way and not suspect to me notary to Thomas Murray in (blank) who handed it to me notary to read out as follows: Patrick Murray of Fawlawhill and lord of the husbandlands of Selkirk to Thomas Murray, George Murray my bailies in that part specially constituted greetings...as is clearly shown that not long ago my honourable father James Murray of Fawlawhill etc has given, granted, sold and heritably alienated to Thomas Jonsone burgess of the burgh of Selkirk, all of a husbandland called "Bogland" lying in ryndail in the bounds of Selkirk [now in the hands of] Thomas Jonsone younger as is fully contained in the charter from my father. I therefore charge you to give sasine of the husbandland called "Boglands" to Thomas Jonsone younger, true and lawful heir of his grandfather the deceased Thomas Jonsone in testimony of which I set my own seal at Hanginschaw on the said day and month of March 1535 before sir Laurence Jonsone, Ninian Brydin chaplain, Adam Murray, James Murray brother of Patrick of Newark. Which precept being read out Thomas Murray bailie gave sasine of "Bogland" to Thomas. Thomas asked instrument before witnesses James Haw in Syntoun, sir Stephen Vylkesone, Simon Shortreid priest, James Keyne, John Scot ["obscrite"], David Jonson, John Keyne.

287. [The whole of the next item has been scored out]

Here are the goods pertaining to David Jonsone and Janet Jonson (illegible)...worth on their mother's death, the final worth of the goods [being] 40 [merks] viz. £[2]7 ... "Imprimis auld bed and bouster, four codis, ane coverynge, ane plaud, ane blankin, ane pair of scheittis, ane rest vorne, ane stands bed vantand ane burd, ane veschel beuk, ane lytill counter, ane rownd kyst with twa burds in the ends of it, ane large auld kyst, ane maskyn falt, twa betin tubbin, ane lytill stand, ane kedding tub for quheit, ane small pot, ane pudir [i.e. pewter] plait, ae bonny roundaill".

The following paid £6 to Janet Jonson and rests in hands of Nicolas Ker until the decease of the forsaid viz. "covering with halff (illegible)…boll de…worth 27 shillings (illegible) six with Elesabecht Brydin 16 shillings, item ane gray meir 20 shillings, (illegible) 25s of item the [vaicit?] (illegible) Kelsoo"

288. **Berkare** 16 March 1535/36 John Haw and David Haw his son and heir apparent…in the presence of witnesses underwritten acknowledge that they have set in tack 4 rigs of their arable land for £10 scots to Thomas Barker burgess of the burgh of Selkirk of which the first rig lies under "le Knowe" between the lands of William Ker on the west and the lands of Patrick Murray on the east; the second over "Crukit Lands" with the lands of Thomas Mynto on the north and Thomas Jonsone on the south; the 3rd rig lies over "Goslodaillis" and [is between the land] called "Burgess Vallis" on the north and the lands of Patrick Murray on the south; the fourth rig lies over in "Fluris (p/t) Heids" with the lands of Thomas Jonson on the north and master John Chepman on the south. So that after payment of the said sum we will that Thomas his heirs and assignees shall freely possess the said rigs for two years after and if it happens that the said Thomas his heirs and assignees are disturbed in their peaceful possession of the same we bind ourselves and our heirs to deliver under a clause of warrandice all the land called "Melross Croft" in peaceful possession at the discretion of the bailies and burgesses for the time being. Thomas Barker asked instrument. Done around 6 pm before John Brydin, John Brydin younger, David Jonsone, James Vilkesone, Patrick Layng our servant and divers others in the tenor of evidents openly shown.

289. **John Mithag, James Scot, bailies on the part of the whole community of Selkirk** 22 March 1535/36 William Chepman writer of the king's court, the sheriff or bailie in that part of our lord king specially constituted by his precept under testimony of the great seal came to the mercat cross and then to the court house of the burgh of Selkirk and then to the south common and then to the north common then in diverse places and in course of time handed the precept to the notary to read out as follows: James by Grace of God, King of Scots, to his sheriff and bailies of Selkirk also to William Chepman, William Burn, Alexander Lauder jointly and severally our sheriffs of Selkirk in that part greetings. Because we know that the evidents, charters and letters of the foundation and infeftment of our burgh of Selkirk and the liberty of the burgesses and community of the same was given and granted by our noble forefather and for the greater part has been laid waste and destroyed by assault of war, pest, conflagration and other means and whereas its use as a market has ceased between burgesses to the great hurt to the common weil and freedom of our foresaid burgh and the damage and prejudice to our inhabitants [regarding] customs and ferme owed to us, we therefore moved by pity and justice, desiring reformation of the commonweil and the buildings within

our realm of new infeft, give and grant from us and our successors
and confirm forever according to the tenor of our charter to the
burgesses and community aforesaid of the burgh of Selkirk in free
burgh as before with all lands, commons and possessions, electing as
now bailies and their officers yearly, and a market [fair] yearly on St
Laurence Day and through 8 [days] of the same, forever, with a court
house, gallows ["patibulum"] and all liberties pertaining to the
same...as is contained fully in our charter made thereon. We charge
and command you to give present sasine to the said bailies, burgesses
and community or their trusted attorney to hold from us, all the lands,
commons, rents, possessions, liberties and privileges thereto...accord-
ing to the tenor of our charter...to the [execution] of which you...our
sheriffs in that part are committed by the power given under testimony of our great seal at St Andrews 4 May of our reign 23.

After reading out the precept, William Chepman bailie in that part
gave sasine, heritable possession corporal, actual and real, to the said
burgh also of all the lands, commons, rents possessions, market [fair],
gallows, court house, liberties and privileges...pertaining to the
burgh... forever...to James Scot, John Mithag bailies, John Chepman,
Mark Ker, James Bradfut, John Broun, James Bridin, Alexander
Gledstanes, James Keyne burgesses personally present and accepting
for themselves and in the name of the whole community of burgesses
and indwellers of the said burgh and according to the tenor of the
charter and precept of sasine made, directed and exhibited
thereon...of new invested them in the same heritably in perpetuity.
John Mithag and James Scot and their fellow burgesses for themselves
and the whole community asked instrument from me notary public.
Done on the ground of the burgh lands and commons singly and in
order between 1 and 2 pm...before witnesses George Michilhill, John
Scot, James Murray, Thomas Ker, John Turnbull, Peter Moffat, Mungo
Crukschankis, Adam Veighame, William Weghame, John Andersone,
Thomas Vilkesone, John McDuell, David Jonsone, sir John Bridin
[chaplain] and notary public.

290. "M C [or L] in Edinburgh tenends to our soveran of the lands of S with
consent of [M?] for his entress. To our lovyttis P Gray ouris officiaris in
that part coniunctlie and severaly specially constitut gretting. It is oure
will and we chairgis yow straitly and commandis that incontinent theis
precept seyne ye pass and lawfully warn and chairge W. (illegible)
pretendit tenentis occipyars of our steding or heretaigis M. lyand
within etc pertening to me in heritaige or lyf rentis to flit and remoif
thaim salffs servandis and gudis furtht of my saidis lands (illegible) the
pertinentis at the fest and terme of Witsonday to cum efter the dait of
thir presentis and to leif the samyn wod and red ilk ane of thaim for
thair awin part respective to be browkit, joissit, occupiet, sett, ussit,
disponett be the saids N.B. and hir spouse for his entress as thai sall
think expedient in tyme cumyng conforme to the new actte of parlia-

ment maid anant varnyng of of (*sic*) certeyng the saids pretendit tenends, occupiars coutairs and thai failze that thai salbe haldin and reput as wiolent possessors thereof and salbe actit and persewit thair for conforme to the said act or uther wais as accordis to the lawe and this one na wys ye leif undone as ye vill answr to uss and that ye deliver ane awtentik copy heirof to the said personis geif thai be personaly apprehendit and failyeing thereof to their wiffis, bairnes or servandis in thair name or elles that ye affix the samyn and leiff the samyn upon thair durris one thair dwelling placess of the saides land geif ther be ony. Alsso that ye upone ane Sounday fourty dais before the said fest of Vitsonday pass to the principal kirk of S. quhar the saidis landis lyes and thair in tyme of Hie Mass or dyvyne service opinly reid or caus to be reid this, our precept in presence of the parochinars thereof and leif ane awtentik copie upone the maist patenit kirk dur of the said kirk sa that the knawlege heirof be manifest to the saidis pretendit tenendis thai allegis to na ignorance as ye vil answer to uss upon the quhilk to doo we commit to ye coniunctlie and severalie our power be this our precept selit and subscrivit with our handis at E(dinburgh) the day of (illegible).

[This has probably been copied from a style book as an example.]

291. *Scot of Aikvod* 26 March 1536 Walter Scot son and heir of the deceased John Scot of Robertoune made and subscribed an aquittance as follows: "I Walter Scot son and air of umqhill Jhone Scot of Robertoune grantes me to have resavit be the handis of maister Michaell Scot of Aikvod the sowme of thre schoire of [pounds] and £10 usuaill mony of Scotland in ful contentationne and paiment of all the stane houss callit the peill and clioss with the [?toure] and the pertinenchis of the samyn of Hirdmenstoun and grantes me be tenor of thir presentis weill contenit satisfiet content and pait and fully pleissit of all the pountis contenit in ane contraik of alienatione of the tour cloiss halff manes of Herdmenstoun maid betwix me and maister Michaell Scot at Selkyrk the sext day of december in the yeir of God ane thousand vc xxx fyv yeirs of the quhilk sowme thre schoir ten pounds and contraik forsaid with mony utheris gratitudis plesouris done to me, I hauld me weil content and pait and dischairgis, quitclaimis the said Michaell Scot his airis, executoris and assignais be tenor of this present acquitans commandand sir Ninian Brydin notar publick to subscrywe thir presentes my hand tweychandis the pen at Aykvod the 26 day of March in the yeir of God [1536] before thir vytness Thomas Scot in Vodburne, Voll Scot in Faldishoup, James Tailyefore, Williem Rannyk, Robert Jaksone millar, Thomas Fergreff burgess in Selkirk, Jhone Vynterhoup, Robert Douscheir in Howfurd, William Rannyk". I, sir Ninian Brydin notary public subscribe the present aquittance on special command of the abovewritten Walter Scot of Robertone not knowing how to write with his own hand at the pen and put as witness my subscription manual.

292. *Jamesone of Lyndene* 28 March 1536 Richard Smyth in
Sonderlandhall acknowledged he owed George Jamesone in Lynden
£6 scots and in exchange for paying the whole sum the said Richard
Smyth made, constituted, created, and solemnly ordained the said
George his true lawful, undoubted and irrevocable assignee in and to
the husbandland with pertinents lying in the town of Sunderland
within the sheriffdom of Selkirk also to all his moveable and immoveable goods belonging to the said Richard or to whomsoever at time of
his decease to no other cousin beside me whomsoever alleging his
consanguinity to the said George his heirs and assignees. George
asked instrument. Done in the porch of the parish kirk of Selkyrk
before sir William Brydin vicar of Selkirk, John Craw, Robert
Hawdene, David Jonsone.

293. *Melross* Same day James Scot bailie of Selkirk, came to the tenement
of the deceased James Melross lying between the tenements of the
heirs of the deceased William Ker on the east, the tenement of William
Mathosone on the west, the king's street leading to Peillhill on the
north and the tenement of Elizabeth Keyne relict of the deceased
Patrick Keyne on the south and the bailie invested the young man
James Melross as true and lawful heir of the said deceased James
Melross after reading evidents, by delivery of sasine of the said tene-
ment. James asked instrument before Thomas Ellot, John Broun,
William Mathosone, William Portuus serjeant, John Muthag bailie.

294. *John Mynto* 21 April 1536 Thomas Mynto burgess resigns out of filial
love, all his tenement with yard lying between the tenement of John
Downe on the east, the tenement of James Keine on the north, the
king's street on the south, the tenement of David (p/t) in hands of
James Scot bailie who invests the young man John Mynto as his true
and lawful heir in and to the tenement with yard. John asked instrument. Done around 10 am before sir William Brydin vicar, James
Brydin, David Jonsone, John Downe, Robert Smyth burgesses, David
Mynto.

295. *Marion Burnet* Same day and place James Scot bailie came to the
tenement of John Mynto younger as above and there on the ground of
the same the said John with consent of [his father] Thomas freely and
on account of motherly and brotherly affection, resigned the tenement
with malt kiln, houses and yard for her own sustenance to Marion
Burnet spouse of the said Thomas in liferent and conjunct fee to sustain the said John and his brothers. Observing that the said Marion
should not herself gather (p/t) she should [return?] the goods contained in the tenement at time of making if she does not observe the
said sasine (p/t) and be put out of the tenement. (p/t) asked instrument before witnesses abovewritten.

296. "Sir William Brydin in the name and community of the burgh of Selkirk" [Text ends here.]

297. *Prechour and Lermonte* 20 July 1535 Thomas Prechour and Janet Lermonte, his wife, presented a precept of sasine under the seal of the venerable brother William Lermonte of the Dominican Order in Sterlying to Robert Chepman bailie of Selkirk which was handed to the notary to be read out as follows: the venerable brother William Lermonte of the Order of Saint [Dominic] in Sterlying, to Robert Chepman and James Keyne and all jointly and severally of the burgh of Selkirk, greeting. I have granted, given, and alienated to Janet Lermonte my sister and Thomas Prechour my brother-in-law and their heirs, all my tenement in the Peilgait in Selkirk between the tenement of John Curror on the east, the bog on the south, the king's street on the north and the tenement of Andrew Schortreid on the west, to be held of our lord king and his successors as in my charter made thereon we therefore order and command you to give sasine of the same to the said Janet and Thomas or their lawful attornies...in testimony of which I set my seal and sign manual at Missilburgh 10 May 1535 before witnesses Thomas Vallanch, William Baxstair, Thomas Suert, John Suert (illegible) and brother William (illegible).

And having read out the said precept the bailie...gave sasine to the said Janet as above before witnesses James Keyne, John Curror, David Jonson, Thomas Melrose.

298. William Brydin vicar came to Patrick Murray and questioned him about the sheriffdom of Selkirk.

Patrick Murray of Fawlawhill 30 April 1535 Patrick Murray declared that his forebears and his tenants were in peaceful possession of all the common of Selkirk with our herds by reason that we do not want to withdraw from the common pasture unless lawfully called before the lords of council and discharged therefrom. Patrick asked instrument. Done around 6 pm before witnesses Patrick (p/t) of Caberstoun, William Murray, John Curror, Simon (p/t), Patrick Dobsone, Adam Murray, George (p/t).

On the same day the said Patrick declared that his men had not come with sticks, swords (p/t) in contempt of the king and queen, nor the burgh of Selkirk but because it was possessed by our ancestors. Before witnesses abovewritten.

On the same day Patrick offers to the bailies and the whole community of the burgh of Selkirk to pass to the common and to discharge and distrain those found there having no interest according to the tenor of the book of burgage and common.

299. *Louche* 6 May 153[5] The young man John Dounaldsone son and heir of the deceased Ninian Dounaldsone made, constituted created and solemnly ordained Andrew Louche his true and lawful assignee in and for taking sasine of all the tenement lying in the burgh of Selkirk between the tenement of John Lumisden on the east, the king's street on the south, the tenement of John Downe on the west and the yard of Robert Thomsone on the north for a certain sum of money and for [deeds] done and to be done. Andrew asked instrument. Done near green head ["viride capudi"] before Alexander Broun, Alexander Vylsone, (p/t) Jonsone.

300. *Keyne on the part of Thomas Ker in Yair* ( ) 1536 James Keyne burgess of Selkirk procurator in the name of Thomas Ker in Yair came to Andrew Ker of Prumsydlouch and to the said Andrew delivered the sum of £40 scots for the redemption of lands called "Kyngcroft" and [Ca...ham]land lying in the bounds of Selkirk according to the tenor of a letter of redemption under the seal of Ralph Ker containing the said sum. Then the said Andrew and Gilbert his son and heir in one voice declared they did not have (p/t) of the said lands or delivered sasine to James Keyne being stripped of all possession [by intromission?] of the said lands, all right claim possession and ownership...in and to the said lands... and delivered all evidents by us or any other so that it should [not?] be broken void or falsified by virtue of this instrument. James in name of Thomas Ker in Yair asked instrument. Done around 7 [am?] in the chamber called "Grenheid gren chalmer" before James Ker of Auldroxburgh, (p/t) Loucht, William Thomsone, Thomas M(p/t).

301. *Loucht* 15 May [1536] John Mithag bailie of Selkirk came to a tenement of John Dounaldsone young man and heir of the deceased Ninian Dounaldsone lying in ["Caponlands" scored out] the said burgh between [boundaries as no. **299**] and there on the ground of the same John resigned the tenement and yard in hands of the bailie humbly requesting him to give sasine of the said tenement and yard to Andrew Louche. Andrew Louche asked instrument. Done around 5 am before Henry Yong, John Paito, (p/t), Andrew Estoun, Alexander Browne, Quintin Yong, (p/t) Symsone.

302. *McDuell* (p/t) May 1536. John Mithag bailie of Selkirk at the request of John Cant burgess, came to his tenement lying in "Kirk Vynde" between the king's street leading to Peilhill on the east, the tenement of Nicholas Ker and Marion Brydin on the south, the yard of sir William Brydin on the west and the tenement of Robert Chepman on the north, and there on the ground of the same resigned it in hands of the bailie humbly requesting him to give sasine to Andrew McDuell burgess. (p/t) asked instrument (p/t) am before (p/t), James Neulandis, Andrew Bradfut, (p/t).

303. *Mithac* 9 June [1536] John Mithag bailie declared that a royal letter was lawfully proclaimed around 12 noon before me [notary public] and witnesses James Ker of Auldroxburgh, William Hog of Prestoun, Richard Houme, master Michaell Scot in Aikvod, Alexander Scot in Kyrkhope.

304. *Vatsone* 2 June 1536 John Mithag bailie came at the request of sir John Brydin chaplain of the altar of St (p/t) situate in the kirk afore-said, to his tenement lying in the south side of the burgh of Selkirk between the street leading to the Peilgait and the said blessed altar on the east and west and the lands of George (p/t) on the south and there on the ground of the same resigned the said house in hands of the bailie who gave sasine of the forehouse and yard containing eleven ells to Thomas Vatsone. Thomas asked instrument. Done around 4 pm before (p/t) Freir, Walter Dunhoup, James Robeson.

305. Note in Scots (illegible).

Book D
The Protocol Book of John Brydin
1530–1537

From the original page numbering in this volume it would seem that all but the first page has survived. The first 13 pages are particularly fragmentary and this volume is one of the poorest, in terms of condition, of all the protocol books in the collection.

1.   [Very fragmentary and the first part of the deed is missing.]

"...browk and joyss the tane halff of (p/t) fruttis, multuris, emoluments, profetis and [dewties] all and hail the myl of lilliscleiff with the (p/t) certain sowm of moneye that is to say (p/t) usual money of the rome [i.e. realm] of Scotland (p/t) sowme of £40 we grant us to haif (p/t) be the handis and deliverance of the said (p/t) be the handis and the deliverance of the said Wa[lter] quhilk we hald us content and pait and be (p/t) Walter his ayris executouris and assignais (p/t) we discharge the saming for now and ever. Thai[rupone] (p/t) joyss the said tane half of the fruttis, multuris, profettis and dewitis of the forsaid myl (p/t) the pertinents to be peceably and continuale (p/t) Walter his ayris and assignais fra (p/t) Beteriche his spouss thair ayris and (p/t) quhil the saidis William, Beteriche (p/t) procreat of hir first husband (p/t) ayris or assignais (p/t) and ganging to (p/t) in foresaid sowme of (p/t) rome of Scotland (p/t) Walter, his ayris executouris (p/t) ninianes altar situat within [the parish kirk of Selkirk] (p/t) ten dais warning (p/t) geiff the said Walter his ayris executouris (p/t) unlauefully absentis thaim thai beand lauchfully (p/t) as said it sall be leful to the said William his spouse and hir barnis procreat of hir first [husband] William Ailmer forsaid, thair ayris and assignees (p/t) fre regres and lefull intrometting in and to al foresaid tane half of the fruttis, multuris, emoluments, profettis and dewittis of the forsaid milne of lilliscleif (p/t) had befor the making of this contrac al fraud and gyl excludit. Nevertheless the forsaid sowme of £40 (p/t) for the profett of the saidis Walter his ayris executoris and assignais souerly to be put and efter payment [of the said] sowme of £40 usual money of Scotland (p/t) said Walter his ayris and assignais sal have nane (p/t) intrometting kindness nor claim to the said tane halff (p/t) profettis of the saming in tyme to cum (p/t) the saids William and Beteriche and hir barnis procreat (p/t) husband said as sal defend and warand (p/t) assignais in peceable joysing and browking (p/t) the saidis William Beteriche his spouse (p/t) forsaid first husband (p/t) content and paye to the assignais the sowme of £40 (p/t) in effec as is abone writing (p/t) in said Villiam or Beteriche his spouse or hir barnis procreat (p/t) forsaid, thair ayris or assignais to the tothir half analy (p/t) of the fruttis of the mil forsaid of the saming the said Walter sal haif it before

143

(p/t) he geiffand befor that ane uther will geiff". Walter Scot asked instruments. Done in the chamber of sir William Brydin [vicar] of Selkirk around the hour of 4 pm before sir William Brydin vicar of Selkirk, sir Thomas Skwne chaplain, Simon Farle bailie of the said burgh, [Adam] Gledstanis.

Same day...[Walter Scot] in Ashkirk on the one part and William Scot brother of the said Walter and Beatrix Sinclar spouse of the said William on the other holding in their hands documents written on paper in form of a bond (p/t) and reversion handed them [to the notary] to be read out, copied onto parchment, transcribed and reduced as follows in the vernacular: "the yeir daye plaice and [tyme] abone writting" wholly in words of a protocol instrument. Beatrix asked instrument for herself and her spouse. Done at the house of sir William Brydine, vicar of Selkirk at 5 pm before sir William Brydine, vicar of Selkirk, sir Thomas Skwne chaplain, Simon Farle, bailie of the said burgh and Adam Gledstanis.

Subscription of sir John Brydine, subdeacon of the diocese of Glasgow and notary by apostolic authority.

2.   9 May [1530?] William lawful and undoubted heir of his grandfather John Lauder [gave] granted and sold forever his tenement lying in bounds of Selkirk with the lands of George Chepman on the east, the lands of Thomas Mynto on the south, the lands of Andrew Ker on the [west] and the king's street on the north to James Keyne paying to the said William (p/t) 4d scots [annualrent?]. James asked instrument. Done around 11 am in the back chamber of (p/t) burgess before Robert Chepman, (p/t).

3.   Same day, year, month, before notary and witnesses underwritten... William Lauder kinsman and heir of the deceased [John] Lauder burgess of the burgh of Selkirk came to a tenement of land with pertinents within the said burgh on the south side of the north street between the lands of George Chepman on the east, land of Thomas Mynto on the south, the land or tenement of Andrew Ker of Primsydlocht in the west and the said north street on the north and there on the ground of the same delivered all the lands fore and back with barn and yard thereof in hands of the bailie Robert Chepman...in favour of [James] Keine...and Robert Chepman gave sasine of the same to the said James Keine. James asked instrument. Done at around 1 pm in Selkirk before sir John Chepman, (p/t) Chepman, Robert Portuis burgesses of the said burgh, Alan Keyne, John (p/t), William Portuis, burgess of the said burgh, George (p/t), James Newlandes, George Lamb.

4.   *Ingliss Brydine* 4 June 1530 Christian Ingliss with consent of her [spouse Thomas] (p/t) of Philhop acknowledged that she had sold [the land contained] in the charter to sir [William?] Brydine, vicar of

Aldroxburgh (p/t) for the sum of money of £16 which she had received from the said sir William in counted money. Also she appoints as her procurator James Scot, burgess of Selkirk in all legal duties compearing to seal her charter and give sasine in my name and that of my spouse also all and any other duties which a true procurator is appointed to do. William asked instrument. Done at the house of Janet Portuus, spouse of (p/t) Brydine, burgess at around 1 pm [who] asked instrument before James [Scot], George Scot burgess, Cuthbert (p/t), Patrick Freir and others.

5. ***Murray Lauder*** 29 Oct 1530 Patrick Murray of Faulohill and lord of the land of [Selkirk] and sheriff of the same came at the request of [William] Lauder burgess of Edinburgh to a husbandland lying on the east of the said burgh which the deceased (p/t) John Keine burgess of the same held and which land the said William Lauder has in tack... and there on the ground of the said husbandland the said Patrick gave sasine of the same with pertinents to the said William. William asked instrument. Done at the husbandland around 3 pm before James Scot bailie, sir John Michilhill chaplain,(p/t) Brydin, John Hall and George Chepman, burgesses of the said burgh, Adam Wilkesoune, Ninian Bryding n.p.

6. ***Tait*** (scored out) ***Scot Murraye*** 8 Nov 1530 sir John Scot vicar of Hawik procurator in the name of and by authority of the underwritten viz., James [Gibson], Thomas Dikesoune, William Scott, John Wode and Thomas Bullerwell produced royal letters under the signet to Patrick Murraye lord of Faulohill and sheriff of Selkirk inhibiting, discharging, annulling and breaking the privilege and office and benefice as sheriff of the royal lands which the said Patrick holds and after the said letters were read out the said sir John asked the said Patrick to return them and he refused. Sir John Scot asked instrument. Done at the burgh Court House of Selkirk around 1 pm before Sir Walter Scott of Branxholme knight, John Crenstoun of that ilk, Ninian Brydin chaplain and notary, James Hoppringill in (p/t) and sir John Michilhill chaplain.

7. ***Tait Scot*** Same day. Alexander Tait, lord of the lands of Pirne procurator and in name of Katherine Rutherfurd, lady of (p/t) contrary to [what] sir John Scot above...alleged...that royal letters which he showed, were of no effect or power in respect of the discharge of Patrick Murray from his office of sheriff. Alexander asked instrument. Done at the court house of Selkirk before sir Walter Scot of Branxhelme knight, Robert Hoppringill in [New Hall?], James Hoppringill in Tynneis, sir John Michilhill.

8. ***Murraye Scot*** Same day. Patrick Murraye lord of Faulohill and [sheriff] of Selkirk...within his privilege as sheriff...was handed the royal letters and gave them to the notary to read out, after which the said

Patrick [acknowledged] these vicious and unwarranted letters were demanded on behalf of and with the knowledge of the sheriff in that part and that he would cite the said letter if any harm or prejudice came to him in the future. Patrick asked instrument before witnesses abovewritten.

9. **Tait and Scot** Same day. sir John Scot vicar of Hawik procurator and in name of his brothers and others against [Alexander] Tait, lord of Pirne procurator and in name of Katherine Ruthirfurd lady as above... of his own free will granted...that the said William Scot inhabited and manured..."le forest steid" called "Craggischank" and received the benefits of the same...throughout a period of 12 weeks. [sir John Scot] asked instrument before witnesses as above.

10. **Chepman Brydine** 3 October 1530 sir William Brydine vicar pensioner of Selkirk came to an annualrent of 4 shillings scots uplifted from a tenement of land of John Chepman burgess in Edinburgh...lying on the west of the mercat cross between the tenement of land of Robert Brydine on the north, the tenement of land of William Lauder burgess of Edinburgh on the south and the tenement of land of John Mithag on the west and there on the ground of the same resigned the said annualrent in hands of the bailie who gave sasine to master John Chepman, his heirs and assignees. Master John asked instrument before John Chepman, James Keine and William Chepman.

11. **Wilkesoune Johnestoun** 28 May 1531 Adam Wilkesoun burgess of Selkirk on the one part and John Johnestoun on the other with regard to all the accounts, debts, arrears up to that day made between them... the said John Johnsoun acknowledged that he was content that Adam and his spouse had paid all the aforesaid...and said Adam, his spouse had paid in full and they, their heirs and assignees were discharged of all claims forever. Adam asked instrument. Done at around 2 pm before Thomas Purde, Adam (p/t), George Michilhill burgess, James Wilkesone.

12. **Trumbill Ker** 1 June 1531 Robert Trumbill acknowledged to his grandson John Trumbill tutor of the lord of Phillophaucht, that he had given, granted and set in tack those 5 poundlands lying within the town and pasture of Phillophaucht and by ferme demitted for the space of 5 years to Mark Ker burgess of Selkirk as is fully contained in a letter of tack to the said Mark made by the said Robert by which said tack Robert bound himself to ensure that Mark had peaceful possession to occupy and manure the lands for the abovesaid duration. Mark asked instrument. Done at around 5 pm before James Bradfut, John Chepman, Thomas Hesilhop burgesses of the said burgh, sir Ninian Brydine notary and John Ker.

13. **Scott Scott** 5 Jan 1531/2. John Scott in Myris...of his own free will...all fraud and guile excluded, resigned all right, claim, possession, ownership, occupation, kindness, freedom and tenure ["manutenentus"] of Myris which for the time is in his hands being that fourth part of the lands of Myris with pertinents lying on the west of the place of Myris set in tack to the said John by the reverend father in Christ Gavin archbishop of the diocese of Glasgow and his predecessors and occupied and manured in that time by the said John, in hands of his cousin Walter Scot tutor of the lord of Haning for the love he bears him and according to the tenor of this present instrument resigns all right and claim...in future from himself, his heirs and assignees. Also Walter Scott tutor as above according to the tenor of this instrument binds himself his heirs executors and assignees to pay the said John Scot £14 scots at the following terms viz. 30s at Shrove Tuesday next after in date of this present and the remainder of the sum at Whitsunday next following the said Shrove Tuesday, all fraud and guile...excluded. John and Walter asked instrument. Done here at the house of sir William Bridine, vicar of Selkirk around 2 pm before sir William Bridine chaplain, Robert Trumbul tutor of Holdene and John Brydine.

14. **Memorandum Hesilhoip Brydine.** "The 24 daye of februar in the yeir of god (p/t) 1531 yeiris I schir Johne Brydine sone and ayre [to] James Brydine set in assedatioune for mail to Thomas my foir houss in the peilgait wyth thre cupill of aik and wyth [al and] haill pan frist bakis sper and buggerinne efferand thereto wyth [speirs] and butellar wyth ane dormont geist and ane smallar geist one the bay wyth ane rannyll tre ane halland ane counterdeiss wyth twa durris and windoiss ane veshal almery set wythin the wall wyth ane bakhouse wyth thre standand cupill wyth an est gawill to the panniss the vestand gawill vantand wyth pan frist bak and sper efferand thairto excep ii pannes vantand for al the days and termiss of threttene yeiris nixt followand the dait heiroff the feist of witsondaye that nixt followis the dait of thir q[uarter]lly presentis to be the said Thomas entrie payand to me (illegible) in maner of mail his ayris or assignais xxiiii shillings of usual money of the rome and to uphald [yeris] the samen induring the said spaice of threttene (p/t) in all things necessar befor thir witness Mark Ker bailye for the tyme, James Helme, William [Scott], James Braidfut, James Scott.

Item the said daye and plaice I James Scott befor thir wytness Mark Ker, James Bradffut, [William] Scott and James Helme to taik na thing off the g[avill?] of the forsaid houss off schir John Brydine na [mair?] to tribill him na yit molest na inwaid him [or his] tenandis or subtenandis fra that [daye] furtht the said schir John payand to me iii yeris mail off the sayd tenement and na mair".

15. ***Brydine Portuiss and Portuis*** 26 Feb 1531/2 John Brydine son and heir of the deceased Thomas [Brydine] on the one part and Janet Portuiss and Elizabeth [Portuiss] on the other made a compromise between them which they ordained to be inserted in the burgh court book as follows: "the fourtene daye of februar in the yeir off God 1531 it is appointit and finaly acgreit betuix honorabill personis that is to saye Jenot Portuiss and Elizabetht Portuiss ayris of wmquhill William Portuiss in to ane part and John Brydin ester one the tothir part in manner forme and effec as efter followis that is to saye the saidis Jenot and Elizabetht sal have entress in and to all landis of thair prediessoris deit vestit and sesit of wythout impediment [frae] the said John Brydin as fer as lawe requiris wyth thir condicionis wnderwritting that the foresaidis Jenot and Elizabetht [and] thair ayris sal pay betwix this and midsoumer to John Brydin his ayris executouris and assignais the sowme of six libras gud and usual money of scotland haiffand the cours of paiment for the tyme. Alsua it is comprommitit faithfully betuix the forsaidis parteis and sa happin the said John Brydin ester his ayris executouris and assignais may get heirefter cler certificatioun and [siker] wnderstanding be just men of law ryply awisit and vyll tak it apone thair saullis that land or to ony part of it that umquhill Rychert Brydin and Jenot his douchter deit vestit and [finally] saisist of may have rycht therto than immediately the said John sal refound and paye thankfully the forsaid sowme of vi lib to the Jenot and Elizabetht and than intromet efter notory certificatione and payment off the forsaid sowme bath Jenot and Elizabetht thair ayris executouris and assignais bindess and obliss thaim fathfullye be the tenor off this compromit but fraud or gill to enter the forsaid John his ayris or assignais heretabilly siclik as men off law deliveris or ellis geiff to him his ayris executouris or assignais als mekill awaill for the landis or ony part of thaim efter the sicht and decreit of Andro Ker of Prumsydloucht sir William Brydine vicar of Selkirk sir Ninian Brydine. In wytness off the quhilk thing bath Jenot and Elizabetht hes subscribit this present compromit wyth thair handis at the pen befor thir wytnesses sir John Brydine notar sir John Michilhill notar John Smyth William Brydine". After which Janet and Elizabeth promised to observe the said compromise in all articles and clauses. John Brydin asked instrument. Done around 10 am before William [Brydine], sir John Michilhill, Ninian Brydine.

16. ***Brydine*** Same day. sir William Brydine vicar of Selkirk speaking for and in name of Janet and Elizabeth Portuiss presented a certain royal brieve [in margin: "indorsed"?] the said Janet and Elisabeth had procured to Patrick Murray sheriff of Selkirk in the court house of the said burgh lawfully... held on that day and asked the same be executed immediately and taking the brieve in his hands the sheriff handed it to the clerk of the court to read out after which reading out, pronounciation, indorsing, affirmation and election of a suitable inquest John

Smyth depute sheriff on that day went to the door of the court house and three times warned by proclaimation to all having an interest or objecting and contradicting and opposing whatsoever the proposals henceforth they should assemble at that time or never object to the said brieve. After which proclamation sir Ninian Brydine chaplain and speaking for John Brydine his brother showed how there was a compromise made between Janet and Elizabeth on the one part and John Brydine on the other and faithfully entered in the burgh court book of Selkirk declaring that if it happened that the said Janet and Elizabeth did not observe all articles, clauses and points contained in the compromise then the execution of the said brieve would be null and void...nor would it turn to the said John Brydin in prejudice or damage whatsoever. Done in the court house around 11 am before sir John Michilhill, Master Thomas Ker in Sunderlandhall, Master Michael Scot, sir William Brydine, James Braidfut, John Chepman, Mark Ker.

On the same day master Thomas Ker, Walter Scot in Sintoun, Walter Scot tutor of Haning, Robert Trumbul tutor of Philphophaugh, Adam Scot in Fawsyd, William Scot in Catslack, Thomas Murray in Newhall, George Scot of Well, Mark Ker bailie of Selkirk, William Keine, John Hall, Robert Portuiss, James Braidffut chosen and sworn inquisitors being asked by the sheriff if the brieve could be put into execution... the said Mark Ker for all the other inquisitors declared he and the other inquisitors had made and promulgated articles and decreet of retour for execution and no objectors to the said brieve had come forward at that time declaring that execution of the articles and decreet of retour made by them should not hereafter turn to their prejudice or damage. Mark Ker asked instruments in name of the inquest. Done around noon at the court house before sir John Michilhill, Ninian Brydine, William Brydine chaplain, James Scot, John Chepman, James Helme, William Brydine.

17. **Brydine** 4 April 1532 sir William Brydine vicar of Selkirk warned and earnestly required Alan Keine serjeant of the burgh of Selkirk...by virtue of his office and in the name and authority of the king, alderman and bailies...to prohibit...George Michilhill burgess of Selkirk from the kirklands of the vicarage which the said George has occupied and manured and in particular a certain quarry within the said lands which the said George had opened, hewn and dug out and the serjeant inhibited the said George by above authority from the said lands and quarry...and he resisted...by repudiating him and turning his back and disobediently gesticulating with a rod in his hand in a sign of reviling repudiation...and made a speech using infamous remarks and in contempt of the king and the alderman and bailies. Sir William vicar asked instrument. Done on the ground of the said kirklands around 5 pm before Adam Bowmakar, David Coltart, Alane Keine, John Clerkine.

Same day. the said George acknowledged he was a tenant of the kirk-lands and that he paid his ferme and grassums on time and protested that the objections, contradictions and allegations should not turn to his prejudice.

18. ***Williamsone in Melross*** 24 May 1532 master John Williamsone, master of arts, of the parish (p/t) of Melross viz. of the chapel of Blessed Mary situate there humbly confessed he was given (p/t) and his [election?] and favours of the said chapel. Before Robert Middilmest, Andra Davesone.

19. ***Keine Trumbill*** 6 June 1532 William Keine younger, burgess of Selkirk humbly requested John Trumbill and openly warned him to receive and uplift all the victuals on the appointed day of collection being debts and arrears from the said William to John and especially on that day to receive and uplift 6 bolls of branches ["brachii" – probably a mispelling for "brasii" i.e. malt which appears later in the text]. William openly acknowledged that he had put aside the 6 bolls of malt [as] damages, expenses and deterioration not to be taken up and that he will surrender, give up, sell...the most costly of the six bolls to be discharged and demitted according to the tenor of these presents. William asked instrument. Done at noon before Mark Ker bailie, John W(p/t).

20. ***Murraye*** (p/t) July 1532 Isabel Murraye spouse to the deceased Philip Scot in Edschaw showed how (illegible) on 24 July it was settled between her and James Hoppringill and Walter Scot in Sintoun her chosen arbiters on the one part and Walter Scott in Eidschaw son, heir and executor of the said Philip lord of Riddaill and William Scott in Hardene his chosen arbiters on the other part and Walter Scott and his arbiters agreed to convene on the appointed day in the cause moved between Isabel and Walter. And that Isabella and James Hoppringill her arbiter were present then and prepared to submit to the decision... but Walter and his arbiters in no way compeared at the appointed day and now protesting that the absence of the said Walter and arbiters should not turn to her prejudice Isabel asked instrument. Done around noon in the aisle of the cross of Selkirk before Mark Ker bailie of Selkirk, Master Patrick Wrycht.

21. ***Brydine Ker*** 25 July 1532 Andrew Brydine...of his own free will bound himself, his heirs, executors and assignees to pay Mark Ker in Selkirk or Elizabeth Gledstanis, his mother, the sum of £40 usual money in the name of...Walter Scot knight in Branxhelme at the terms underwritten viz. £20 at the feast of St Bartholomew next and £20 at the feast of St Andrew all fraud and guile excluded. Elisabeth asked instrument. Done in Selkirk around 3 pm before Adam Scott in Fausyd, Walter Scott in Haning and James Bradffut, burgess of the said burgh.

22. **Murraye Loure, King's Messenger** 3 Oct 1532 John Murraye in name and authority of his master and cousin Patrick Murraye lord of Fawlohill acknowledged that David Loure king's messenger without any right or title and against the order of law seized and distrained moveable goods viz. oxen and cows in number 22 [written "xxduo"] belonging to Patrick and his tenants...and brought and assigned them to master Patrick Wrycht, chamberlain of the forest feus of our queen mother for arrears owed...to the said queen by the said Patrick [Murraye] and for her ferme for the term of St Bartholomew in the said year and the said Patrick on account of the said arrears of his ferme was distrained under the provisions of canon law by the said lady queen and was put under ecclesiastical censure for the said sum for the said term promising to pay within 15 days, requiring them to return the said distrained goods to him and his master. The said David by no means did so and usurped and seized the said oxen and cattle with force of law and in name of the said Patrick [Wrycht] protesting that this was perpetrated illegally against the queen and it would turn in prejudice to his master. John asked instrument. Done around 8 am in the sanctuary* of the kirk of Selkirk before sir John Michilhill,notary, James Trumbill, Robert Wilsone.

[*"Sanctuarium" means sanctuary, shrine or kirkyard]

23. **Hopringile Hoppringle** 4 Nov 1532 David Hoppringill in Yair...of his own free will...[sets in tack] to Margaret Ker, daughter of the deceased William Ker in Yair for grace and favours which she has borne him all the 5 poundlands of Slegdene within the district of the "Merches" in the sheriffdom of Berwik with pertinents from the said David as in his letter of tack containing a special assignation made, constituted and solemnly ordained renouncing all right, claim, ownership, possession, kindness, freedom and tenure which he has or will have to the said Margaret of the 5 poundlands of Slegdene forever from himself, his heirs and assignees to the said Margaret, her heirs and assignees. David and Margaret asked instrument. Done in the sanctuary of the kirk of Selkirk around noon before sir William Brydin, vicar of Selkirk, notary John Brydine.

24. **Rannik Murraye** 19 Nov 1532 James Rannik in the court house of Selkirk before Mark Ker sheriff depute swore his great oath purging himself and his whole family to be innocent...of taking accepting unlawfully holding...or any art or part in the theft of two ewes from James Murray prosecuted openly in the sheriff court of Selkirk about which theft of the two ewes James Rannik with his compurgators John Hog, William Chessame, John Clerk, David Cogburn, David Scot, James Craufurd swore their great oaths by touching holy scriptures in the said court lawfully purging all the foresaid and that he was shown to be acquitted...protesting that the said criminal prosecution did not turn to his prejudice. James Rannik asked instrument. Done in the

court house around noon before Andrew Ker of Prumsyd loucht, Mark Ker, deputy sheriff, William Brydine, vicar of Selkirk, John Michilhill, Ninian Brydine, chaplain and notary.

25. **Scott Scott** 31 Jan 1532/3 Margaret Scott spouse of John Scott burgess in Selkirk presented a precept of sasine to James Scott bailie in that part who gave it to the notary to read out as follows: John Scott burgess of Selkirk lord of a fourth part of land wadset to himself of Est Haning, to James Scott and William Portuiss my bailies in that part greeting. Because I have given, granted and demitted to my spouse Margaret in conjunct fee for her lifetime, all of one half the said fourth of the lands of Est Haning with pertinents and especially those 20 shillinglands and a redemption on the same from Robert Todrig who manures and occupies them reserving to me free tenement as long as I live, [all lying] within the said place of Est Haning and lordship of Ettrick Forest and sheriffdom of Selkirk as is fully contained in my charter to Margaret thereon. Therefore I order and command you to give sasine of the above 20 shillinglands and pertinents without delay and a redemption of the same to Margaret or her lawful attorney according to the tenor of my charter...in testimony of which sir William Brydine has placed his seal lacking her own on the 31 Jan 1532. After which the bailie gave sasine of the said lands to the said Margaret in conjunct fee etc. Margaret asked instrument on the ground of the same around 3 pm before [William] Brydine, David Scott, chaplain, William Scott, Robert Todrig, [James] Helme, William Portuiss.

26. **Scott Scott** 31 Jan 1532/3 Walter Scott, son and apparent heir of John Scott burgess of Selkirk presented a precept of sasine to James Scott bailie in that part who gave it to the notary to read out as follows: John Scott burgess and lord of a fourth part of the lands wadset to him of Est Haning to James Scott and William Portuiss my bailies in that part specially constituted greeting. Because I have given, granted and demitted to my son and apparent heir all the said lands wadset to me being the fourth part of Est Haning with pertinents and reserving a redemption to my spouse Margaret Scott of the same lands as long as she shall live and reserving free tenement of the same to me as long as I shall live, lying within the said place of Est Haning and lordship of Ettrick Forest and sheriffdom of Selkirk as contained in full in my charter to Walter made thereon I firmly command and order you to give sasine of the lands to Walter Scott or his lawful attorney in testimony of which I have procured the seal of the venerable William Brydine chaplain my own being missing at Selkirk 31 Jan 1532. After which James Scott bailie delivered sasine of the same to the said Walter, his heirs and assignees. Walter asked instrument. Done at the ground of the said lands around 3 pm before sir William Brydine, David Scott chaplain, William Scott, William Portuiss, Robert Todrig, George Helme.

27. **Todrig** 31 Jan 1532/3 as in the preceding protocol, Robert Todrig
showed how he had the use of the 20 shillinglands wadset to John
Scott burgess of Selkirk lying in Est Haning and that he was specially
tenant of the same so long as, he asserted, the said lands remained
unredeemed protesting that any sasine of the said lands or any contract given should not turn to his prejudice. Robert asked instrument.
Done here at the said lands around 3 pm before sir William Brydine,
James Scott.

28. **Brydine Trumbull** 4 Feb 1432/3 sir William Brydine chaplain
declared by proclaiming to those then present that David Brydine and
Janet Trumbill wished to be joined in marriage and by warning those
then present that if the said David and Janet had any impediment they
should let it be examined...and sir John Brydine chaplain announced
there was an impediment in law, alleging that the father of the said
David had raised the said Janet over the holy font [i.e. he was her
godfather] and so, by reason of spiritual affinity, their desire could not
be fulfilled. To which the said sir William Brydine presented a dispensation from the apostolic see written on parchment and sealed...and
handed it to me the notary to read out as follows: To the venerable
father in Christ the archbishop of Glasgow or his vicar or official in
spiritual matters Silvester Darius [Lucan?] chaplain of our holy lord
pope and auditor of causes in the holy apostolic palace to James king
of Scots and messenger of the said pope and of the apostolic see,
greeting in the lord. On the part of David Brydine layman and Janet
Trumbill living in the diocese the petition brought contains that...the
same desire to be joined in marriage but because David's father held
the said Janet over the font their desire cannot be fulfilled and so they
make supplication for a dispensation of the apostolic see...to provide
a remedy to the above. Therefore we grant indulgence to the underwritten by letters of the said see from us and our assertion should be
sufficient in all things...and concede that the impediment of spiritual
affinity arising from the aforesaid should be no obstacle to their mar-
rying and remaining validly married thereafter freely and lawfully by
this merciful dispensation provided that the said woman has not been
taken by anyone on this account to have offspring issuing therefrom
decreed legitimate. Which...through our secretary I subscribe and seal
dated Edinburgh in the diocese of St Andrews ad 1532 January 7

After which, David and Janet celebrated the marriage. Sir William,
David and Margaret [asked instruments] in the chapel of Blessed Mary
of Selkirk around 11 am before Robert Trumbill, James (p/t), John
Michilhill, Ninian Brydine, Richard Brydine chaplain, David (p/t)

29. **Sinclelr Wonterhop** 6 Feb 1532/3 William Wonterhop...of his own
free will...binds himself to give a certain tenement which was then
inhabited by Thomas Dunne to Marion Sincleir his future wife irrevocably for her lifetime...to be conferred at the feast of Shrove Tuesday

next after, the same being given all fraud and guile excluded. Marion asked instrument. Done in the kirk of Selkirk, around 4pm before John Chepman, Robert Chepman burgess, master Patrick Wrycht, Edward Sincleir.

30. **_Helme Hawe_** 18 Feb 1532/3 John Helme demanded by what right James Haw then present did put himself above any law, title or ordinance of the burgh court to arrest and escheat, alleging that the said John under cover of night attacked his door without lawful reason and broke it and spoke threatening words...and the said officials [of the court] had promised him and up to the said statutory day affirmed that admissions were completed and...witnesses called and by throwing out, reducing and annulling the lawful cause of the said John, he voluntarily...offered himself to the will and decreet of the inquisitors in the presence of the bailies and alderman which the said James said was not suitable evidence and protested he was innocent...of any crimes, malicious acts etc and did no damage...Done in the court house of the burgh of Selkirk around noon before sir Ninian Brydine notary, Mark Ker bailie, Robert Chepman bailie, John Mithag, James Scott, John Curror.

[Note in margin: "nulla citatione canonicali et civili non seu (?) ecclesiatione seu [quibus]cumque non et distring[?]". No canonical, civil or whatever ecclesiastical summons and distraint(?).]

31. **_Murraye Murraye_** 20 Feb 1532/3 Roger Murray burgess of Selkirk showed how he was in old age, deprived of strength...and cast down and despoiled by thieves for which reason he was now in great penury and suffering hardship and under lamentable proclamation to certify promises at the altar of the Holy Sacrament by him...he sells and alienates his tenement of land and his moveable and immoveable goods and an annualrent and lands at "le riggis" with pertinents in order to sustain himself in his pitiful life forever and the said Roger gives and confirms all his tenement with looms ["utensilis"] and household goods, heritable goods moveable and immoveable with back houses and yard thereto also seven "le riggis" of land with pertinents and an annualrent of 9 shillings uplifted from and annexed to the tenement to the south of him, to his younger son James Murraye for a certain sum of money viz. £20 scots. James asked instrument. Done around 3 pm before Mark Ker, (p/t) bailies, James Keine, John Smail, Thomas Curror.

32. **_Murraye Murraye_** 24 Feb 1532/3 Roger Murray burgess of Selkirk came to his tenement of land with pertinents within the said burgh on the east side of the street called "le kirk wind" between the land of George Jamisoun on the east, the land of the heirs of Robert Scott burgess in Edinburgh on the south, the land or tenement of John Chepman on the north and the kirk wind on the west...together with

seven rigs lying in ryndail and an annualrent of 9 shillings uplifted from a tenement of the heirs of the deceased Robert Scott and his moveable and immoveable goods...and by delivery of earth and stones on the ground of the same resigned the said in hands of the bailie who gave sasine of the same to his younger son James Murraye. James asked instrument. Done at the said tenement at around 10 am before William Portuiss, John Smail, Thomas Broun burgesses, master Patrick Wrycht, George Clerk, William Scott.

33. **Scott** 10 March 1532/3 Walter Scott son and apparent heir of the deceased John Scott of Robertoun his father, presented a certain brieve of right to Mark Ker depute sheriff and demanded that it be lawfully endorsed and made public...who gave it to the notary to read out as follows: James by Grace of God to his sheriff and bailies of Selkirk, greetings. We command and charge you that you cause a faithful inquest to be made by worthy men of the district by whom the better truth can be known, after swearing a great oath, of what lands, [annual] rents with pertinents, the deceased John Scott of Robertoun father of Walter Scott bearer of the present [instrument] died last vest and [seised] as of fee at our peace and faith within your jurisdiction and if the said Walter is the lawful and nearest heir of the deceased John Scott...and if he is of lawful age and of what value are the lands in time of peace, of whom held and for what service are they held, in whose hands they now rest, in what way, from what time. And whatever is done by the said inquest faithfully and dili-gently...under your seal and the seal of the inquest, you send to our chancery. At Edinburgh 10 Feb 15[32]. After the brieve was read out...John Scott serjeant at the court house door...declared that anyone with an interest, objection or contradiction to the said brieve [make himself known] and...no objections being forthcoming...the said Walter humbly declared that he should have a form of decreet or deliverance or retour under the seal of the said inquest. Walter asked instrument. Done at the court house of the burgh of Selkirk around noon before sir John Michilhill notary, Master Michael [Scott], John Dikesoun, Thomas Ker in Yair, Walter Scott in Sintoun.

34. **Scott and Douglaice** Same day. Stephen Scott procurator in the name of Isabel Douglaice showed how the said Isabel held certain lands in conjunct fee with her deceased spouse John Scott of Robertoun as contained in an instrument of sasine and a confirmation of the queen and he protested that the sasine, tack or title of confirmation held on the said land should not turn to her prejudice during her life-time by right and title of her conjunct fee. Isabel asked instrument. Done in the court house of Selkirk before sir John Michilhill, chaplain and notary, master Michael Scott, Mark Ker, Thomas Ker in Yair.

35. **Scott** Same day. master Michael Scott, master of arts, declared that he and the other inquisitors gathered to execute a certain brieve of Walter

Scott, son and apparent heir of the deceased John Scott in Robertoun
his father, at the sheriff court in Selkirk and the which brieve was
taken, read out and judged in all its articles and discussed and
decerned and deliberated all that was known on the matter faithfully
and the said inquest...found no voluntary error incurred in the execution of the said brieve. Master Michael asked instrument. Done at the
hour and place above before witnesses abovewritten.

36. **Chepman** Same day. the widow Elizabeth Chepman showed how
John Scott her deceased spouse in contesting a lawsuit, improvidently
made her executrix of his will, therefore the said Elizabeth alleges that
she will not undertake willingly all the duties as executrix of the said
John...and that she neither has nor had nor has intromitted with the
said goods as it was known by many that she had taken her great
oath on the premises and with consideration and mature judgement,
Elizabeth renounces and abdicates herself forever from the debts,
expenses and duties of the said John and whatsoever lawsuits, evidents, duties as executrix or testaments...incurring no damage from
the burden of executrix. Elizabeth asked instrument. Done in the
house of John Chepman around 3 pm before Robert Trumbill tutor of
[Houdene], master Patrick Wrycht master of arts and notary, Walter
Scott, Simone Farle, Thomas Forest, John Chepman.

37. **Howatson** 31 May 1533 [John] Howatsone showed how John
Achesone son and heir of the deceased (blank) Achesone burgess of
Selkirk had sold, alienated and for a certain sum of money pledged to
John Howatsone his tenement lying in the said burgh binding himself,
his heirs and assignees to pay John Achesone the said sum on the
appointed day viz. the feast of Whitsunday and the said John
Howatsone to pay thankfully the said John for selling, pledging and
resigning the said land to him on the said day...requiring Robert
Chepman bailie of the said burgh then present to expel and discharge
the inhabitants and occupiers of the said tenement warning those
having interest that five days after the date of these presents he, his
heirs and assignees being satisfied with the said sum, the tenement
with pertinents will be [handed over] under the form of obligation
resigning it from the said John [Achesone] to John [Howatsone]. John
Howatsone asked instrument. Done at the said tenement around 4 pm
before Robert Chepman bailie,James [Jonsone], Robert Trumbill
burgess, John Chepman, John Brydin.

38. **Ker** 10 June 1533 master Thomas Ker in Sunderlandhall [Blacklaw –
scored out] showed how he was occupier and lawful tenant of the
moiety [of the lands] of Sunderland with pertinents and the said [lands]
extending...to the sum of [£10*] yearly...which sum the same master
[has paid] in whole to lady Margaret in ratification as feuar of the said
lands and Master Thomas asked instrument. Done at the court house
of Selkirk before William Duncan, depute sheriff for the day undoubt-

edly admitted, [Andrew] Ker of Primsyd, master James John[soun], Ninian Brydine, notary.

*[See next item no. **39**]

39. ***Mariorebankes Flemynge*** Same day. master Thomas Mariorebankis, master of arts, showed how master Thomas Ker in Sunderlandhall by his own admission acknowledged that he was and is occupier and specially tenant of the moiety of lands of Sunderland with pertinents extending to £10 yearly and...then master Thomas Mariorebankis procurator for the foresaid James Flemynge presented a document in the form of a claim, viz. for the sum of £40 yearly uplifted from the said lands to William [Duncan] sheriff depute (p/t) for assigning a lawful day for approbation and witnessing and ratification of the said document and that on that day the said master Thomas tenant as above should present lawful warrandice in his defence and on that, that the said master Thomas had presented no evidents or legal titles to defend himself and the sheriff William Duncan with consent of parties said he would make his judgement on the said pledge and promise on the second last day of July and immediately following days. Master Thomas asked instrument at 10 am before witnesses abovewritten.

40. ***Doby Dwnne*** 31 July 1533 John Dwne burgess of Selkirk bound himself, his executors and assignees to pay James Doby the sum of xii [12] (p/t) [pounds?] within the next year...viz. six and a half said sum at the feast of Saint Martin next after and the rest on the last day of July, "viz. in penny and pennyworchtis". James asked instrument. Done about (p/t) pm at the house of Marion Dwne widow before witnesses John Bellendayne and John Th[omsone].

41. ***Ker Brydine*** 2 Aug 1533 William Ker in Sanct Helenes Schaw and Adam Ker his son and invested ["investitus"] heir, came to his tenement in the burgh of Selkirk on the south of the king's street between the lands of John Brydine on the east, the lands of master John Chepman on the south, the lands of John Lumisdane on the west and the king's street on the north and there on the ground of the same gave sasine of the tenement containing (40 – scored out) feet in length from the front to the south boundary, to David Brydine and his spouse Janet in liferent and their heirs without revocation forever. David and Janet asked instrument. Done on the ground of the tenement around noon before John Lumisdane, Thomas Mynto burgesses, David Brydine, John Brydine, Walter Haw, John Pacok.

42. ***Farle*** 9 Sept 1533 Adam Farle on the one part and Simon Farle, brother of the said Adam, on the other, held in their hands a certain document on paper in the form of a contract and bond between them...which they gave to me notary public to read out and transcribe on to parchment in form of an instrument as follows: "At Selkirk, the

nynt daye of september the yeir of god 1533 yeres, it is appoyntit
componit and irrevocabilly acgreit betwix thir tua personis underwritting that is to say Simon Farle one tane part and Adam Farle his
bruther on the tothir part in maner forme and effect as efter followis
that is to saye the said Simon bindis and oblisis [himself] ayris, executoris and assignais to content and paye to Adam Farle, [his ayris] and
executoris and assignais the sowme of fourteine merkis usual Scots
money at thir termis underwritting that is to saye sax merkis of the
said sowme within aucht days nixt efter the date of this presentis and
foir merkis at paische nixt efter and the tother foir merkis att lammas
nixt thereafter and atour the said Simon and his ayris to possess from
the said Adam and his ayris frely and quietly vithout ony exactionnis,
byrowis, malis and annuelis quhatsumever in ane tenement of land
lyand in Hawilk and the said Adam and his ayris to sit mail fre in ane
houss of the said Simon and his ayris ay and quhill he be frely and
peceabilly possessit in the foresaid tenement baitht the saidis parteis
exonerand and forgeiffand thereof al things bygane, present and forto-
come be the vertue of contrak maid at Selkirk in the chalmer of the
said Simon the same daye and yeir above writting befor thir witness
sir Robert Ker vicar in Lyndene. sir Wilyiam Bradffutt, Robert
Chepman, John Mithag, John Farle".

43. **Ker Kere** 9 Sept 1533 William Ker in Quhitmurhawe bound himself,
his heirs and assignees by virtue of this instrument in this way viz. that
John Ker his well beloved cousin has...used, enjoyed and possessed
within the ground of the loch ["stagnum"] of Quhitmurhall sufficient
space to build a house with pertinents...lasting for the space and term
of a tack from William Ker to the said John...also to build on the tack
a barn and yard freely and without obstacle as he has possessed. John
asked instrument. Done in the house of sir John Brydine around 7 pm
before Mark Ker bailie, sir Robert Ker vicar in Lyndene.

44. **Trumbull Helme** 21 Sept 1533 James Helme of his own free will
resigns, releases and quitclaims all wards, marriage contracts, reliefs,
evidents, letters, rights and claims of his lands in hands of [his cousin]
George [Trumbill]. George asked instrument. Done around 3 pm in the
room of sir John Michilhill [before] sir John Michilhill, Thomas Skwn,
chaplain and others.

45. **Scott Murraye** 24 Sept 1533 Isabel Murraye of her own free will with
the consent of Alexander Ellot her spouse leases and sets in tack amicably the lands, possessions and common pastures of Kersshop which
she lawfully holds in conjunct fee and liferent lying within the lordship of Ettrickforest and the sheriffdom of Selkirk, to her brother-
german master Michael Scott for the duration of her conjunct
infeftment. The said master Michael Scott, his heirs and assignees
paying to the queen the rent used and wont and 30 shillings yearly to
Isabel. Master Michael asked instrument. Done at the manor of the

said master Michael around 8 am before Alexander Ellot, John Hoye, Janet Scott, James Rannik and others.

46. ***Murraye Murraye*** 3 Oct 1533 Roger Murraye freely demitted, renounced and by virtue of this instrument irrevocably demitted from himself, his heirs, executors and assignees forever his tenement and 7 rigs of his own lands annexed thereto and an annualrent of 9 shillings with pertinents in favour of his younger son James Murraye...and invested the said James in the said lands by tenor of this charter and sasine made thereon paying to the said Roger 20 shillings if asked. James asked instrument. Done in the house of James Helme around 7 pm before John Smaill, James Helme and others.

47. [A note at the top of the page preceding the next instrument reads: "A note of the mortification of an annualrent to the shrine of The Holy Rood..."]

Gledstainis 22 Oct 1533. Elizabeth Gledstanis spouse of the deceased Robert Ker burgess of Selkirk...of her own free will taking leave of this world repenting (p/t) fearful and also considering the vain changeable wavering inconstancy [of life?] turning kindly eyes towards the soul of her said spouse and the salvation of herself and their offspring and the kings of the Scots and singular (p/t) the faithful, resigned a tenement which she had for her lifetime lying in the burgh of Selkirk on the south side of the king's street which leads to the well on the one part between the tenement of the said Robert Scot previously donated and annexed to the service of the Blessed Virgin Mary situate in Selkirk on the other on the west, the said king's street on the north, the tenement of James Brydin on the east and the lands of George Chepman on the south in hands of her son Mark Ker and the bailie James Scott requiring this present [instrument] in the form of a mortification to annex, donate and mortify the said tenement and orchard with pertinents for the service, care and ministry and altar of the Holy Rood in Selkirk to the profit and use and sustentation of sir John Brydin for that time chaplain ministering at the said altar and his successors...and the foresaid Mark, succeeding as heir to the foresaid tenement, with consent (p/t) of Elizabeth his mother resigned the said tenement with (p/t) orchard in hands of the bailie who gave sasine of it and its orchard with pertinents for ever to an image of the Cross and to sir John serving the altar (p/t) and his successors according to the tenor of the foresaid foundation and mortification of the same. Sir John asked instrument. Done here on the ground of the tenement around 3 pm before sir John Michilhill, William Brydine, John Brydine chaplains, James Bradfut, John Chepman, George Michilhill burgesses, Master Patrick Wrycht and William Scott.

48. 19 Nov 1533 sir John Brydin procurator and in the name of Elizabeth Gledstanis produced and published a charter and instrument of her

lands of Wra... [given] in the court of the barony of Hundils[is]hop
before bailie James Gledstanis and lord superior of the same before
witnesses Patrick Murray of Fawlohill, William Scott in [Tussilaw],
[Richard?] Gledstanis, John Gledstanis, William Diksone, (illegible),
John Scott, William Scott and on which [asked] instrument sir John
Brydin and sir William (p/t).

49. **Freir Fairle** 22 Nov 1533 the young woman Janet Freir, apparent heir
of John Freir her brother with the consent of her mother Marion Freir
brought certain evidents viz. a letter of reversion [resigning] all right,
claim, kindness and possession which she has, had or will have to the
tenement of Caldshielis with pertinents and a shrine ["oraculo"] in
hands of Simon Fairle burgess of Selkirk and in favour of the said
Simon for a payment 40 shillings to the said Janet. Simon asked instrument. Done around 11 am before sir William Brydin and sir John
Michilhill.

50. **Mark Widow ("Vidua")** 12 Dec 1533 the widow Marion Moris with
the consent of her son freely constituted Mark Ker in Kippielaw and
William Hog special assignees to her land viz. to "half a land" called
"Hil land" and to two (illegible) and "landis lyand in ryn daill" within
the bounds of Midlame...and renounced all right and claim thereto.
Mark and William asked instrument before (page torn to end of instrument).

51. **Scott Wrycht** 25 Jan 1533/4 Thomas Scott in Aikwode ester for himself and all other tenants living in "le Aikwode" paid gave brought and
delivered the sum of £10 scots for his part in the occupation and
appropriation of grain, comestibles and arrears and in the interest and
vicinity of "le Hartwod myris" with pertinents to master Patrick Wrycht
the queen's chamberlain of Ettrick forest by which sum the said
master Patrick in name of the queen Margaret infeft of the said forest
and her spouse Henry lord Methven was paid in full as agreed beforehand [and] if the said Thomas and tenants of "ester Aikwod" fall into
poverty [or] the said Thomas and the tenants be distrained or compelled civilly or canonically, to defend, relieve and give them indemnity and answer for them or for satisfying and relieving the said
Thomas and tenants of the said sum. Thomas Scott for himself and
tenants asked instrument. Done at the chamber of sir John Michilhill
chaplain in Selkirk around 3 pm before sirs William Brydin, John
Michilhill, Ninian Brydin notary, Thomas Johnesoune, sir Stephan
Wilkesoune.

52. **Notman Lauder** 11 Feb 1533/4 William [Lauder] burgess of
Edinburgh came to his tenement of land with pertinents lying within
the burgh of Selkirk on the east of the king's street which leads to the
well between the land of the heirs of Patrick Kene on the south, the
said street on the west, the other king's street which leads to the well

on the north and the lands of the said William (p/t) on the east and
there resigned all the tenement of land fore and back with the house
called "le Peil" and yard adjoining it with pertinents as is customary by
delivery of earth and stones on the ground of the same, in hands of
John Mithag one of the bailies of the said burgh who gave sasine to
the widow Marion Notman according to the tenor of a charter to
Marion and her heirs from William Lauder made thereon. Marion
asked instrument. Done on the ground of the same around 11 am
before John Lauder, William Portuis burgesses, James Melros, sir
Bartholomew Robesoune.

53. **Melross Lauder** Same day. William Lauder came to his tenement of
land on the south of the king's street leading to the well between the
land of the heirs of the deceased William (p/t) on the east, the lands
of the said William Lauder on the west, the said king's street on the
north and the lands of the heirs of the deceased Patrick Kene on the
south... and there on the ground of the same resigned the tenement
containing in length nine and a half ells with yard adjoining and of
equal width in hands of the bailie John Mithag who gave sasine to
James Melros, before witnesses above [no. **52**].

54. **Caidzo Lauder** Same day. William Lauder burgess [came] to his tenement of lands in the burgh of Selkirk containing ten and a half ells in
length between the land of Marion Notman called "le Peil" on the
west, the king's street leading to the well on the north, the lands of
the said William on the east and the yard of the said Marion on the
south and there on the ground of the same [resigned it] in hands of
John Mithag who...gave sasine to James Caidzoo before the same witnesses [no. **52**] and at the hour above.

55. **Hall Wonterhop** Same day. James Hall on the one part and William
Wonterhop on the other presented a document in the form of a bond
and contract and reversion as follows: "At Selkirk the lewint day of
februarii the yeir of god 1533 yeiris it is appointit and aggreit betvix
James Hall one ane part and William Wonterhop one the tothir part in
maner [followand] that is to saie the said James sal be (crossed out)
peceably brouk [ane] tenement of land with the pertinentis pertening
to the said William Wonterhop the quhill the said James duellis in and
occupyis the samyn be verteu of sesing ay and quhilk the said William
or his ayris executoris or assignais content and paye in usual money
to the said James his ayris executoris or assignais upone ane daye
betwix the sone rysing quhatsumever tyme and plaice thai be warnit
thairto the sowme of 40 shillings of the quhilk sowms of fourty
shillings the said William haldis him content and pait and dischargis
the said James his ayris (illegible) and the said William til uphald the
tenement forsaid [in all] thingis necessaris in and howsumever that the
saidis William his ayris, etc pais and contentis the said James his ayris
etc, the forsaid soume of 40 shillings the said James his ayris etc sal

discharge thaim of all richtis saising ingres clames thereto [in] the said
tenement with this condicioune the said James his ayris etc to pay the
annuallrent to oure lard and to brouk the samen tenement tua yeris
efter the (illegible)". The which read and seen the said William
[resigned] the tenement to John Mithag bailie who gave sasine to John
Hall and his heirs... done on the ground of the same around 4 pm
before William Portuiss, Cuthbert Hall and John Mithag.

56. **Steward Murraye** 5 March 1533/4 Patrick Murraye of Fawlohill on
the one part and William Steward (illegible) on the other [brought] a
document on paper in the form of a bond, commission or contract...
and gave it to the notary as follows: "At Selkirk the fift daye of the
monthe of marche"

[Instrument ends here.]

[The next group of pages (xlvii – lviii) is bound out of sequence.]

57. **Steward** Same day. William Steward lord of Tracquhair binds himself,
brothers, friends, cousins and tenants that if it happens that Patrick
Murray and his cousin, kin and tenants to (illegible) or object the reasons, allegations, pledges (illegible) the said William and his friends
and abovewritten to clear themselves lawfully (illegible) by circumspect [men] and other friends (illegible). William asked instrument.
Done at the same hour, day, month before witnesses James Gledstanis
of that ilk, master Michael Scott in Aikwod, William Scott in (illegible),
John Michilhill. Or subject him to a decreet of arbitration requiring
[him] to compromise [and be] content and that the said Patrick had
finally done.

58. **Murraye** Same day. Patrick Murray in Fawlohill declared that he and
William Steward had made a compromise and contained in it was a
declaration that the said William, his brothers, friends would not
molest or injure him in words or deeds and to be content for the
duration of the decreet of arbitration. William asked instrument before
witnesses above written.

59. **Brydine** 11 April 1534 James Scott bailie of Selkirk came to a chamber
and house in the west thereof called "le lang stabill" which was inhabited at the time by sir William Brydine, vicar of Selkirk and there on
the ground of the same gave sasine to William Brydine son and heir
of Robert Brydine by delivery of earth and stones, reserving however
free tenement of the said land to sir William Brydine as long as he
lives. The said William asked instrument. Done here at around 11 am
before sir William Brydine, David Scott chaplain, William Portuis,
(p/t), Thomas Ker, Thomas Dinghop.

60. **Brydin Brydin** 11 April 1534 William Brydine son and heir of Robert
Brydine his father came to the house then inhabited by sir William

Brydine vicar of Selkirk, brother-german of the said Robert, being known as "the lang stabill awester" with pertinents lying between the land of John Mithag on the west, the land of William Bennat on the north, the lands of the said William on the east and the lands of master John Chepman on the south...and resigned the chamber and "lang stabill" tenement in hands of the James Scott bailie who gave sasine to his brother-german John Brydine for his lifetime according to the tenor of his charter made thereon...and reserving the free tenement [as above]. Done at the hour as above.

61. **Helme Curll** 15 April 1534 John Curll burgess of Selkirk showed how he and his spouse Margaret Curll were by their old age and weakness of bodies...thrown into destitution and poverty...and compelled by necessity, John with the consent of his spouse, of his own free will... sold to John Helme, one iron anvil, a "foir hammer" and a carved table with forms and trestles ["mensam cilaris cum formalis et tripodibus"] for the sum of 47 shillings and 8 pence and discharged the same forever. John Helme asked instrument. Done at the smithy of the said John around 4 pm before James Craufurd, Stephen Loremer burgesses, (p/t) and Patrick Spens.

62.

"the ryding off the comon [of] Selkirk". [The rest of the page is blank although crossed and signed by [R.] Scott showing it has been examined for fraudulent insertion before the Lords of Council.]

63. **Scott, procurator for Peter Portuiss** 5 May 1534 James Scott bailie of Selkirk, procurator in the name of Peter Portuiss his cousin, showed how the said Peter was lawfully seised of a maltkiln and yard annexed with pertinents then occupied and inhabited by the deceased [Robert] Portuis, his uncle and that he was the lawful heir of the said Robert and at an inquest of the burgh no impediment was found...or protest was forthcoming...and occupation of the said malt kiln or yard was conferred on him. James asked instrument. Done at the court house about noon before John Mithag bailie, John Chepman, James Keine, William Portuis, George Michilhill, James Scott, burgesses of the said burgh.

64. **Brydin** Same day of the month of May as above. sir Ninian Brydin speaking for and in name of John Brydin his kinsman showed how he had given a false sasine to Peter Portuis alleging that the same was of no value concerning the said [maltkiln] and yard with pertinents and from this that Peter Portuis was not...seised of the said maltkiln, yard and pertinents as he asserted, requiring then the said Peter Portuis to present evidence of sasine and if he was given by Robert Portuis the said maltkiln yard and pertinents on which the said Peter now [shows] them. Sir Ninian asked instrument as above.

* Two loose pages are inserted here listed as **66** and **67**.

65. ***Portuis*** Same fifth day of the month and year above. James Scott bailie came to the tenement of which the said Robert Portuis died last vest and seised and there gave sasine of the said tenement with pertinents...in the form of a testimonial letter by James Kene then bailie under the common seal of the burgh given to the said Robert Portuis by his father James Portuis...the which letter was fully delivered to me, notary for reading out by the said Peter before the present inquest.

66.   [Originally a separate sheet]

"The xiii day of july Robert of of (*sic*) howpaslot and niniane andersone hes grantit in thir presens of the vytness undervrytting that thai haif resavit in nayme and behalff of M. Thomas Mairiorebankis sevin schoir and xv yowes and vi xx [six score] and xiiii yeild scheip fra patrik murray sanders murray and James greff and hes markit and keillit [i.e. marked with ruddle] the gudes forsaid to utilite and profett and the said Patrik Murray of hes fre vyll be supplication of Robert Scot grantit to gef the saidis gudis geris ane yeir mal fre and ferder induring the said patrik vyll [text ends here].

Reverse of 66. "The quhilk day Patrik Murray of Fallawhill in presens (illegible) undervrytting exponet that Villem [Mur] and archebauld hereot messengeris hes caussit to appris sevin schoir of milk yowes and xv and six schoir of yield scheip and foirtene of his for certane sowmes awud be the said Patrik to the king's graice and now master Thomas Mairiorebankis hes coft and cell the forsaidis gudis fra maister hendre bonayes thesaurer clerk and the said patrik murray and Sanders Murray James greife borrowis for the saidis gudis hes deliverit the saidis gudis haill and fere to Robert Scot and Niniane Andersone in nayme and behalff of maister Thomas Mairiorebankis". On which Patrick Murray asked instrument.

67.   [Originally a separate sheet].

"The secund day of Ianuar in the yeir of god ane thousand vcxxxix [1539/40] we Gilbert Ker of Prumsydlocht and Mairyone Hoppringill his moder coniunctly and severaly bindis ws be tenor of thir presentis and instrumentis to be tane therupone to purches and get the nonentres fre to Jenot Neuton lady of Dalcoif and Ad[am] Ker hir spous ther airis betuex this and witsonday nixt to cum efter the dait of thir presentis of fyv lib landis lyand in Town Yethame pertenand to the said Jenot and hir ayris under the pane of thre hundrecht merkis gud and usuaill money of Scotland. Elyk wys William Ker of Shawe and Ad[am] Ker his sone bindis and oblys thayme coniunctly and severally to geif Gilbert Ker and Mairyone his moder the sowme of fourtty merkis usuaill money for coftis, travelle and expensis maid be the said Gilbert in the purchesching of (illegible and torn) betuex this and witsonday next to cum under the payne of thre hundretht merkis (p/t) saidis

William, Ad[am] and Jenot remittis and quhort out quhictis all intromit-
ting (p/t) be the said Gilbert and his gudschir and fader of the said fyv
lib lands thir [presentis] complect wrytting at Grenheid the said day
and plaice befor thir vytness G[eorge Ker of] Lyntoun, Andrew Loucht,
sir John Blyth, sir Ninian Briden and subscribit with bath the parteis
handes, Gilbert Ker in Grenheid, Maryone Hoppringill with my [hand],
Adam Ker with my hand, Woll Ker with his hand at the pen".

Reverse blank.

68. ***Portuis*** 5 May [1534] Peter Portuis lawful heir to Robert Portuis his
uncle presented a testimonial letter sealed under the common seal of
the burgh of Selkirk to James Scott then bailie requiring the same to
infeft and seise the said Peter in and to all the lands of which the said
Robert died last vest and seised and the bailie gave the letter to the
notary to read out as follows: "Sen neidful thing is to beir witnes to
suchtfastnes and speaceli in thai thingis that maye gener preiudice to
innocent personis heirffor I James Kene bailye in the burcht off
Selkirk beris leill witness that the sewint daye of Januar the yeir off
our lord 1496 yeris that day personalye comperit ane honorabill man
James Portuis burgess in Selkirk and that daye in presens off thir
witnes underwritting puirly and sympilly resignit and upgaiff be erd
and stane in the handis off me the forsaid bailye James Kene ane certane of his land that is to say the est syd off his clois fra the foirhous
extendand to robert scottis land and (illegible) watsonis land one the
est syd and the said James landis one the norcht and vest parteis with
fre usche and entre to the foirgait sa at the throuchtgang ower the foir
gait be (p/t) futtis one breid. At the favor and requeist off hes [wel-
belovit] sone carnal roben portuis and this resignatione sa maid I the
forsaid baillye gaif heritabll stait sasine and possession to my belovit
frend roben portuis forsaid to him, his ayris executouris and assignais
imperpetuall and until al and sundry quham it efferis I maik it knawen
be thir my present lettres off testimoniall. In wytnes of the quhilk
thing I the forsaid bailye James Kene because I had not ane seill
(illegible) proper present off my awin I haif with instance procurit the
common seill of the burcht of Selkirk to be hungin to this present lettres off testimoniall daye and plaice forsaid and befor witnes that is to
saye sir John Brydin chaplain, sir James Portuis, Johne of Lauder elder,
Johne of Lauder younger, William Mayne, Cuthbat Trumbill, Rinyen
Graye, Thomas Tailyer, Thomas Graye, William Richertsone, George
Scott"... the which having been read out, the bailie by virtue of his
office gave sasine of "le est syd of the cloiss" with pertinents to Peter
Portuis...[heir] of the deceased Robert aforesaid by delivery of earth
and stones saving the right of anyone, with free tenement...for his
lifetime. Peter asked instrument. Done at the said close around 4
pm...before John Chepman, William Portuis, William Scott, George
Chepman, James Kene, John Loremer burgesses of the said burgh.

69. **Chepman Bane** Same day. John Chepman in the name of his wife
Elizabeth Bane asked an instrument to say that the said Elizabeth
[knew of] no impediment...why on account of the said Peter she
should be disinherited, expelled and her right of a liferent of the east
side of the close be removed according to the tenor of the letter of
testimonial...about which the said Peter acknowledged the said
Elizabeth should not be molested in the said [liferent] while she lived.

70. **Hoppringill Scott Mithag** 10 May 1534 George Hoppringill in
Torretle had prosecuted a certain woman Elizabeth Fawlaw in his custody because an act of theft was discovered and the bailies of Selkirk,
James Scott and John Mithag and their officers had arrested...the
woman and the said George under the laws regarding goods received,
"ane gowne of russett, ane browne clok, four ellis off quhit [cloth], ii
[2] pair off womannis hoiss maid ane quarter off braid reid, ane pair
off new lynning scheitis, a curche and colar, ane ald serk with ane lin-
ning scheit" the said George promised and obliged himself to answer
with respect to the said woman and goods as the law demanded and
required. George and the bailies asked instrument. Done at the market
cross around 5 pm before Master Thomas Ker in Sunderlandhall,
James Ker (illegible), William Brydine, John Brown, William Scott,
Alexander Gledstanis.

A note appears at the top of the next page : "The Compt off delyver-
ance of Selkirk".

71. **Murraye** 10 May [1534] Patrick Murraye of Fawlahil, sheriff of Selkirk,
declared that a certain woman in his custody Elizabeth Fawlaw for an
act of theft was delivered to him in order that he should execute his
office and prosecute in the sheriff court and a proclamation was made
in Selkirk that anyone with a grievance against Elizabeth Fawlaw
should compear at a certain time in the morning of the prosecution
which having been done and no one coming forward and the said
Patrick being present and ready to do justice protested that the theft
by the woman was alleged and that it should not turn to him and his
heirs and assignees in prejudice or harm that no one prosecuted.
Patrick asked instrument. Done at around noon before Mark Ker in
Kippelaw, Adam Scott in Fawside, James (p/t)myddall, David Pringill,
Adam Dalgless.

Some faint writing appears at the top of the next page overwritten
with the main text "Thomas Cort wythe my hand at the pen led be me
the xix daye of mai..."

72. **Ker Maitland** 30 May 1534 Andrew Ker son of Mark Ker in Litildene
showed how [John] Maitland when of late an officer of the said
William (p/t) Castellawe unjustly and against title of law distrained
and seized his moveable goods in erin heuch alleging that the said
goods pertained to Andrew and not his father Mark, which things

mentioned before, pronounced by the said Andrew taking on him the the burden of law, he took away the same [goods] from John and William and conversely the said John Maitland and an officer alleged the said goods pertained to Mark father of Andrew and not to him and the said [goods] were to be distrained and seized as well as the (illegible) belonging to the said Mark it should be done. Andrew and John asked instrument. Done on the king's street in the burgh of Selkirk around 6 pm before master (p/t), John Cob, George Michilhill.

73. **Waucht Heip Ker** 17 June 1534 John Waucht lord of Heip and Elizabeth Ker...made an agreement between them that Elizabeth resign all right and claim she has to a third part of the lands of Heip and also Cragwod in "water off roull" lying within the sheriffdom of Roxburgh, in hands of John Waucht and his heirs in the form of an instrument of compromise and quitclaim and so the said Elizabeth demits and discharges forever all the above lands with her moveable and immoveable goods, debts, ferme and arrears forever to the said John his heirs executors and assignees paying to the said Elizabeth her heirs executors and assignees the sum of ten merks at the following terms, 4 merks at Martinmas next, 3 merks at Whitsunday next 3 merks at Martinmas following that. John Waucht asked instrument. Done in the parish kirk of Selkirk around 5 pm before John Reddaill of that ilk, George Ker in Lyntoun, George Tait in Pyrne, Walter Scott in Syntoun, Thomas Ker in Yair, sir Richard Wauch.

74. **Brydin Mithag** 8 July [1534] James Brydin and John Mithag burgesses of the burgh of Selkirk showed how the said James and John in respect of a certain inquest into the value of the lands of the lordship of Selkirk pertaining heritably to Patrick Murray elected, summoned, called, swore and decreed with other inquisitors at this a retour be made by those elected for the court with seal attached protesting that the said sealing would not turn to their prejudice. (p/t) asked instrument. Done around 4 pm before witnesses (p/t).

75. **Curror Chepman** 18 Aug 1534 John Curror burgess of Selkirk son and heir of the deceased Walter Curror came to his tenement of land lying in the said burgh on the south side of the king's street which leads to the loch between the land or tenement of James Mithag on the east, the land or tenement of William Lermont on the west, the place called "the Bog" on the south and the king's street on the north...and there on the ground of the same resigned the said tenement of land with backhouses and yards lying outside the gate on the south side of the king's street which leads to the loch in favour of his spouse Janet Chepman in conjunct fee for her lifetime and there on the ground of the same the bailie James Scot gave sasine of the same according to the tenor of a charter made thereon. Janet asked instrument. Done on the ground of the tenement around 3 pm before

William Portuis serjeant, (p/t), John Chepman, Patrick Freir, Alan
Mithag, burgesses of the said burgh and William Chepman.

76. **Murraye Dowglaice** 6 Oct [1534] Patrick Murraye of Faulohill sheriff
of Selkirk, in name of the king required William Douglace of
Bonjedward [to compear] within his court at an agreed time to proceed with an inquest and with others decide and discern what were
the royal requirements. The said William prepares (p/t) and Patrick
sheriff (p/t) gestured with his hand breaking (p/t) over the said
William. Patrick asked instrument. Done around noon before witnesses (p/t).

77. Same day. William Douglace of Bonjedward acknowledged that he
was required by Patrick Murraye sheriff of Selkirk to plead at an
inquest declaring himself prepared to be obedient (illegible) to the
service of our supreme lord king...and William declared he was superior to the sheriff [and] that no service ought to be given by the
inquest. William asked instrument at the hour above.

78. **Chepman** 13 Oct 1534 John Dwne and Marion Chepman of their own
free will held in safekeeping the heirship goods of Janet Scot son (*sic*)
and heir of the deceased George Scott burgess of Selkirk viz. "ane
meit almery, [ane] kist, hir faders bed with pertinents, ane pot, ane
pulder [pewter] plait and ane chandilar" which were received and the
said Janet faithfully agreed to keep her said goods in [their safekeep-
ing]. John Chepman grandfather of the said Janet in the name of Janet
asked instrument. Done in the chamber of said John Chepman around
4 pm before James Scot, James Bradfutt, William Scott and John Dwne
burgesses.

79. **Hall** 27 Oct 1534 the young man David Haw son and heir of [John
Haw] burgess in Selkirk of his own free will...binds himself to resign
and quitclaim without delay a tenement with croft and pertinents
which the said David has from the abbot and convent of Melrose [set
in tack] to his father John. John asked instrument. Done at the chamber of sir John Michilhill chaplain around 2 pm before sir John
Michilhill notary, James Wilkesone, George Michilhill burgesses and
John [Michel]hill.

80. **Brydin** 10 Nov [1534] sir Ninian Brydine procurator in the name of his
kinsman ["nepos"] John Brydin alleged that a false sasine was given by
James Scott bailie to Peter Portuis of certain lands pertaining heritably
to the said John...and that the said bailie did not see a letter of infeftment of the deceased Robert Portuiss uncle of the said Peter. sir
Ninian chaplain asked instrument here at the court house of the burgh
of Selkirk around the hour of eleven am before [Robert Chepman],
James Keine bailies, sir John Michilhill notary, David Brydin.

81.   ***Graham***   10 Dec [1534] Walter Scott tutor of Hanyng promises and binds himself to be subject to...all contracts made between Thomas Graham and John Brown and to reply and respond for the said Thomas in law and the same to be upheld in all things. Done around 5 pm before witnesses (p/t).

82.   ***Brydin***   15 Dec [1534] sir Ninian Brydin chaplain speaking in the name of Thomas Johnson his kinsman ["nepos"] declared that James Craufurd burgess of Selkirk with sir Hugh Riddaill and their accomplices...after an arrestment or royal escheat laid on the said Thomas by a royal officer on a bed and press artificially [skilfully?] carved in wood pertaining and belonging to the said Thomas as heir they had broken and held in contempt the arrestment lawfully laid on and burdening them and, against our title to the said bed and press as aforesaid, as arresters had taken them away and removed them as he asserted and they accepted. Ninian asked instrument. Done here in the burgh court house around noon before Robert Chepman, James Keine bailies, John Mithag, James Bradfut burgesses.

Same day. the said Ninian asked from sir John Michilhill the best gown of the deceased master James Johnson...the which [gown] the said sir John Michilhill acknowledged he had and was given to him for debts in hands of [Thomas] Johnsone elder.

83.   ***Hendersone Burne***   16 Dec [1534] Robert Chepman, James Helme, John Smaill, Andrew Mcdowell arbiters for Thomas Hendersone and Katherine Burne unanimously decided to divide the underwritten goods between the said Thomas and Katherine thus: seven ewes to Thomas and six ewes to Katherine, six hogs to Thomas and six to Katherine, ane stot and ane stirk to Thomas and a cow to Katherine, six stone of butter and six quarters of cheese to John Hendersone son of the said [?Thomas], 15/6d to Katherine and 13 shillings to Thomas and thirteen shillings which the said Katherine shall pay to the said Thomas between now and the feast of Kentigern next after, thirteen ells of fulled cloth ["panni fulli"] to be equally divided, the said Thomas to pay a debt of a boll of flour and the said Katherine another, equal shares of two tables and other household goods and utensils...done around 4 [pm] before William Portuis, Patrick Graden, and James (p/t).

84.   ***Helme***   30 Dec [1534] James Helme resigns in hands of Robert Chepman bailie in favour of his son George Helme, his forge, anvil, bellows and all his iron and non-iron instruments for the craft of forging and the said bailie gave sasine to the said George Helme and his heirs failing which to James Helme and Paul Helme his younger brothers reserving a free tenement to the said James while he lives. Done at the forge around 2 pm before William Brydin, Stephan Loremur, William Flecher, James Cant burgesses, Alexander Scott,

William Mathosone. "memorandum George ane kist the maist with ane stand bed".

Same day. James Helme with the consent of his spouse Janet Curll resigned in favour of his son George Helme a croft in the lordship of Selkirk with pertinents lying between the lands of Thomas Morlaw on the east, the lands of William Brydin on the west, the lands of John Chepman on the north and the king's street leading to the town ["casa"] loch* [on the south] and the bailie delivered sasine of the same to the said George.

Same day. James Helme with the consent of his spouse Janet Curll resigned the tenement in which he was living in favour of his sons James and Paul together with houses, backhouses and yard and the bailie gave sasine to the said James and Paul "fra the durris [ben?] with the west syd of the closs and yard" to James Helme and "fra the durris but with the est syd of the cloiss and yard to Paul Helme".

Memorandum : Paul Helm sal haif the mekil pot, ane skift with ane stand bed and James (p/t) with the burd and tr[ests].

* The Haining Loch; burgesses had the right to use the water from it until the nineteenth century.

Next page blank and cancelled.

85. **Murraye** 26 Jan [1534/5] Patrick Murraye sheriff of Selkirk showed how he held his own court lawfully in the court house of Selkirk and [affirmed that he] had always held his court openly in the place of the said court house and by no means had he impeded the bailies of the said burgh from holding their court but the place was open to them at the lawful hour and day. Patrick asked instrument. Done around 2 pm before Mark Ker, sir Ninian Bridin notary, George Ker, James Scott and George Michilhill.

86. **Brydin** On which day Ninian Brydin in the name of Thomas Johnsone alleged that Robert Chepman had broken a certain arrestment of a stack of grain. Ninian asked instrument before James Kein, John Muthag, William Portuis.

87. **Chepman** The same day Robert denied the arrestment was broken and the said stack of grain was present within the bounds of the burgh.

88. **Lauder** Same day. William Lauder procurator in the name of sir Hugh Reddaill showed how an arrestment laid on a certain bed and wooden press of Thomas Johnsone had now been broken by James Craufurd with his consent before witnesses Mark Ker, James Keine, William Keine, master John Williamson.

The same day Ninian Brydin procurator for Thomas Johnsone alleged that James had violated the burgess oath [when] he in a partisan manner broke the royal arrestment brought on his house and did not serve justly.

89. **Brydine** [The name of Ninian Brydin is scrawled across the top of the page] 2 Jan [1534/5] William Brydin burgess of Selkirk showed how slander and murmur by certain of his fellow citizens had been promulgated alleging that the said William had unlawfully taken two ewes and had sold them to two wool merchants ["laniatoribus"] of the burgh about which the said William pledges his faith and swears his innocence...by the tenor of this instrument with the said wool merchants viz. Robert Smyth and Thomas Hog and he was acquitted by the worthy burgesses underwritten Mark Ker, James Brydin, James Scott, William Portuis, John Chepman, William Scott, sir William Brydin, James Bradfut, Robert Chepman and many others and purged by touching the holy evangel of God. William asked instrument. Done in the church of Blessed Mary of Selkirk at the time of High Mass before witnesses sirs John Michilhill, Ninian Brydin notaries, Adam Scott in Fawsyd, William Scott in Faldishoip, John Lauder, John Browne and David Mithag.

[Next page is blank and cancelled.]

90. **New Protocol Brydin Brydin** 12 Feb 1534/5 James Brydin burgess of Selkirk came to two rigs of land [lying] in Dunsdalis within the lordship of Selkirk and the sheriffdom of the same between the lands of Patrick Murray of Faulohill on the west and the lands of John Scott on the east, the lands of John Hall on the north and south and resigned the rigs in hands of the Robert Chepman bailie who gave sasine to John Brydin [brother?] of the said James. John asked instrument. Done on the ground of the same around 4 pm before Alexander Smyth, James Keine, (illegible), Thomas Wilkesone.

[Next page is blank and cancelled.]

91. **Bradfut Scott and Scott** 4 March 1534/5 Alexander Scott burgess of Selkirk came to his tenement of land in the said burgh then inhabited by James Bradfutt between the tenement of Patrick Murray then inhabited by Janet Scott relict of the deceased George Scott burgess of the said burgh on the east, the lands of the said Patrick on the north, the tenement of the heirs of the deceased Cuthbert Trumbull on the west and the king's street on the south and resigned the tenement in hands of the Robert Chepman bailie who gave sasine in favour of Thomas Scott son and apparent heir of Alexander Scott forever and the said Thomas without delay resigned the tenement in [blank and cancelled page here] hands of the bailie who gave sasine in favour of James Bradfutt according to the tenor of his charter. Thomas and James asked instrument. Done on the ground of the said lands around

[ten] am before John (illegible), William Bennat, George Michilhill burgesses of the said burgh, (illegible) Johnestoun, William Scott.

[Part of next page cancelled]

92. **Murraye Helme** 24 March 1534/5 James Murray resigns in favour of his spouse or Christian Helme half of his fore house viz. "fra the durris but" with the barn annexed on the north with free entry and ish to the yard and the bailie gave sasine of the said house with barn to the said Christian for her lifetime in conjunct fee. Christian asked instrument. Done on the ground of the said tenement before Adam Bowmaker (p/t).

93. **kune Gren heid Ker** 3 April 1535 sir Thomas Skune chaplain in name and authority of Thomas Ker in Yair publicly warned Andrew Ker in Prumsydloucht at his place called Grenheid according to the tenor of a [reversion] to compear within 40 days within the sanctuary of the kirk of "Selikirk" to receive a certain sum of money from the said Thomas. Sir Thomas asked instrument. Done in the hall of the said place around noon before Robert Ker, (illegible) Andersoune, John Hesilhoip and Andrew Fairle.

[Next page blank and cancelled.]

94. **Michilhill Bennat and Ker** 16 April 1535 Mark Ker in Kippelaw binds himself his heirs, executors and assignees to relieve and discharge the worthy men underwritten viz. George Michilhill and William Bennat in respect of acts, instruments and contracts [he had] made through the said George and William as well as acts made with the abbey and convent of Melross through John Scott in Thirlstane. George and William asked instrument. Done in the chamber of John Brydin chaplain around 2 pm before William Douglass, John Andersonne, John Scott in Thirlstane, Simon Gledstanis.

95. **Wrycht Rutherfurd** 22 April 1535 David Rutherfurd attorney in the name of John Rutherfurd of Honthill presented a precept sealed under the great seal of our lord king to master Patrick Wrycht, master of arts, in hands of the bailie in that part who gave it to me notary to read out as follows [page blank and cancelled. No detail of precept given] asked instrument. Done on the ground of Blakhauch around one pm before sir George Wallace chaplain, William Johnsonne, Robert Michelsone, Adam Blaik[hop].

96. **Rutherfurd** Same day. master Patrick [Wrycht] (p/t) publicly warned all the indwellers of the royal lands of Blakhaucht between now and the feast of Whitsunday next following the date of these presents...and that all the indwellers [there] of the lordship of Ettrick Forest were summoned and warned by royal letters to flit at the said feast. Adam Rutherfurd asked instrument. Done wholly as before.

97.   *Ker* 15 May 1535 Thomas Ker in Yair showed how he had lawfully warned Andrew Ker in Prumsydloucht at his dwelling place called Grenheid on 3 April last through his procurator sir Thomas Skune to compear within 40 days at the sanctuary of Selkirk to receive a certain sum of money according to the tenor of a reversion produced and shown by the said Thomas and the said Thomas compeared with an authentic copy of the reversion...and handed the money in gold and silver lawfully counted into the custody of the bailies of the burgh of Selkirk, Robert Chepman and James Keine...and the said Andrew not compearing to receive the said sum according to the reversion, the said Thomas protested that his return to the lands contained in the reversion in the absence of the said Andrew and his heirs should not fall to his prejudice. Thomas asked instrument. Done in the sanctuary around 10 am before Mark Ker, James Keine, (illegible) Michilhill, Thomas Murraye, William Wod, Robert Chepman, (illegible), sir Thomas Skune.

98.   *Scott in Edschawe* 21 May 1535 Walter Scott in Edschawe showed how there was a false sasine taken by him and made by Isabel Murraye his stepmother ["novercam"] on and for him [narrating] that the said Walter with his arbiters in form of a said contract made between himself and the said Isabella did not compear at 9 o'clock on the 24 July 1532 to make a decision in the causes contained in the said contract as the said Isabel asserted. The said Walter alleged the opposite [that] it was not the agreed said hour, day and month for making a decision on the causes but the said Walter had observed, as he asserted, all the three days agreed for the decision making and the said Isabel brought and presented an arbiter at the said alleged hour when she should have brought and presented two arbiters protesting that in the alleged absence of her and of her arbiters it should not fall to him, his heirs, executors and assignees in prejudice or damage concerning the contents of the said contract. Walter asked instrument. Done at the house of Thomas Heisloip around 5 pm before Walter Scott in Haining, Walter Scott in Ashkirk, Cuthbert Curror, William Fawsyd, Robert Patersone.

99.   *Sheriff Court of Selkirk held and begun in the court house on the behalf of the sheriff on the first of June 1535.* On which day suits called and the said court lawfully fenced master Patrick Wrycht procurator for Margaret, queen of Scotland lady of Ettrick Forest and her spouse Henry, lord of Methven gave and showed a certain letter of commission under the signets and subscription of Margaret and Henry to Patrick Murray sheriff of Selkirk, to repledge John Rutherfurd of Hunthill from the said court to the liberty and privilege of the said lordship and also humbly required this by admission of the said commission. The sheriff received the said commission and read it out aloud and the said sheriff not admitting it the said master Patrick procurator openly offered and promised [to appear?] for the assignation of a court on whatever days and at suitable places and also for deputing a judge not doubted and not suspect to either of the parties viz. Alison Douglace relict of David Hume of Vedderburne on the one part and John Rutherfurd of Hunthill on the other for decerning, determining and concluding (p/t) the cause or causes raised between the foresaid parties or (p/t) at the place of Blakhauch with pertinents feued by the said queen Margaret, protesting that the said pretended non admission of the commission and any other acts and deeds whatever (p/t) done or to be done in the said sheriff court should not fall (p/t) to the prejudice or loss of the queen and her spouse and the said John and the freedom of the lordship. Master Patrick asked instrument. Done in the court house around 11 am before Andrew Ker in Primsydloucht, George Ker in Lintoun, Mark Ker in Kippelaw, sir John Michilhill and Ninian Brydin notaries...and the said master protested that the admission of a certain letter of assedation of the place of Blakhaucht should not fall to the prejudice of the said queen for reasons to be proponed in [due] time and place.

Same day. Patrick Murray sheriff of Selkirk showed how a letter of our supreme lord king was presented to him to take cognizance of the cause raised between Alison Douglass and John Rutherfurd and that master Patrick Wrycht procurator for Margaret queen of Scotland had shown and given him a certain letter of commission under the signet (p/t) for repledging the said John Rutherfurd from his court and therefore on this Patrick on the admission of the said commission called the worthy barons of his sheriffdom as suitable interlocutors and ordained them to decern and the said interlocutors along with the said sheriff Patrick decerned and gave deliverance that the said commission should not be admitted for the reason that the said letter of our supreme lord king was given and shown to him sheriff Patrick in stricter form and that [neither] the said queen and her spouse nor anyone else (p/t) in their name had given or produced letters of our supreme lord king to discharge and exclude the said sheriff Patrick from sitting and decerning in the foresaid cause and that there was never any custom nor practice in the foresaid court of admitting any commission of repledging to the liberty of the said lordship of Ettrick Forest. Also the said Patrick said he was not sitting to decern in the case in lesion or contempt or (illegible) of the said liberty but only in obedience to the king's letter and in execution of it, protesting that anything done and to be done by himself, the inquisition and other members of the court should not fall to his or their prejudice or loss... before above witnesses.

Same day. George Hume of Vedderburne protested that the plea moved between his mother and John Rutherfurd should not turn to prejudice or damage of him and his infeftment in Blakhaucht.

(p/t) Also on the same day sheriff Patrick said that he (p/t) had not seen at all presenting...of the liberty (p/t) nor any kind of proof (p/t) of the reading(?) (p/t) of the said book (p/t).

100. **Blakstok** On the above day master Andrew Blakstock procurator and in name of Alison Dougliss relict etc presented a letter of tack of the said Alison of the place of Blakhauch lying in the lordship of Ettrick forest and sheriffdom of Selkirk made with signet and subscription of Margaret queen of Scotland and given to Alison on 24 April 1525, to last until her son George Hume reaches the age of twenty one, to Patrick Murray sheriff of Selkirk and the inquest subscribed, elected and sworn and read out [the same] to the said sheriff and inquisitors requiring them to make a decision in the forementioned according to the tenor of royal letters, whether Alison is in possession of the place of Blakhaucht and whether her son was made a promise of the said place in the letter of tack and whether the said letter had come to the end of its duration.

The Inquest

Andrew Ker in Prumsydloucht, chancellor of the assize.

George Ker in Lintoun, Patrick Murray, Simon Farle, master Thomas Ker in Sunderlandhall, William Murray, Robert Chepman, Alexander Hoppringill in Cragleche, James Brydin, John Hall, William Ker in Quhitmurhall, James Scott, James Ker in Farnele, James Keine, James Trumbill...who made [judgement] on the said letter that Alison was in lawful possession of the said place and that in their view the end of her term [had not come] because George Hume had not reached 21 years according to the date of the letter and Andrew Ker chancellor for himself and the other inquisitors said that the aforesaid decreet should not fall to his or their voluntary error or prejudice and that nothing was decided in the forementioned unless it was set before their eyes in the said tack. Andrew Blakstok and Andrew [Ker] asked instruments done around noon before above witnesses.

101. **Rutherfurd** Same day. sir William Rutherfurd chaplain procurator in name of John Rutherfurd of Hunthill showed and asserted that a false letter of tack of the place of Blakhaucht produced by the said Alison Douglas was of no effect and that the letter of tack was made to the said Alison by Margaret queen of Scotland without consent of her spouse...that the said William made to be read out did not give her the heritable possession of the said place alleging Patrick Murray sheriff and his inquisitors ought not to decide in the foregoing on account of their voluntary error incurred which was committed by them conjunctly protesting that whatsoever acts...done in the sheriff court of Selkirk should not fall to John Rutherfurd, his heirs and assignees in prejudice of his heritable possession. William asked instrument. Done at noon before witnesses as above.

102. *Scott Scott* 4 June 1535 Robert Scott in Howford openly warned John Scott in Dringstoun then present, to flit from his dwelling house, place and lands of Dringstoun with pertinents and thereafter to desist from occupation and intromission with the said place and lands...the said Robert alleging that the said John had already been lawfully warned to remove from the said place of Dringston belonging heritably to Robert and that the said John was in violent possession of the same and that the said occupation should not turn to his prejudice regarding his heritable feu. Robert asked instrument. Done on the ground of the same around noon before Robert Scott in Blindhaucht and (p/t) Boill.

103. *Scott* Same day. John in Dringstoun protested that a false premonition of removal was made by Robert Scott and...John would not yield to him or prejudice his title of possession...and he was within the terms pertaining to the fermes, money and customary dues on the said place of Dringstoun agreed to be paid to the said Robert also alleging that the said John was never before that time lawfully warned to flit. John asked instrument. Done at time and before witnesses above.

104. *Kene Chepman, bailies of [Selkirk]* 17 June [1535] James Kene and Robert Chepman, bailies of Selkirk with the consent of the whole community advised and warned all non-burgesses and those indwellers without the freedom of the burgh, that they shall not sell goods ["mercimonia"] within the bounds of the burgh according to the tenor of royal letters to the bailies and community...especially warning the indwellers of the town of Gallo[sheillis]. Bailies asked instrument. Done at the hour of noon before sir James Davesone, William Portuis, (p/t) Bradfutt.

105. *Trumbill Brydin* 5 August 1535 sir John Trumbill chaplain vicar pensioner of "le barechy Benedochy" [i.e. the parish of Benedochy] gave to the notary to read out and render in the form of an instrument a certain letter of legacy written in his own hand...as follows...in latin [Text ends here. Rest of page is blank and cancelled. Continues on next page] ...in latin 5 August 1535 I John Trumbill vicar pensioner of the parish church of Benedochy give and leave all my moveable and immoveable utensils and household goods not yet left to my servants and the poor: My last will without any revocation if I should pass away intestate [I entrust] to John Brydin and my sister. Before witnesses Robert Trumbill, John Jak, John Symsone, John Brydin notary. John asked instrument.

[Reverse of this page blank and cancelled.]

106. *Helme Roger and Murraye* 26 August 1535 George Murraye and his spouse Janet Rog[er] jointly and severally bound themselves and their heirs to render all moveable and immoveable goods of the deceased James Trumbill to his said heirs, offspring and friends at lawful value and to render just account of the said goods. James Helme on the part of the heirs took instrument done around 5 pm in the chamber of sir John Michilhill before witnesses sir John Michilhill notary and George [Brokess?].

["mutatio indictionis vigesimo q[uinto] mensis septembris indictio nona" appears above the next entry.]

107. *Murraye Brydine* 4 October 1535 James Murray came to his annual-rent of nine shillings uplifted from a tenement of the heirs of Robert Scott at Kirkwind and there resigned the annualrent in hands of Robert Chepman bailie who gave sasine to sir John Brydin by delivery of one penny. Sir John asked instrument. Done on the ground of the said tenement around ten am before John Smaill, James Chepman, John Michilhill notary in the premises.

108. *Scott Huntar* 5 October 1535 Walter Scott lord of Robertoun of his own free will by way of satisfaction and in form of penance for bear-ing openly a bare sword with a point compeared before Robert Huntar on bended knee...asking for clemency of almighty God the father and from the said Robert, his parents, friends, cousins, acquain-tances etc... for indulgence in the injurious and violent killing of the deceased John Huntar brother of the said Robert which the said Robert received thankfully with all his heart remitting all rancour towards the said Walter and his family etc. and the said Robert binds himself and the foresaids not to pursue the said Walter for the killing in future in civil or canonical court. Walter asked instrument. Done in the parish kirk of Selkirk around 5 pm before sir John Michilhill notary, Robert Trumbill tutor of Holdene, George Michilhill, Thomas Ellot burgesses and sir Mathew Ellot chaplain.

109. *Ker Trumbill* [scored out] 14 October 1535 It is appointed and agreed between...Mark Ker of Kippelawe on the one part and Robert Trumbill on the other in the following form...that the said Mark to enjoy peaceably without molestation from the said Robert [all the text to here has been scored out and in the margin written the following note "all allegations and [?arrears] viz. debts, objections, (illegible)"] a half part of the wardship of the lands of Philhop lying within the sher-iffdom of Selkirk and their lawful pertinents and the said Robert shall peacefully enjoy the other half of the same with pertinents granting freely the profits and income of the said parts of the wardship until the entry of John Trumbill son and apparent heir to the deceased Ralph Trumbill deceased lord of the said lands of Philhop and the said Mark and Robert shall not lease the said lands during their wardship to powerful men or lords or their like by reason of agreement. Mark and Robert asked instrument. Done in the burgh of Selkirk around noon before sir John Michilhill notary and James Bradffutt, sir Adam Trumbill chaplain.

Also the said Mark and Robert in accordance with their wardship, bind
themselves in the sum of 50 merks to resign, quitclaim and renounce
all right and claim to ownership and possession of the said tack to the
said John heir of the above before the same witnesses.

110. **Ker Trumbill** 14 Oct 1535 Mark Ker and Robert Trumbill one by one
showed asserted and confessed according to the tenor of this present
instrument...that the same were...agreed on all causes between them
without exception or allegation, all opposition, cavil and allegation
excluded so that the said Robert shall enjoy peaceably a half of the
lands of the wardship of Philhop with pertinents and the said Mark
peaceably enjoy the other half of the [same] up to the entry of John
Trumbill heir of the said lands and that they should not lease their
said halves of the lands to powerful men or lords or their like by
means of agreement. Before witnesses and at hour above.

111. **Ker** Same day. Mark Ker made constituted and ordained the said
Robert his true and lawful assignee in and to the half wardship of ten
poundlands of Philop etc now reasonably in hands of the said Mark
excepting his holding in marriage ("maritagium").

112. **Scott Baillie Ker** 9 November 1535 James Scott one of the bailies of
Selkirk came at request of William Ker son and apparent heir of the
deceased William Ker burgess in Edinburgh his father to a tenement of
land in the said burgh to the south of the mercat cross between the
lands of Lancelot Ker or Thomas Crukschankis on the east, the lands
of George Jamesone and James Murray on the south, the lands of
George Chepman on the west and the king's street or mercat on the
north, and then to a tenement "le onseit" called "Alisonis Landis" with
pertinents lying in the said burgh between the lands of the heirs of
George Halden on the west, the lands of Patrick Murray of Faulohill
and William Ker in Schaw on the north, the lands of the same William
Ker on the east and the king's street on the south and then to a tenement lying in the said burgh between the lands of Thomas Mynto on
the east, the lands of Peter Portuis on the west and north and the
king's street on the south and then to a tenement lying between the
lands or tenement of James Craufurd on the east, the lands of Patrick
Murray on the south and the lands of Thomas Forest, heir of said
Patrick and James Melros on the west and the king's street which
leads to the [well?] on the north and then to an annualrent worth 12
shillings uplifted yearly from a tenement of the said Thomas Mynto
lying in the said burgh on the north of the king's street leading to the
well, then to an annualrent of nine shillings uplifted yearly from a tenement of the heirs of the deceased Peter Keine on the east of the
king's street leading to the Foulbrig then finally to an annualrent of 10
shillings uplifted yearly from a tenement of Stephen Loremer lying in
the Peilgat, and there the bailie entered William Ker into the tenements and annualrent as known heir of the deceased William Ker his

father according to the tenor of the old infeftment and gave sasine of the said tenements called "le onseit of Alisonis Land" with crofts, pasture and pertinents lying in ryndaill within the bounds of the burgh [and all other] tenements and annualrents [as above] to the said William reserving a conjunct infeftment to Katherine Curll spouse of the deceased William his father as long as she lives and the bailie gave sasine of the same to the said William. William asked instrument. Done on the ground of the said tenements around 2 pm before George Michilhill serjeant, John Scott, John Dwne, Thomas Henry and John McDowell, William Elphinstoun.

Same day. Katherine Curll spouse to William Ker protested that the sasine given to her son William should not turn in prejudice to her conjunct fee according to the tenor of the sasine which she has. Katherine asked instrument. Done at the same hour and before witnesses as above.

113. **Mynto Ker** Same day. the said William Ker came to his tenement of land lying on the north side of the king's street which leads to the well between the lands as above and there on the ground of the same resigned all the tenement with yard...in hands of James Scott bailie in favour of David Mynto and the bailie gave sasine of the said tenement by delivery of earth and stones. David asked instrument. Done at the above hour before Thomas Mynto, William Elphinstoun, William Brydin and others.

[Reverse of page blank and cancelled.]

114. **Craufurd Ker** 9 Nov [1535] the same William Ker came to his tenement of land lying in the burgh of Selkirk on the south of the king's street leading to St Mary's Well between the lands of James Craufurd on the east, the lands of Patrick Murray of Faulohill on the south, the lands of Thomas Forest heir of Patrick [Forest?] and James Melros on the west and the said street on the north...and there on the ground of the same resigned the tenement with yard in hands of James Scott bailie in favour of James Craufurd...and the bailie gave sasine of the tenement with yard and pertinents. James Craufurd asked instrument. Done on the ground of the same around 3 pm before William Brydin, George Michilhill, William Elphinstoun burgesses.

115. **Scott Ker** Same day. William Ker came to his tenement called "le onseit of Alisonis" [land] [boundaries given as in no. 112]...and resigned the tenement reserving to William the yard, crofts, rigs and pastures in favour of John Scott and James Scott bailie gave sasine of the same done at "le onseit" around 3 pm before George Michilhill, Henry Young, John Hall and William Brydin.

116. **Brydin, Bradfut, Ker, Curll** 9 Nov [1535] William Elphinstoun and Katherine Curll his spouse in their own interest and William Ker

invested heir of the deceased William Ker in Edinburgh (p/t) on the one part to sir William Brydine chaplain and to James Bradfutt on the other irrevocably entered into a compromise the form of which follows that the said sir William Brydine chaplain and James Bradfutt, his heirs and assignees shall peacefully enjoy all the husbandland called "Alisonis landis" with crofts, rigs, open fields and pertinents thereto reserving "le oinseit" of said lands to William and Katherine for their interest...and William [and Katherine] shall peaceably enjoy the same also the said husbandlands, crofts, rigs and open fields with pertinents but they reserve [the right] led by god ["deo duce"] while parties to the compromise by custom of tenantry [that] they will occupy and manure the lordship of the said William and James, [and shall] not be regarded as criminals, rebels or transgressors, paying yearly to William and Katherine for their interest and to William Ker heir to the said lands the sum of 40 shillings at the customary two terms.

Also if it happens that in the remaining term the ferme for any husbandland lying in the said territory is raised higher or reduced then it will be allowed to the said William and Katherine for their interest and to the foresaid William Ker heir to raise or reduce the ferme for their husbandland likewise except if the said William Ker intends to occupy the lands personally. Sir William and James Bradfutt asked instruments. Done in the chamber of sir William Brydin around 5pm before William Brydin, James Scot, Thomas Mynto.

Also the said William, Katherine and William and his heirs are granted indemnity by William and James and heirs to warrant and defend them in peaceable occupation and manuring of the said lands and against all men. Also that entry to the said lands shall be at the feast of Martinmas.

117. **Hall, Berkare** 10 Nov [1535] John Hall came to his rigs lying above "le Goslawdalis" within the bounds of burgh of Selkirk between the lands of the heirs of George Halden on the north, the king's street leading to the Stobstane Gait on the east, the land of John Young on the south and the lands of Patrick Murray and James Scott on the west also to a butt of land lying in Crukitlandis and there on the ground of the same resigned all the rigs and the bounds above Crukitlandis in hands of James Scott bailie who gave sasine to Thomas Berkare. Thomas asked instrument. Done on the ground of the said rigs around 8 [am] before James Wilkesone and John [Brydin].

118. **Crenstoune Scot** 16 November 1535 Janet Scott relict of the deceased Walter Scott came to three husbandlands now occupied by William Davesone, Archbald Trumbill and James Hopkirk with pertinents lying in the town of [Dennum?] in the barony of Caveris in the sheriffdom of Roxburgh and presented to William Crenstoun and James [Spuin?] bailies in that part, a precept of sasine under the seal of John

Crenstoun of that ilk which the notary read out as follows: John
Crenstoun of that ilk etc greeting. Because I have sold etc three hus-
bandlands now inhabited by John Daveson, Archibald Trumbill and
[James] Hopkirk lying in the town of [Dennum?] in the barony of
Caveris etc…and James [Spuin?] bailie gave sasine of the same to the
said Janet. Janet asked instrument. Done here on the ground of the
lands around 9 am before James Scot, William Davesone, Archibald
Trumbill and James Hopkirk.

119. *Brydin* 23 November 1535 sir Ninian Brydin showed how the inquest
measured the tenement of Thomas Hendersone (p/t) by 5 feet the
which tenement to his nephew. Witnesses George Michilhill, (illegible).

120. *Michilhill* [12?] Nov [1535] This instrument is very fragmentary.
Reference is made to sir George Michilhill who made a declaration
concerning Alan Mithag, Oliver Dwne and John Murray and his brand-
ing [of their cattle?].

[Reverse of page blank and cancelled.]

121. *Wallance, Johnesone* 27 Jan [1535/6] sir Laurence Johnesone showed
how there was a disagreement [over] a yard between the same lord
and Adam Vallanche but that the said Adam had not been pursued for
his disagreement, injury, menaces or words against the said sir George
and he himself had not been the cause for disagreement and litigation
cordially remitting his rancour and contempt against the said Adam
and conversely the said Adam remitting his rancour and contempt for
sir George amicably (p/t) for consideration in future and that neither
should pursue the other maliciously for the disagreement civilly or
canonically. Adam asked instrument. Done in the house of John Dwne
burgess of Selkirk around 2 pm before William Wod, John Baxstair,
(p/t) Murray and George Wallance.

122. *Scot attorney* James by grace of God king of the Scots to all worthy
men…greetings. We have accepted John Scott or any other attorney or
attornies of my cousin Henry lord Methven in all his negotiations,
deliberations, pleas, [or] quarrels moved and to be moved, touching
the said cousin and on whatever days or places against anyone
whomsoever and we command and order you the said [John Scott] or
any other attorney to be present [whenever] it befalls the said attorney
to receive these presents from me after a year [being] no less valid in
whose [hands] these our letters may be brought to him [and] we make
them patent at Edinburgh 29 [Jan] in the 23rd year of our reign.
[1535/6]

123. *Scot attorney* 31 Jan 1535/6 John Scott attorney of Henry lord of
Methven, came to the places of Galloways schele and Mosele with
pertinents and pendicles thereof lying in the lordship of Ettrick Forest

within the sheriffdom of Selkirk and there presented a precept of
sasine given under the testimony of the great seal to Gilbert Scot bailie
in that part...and requested the bailie to accept the precept. He
passed it to the notary to read out as follows: James by the grace of
God, king of Scots to his sheriff and bailies of Selkirk also to Gilbert
Scott and William Murray bailies in that part, greetings. Because on
the advice of our queen of Scots, liferentrix of the said lands, and our
comptrollers ["compotorum"] of the rolls we give and grant and demit
in heritable feu ferme to our...cousin...Henry of Methven all the lands
of Gallowayschellis and Mosele with [pertinents] and pendicles as is
fully contained in his charter made thereon...and we command you to
give sasine of the said lands to Henry lord of Methven without delay
to be held of us according to the tenor of our charter. Done at
Striveling under the testimony of the great seal 6 Jan 1535/6.

After which the bailie Gilbert [Scott] gave sasine of the said lands to
John Scott attorney of Henry lord of Methven and the said Henry
asked instrument. Done on the ground of the said lands before witnesses sir Thomas Hoppringill, John Harve, William Hiltsone, William
Wonterhop, Robert Patersone.

124. **Ker Johnesone** 10 Feb 1535/6 Marion Johnesone in her own right
according to the tenor of these present instruments acknowledged she
could by no means pay the £4 left mistakenly in the will of her
spouse Nicholas Ker to David Johnesone but can only pay 40 shillings
of the said £4. Nicholas asked instrument. Done around 2 pm in the
house of Nicholas before John Smyth. John Curror and Thomas
Johnesone.

125. **Berkar Hall** 22 Feb 1535/6 John Hall came to his rigs of land lying
over "le Know" within the bounds of Selkirk between the lands of
Patrick Murray on the east, the king's street which leads to the church
of St Helen and to the water on the south [Bridgelands road], the
lands of William Ker on the west and "le Mylsydheucht" on the north
and there on the ground of the same resigned all the rigs in hands of
the James Scott bailie who gave sasine to Thomas Berkar according to
the tenor of a charter made thereon. Thomas asked instrument. Done
on the ground of the same around 4 pm before James Wilkesone and
Robert King.

126. **Brydin Ker** 4 March 1535/6 sir Ninian Brydin on the one part and
Nicholas Ker on the other showed that they came to an agreement
concerning the matters, cases, moveable and immoveable goods,
arrears, damages and expenses between them especially concerning
the disposal of goods of the deceased Marion Johneson concerning
which the said made agreement and quitclaimed and discharged himself...and the same Nicholas acknowledged that he owed sir Ninian
£4 10s to be paid between now and the feast of St Kentigern and

Ninian acknowledged he had received and held the goods of John
Johnesone in the sum of £6. Ninian asked instrument. Done around
(p/t) am before John Mithag, George Smyth, David Johnesone.

127. **Vonterhop Fawsyd** 6 March 1535/6 William Vonterhop came to the
house then inhabited by him lying in the burgh of Selkirk between the
lands of sir William Brydin heir of Robert Brydin on the south and the
lands of William Bennat on the west and north, the lands of John
Ingliss on the east and there on the ground of the same resigned the
house in hands of James Scott bailie who gave sasine to William
Fausyd. William Fausyd asked instrument. Done on the ground of the
said lands around 10 am before sir John Michilhill notary, George
Michilhill and James Johnesone.

128. **Johnesone Scott** 8 March 1535/6 Thomas Johnesone came to a hall
and yard and others pertaining to him by right, which was built by the
deceased master James Johnesone and to a house on the east of the
close between the lands of Simon Fairle on the west and north, the
king's street on the east and the lands of the said Thomas on the
south and west and resigned the hall with yard and pertinents and the
chamber with pertinents in hands of John Mithag bailie who gave
sasine to Janet spouse of the said Thomas in liferent. Janet asked
instrument. Done around 8 am on the ground of the same before sirs
Ninian Brydin, John Michilhill notaries, sir Stephen Vilkesone, James
Doby.

129. **Dwne** 21 March 1535/6 John Dwne showed that he has and had not
any interest, concomitance, resistance or favour with Robert Landreth,
only in claiming his property for debts [owed to] him the said John.
John asked instrument. Done in Selkirk around 3 pm before John
Broune, George Michilhill, Alexander Gledstanis, James Scott bailie.

130. **Sasine of the Burgh [of Selkirk]** 22 March 1535/6 William Chepman
on the part of James Scott and John Mithag bailies received a precept
of sasine which was handed to the notary to read as follows: Sasine of
the burgh of Selkirk 22 March 1535...in the presence of the notary
[note in margin "Ninian Brydin other notary and witnesses came".]
Ninian Brydin, James Scott and John Mithag bailies, John Chepman,
Mark Ker, James Bredfutt, [John] Cruk[schankis], Alexander Gledstanis
burgesses and the whole community of the said burgh and the south
and north commons thereof and there presented a precept of sasine
to the bailie in that part William Chepman...who handed it to the
notary to read out as follows: "James by the Grace of God to his sheriff and bailies in Selkirk and to his bailie William Chepman, greeting.
Since we know that evidents of the charter and old letters of the foundation and infeftment of our burgh and the liberties of the burgesses
of the same bestowed by our noble progenitors through wars,
assaults, plague and fire...have been destroyed whence the trade

between the burgesses has ceased to the detriment of the burgh and community through loss of ferme etc...out of mercy and justice and desiring the foresaid reforms, we infeft anew, give, grant and from us and our successors according to the tenor of our charter confirm forever...to the burgesses and community (p/t) of the burgh of Selkirk in free burgh as before... all lands, commons and possessions pertaining to them, their bailies and necessary officers anually elected on the day of St Laurence (p/t) for eight days yearly and having forever a court house, a gallows and all freedoms pertaining as contained fully in our charter made thereon and we charge you and command you to give to the bailies, burgesses and community of Selkirk or to their lawful attorney sasine of the above our seal appended at St Andrews 4 March [1535/6].

After which, sasine of the above was given. On which James and John bailies, Mark [Ker], John Chepman, John Brown, Alexander Gledstanis burgesses for themselves, other burgesses, the whole community and others living in the said burgh asked instrument...Done at the mercat cross in the said burgh and in the north and the south commons around 2 pm before George Michilhill, John Scott, James Murraye, Thomas Ker, Peter Moffet, John Trumbill, John McDowell, Mungo Crukshankis, Thomas Crukschankis, Thomas Dunghop.

131. *Cranstoun Sheriff Murraye* 29 March 1536 master Thomas Crenstoun second son of the deceased William Crenstoun of that ilk came to the lands and place of Elburne alias Voststeid [of] Langhoup and there presented a precept of sasine under testimony of the great seal to the sheriff in that part Thomas Murraye who gave it to the notary to read out as follows: James by the grace of God king of Scots to his sheriff and bailies of Selkirk also to Thomas and James Murraye my sheriffs in that part greeting. Because with advice of our comptrollers of the rolls, we have given, granted and demitted in feu ferme to master Thomas Cranstoun second son of the deceased William Cranstoun of that ilk all the lands of Elburne alias the Veststeid of Langhoip with pertinents lying in the Ettrick Forest within the sheriffdom of Selkirk extending yearly according to our new rental to £22 which lands were set in feu to the said master Thomas in rental of our noble father for the said sum...shown to us and contained fully in our charter made thereon...and we charge you and command you to give sasine to master Thomas of the said lands with pertinents to be held lawfully from us...given under testimony of the great seal at Streviling on 7 January 1535/6. After which the sheriff gave sasine to the said master Thomas. Master Thomas and Thomas sheriff asked instrument. Done on ground of the said lands around 11 am before sir William Lidderdaill, Ninian Cranstoun and Robert Cranstoun.

The same day master Thomas warned all the inhabitants of the tack of Elburne to remove themselves and their goods from the place and lands of Elburne between this and Whitsunday. On which premonition the said master Thomas asked instrument before witnesses above.

132. **Scott** 6 April 1536 Thomas Scott and (blank) Patersone [came] together to the mercat cross of the burgh of Selkirk and there asked pardon from John Scott regarding the slander on the same Thomas and (blank) Patersone regarding sheep stealing. John asked instrument. Done at the mercat cross around noon before James Scott and John Mithag bailies, William Portuis serjeant, sir William Brydin, Ninian Brydin notary, Mark Ker burgesses.

133. **Ker Trumbill tutor of Holdene** 6 April 1536 it was appointed and irrevocably agreed between Mark Ker on the one part and Robert Trumbill on the other by touching the holy evangel that..."the said Robert Trumbill for him, his ayris, executouris and assignais has resignet and gewin oure al rycht clame properte, interess and possessione that he had, hes or may have at the making of thir presentis belanging and perteining to his tutory of Philhophaucht and holden with the pertinents lyand within the sheriffdom of Selkirk induring the tyme of the said tutory to the said Mark Ker his ayris, executouris and assignais for the behuiff and profett of Johne Trumbill heretour of the samen And alsua the said Robert hes quiteclamit, dischargit and forevermair exonerit and be the tenor of this presentis quiteclames dischairges and for ever exoneris the said Mark Ker his ayris executouris and assignais of xxxii bollis of ferme beir pretenditly askit and requirit be the said Robert and of al uthir thingis that may be mowit be the said Robert or his ayris or assignais in tyme cumming. And atour the said Robert siclik for him, his ayris, executouris and assignais dischairgis for now and ever the said Mark...of all and sundry allegatiounis, obligatiounis, (illegible), instrumentis, contractis, actiounis, debatis, pleus, dettis, restis ald and new or dewties rasit mowit led (illegible) movit askit requirit or maye be requirit be the said Robert...and this done for ane certane sowme of money gewin to the said Robert in his necesite and neid. Alsua in likwis the said Mark Ker hes dischairgit the said Robert of al actiounnis as is above exprimitt and to this effect that the said Mark Ker godwilling sal peciabilly vithout ony impediment molestatioune or exceptione quhatsumever of the said Robert his ayris and assignais sal enter posess and finaly brouk the forsaid tutory of the lands of Philhophaucht and holden with al profettis and dewties thereoff in tyme cumming reserving the witsonday mail of Holdene to nixt to cum efter the dait heirof to the said Robert to gidder with the tend of the said Holdene this instant yeir and na langar and therefter to leiff the said tend with al kind[ness] reserving the stray of the said tend to the said Mark and assignais the entre of the said Mark of the said tutory to be at the dait of the making of this presentis and this to stand ferme and stabell halding

and for to ha[l]d al fraud and gyl excludit and put awaye for ever" on which Mark asked instrument in the chamber of sir John Michilhill notary around 2 pm before James Bradfutt, master Patrick Wrycht notary, Adam (p/t).

A note at the bottom of page includes the names of George Scott and Patrick Murraye.

134. 30 April 1536 George Hog on the part of his spouse Janet Hogekin came to "le ters" of the said Janet being a third part of the lands of Burne Granis [note scribbled between the lines "with Charles Murraye in Lauder..."] with pertinents lying in the sheriffdom of Berwilk and there presented a precept written on paper to the officer in that part Andrew Bonington for authentication...who gave it to the notary to read out as follows: "Janet Hogekine lady of Burne Granis with awiss and consent of George Hog my derest spouse to my lovittis Dand Bonyntoun [blank – for more names?] my serjiandis and officiaris in that part coniunctlie and severally specalie constitut greting my vill is and I charge yow straitlye and command that incontinent this my precept sene ye or ony of yow that beis requirit heirwith pass and in my name and my derest spouse warne Charles Murraye, James Thomsone and al his occupiaris and inhabitatis of my terce and thrid of the landis of Burne Granis with pertinents lyand within the sheriffdom of Berwilk to flit and remove thaim thair servandis and gudis therfra the nixt fest and terme of witsonday and upon fliting frydaye nixt to cum that ye lay furth of thair housis ane stress stule or [chirs?] (p/t) is in streasis and one vitsoun vednesdaye nixt therefter that ye (p/t) thame servandis catal and gudes of my said terce and third of the landis forsaid and hald thaim furtht of the samyn to be peciably broukit and joisit be me and utheris in my name as I pleis in tyme cuming as ye wil anss[er] to me thereupone. The quhilk to do I committ to yow coniunctlye and severalye my full power be this my precept deliverand the samyne for you dewlye executit indorsat agains to the berar in witness of the quhilk thing becauss I nor my said spouss can not write we haiff caussit this notar writing subscrive thir presentis in our name at Halydane the xxii daye of marche the yere of god 1535 yeris befor vitness sir Patrick Craufurd [and] Walter Hog". After which the said Andrew warned James Thomson in his dwelling place and the said Charles personally apprehended in the kirkyard of the burgh of Lauder to flit from "le terss" and third part of the lands of Burne Granis at Whitsunday next after. Andrew asked instrument. Done and sealed on the ground of "le terss" of Burnegranis and in the said kirkyard between the hours of ten and eleven am before William Stewinsone, Andrew Duncane, Charles Gibson, George Murraye, George Vauchoip and John Broderstanis.

135. *Ainslie* April 1536 John Ainslie alleged that all the [common] lying to the east of the burgh of Selkirk extending from "Hilheid Moss" to "le

noltlairburne" pertained to him protesting that the mill of Midlame (illegible). John asked instrument. Done around 2 pm before Mark Ker, David Brydin, John Brown and others.

136. **Michilhill** 23 April 1536 John Michilhill warned Thomas Johnesone to take (illegible) and contained in a certain reversion within this and (illegible) the following witnesses James Helm, John Mithag, George Clerk.

137. **Tudhop Douglace** 27 April 1536 it is appointed and irrevocably agreed between David Tudhope and William Douglas that the said David for his lifetime shall peacefully enjoy and manure sufficient land to yield 18 bolls of oats lying in the bounds of Freirshaw on the east of the place lying in ryndaill paying 2 yearly merks or all the grassums and duties thereto and for his lifetime the said David may lead his oxen and cattle to pasture on the place and meadows of Freirshaw and...the said David should not be in law transgressor on the said place. David asked instrument. Done in the burgh of Selkirk around 11 am before John Scott, William Scott of Kershop and Thomas Henry.

138. **Mithag bailie** 30 April 1536 John Mithag and James Scott bailies of the burgh of Selkirk on the part of the whole community declared...that Patrick Murraye of Fawlohill had come to the common of the said burgh...with a multitude of men in violent oppression with swords, staffs and cudgels and...led away many cattle viz. those belonging to the said bailie and...violated his privilege and freedom [to graze the common] and the said Patrick said it did not turn to the prejudice or loss of the privilege and freedom of the common of the said burgh. The bailies asked instrument. Done at the common before Patrick Murray, George Murray and Andrew Murray.

139. **Murray** On which day Patrick Murray declared that he had not come to the common with many men in contempt of the royal letter and the freedom of the same but with his own servants, tenants and his oxen and cattle not with violent hand or any oppression but only by his ancient right of possession and strength of custom. Witnesses as above.

140. **Ker Murray** 30 April [1536] John Lumisdane and David Brydin...bound themselves, their heirs, executors and assignees to pay James Murraye the sum of £8 between now and the feast of the nativity...at the terms underwritten £3 between now and Tuesday next, 40 shillings at the feast of Peter "ad vincula" [Lammas] next following and £3 at the feast of the nativity next after without any revocation, obstacle or cavil. James asked instrument. Done in the yard of John Crawe around noon before James Bradfutt, William Portuis, Robert Chepman and others.

141. ***Brydin*** Same day. Ninian Brydin procurator for Thomas Johnsone acknowledged the heirship goods contained and inserted in the common book were freely decreed by an inquest to pertain to Thomas Johnsone as his patrimony requiring officers and bailies to arrest these and list the other goods pertaining to Katherine Johnsone the spouse of the deceased Thomas Johnsone which the officers and bailies have now prepared. Ninian asked instrument before witnesses James Keine, John Dwne, (p/t), John Brown.

142. ***Trumbill Craufurd*** 12 May 1536 Robert Trumbill came to his quarter of the lands called Ladylands lying in ryndail within the bounds of Selkirk and there resigned the lands in hands of James Scott bailie who gave sasine in favour of the said James Craufurd. James asked instrument. Done on the ground of the fourth part of the lands around seven am before James Doby, Thomas Forest, David Mynto, Patrick Andersone.

143. ***Mynto*** Same day. Robert Trumbill came to another quarter of his lands called Ladylands and resigned it in hands of the bailie who gave sasine in favour of James Mynto son of the deceased Thomas Mynto. On which day wholly as before.

144. ***Forest*** Same day. Robert Trumbill came to the other half of his lands called Ladylands lying in the north part of the same and there resigned it in hands of the bailie who gave sasine of the same in favour of Thomas Forest. Thomas asked instrument. Done on the ground of the same before the above witnesses.

145. ***Keine Johnesoune*** 24 May 1536 Thomas Johnesoune son and heir of John Johnesoune burgess of Selkirk came to two rigs lying in ryndail over the back of "le Flouris" in the lordship of Selkirk and there resigned the two rigs in hands of John Mithag bailie who gave sasine of the two rigs of land to John Keine. John asked instrument. Done on the ground of the same around 2 pm before Patrick McGrower, William Hall and James Keine.

146. ***Mithag bailie Johnesoune*** 27 May 1536 John Mithag came at the request of Thomas burgess son and heir of the deceased John Johnesoune and his grandfather Thomas Johnesoune to a tenement of James Keine then inhabited by John Thomsoune lying near Fulbrig on the north of the common which leads to the Bog with the tenement of the deceased Thomas Johnesoune on the west and north, the king's street on the east and there the bailie gave sasine and entered Thomas Johnesoune as known heir to John and Thomas in an annualrent of 4 shillings uplifted yearly at two terms from the above tenement by delivery of one penny...Done on the ground of the same at 8 am before William Mithag, Patrick Hesilhop and John Keine.

Same day. Thomas resigned the annualrent to the bailie in favour of James Keine and sasine was given by delivery of one penny.

147. **Ker Murray** 3 June 1536 Patrick Murray of Faulohill came to his husbandland occupied by Alexander Scott with tenement and pertinents in the lordship and sheriffdom of Selkirk lying in ryndaill and then to another husbandland called "le Bogland" with pertinents lying in ryndaill...and there gave sasine of the two husbandlands with tenements pertaining thereto to Mark [Ker]. Mark asked instrument. Done on the ground of the same around [3]pm before master Patrick Wrycht, sir John Michilhill, (p/t), Thomas Hendry, George Michilhill, Adam Murray, James Wilkesoune.

148. **Murraye** Same day. Patrick Murray of Fawlohill produced and caused to be read out a reversion to redeem one husbandland occupied by Thomas Johnsoune for the sum of money contained in the said letter and that the said Thomas Johnesoune was lawfully warned according to the tenor of the said reversion...to receive the said sum and that if the said Thomas his heirs or his assignees did not compear to receive the said sum then Patrick would place the £12 in the safekeeping of James Ker burgess of Selkirk in use and commodity of the said Thomas...protesting it should not turn to the prejudice of the said Patrick and his heir regarding the return of the same. Patrick asked instrument. Done in the parish kirk of Selkirk at around 2 pm before sir John Michilhill, Robert Chepman, Alexander Gledstanis and James Bradfutt.

149. **Ker** 15 June 1536 master George Ker showed how the Royal chamberlain and the steward of Kelso and their factors against the order of law both royal law and the decree of the lords of Council collected and received the Dean's* lambs of Selkirk pertaining to him by virtue of assedation and master George Ker protested that the said collection should not turn to prejudice of the said assedation. Done in the kirk of (p/t) around 10 am before sir Simon Shortreid, George (p/t).

* [i.e. Dean of Christianity]

150. **Berkare** 31 July 1536 John Bellendane came to two rigs of his lands lying over "le Crukit Briglandis" between the lands of William Brydin on the west, the lands of James Murray on the east, the king's street on the south and "le Heucht" and the Water on the north and there the said John resigned the two rigs in hands of the John Mithag bailie in favour of Thomas Berkare and the bailie who gave sasine to the said Thomas...and the said John relieved and granted indemnity to the said Thomas his heirs and assignees against an annualrent on the said lands. Instrument done on the ground of the lands around 4 pm before sir John Michilhill chaplain and notary and James Wilkesoune.

151. *Johnesoune Ker Murraye* 4 August [1536] Thomas Johnsoune resigned the husbandland called "Bogland" with pertinents to Patrick Murraye, his heirs and assignees and quitclaimed all right, claim etc he has or had to the lands. Patrick asked instrument. Done around 8 am before [sir] John Michilhill, James Keine and Robert Chepman.

152. *Wrycht Trumbill* 17 Sept 1536 master Patrick Wrycht chamberlain of the Ettrick Forest presented a letter of tack of Uter[all]burne in hands of Margaret Trumbill on the following condition that if she should provide an account or testimonial note that her father or begetter of the said Margaret held at last [i.e. at his death], the said place of Uterall burne and tenancy, customary kindness and feu of the same from our king or queen he would hold the said letter valid and of lasting strength. Margaret binds herself to be content. Master [Patrick] asked instrument. Done in the chamber of sir John Brydin notary around 2 pm before witnesses John Brown and John Michilhill.

153. *Wrycht Trumbill* On the same day master Patrick Wrycht presented a letter of tack of the place and lands of Uterall burne on this condition that if the account and note underwritten were that the deceased Robert Trumbill father as noted held the said place and lands...in feu [as] asserted [he would] validate the said letter of tack...and otherwise there should not be recovered from the said Margaret (p/t) £10.

154. (p/t) September 1536 sir Simon Shorthreid gave a letter of assedation of master Richard Bothuell to be read and copied of which the tenor is as follows: "maister Richert Boithwell parsoune of askirk grantis me til have sett and for mail lattine and be the tenor haroff settis and for mail lattis ane part of my kirk land of askirk callit the clewis and kempis knowis to ane discrett man my servand schir Simond Shortreid for al the dayis and termis of thre yeris nixt followand the dait of thir presens the entre of the said sir Simont to be at witsondaye nixt following the dait heroff payand to me yeirlye therfor the sowme of twenty shillings usual money. In wytnes of the quhilk thing I have subscrivit this my letter of assedation the 15 day of September the yeir of God 1536 yeris befor vitness schir John Michilhill, schir James Davesone, schir David Brownfeld chapellanis and William Montgomery"... after which sir Simon protested that the letter should be copied and transcribed in form of an instrument. Done in the house of James Scott bailie around 3 pm before sir James Davesone, James Scott, Walter Scott and [Robert] Watsoun.

155. *"Cassatur"* Portuiss Ker* 19 October 1536 Peter Portuis nephew and heir of the deceased Robert Portuis his uncle came to his maltkiln and yard with pertinents lying in the burgh of Selkirk with the lands of David Mynto on the east, the king's street on the south, the lands of Andrew Davidsone on the west and the land of the said Peter on the north...and there on the ground of the same resigned the maltkiln,

yard and pertinents in hands of James Bradfutt bailie who gave sasine
of the same to Mark Ker burgess of Selkirk according to the tenor of a
charter made to him. Also the said Peter bound himself and his heirs
to relieve and pay the said Mark and his heirs the sum of money
given to him and allow the said Mark peaceful possession of the
maltkiln, yard and pertinents and gave as warrandice sasine of his hall
in the close. Mark asked instrument. Done on the ground of the
maltkiln and yard around 11 am before James Wilkesoune, William
Portuiss burgesses and [Robert?] Ker.

* ["Cassatur" indicates that the sasines are broken.]

156. Ker Portuis Cassatur* 10 Nov 1536 Peter Portuis heir as above
came to his hall and barn viz. "le est syd of his cloiss" lying in the said
burgh between the lands as above and there on ground of the same
resigned "le hall and berne" with pertinents viz. "le est syd of the
cloiss" in hands of the James Bradfutt bailie who gave sasine to Mark
Ker with a clause of warrandice in the sum of 6 merks for the said
Mark to enjoy peaceful possession of the maltkiln and yard. Mark
asked instrument. Done on the ground of the lands around 11 am
before James Scott, Thomas Wilkesoune, Adam Ewartt and others.

157. Wrycht 2 Nov 1536 master Patrick Wrycht came to [a cornfield?
"bladum"] yard (p/t) grain and there arrested and escheated and
fenced all the grain within the ward of the [Ettrick] Forest pertaining to
Patrick Murray of Fawlohill by virtue of a precept of lady Margaret,
queen of Scotland shown to me and given as follows (p/t)…then
came to 9 score of ewes and arrested them until the said Patrick paid
the Queen 8 score pounds of money for the sheep and the said
Patrick surrendered to the arrest and to the caution of James Grieff
and gave up the said ewes. Patrick took instrument. Done on ground
of the Ettrick Forest around noon before Oliver Dwne, William Dwne,
John Fergreff.

158. Edmont 24 Jan 1536/7 William Edmont judicially committed in old
age on account of his evil deeds showed how John Edmont was and
is innocent of whatever criminal acts perpetrated by the said William
and has taken no part in them protesting that the slander against the
said John was done by William and should not turn to him or the said
John in slander or prejudice. John asked instrument. Done in the
burgh courthouse around noon before Master Thomas Ker, Gilbert
Bowe, William Murraye sheriff depute, James Bradfutt, George
Michilhill, Adam Scott in Fawsyd.

Same day. James Bradfutt bailie of Selkirk showed how it was alleged
by William Scott in Hartvood [that] the same [William or John?] was
selling stolen skins openly in the market having no suspicion the skins
were stolen…and that the said William Edmont frequented the market
of Selkirk…to sell openly his merchandise without suspicion…and

that it should not turn to him in prejudice and slander. James asked instrument.

159. **Brydine** 25 Jan 1536/7 William Brydine required and asked Thomas Dunhop to receive a measure of malt sufficient to repay a debt to the same Thomas which he by no means wanted to receive. William asked instrument. Done around 8 am before John Cruk and John Lumisdane.

160. **Vilkesoun Todrig** Same 5th (*sic*) day of January it is agreed between sir Stephen Vilkesoun on the one part and David Todrig on the other to complete and contract a marriage between Helen Vilkeson daughter of the said Stephen and the said David between now and the feast of the finding of the Holy Rood [3 May] under pain of a fine of three pounds...and the said David after the marriage contract is sealed will give the said Helen her own tenement providing the said sir Stephen pays David the sum of £10 scots at the terms underwritten viz. £3 between now and Easter Monday ["feria secunda pasche"] next after and the rest within the space of five years. Stephen asked instrument. Done at Selkirk at the house of Marion Caverhill around (illeg?) pm before William Flecher, William Trumbill, William Flecher younger and Simon Flecher.

161. **Anguiss** 30 Jan 1536/7 James Bradfutt bailie, James Scott, George Michilhill, Matthew Vatsoun, Thomas Hery, Peter Moffet, Alexander Gledstanis and John Smail were attested in the lord and showed, declared, clarified and made public according to the tenor of this present instrument, testify in the lord, show, declare, clarify and make public that the deceased William Edmont judicially committed on account of his evil deeds and at the moment of death...apologising piously for his faults and taking care to (illegible) the innocence of others in an authoritative voice and with contrite heart on account of his faults and especially the terrible slander of John Anguiss and attempts to cause his death and humbly asked pardon from God and from the said John absent or present and he asserted and verified the same John is innocent of all theftuous acts perpetrated by the said William protesting that scandal should not fall in prejudice or loss to the said William as John Anguiss was innocent before God and men. John asked instrument. Done at Selkirk around 1 pm before Thomas Gras[on], Alexander Craw, Ninian Moffet.

162. **Keine** Feb 1536/7 William Keine lawful son and heir of the deceased Richard Keine his father and possessor of the underwritten lands by reason of receiving the rents of the same came to those 7 rigs of land and pertinents occupied by John Chepman in tack ["assedaliter"] and also two rigs of land lying in "le dunsdaillis [ly norcht]" occupied by sir Ninian Brydin and his substitutes lying within the sheriffdom of Selkirk in ryndaill and there James Bradfutt bailie of the same

burgh...gave sasine to and entered the said William Keine as true
reckoned ["comptum"] heir and known possessor of the seven rigs of
which one lies "on the forsyd of the layis", another on the west side
of the "reidheid", a third on the east side of "Thurllydane", the fourth
on the east side of "dunsdaillis", and the other three on the east side
of "Kingis Medoss" and two of those rigs in the hands of sir Ninian
Brydin save the right of whomsoever. William asked instrument. Done
on the ground of the same around 10 am before John Chepman and
Simon Farle.

163. **Ker Trumbill** (illegible) Feb 1536/7 the young man John Trumbill
(illegible) of Philop and lord of the lands of Holdene and
Philop[hauch] of lawful age and of his own free will appointed his
uncle Mark Ker in Kippielaw his true and lawful curator in and to all
his lands, annualrents, fermes, moveable and immoveable goods as is
customary in the realm of Scotland whom failing he appoints Andrew
Ker of Aldroxburgh curator of the lands above etc as above. Mark
asked instrument. Done in the kirk of Selkirk around 1 pm before
John Chepman, James Bradfutt, Alexander Gledstanis, (illegible)
Brown and Mathew Watsoun.

164. **Keine** 23 Feb 1536/7 Thomas Mynto procurator in the name of
William Keine came to seven rigs now occupied by John Chepman
burgess of Selkirk, two rigs rented to William Kene son of the
deceased Adam Kene of Had[erlie] and to two rigs occupied by sir
Ninian Brydin and there gave a letter of procuratory under the seal
and subscription of the said William to James Bradfutt bailie who gave
it to the notary to read out as follows: "be it kend I [make etc.]
Thomas Mynto my procuratoris to pas and (illegible) resigne thai
sewin riggis of land with the pertinentis ane lyand on the vest lays
betuex the landis of Andro Ker on the souchtsyd and landis of maister
John Chepman on the norcht syd over the vest part the pot lok sik
[Pot Loch Syke]" one over the east side of "le Thirllydane", the third
on the easter Reidheid, the fourth over "le dunsdaillis bacis" and the
other three...in two "dalis" at the "kingis medos", then came to two
rigs of land lying on the west side of "le dunsdalis" near the river in
hands of sir Ninian Brydin" and there Thomas procurator resigned
them in hands of the James Bradfutt bailie in favour of James Keine
procurator of master Thomas [see no. **167**]. Done around 8 am before
John Hall and William Burne.

165. **Ker** Last day of February 1536/7 William Wod procurator came to
those two rigs of land occupied by Ninian Brydin and his nephew
John Brydin and also those seven rigs of land occupied by John
Chepman lying as above written and there the said William on the
part of Thomas Ker in Yair broke a certain false sasine given to
Thomas Keine by breaking a dish as is the custom. William asked

instrument. Done on the ground of the same around 2 pm before John Hall, James Bradfutt, John Chepman and John Mithag.

166. **Kene** 6 Feb 1536/7 James Bradfutt bailie came at the special command and request of William Keine son and lawful heir of the deceased Richard Keine to nine rigs of land now occupied by the persons underwritten within the bounds of the burgh of Selkirk one lying over the "west lays" between the lands of Andrew Ker on the south, master John Chepman on the north and the "Pot Locht Sik" on the west, another on the east of "Thurlindone burn" between the lands of sir William Chepman chaplain on the east and the said burne on the west, the third over "wester reidheild" between the lands formerly of the Earl of Angus on the west, the lands of master John (p/t) on the east, the fourth over the "dunsdaill baks" extending and leading to "yperlawis pecht" between the lands of the former Earl on the east and the lands of William Portuis on the west and the other three within "Dunledalis" of which one lies on the east side of "kingis medows" between the lands called "Alisonis land" on the east and the lands of the said Andrew on the west..."the battis" on the north and the other "le dail" lying near the "kingis meadow" between the lands of the said Andrew on the west, the lands of the said former earl on the south, "the battis" on the north and "le Brawne Mur" on the south which is now occupied by John Chepman (p/t) on the west part (illegible) near the banks of the river between the lands of the former Earl on the east and the [Ettrick] Water on the north, the said burn on the west which is now occupied by sir Ninian Brydin chaplain and John Brydin his brother's son...and there the said bailie entered the said William as known undoubted heir of the deceased Richard his father in all the said rigs as the custom is by giving sasine one by one of the said rigs with pertinents. William asked instrument. Done on the ground of the lands around 10 am before John Chepman, Simon Fairle and James Keine younger, burgesses of the said burgh.

167. 23 Feb 1536/7 James Bradfutt bailie came to the ground of the above lands and there Thomas Mynto burgess of the said burgh, procurator for the said William by letters under his seal and subscription manual resigned and renounced all right and claim which the said William had or has in and to the said nine rigs and the bailie gave sasine thereof to James Keine procurator for master Thomas [Ker or Keine?] according to the tenor of the charter from the said William to master Thomas. Done on the ground of the same around 8 am before John Hall and William Burne.

168. **Scott** 7 April 1537 Walter Scott in Sintoun showed how Thomas [Scott] procurator for Andrew Ker in Greinheid had warned the said Walter to remove himself, his goods and [servants] from 20 merklands with pendicles in (illegible) with pertinents between now and the feast of Whitsunday next after which 20 merklands as the said Walter alleges

(illegible) to have been known protesting I will deem that the said
Walter violent possessor of the said lands. Done around 1 pm before
Master Thomas Ker, Walter Scott, and Walter Scott.

169. **Scott** 28 April 1537 sir Simon Shortreid chaplain of the diocese of
Glasgow by touching the kirk door, the font, the altar, the chalice, the
books and ornaments of the parish kirk of Rankilburne, invested
Simon Scott clerk of the diocese of Glasgow in the possession...of the
fruits, rents, income ["proventium"], teinds, oblations, obventions and
emoluments of the benefice of rector ["rectorie"] of Rankilburne kirk.
Simon asked instrument. Done in the sanctuary of the said kirk
around noon before Andrew Shortreid, John Wache, David Damhoy,
Walter Scott of Sintoun, John Ingless.

170. **Portuiss** 22 May 1537 Mark Ker of Kippelaw of his own free will...
resigned all right and claim which he has or had to a maltkiln with
[pertinents] also a clause of warrandice on the same from him, his
heirs and assignees in favour of Peter Portuiss, his heirs and assignees
forever. Done in the said burgh of Selkirk around (p/t) before [James]
Portuiss, Thomas Henry[son].

171. **Newtoun** 23 May 1537 viz. Wednesday [after] Whitsunday James
Newtoun officer of Janet Newtoun with the consent of her spouse
Adam Ker in St Hel[en] Schawe came to the place and whole tenandry
of Dalcoiff lying in the sheriffdom of Berwilk and there by virtue of a
precept read out by me [notary] to James Ker of Mersingtoun his servants and friends and (p/t) and tenants of Dalcoiff door by door themselves and their goods and by name were removed and ejected from
the said place, manor, tenandry and town of Dalcoif also the same
James came to Newtoun and Newtoun Cruik with mill and there
removed and ejected [James] Wilkesoun and all tenants door by door
and by name themselves and their goods from the said place and mill
and then came to Cesfurd Mains lying within the shire of Aldroxburgh
and there removed and ejected all the tenants therefrom by virtue of
the same precept. James asked instrument. Done one by one between
9 [am] and 4pm before (p/t) Ker chaplain, William Tait.

172. **Trumbill** (p/t)[May] 1537 Elizabeth Gle[dstanis?] promises to observe
faithfully all the points in a letter of assignation from the said Elizabeth
to Robert Trumbill regarding wards, reliefs and the non-entry of
Philop[hauch] according to the tenor of the said letter without revocation and (p/t) and renounces all right and claim the she has had or
will have in favour of the said Robert. Robert asked instrument. Done
at the dwelling place of the said Elizabeth in Selkirk around 2 pm
before Walter Scott, Mathew Watsoun and [John] Smyth.

173. **Loucht Portuiss** [2]3 May 1537 Peter Portuiss grandson and apparent
heir of the deceased Robert Portuiss came to his maltkiln with yard
and pertinents lying in the north of the burgh (p/t) which leads to the

Lady well between the lands of David Mynto on the east, the lands of
the said Peter on the north, the lands of Andrew [?Ander]soun on the
west, the said street on the south and (p/t) and there resigned the said
maltkiln and yard in hands of James Bradfutt one of the bailies who...
gave sasine of the same in favour of Andrew Loucht forever. Andrew
asked instrument. Done on the ground of the lands around 5 pm
before William Portuiss, sir John Rankin, Patrick De(p/t).

The same day the said Peter came to the barn and "le peithouse" and
the rest of his lands which he had sold and there resigned all the
barn, "peithous" and lands sold in hands of the said James and under
a clause of warrandice of six merks in favour of Andrew Loucht and
the bailie gave sasine of the said barn, "peithous" and lands sold at
that hour lying in the close of the lord of Grenheid next to the
maltkiln in the clause [for] 6 merks to Andrew Loucht. Andrew asked
instrument. Done on the ground of the same with witnesses above.

174. *Cant Mathesoune* 30 May 1537 William Mathesoune came to his tenement and yard lying in the burgh of Selkirk on the south side of the
king's street leading to the Lady well between the lands of the heirs of
James Melross on the east, the tenement of James Caidzo on the west,
the lands of the heirs of Patrick Keine on the south and the said street
on the north and there on the ground of the same freely resigned the
tenement with yard in hands of James Bradfutt bailie who gave sasine
of the same in favour of James Cant his kinsman ["geniti"] for the sustenance of one of the said William's children rendering yearly to
William Lauder of Todrig and his heirs the sum of 14 shillings in name
of annualrent. James Cant asked instrument. Done on the ground of
the tenement and yard around 7 am before Andrew McDowill, William
Portuiss serjeant.

175. *Bradfutt* 21 June 1537 James and Badb (p/t) Scheill conjunctly and
severally of their own free will became cautioners and debtors to
James Bradfutt his heirs and assignees in the sum of £29 [written "xix
decem"] scots and are to pay to the said James and his heirs the said
sum between now and the feast of St Bartholomew next after viz. £8
within 15 [days]...and the rest by the said feast day. James asked
instrument. Done at (p/t) around 1 pm before sir(p/t) Brydin, Patrick
Roull, Patrick McGro[wer], master Patrick Wrycht.

176. *Loucht on the part of Andrew Ker* (p/t) June 1537 Alexander (p/t)
alias Fakland (p/t) and James K(p/t) messenger a certain (p/t) of the
goods (p/t) viz. all "ald and ying" (p/t) Ker of Primsydloucht surveyed
according to the tenor of the royal letter at (p/t) score and £16 usual
money [witnessed by?] the underwritten viz. David Brydin, John
Dwne, (p/t) Chepman, John Hog.

Also...the goods of Katherine Scott in the interest of herself [and] her sister assigned a quantity of goods worth six score and sixteen [pounds?]...[the rest of this entry is illegible].

177. [This entry is very badly torn.]]7 July 1537 Katherine [Scott] in her own interest and in the interest of her sister Janet Scott reasonably (p/t) to Alexander Carmaig (p/t) sufficiently (p/t) from the goods. Katherine asked instrument. Done at the [house] of John Chepman around 4 pm before Walter Scott in Assindane, Walter (p/t), John Donaldsoun, and Adam Scott in (illegible).

178. *Scott* 9 July 1537 Walter Scott in Fau[syd] showed how John Cob messenger and sheriff in that part Alan Hoppringill and Patrick Kn(p/t) according to the tenor of a false decreet obtained by Margaret Hoppringle against the law valued and seized her moveable goods viz. her cows (p/t) and led away the same...the said Margaret alleging...to her loss (illegible)

179. *Brown* (p/t) 1537 Janet Chepman with the consent of her spouse (p/t) Yowng resigned her backchamber with cellar below (p/t) behind and maltkiln (p/t) [in favour of] John Brown (p/t) and apparent heir renouncing all right ownership and possession but reserving to herself the forehouse on "le est syd of the clois" for as long as she lives according to the tenor of her conjunct infeftment paying yearly an annualrent of 5 [shillings]. Done on the ground of the said lands around 5 pm before Thomas Henry, John Chepman, John Scott, (p/t), James Daveson, Bartholomew Mathesoun chaplain and Quintin Yong. With free ish and entry to the fore house.

Same day. She protested that [the above] should not turn to her prejudice with respect to the rest of her conjunct infeftment.

180. *Ker Brydin* William Ker heir of the deceased William Ker burgess in Edinburgh (illegible and torn).

Explanatory Note to Indexes

Two separate indexes have been created. The first covers 'persons and places' and the second deals with 'subjects'.

The references are to instrument numbers not page numbers and all are prefixed by a letter, A, B, C or D. These letters refer to the individual protocol books, i.e.

A   John Chepman 1511–36, 1545–47
B   John Chepman 1536–43
C   John Brydin, Ninian Brydin and others 1526–36
D   John Brydin 1530–37

Therefore an index entry 'A54' refers to the Protocol Book of John Chepman 1511–36, 1545–47, instrument numbered 54.

INDEX OF PERSONS AND PLACES

Appletreehall (Apiltrehall) [NT5217],
B12

Archibald, John, C19

Armstrong (Armistrang, Armstrang),
David, in Elrig, C208
Ninian, C100
Simon, of Whitehaugh C100
William, A5

Arran (Araynne), James, earl of, and
lord of Floors, C18

Arras, John, in Stow, A56

Ashkirk (Askirk, Askyrk) [NT4722],
C138, 143, 258, D1
parish: parson *(named)* of, D154;
rector *(named)* of, A23, 78;
vicars *(named)* of, C18, 22, 32,
181, 245, ?A 24
Scott in, *q.v.*

Ashybank (Eschebank, Esschebank)
[NT5417], B5

Assindane *see* Hassendean

Atkin, William, A36, 38

Atric Water *see* Ettrick Water

Auldroxburgh *see* Old Roxburgh;
Ker of, *q.v.*

Baillie (Bailye), (Master) Bernard,
rector of Lamington, B52

Bain (Bane, Bayne), Elizabeth,
widow of Robert Porteous *q.v.*,
C255; *(same?)* wife of John
Chapman *q.v.*, D69
George, C102

Baird (Bard) James, B13
John, Laird of Posso, A78

Bannatyne (Bannantyn), Andrew, A5
Patrick, C123
William, A6–8, 67

Bard *see* Baird

Barker (Berkar, Berkare), Thomas,
burgess of Selkirk, C288;
(same?) in Selkirk, D117, 125,
150

(Barre) John, B39

Bartonis *alias* Bartius, Barnard of,
A16

Barnet, Alison, in Stow, A56

Bauld *see* Bold

Bawethorn *see* Byethron

Baxter (Baxstair), John D121
William, C297

Beaton (Betoun, Betone),
Andrew, abbot of Melrose, C231
James, archbishop of Glasgow,
A27, 31, 37; archbishop of St.
Andrews, A56, C119

Beil, Barnard, abbot of Melrose, A6
Cf. Bell

Bekinsyd *see* Birkenside

Bell, Andrew, B8
James, C19, C56
Stephen, C209
Thomas, C15
William, in Appletreehall, B12

Bellenden (Bellendane, Bellendayne,
Bellenden), Alexander, dean of
[Melrose] C93–94
John, D40, D150

?Bendochy (Benedothy) [NO2141],
church: vicar pensioner
(named) of, D105

Bennet (Bennat) Adam, A21
Isabella, wife of Robert, C27
sir James, B5, B35
John, C27; tenementar in Selkirk,
C157, 162, 184
Robert, in Selkirk C25, 27; wife of,
see Isabella
William, in Selkirk, C32, 148, 157,
162, D91 94, 127

Berkar, Berkare *see* Barker

Berwick, sheriffdom of, A67, B25,
36, C179

Bessat *see* Bisset

Best, John, in Selkirk, C16, 154,
210–11

Betone, Andrew, Abbot of Melrose,
C231, C252?

Birkenside (Berkinsyd, Birkinsyd,
Byrkkinsyde) [NT5642], A67,
79; lordship, C179

Birne, William, C210

Brigheucht *see* Bridgehaugh;
   Briglandes *see* Bridgelands
Broadfoot (Bradfut, Bredfutt), *(no
   name)*, D104
   Andrew, C76, 247–8, 302
   Christine, widow of Alexander
      Cruikshank and Thomas, her
      heir, C204
   James deceased, C59; heir of, *see*
      sir William *below*
   James, *(another)* B37, C28, 31,
      59–60, 83–85, 135–6, 164, 168,
      225, 264, D12, 14, 16, 78, 91,
      109, 133, 140, 148, 163; *(same)*,
      baillie of Selkirk, D155–6, 158,
      161, 164–5, 167, 173–5; *(same)*,
      burgess of Selkirk, B43, C131,
      213, 226, 270, 289, D21, 47, 82,
      89, 116, 130; wife of *see*
      Haldane, Isabella
   John, in Selkirk, B38, C12, 92, 218
   sir William, A23, 36, 39, 78, B6,
      10, 23, C6, 209, D42, ?A30;
      chaplain at Fairnilee, B23; heir
      of James, deceased, C59
Broadmeadows (Braidmedois)
   [NT4130], B14
Broadstones (Bradostonis,
      Bradstonis, Brodstanis),
      Alexander, C103
   George in Lauder, B51
   John, D134
?Brokess, George, D106
Browis *see* Bruce
Brown (Broun, Broune) *(no name)*,
   D163
   Alexander B38; *(same?)*, C299,
      301
   Alexander, deceased, in Lauder,
      B51
   Archibald, C258
   David in Selkirk, A11, C63;
      (same), deceased, C98, 141,
      186, 204; wife of, *see* Janet; son
      of *see* William
   George, of Coulston, A57
   Janet, wife of David, C141

Janet *(another)* wife of John Ker
   q.v., C45
John, in Lauder, B51
John, in Selkirk, A50, B42, C21,
   152, 204, 224, 279–80, 293,
   D70, 81, 89, 129, 130, 135, 141,
   152–3, 179; *(same)*, burgess of
   Selkirk, C226, 289; formerly in
   Selkirk, C219; wife of, *see* Hall,
   Janet
Richard and Robert, in Stow, A56
Thomas, burgess of Selkirk, D32
William, son of David and Janet,
   C141
Brownfield (Brounfalld, Brounfeld),
   sir David, priest, C119, 129,
   132, D154
Bruce (Browis, Bruss), John, B25
   Robert, sheriff of Selkirk, C19–20
   Thomas, C83
Bryden, Brydin or Brydon (Brydine,
   Brydyn) *(no name)*, D5, 175,
   179
   Alan, burgess of Selkirk, C150;
      son of *see* James younger
   Andrew, C50, 238, 285, D21
   David, deceased, C238, 285
   David, second son of James,
      C186; *(same?)* C7, 16, 53–54,
      198, 211–2, 266, 285, D28, 41,
      80 135, 140, 176; [mother of],
      see Turnbull, Janet
   David *(another?)* son of late John,
      C285
   Elizabeth, *alias* Howden, widow
      of John, C241
   Elizabeth *(same?)*, C287
   James, baillie of Selkirk, C141,
      148, 152, 156–7, 161–2, 164,
      167–9, 173, 175; *(same?)*,
      burgess of Selkirk, C289, 294,
      D47, 74, 89–90, 100; *(same?)*,
      tenementar in Selkirk, C10, 14,
      62, 141, 185–6, 194, 221, 228,
      242–3, 262, 278; brother of, *see*
      John; sons of, *see* David, John;
      ?wife of, *see* Turnbull, Janet

116, 132; brother-german of
   Robert, D127
William *alias* sir William
   (another?), rector or vicar of
   Old Roxburgh, A39, 46, B20;
   C30, 55, D4; resigns vicarage,
   B19
William, son of Robert, C59–60
Buccleuch (Bukcleuch) [NT3214],
   C199; Scott of, *q.v.*
Buckholm (Bukhame) [NT4838],
   C250, 252; Ker of, *q.v.*
Bullerwell, Thomas, D6
Bulliheuch, Bullisheuch [in area
   Selkirk NT4628] mill of, C217,
   225
Bulman, John, A2
Burn or Burns (Boirne, Burne),
   Katherine, C230, D83
   William, in Selkirk, C277
   William *(same?)*, C289, D164, 167
Burnet or Burnett, David, B25
   Marion (Mariota) wife of Thomas
   Minto, *q.v.*, C295
Burngrains (Burne Granis)
   [unidentified, in area Lauder,
   NT5247], D134
Burnton, Thomas, in Elibank, B50
Byethorn (Bawethorn) [in area
   Selkirk, NT4628], C121
Bykertoun, Thomas, A57
Byrkindalyschank [in area NT3020],
   A63–64
Byrkinsyde *see* Birkenside

Caberston (Caberstoun) [NT3737],
   C298
Cadzow (Caidzo, Caidzow), James
   C82, 180–1 214, D54; in
   Selkirk, D174
   John A2, 22, C12, 74; *?alias* John
   of, C262
   Robert, in Davyk, C24
   Robert, in Selkirk, C5
   Robert, in Wylecleucht, A6–7
   William, C180–1

William, burgess of Selkirk, C31,
   60, 226
William, late tutor of Robert, in
   Davyk C24
Cairncross (Carncroce, Carncross),
   George, son of William [in
   Colmslie], B36
John, brother or brother-german
   of *[same]* William B25, 28, 36
William, in Colmslie, B25, 28, 36
William *(same?)*, C106
?Caiyk *see* Crook
Calco *see* Kelso
Calderwood (Calderwod) [NN6455]:
   lady *(named)* of, C101
Cancardine *see* Kincardine
Cant, James, in Selkirk, C82, 168–9,
   226, D174; burgess of Selkirk,
   D84
   John, C249, 251; burgess of
   Selkirk, C302
Carmag, Carmaig, Alexander, C199,
   D177, ?D176; *(same)* royal
   officer, B29–30
Carmichael (Carmichell), Sibella,
   wife of James Pringle *q.v.*, C101
Carncroce, Carncross *see* Cairncross
Carstairs (Carstars), Alexander, A68
Carterhaugh (Carterhaucht [NT4326],
   A59, C262
Castlelaw (Castellawe) [?NT1451],
   D72
Castleton (Castletoun) [NT3358], A50
Catlands, le, in Smailholm [area
   NT6436], C81
Catslack [in area NT3326], D16
   Scott in, *q.v.*
Caufhill [*now* Calfshaw, NT4633], A65
Caverhill (Caverhyll), Margaret, C128
   Marion (Mariota), D160
Cavers (Caveris) [NT5315], C244, B5
   barony D118
   church: vicar *(named)* of, C253
   Douglas of, *q.v.*
Cawfshawis, le, A8
Ce[?]sis, Angelus of, A16
Cessford (Cesfurd) [NT7323], A71

Katherine, widow of William Ker,
q.v. D112, *(same)*, wife of
William Elphinstone *q.v.*, D116
Thomas, C262
Curror, Andrew, B6, 11
Cuthbert, B31, C214, D98
James, B6, 11, C6, 214, 279
John, in Selkirk, C26, 191, 246,
261 281, 297, D30, ?C74; *alias*
burgess of Selkirk, son of late
Walter, C214, 218, D75, ?D124;
wife of, *see* Chapman, Janet
Thomas, in Selkirk, C117, 219,
224, 253, D31; burgess of
Selkirk, C180, 226
Walter, burgess of Selkirk, C74;
deceased, C214; son of, *see*
John
Walter *(another?)*, C97, 125
William, in Selkirk, C266

Dalcove (Dalcoff, Dalcoif, Dalcoiff)
[NT6432]: husbandlands of, B1;
lady [Janet Newton] of, A83,
D67, 171
Dalgleish (Dalglese, Dalglesh,
Dalgless), Adam, C70, D71
David, C179
George, tenant in Stow, A56
James, A47
James, tenant in Stow, A56
Janet, bailie in Peebles, A47
Janet, A25
Mark, priest, C119
Robert, C20
Thomas, *alias* Thome of, B44–46
Thomas, tenant in Stow, A56
Dalkeith, regality: lord *(named)* of,
A47
Dalkeith (Dalkethe; Dalketht)
[NT3367]: document dated at,
A47
Damphoy, David, C280, D169
Danscheill or Davscheill, Robert,
priest, C129 132

Davidson (Daveson, Davison) *(no
name)*, A26
Agnes, widow of Adam Grimslaw,
C115
Andrew in Selkirk, C59, 213, 230
(same?) C71, D18; *(same?)*,
brother-german of Richard,
B47;
son and heir of James, C213
Cristall, A29
Dand, (or Andrew), heir of late
James, C213
Elizabeth, C158; son of, *see* Forret,
Nicholas
George, in Throgdene, B16
George *(another?)*, A79, B6, 11,
23
George, priest, C95
Henry, B6, 11
James, deceased and Andrew (or
Dand) his son, C213
James *(another)*, D179
sir James, D104, 154
John *(?various)*, A41, B6, 23,
C71–72
Katrina, A41
Ralph (Ralf), C147, 179, 201–203,
225; cousin of Agnes *above*,
C115
Richard B47, C158; ?brother-
german of, *see* Andrew above
Thomas, B6, 11, 23
William, in Denholm, D118
William *(another or others)*, A29,
41, B6, B23
Davscheill or Danscheill, Robert,
priest, C129 132
Deephope (Deiphoup), William,
C244, 249, 251
Denholm (Dennum) [NT5618], D118;
Davidson in, *q.v.*
?Dennerles *see* ?Littledeanlees
Dennum *see* Denholm
Dewar, George, in Lauder, B51
Dickson (Dikesone, Dikkesone,
Dykesone), Adam, tenant in
Stow, A56

Walter, at Evart, C187

Walter *(another or others?)*, A48, D41

William, A78–79, *(same?)* C210, 282–3, D145

William *(another)*, burgess of Edinburgh, brother-german of John, C282–3

Hawick (Hawyk) [NT5014], burgh and lordship, C170

church: alleged rector of C172; vicars *(named)* of, B12, C232, D6, 9

tenement in, D42

Hawickshiel Burn (Hawik Scheilburn) [in area NT5542], A79

Hawthorn (Hairtherne, Hartherne) [NT4033], B9, C20; royal shepherd in, B29

Hay, Agnes, wife of William Stewart of Traquair, B32

Master George, of Yester, A72

John, Lord Hay of Yester, A11

John, A16

Hayte, John, C86; *cf.* Hastie

Headshaw (Edschaw, Edschawe) [NT4622], B38, C100, 138, 143, D20, 98

Scott of *or* in, *q.v.*

Heatherlie (Haderlie, Hadirle) [NT4628]: lordship, C118, 124, 136, D164

Hebburn *see* Hepburn

Heip *or* Heap [NT4915]; lordship, D73

Heisloip *see* Hislop

Helburinsfurd [*unidentified*, in area NT5343], A79

Helm (Helme), Christina, D92

George, son of James, and James and Paul, his brothers, D84; *(same?)*, D26

James, C10–12, 23, 36, 74, 176–7, 214, 218, D14, 16, 25, 46, 84, 106, 136; *(same)*, burgess of Selkirk, C35; *(same?)*, cousin of

George Turnbull, *q.v.*, D44; *(same?)*, smith, D84; sons of, *see* George, James, Paul; wife of, *see* Curle, Janet

James, son of James, D84

John, D30, 61

Paul, son of James, D84

Helmoss [*unidentified*, in area NT5242], A79

Henderson (Hendersone, Hendisone) Alison, wife of Nicholas, C150

Katherine, wife of Thomas, C230

Nicholas A2, *(same?)* C150; wife of *see* Alison

Stephen, C115, 147

Thomas, burgess of Selkirk, A32, C230, *(same?)* D83; wife of, *see* Katherine

William, B47; baillie of Roxburgh, C71–72, 81, 259

Cf. Henryson

Henry or Hendry, Thomas, B53, D112, 137, 179

Henryson (Henresone), Thomas, in Selkirk, A32; (?) D170

Cf. Henderson

Hepburn (Hebburn), Master John, alleged rector of Hawick, C172

Patrick, Master of Hailes, and Patrick his son, A60

Herdmanston (Hermenstoun, Hirdinestoun) [NT4769], C291

Heriot (Hereot, Herrot), Archibald, messenger, D66

David, B51

Thomas, C260

Hervy *see* Harvey

Hery [Henry?], Thomas, D161

Hesilhop, Hesloip *see* Hislop

'Hie Cross' [*unidentified*, in area NT5343], boundary cross, A79

Hill, sir Robert, A27

Hilson (Hiltsone, Hyltsone), Alexander, in Stow, A56

sir Peter, notary, A73

Thomas, B39

Bartholomew, C89
David, of Wedderburn, D99; son
    of *see* George; widow of, *see*
    Douglas, Alison
George, of Wedderburn, B2; son
    of Alison Douglas, D99–101
sir John, notary, C14
John, of Cowdenknowes, C113,
    139
John, of Hutton, C122; heir of *see*
    Alexander
John, baillie of the priory of
    Eccles, C119
Margaret, wife of James Murray,
    q.v., C65, 70
Marion (Mariota), wife of George
    Ker, *q.v.*, A60
Richard, C303
Robert, in Eccles, A83
Hundalee [NT6418], A29
Hundilsishop, D48
Hunter (Hountar, Huntar), Edward,
    A47
Elizabeth, widow of Thomas of
    ?Williamslee, A6–7; heirs and
    son of, *see* James, Robert,
    William
George, C128
James, heir of Elizabeth, A6
Janet, *alias* Lady Janet, nun,
    claimant to the priory of Eccles,
    C119, 129, 132, 140
Janet, widow of Thomas Turnbull,
    C14
John, A54
John, deceased, brother of Robert,
    D108
Margaret, widow of Robert Ker,
    q.v., C106
Robert, and the late John, his
    brother, D108
Robert *(another)*, son of
    Elizabeth, A6
Thomas A47; in Halkburn, A82;
    (same?), C232
Thomas, deceased, husband of
    Elizabeth, A6–7

William (Voll) crofter, C86
William, heir of Elizabth, A6
Hunthill (Honthill) [NT6619], A65,
    D99, 101
Rutherford, of, *q.v.*
Huntlywood (Hontlie Wod)
    [NT6143], C158
Hutlerburn (Uterall Burn)[NT 4123],
    D152–3
Hutton (Huten) [NT9053], C122;
    Hume of, *q.v.*
Hylston, Hyltsone *see* Hilson
Hyndelaw, Hyndlaw [*unidentified*,
    in area NT7726], B4, 40

Inglis (Ingless, Ingliss), Christina,
    C109, D4; husband of *see*
    Geddes, Thomas
John, D127,169
William, in Stow, A56

Jack (Jak) Isabel, crofter, C86
John, A37
John *(another)*, D105
Jackson (Jaksone), James, C249
Robert, C244
Robert *(same?)*, miller, C291
Thomas, C249, 251
William, of *or* in Rutherford, C244,
    249, 251
William, younger, *(another?)*,
    tenant in Rutherford, C244, 249
William, priest, C129
Jak *see* Jack
James IV, king of Scotland, A10;
    death of, C83, 85
James V, king of Scotland, B48,
    C119, 140 D131
charter by, confirming liberties of
    Selkirk, C264–5, 271–3, 275,
    D33, 104, 130, 139
grant of Galashiels by, D123
majority of, B9
James [?]myddall [*unidentified*], D71

William, A68, B2
William *(same?)*, D95
Jolly (Joly), William, in Lauder, B51

Kean *see* Kene
Keir [NS7698], B25, 28, 36; Stirling
    of, *q.v.*
Keir, James, C225
    See also Ker
Kelso (Calco) [NT7233], abbey, C51,
    59
    abbot and convent of, B8, C124,
        D149
    altar of St. Katherine in, C116, and
        of St Salvator C31, 59
    factor of, B17
    Miller's Acres of, C124
Kelso (Calco) [NT7234], burgh:
    baillies of, A70
    church [of St. Mary] in, A46, 70
Kene (Kean, Keine, Keyn, Keyne,
    Keynem) Adam, deceased, of
    Heatherlie, D164; son of, *see*
    William
    Alan, burgess of Selkirk, A33, C57,
        91–92, 118, 136, 154, 157, 230,
        277, 285, D3; sergeant of
        Selkirk, C98–99, 167, D17;
        brother-german of, *see* John
    Andrew, C13–14
    ?sir Andrew, C21
    Elizabeth, widow of Patrick, C293
    Helen, in Selkirk, C266
    James, uncle of John Haw, *q.v.*,
        C178
    James, younger *(another?)*, C178;
        (same?), baillie of Selkirk,
        C241–2, 244, 262, 264–5, 267,
        269, 280, 298, D31, 65, 80, 82,
        86, 88, 90, 97, 100, 104, 141,
        151, 164, 167, ?D176; *(same?)*
        burgess of Selkirk, C282–3, 286,
        287, 300, D63, 68, 145–6, 148,
        166; resident in Selkirk, C210,
        222, 294, D3, 10; ?son of the

late William, C278; *(same?)*
    C21, 31, 41, 109, ?C91
John, A28,C267, 282, 286, D145–6;
    son of Patrick, C283
John *(another)*, deceased, burgess
    of Selkirk, C110, D5,
sir John, A78, C109; *(same?)*,
    chaplain in Glasgow, C91;
    brother-german of, *see* Alan
Patrick, C278
Patrick *(another)*, deceased, C283,
    293, D52–53, 174; son of, *see*
    John; widow of, *see* Elizabeth
Peter, in Selkirk, deceased, D112
Richard, deceased, father of
    William, D162, 166
Robert, A31
Thomas, *alias* master Thomas,
    notary, B52, C260, ?D165
William, elder, in Selkirk, C182;
    (same?) late burgess, C278,
    285, D16, 88, 164; *(same?)* C88,
    117; son of, *see* James
William, younger, C182, ?C255;
    burgess of Selkirk, D19
William *(same?)*, son of late
    Richard, D162, 166
William *(another)*, son of late
    Adam, of Heatherlie, D164
Ker or Kerr, *(no name)*, A16, B4, C4,
    64, D179; chaplain, D171
Adam, of Shaw *alias* of St.
    Helen's Shaw, A83, C37, 53–54,
    87, 127, 150, 216, 221, 228,
    233, 266; son of William, of
    Shaw, C78, 121, 148, 194–6,
    D41, 67, 171; ?husband of Janet
    Newton, D67 171; *(same?)*,
    C159
Adam, clerk, C216
Adam, younger, C228
Andrew, of Cessford, A5, 49;
    deceased, A58; son of, *see*
    Walter: wife of, *see* Cranstoun,
    Ann
Andrew, of Fairnilee, A29,
    ?A36–37

Moush, Mouss, Moussee *see* Moyes
  or Mouncey; *cf.* Morris
Mowat, George, sheriff-depute of
  Selkirk, John, and Thomas, B48
Moyes or Mouncey (Monse, Moush,
  Mouss, Mousse), Helen, heir of
  John, C53; *(same)*, C7
  James, C178, 262; *(same)*, burgess
    of Selkirk, C41
  John, B38; *(same?)* burgess of
    Selkirk, deceased, C3, 7, 36,
    53–54 ; heir of *see* Helen,
    Marion
  Marion (Mariota), heir of John,
    C54, *(same)*, C3, 7
  Cf. Morris
Mude, Mudy *see* Moodie
Muir (Mor, Mur), John, A21
  Marion [*?alias* Margaret or 'Mege'],
    sister of Robert Howden, *q.v.*
    and executor of Alexander
    Howden *q.v.*, C220
  William, messenger, D66
  Cf. Mar
Muircleuch (Morcleucht, Murcleucht)
  [NT5145], B25, 28; Pringle in,
  q.v.
Muirhouse (Murhouse) [NT4644],
  B55–56
Murray (Murraye), *(no names)*,
  D121; [?Patrick], C109
  Adam, C286, 298, D147
  Alexander (Sanders), D66
  Andrew, D138
  Charles, A73
  Charles, *(another?)*, in Lauder,
    B51, D134
  Christina, wife of late Thomas, of
    Bowhill, B8
  David, A61
  Elizabeth, C171
  George, in Howden, C227
  George *(another)*, D134, ?D138
  George *(same?)*, B25, 28, C286,
    ?C298; *(same?)*, and Janet
    Roger, his wife, D106
  Helena, in Stow, A56

Isabel (Ysabella), daughter of
  James, of Bowhill, C83–85;
  uncle of, *see* Scott, Master
  Michael
Isabel, wife of Alexander Elliot,
  cousin, of Master Michael Scott,
  D45
Isabel, wife of Philip Scott in
  Headshaw, D20; stepmother of
  Walter Scot in Headshaw, D98
James, of Bowhill, C83, 85;
  daughter of, *see* Isabel
James of Falahill, C17, 65, 70;
  father of Patrick, C286; wife of,
  see Hume, Margaret
James, of Philiphaugh, sheriff of
  Selkirk, C9, 34–35, 55, 57, ?D
  131
James A22; *(same?)*, A63, 64
James, *(another)*, A63
James, brother of Patrick, C286
James, in Selkirk, C73–74, 92, 107,
  227, D92, 107, 112, 130, 140,
  ?D131
James, second son of Roger, C117,
  D31–32, 46
John, of Falahill [Bold and
  Philiphaugh], A10
John, in Howden, C227
John, of Kershope, C197
John, of Lewinshope, C9
John, in Stow, A56
John, D120
John, cousin of Patrick, D22
Patrick, of Falahill, A59, 61–64,
  C102, 110, 112, 118, 121,124,
  126, 136, 148, 187–8, 285–6,
  298, D22, 48, 56–58, 66, 74,
  90–91, 112, 114, 117, 125, 133,
  138–9, 147–8, 151, 157; *(same)*,
  C182, 214, 223–4, 228, 238,
  240, 255–7, 278, 283, 288,
  ?D100; lands of, in Selkirk,
  C121; sheriff of Selkirk, B43,
  C242–3, D5, 16, 76–77, 85, 99,
  discharge of, attempted, D6–8,
  71; son of James, C286; brother

James, of *or* in Tinnis, D6–7;
  brother-german of Master
  Robert, C89 250; son of, *see*
  James, wife *(named)* of, C101
James, of Whitebank, A80
James , son of David, C44, 89, 95
James, son of James, of Tinnis,
  C250, 252
James, son of John, of Blindlee,
  B34
James, C66–68
James *(another?)*, D20
Janet, daughter of David, A57,
  C89
Janet *(another)*, A26
John, of Blindlee, deceased, B33;
  sons of *see* James, John, Robert;
  wife of, *see* Spottiswood,
  Elizabeth
John, of Galashiels, A35; *(same?)*,
  A47, 55; ?son of David, A65;
  [?*alias* John of Smailholm, John
  son of David], *see these entries*
John, in New Hall, B2
John, of Smailholm, [?*alias* of
  Galashiels], A80, 82, B51–52;
  wife of, *see* Gordon, Margaret;
  cf. John , son of David
John, in Tinnis, C93
John, in Torsonce, B56
John, brother of George, of
  Torwoodlee, B2
John, son of David, C44, 89 95;
  [?*alias* John, of Galashiels or of
  Smailholm] *see those entries*
John, son of John, of Blindlee and
  Elizabeth his wife, B33–34;
  brothers of, *see* James and
  Robert
Margaret, daughter of David, A57,
  C89
Margaret *(same?)*, D178
Marion (Mairyone, Mariota), lady
  of Greenhead, B47; mother of
  Gilbert Ker of Primside Loch
  D67; wife of Andrew Ker of
  Greenhead, C77

Robert, of Blindlee, brother-
  german of Adam, B25; brothers
  of, *see* James, John; son of John
  and Elizabeth, B33; son of, *see*
  Adam
Robert, in Muircleuch, B25, 28
Robert, in New Hall, C20, ?D7
Robert, in Stow, A56
Robert, father of Alexander, B29
Master Robert, rector of Morham,
  A82, C89, 93 ?C95; brother-
  german of, *see* James
Robert *(another)*, C95
Roger, A8
Thomas, in Torwoodlee, A8
sir Thomas, A56, 65–66, 73,
  (same) D123; chaplain, A57
Walter, of Blindlee, A80
William, of Tofts, A35
William, in Lauder, B51
William in Stow, A56
William, rector of Morham, B52
William, A8
William *(same?)*, A8, 23, 27, 30,
  42, 82, B51–52, ?C16
Purdie (Purde), Thomas, D11
Purves or Purvis (Purvess), George,
  A75
  John, C260
  Kentigern, A79
  Master Robert, curate of
    Aldroxburgh, A38
  William, B25
Purveshill [?Purves Hall, NT7644],
  grant of, C260

Quhit *see* White
Quhitlawislandis [NT 5130, now
  Whitlaw], A10
Quhitmurha *see* Whitmuir
Quhitslaide *see* Whitslaid
?Q...utshill, ?*alias* Calfhill [now
  Calfshaw, NT4633], A65
Quhithaughbra [*now* Whitehillbrae,
  in area NT 4024], B31

John, in West Mains of Lilliesleaf, C62

John, baillie of Selkirk, C78, 88

John, burgess of Selkirk, D25–27, *(same?)* D90, 115, 130, 132, 137, 179; *alias* John in Peelgate, C59, 64, 245; deceased, C279; son of, *see* Walter; wife of, *see* Margaret

John, burgess of Selkirk *(another)*, C88; deceased, D36; widow of, *see* Chapman, Elizabeth

John, in Hawick, C235–6; daughter of, *see* Janet

John, in Selkirk, C161, 180, 215, 218, ?C189; deceased, C228; wife? of, *see* Porteous, Elizabeth

John, C278, 286

John, royal attorney, D122–3

John, sergeant of Selkirk, C121, 146, D33; *(same?)*, C232, 278

John, *alias* sir John, vicar of Hawick, B12, C232, 236–7, D6–7, *(same?)* C14, 113, 139; his brothers, D9

John, C148, 215, 257

John *(another or others?)*, C6, 14, 22, 33, 69, C78, 97, 235, 238, 259, D48

Katherine, D176–7; sister of, *see* Janet

Margaret, wife of John, C245, D25–26

Master Michael, of *or* in Oakwood, C18, 83–85, 103, 106, 133, 193, 227, 291, 303, D16, D33–35, 57; *alias* Master Michael, in Bowhill, B31; brother-german of Isabel Murray *q.v.*, D45; son of, *see* William

Michael *(another?)*, C8

Philip, in Dryhope, C197

Philip, in Headshaw, C100, 138, 143, D20; son of, *see* Robert; wife of, *see* Murray, Isabel

Robert, in [Blindhaugh], D102–3

Robert, in Haining, C54; son of, *see* Thomas

Robert, in Headshaw, son of Philip, C138; *(same?)*, brother-german of Walter, of Headshaw, B38

Robert, in Howford, D102–3

Robert, of Howpasley, C28, 197, D66, ?B12; *alias* tutor of Howpasley, C165–6; lord of Birkenside, C179

Robert, deceased, burgess of Edinburgh, D32

Robert, in Selkirk, D68; ?*alias* Robert in Kirk Wynd, D107

Robert, nephew of William, of Ormiston, C138

Robert, C197; *(same?)*, C172

Robert *(another?)*, A67

?Robert C57, 92; heir of, *see* Elizabeth

Rolland, B12

Simon, B12

Simon *(another?)*, rector of Rankleburn, D169

Stephen, D34

Thomas, in Oakwood [or Oakwood Easter], C83–85, D51

Thomas in Woodburn, C291

Thomas, baillie of Hawick, C235–7

Thomas, in Selkirk, D132; *(same?)*, D168

Thomas, son of Alexander, D91

Thomas, son of Robert, C54; *(same?)*, C56, 96; ?*alias* Thomas, younger, C105

Thomas *(another)*, A17–18

Walter, of *or* in Ashkirk, C138, 143, 171, 174, C280, D98, ?D154

Sir Walter (of Buccleuch), *alias* of Branxholme, C18, 32, 113–4, 139, 172, 199, D6–7, 21

Walter, [?in Denholm], deceased, D118; widow of, *see* Janet

Scott in or of, *q.v*

Synton (Syntoun), James, royal
    shepherd, B29

Tailor (Tailyer, Tailyr), *(no name)*,
    A56
    ?David, in Stow, A56
    Thomas, A13, D68
Tailyefore *see* Telfer
    Cf. Tailor
Tait, Alexander, of the Pirn, A10,
    50–51, D7, 9; wife of, *see*
    Rutherford, Katherine
    Alexander *(another?)*, and
        Isabella, his daughter, B13
    Andrew, A35
    Anthony, A51
    Elizabeth, in Tait's Hill, C54
    George, of ?Canterus, B24
    George, in the Pirn, D73
    George, B1
    Isabella, daughter of Alexander,
        B13
    James, A53, 68, B39, C215
    James *(another)*, in Stow, A56
    John, B51
    Marion (Mariota), in Stow, A56
    Robert, A56, B51–52, C77, 147
    Roger, A36
    Simon, B29
    Thomas, B25, 28
    William, in Stow, A56
    William *(another or others)*, A27,
        42–3, 55, 61–62 B15, 19, 32,
        D27, 171
Tait's (Taitts) Croft, C7
Tait's Hill (le Taittis Hyll) [now in
    Selkirk], C54, 148
Telfer (Tailyefere), James, C291
Tennis *see* Tinnis
Teemside (Teemsid), Robert, B4
Teviot, river, C170
Teviotdale, archdeaconry, A13–20,
    25–28, 30–31, 39, 43
    books of, B12, 20
    official of, C95

Teviotdale, commissary, B12
Teviotdale (Tevidale), sheriffdom,
    C147
Thankerton (Thankertoun) [NS9738],
    parish: rector of, A31
Thin (Thyn, Thynn), Archibald, *alias*
    Arche, B49–50
Thirbrand or Thorbrand, James,
    C124
    Robert, in Stow, A56
Thirlstane [NT2813], D94; Scott in,
    q.v.
Thomson (Thomsone), Charles and
    David, in Stow, A56
    James, in Burngrains, D134
    James, in Stow, A56
    James *(another)* in Stow, A56
    John, C136, 178, 262, 278
    John *(another)*, ?gardener, B36, 41
    Patrick, priest, C129, 132
    Robert, in Selkirk, C52, 182–3,
        210, 299; *(same?)*, baillie of
        Selkirk, C8
    Patrick, priest, C129, 132
    Robert, in Selkirk, C52, 182–3,
        210, 299; *(same?)*, baillie of
        Selkirk, C8; *(same?)*, uncle of
        John Acheson, *q.v.*, C187
    William, in Stow, A56
    William *(another or others)*, B7,
        30, C101, C300
Thorbrand *see* Thirbrand
Threepwood Shaw
    (Threpwodschaw) [NT5142],
    A79
Throgdane *see* Frogden
Thyn, Thynn *see* Thin
Tinnis (Tennes, Tennis, Tynnis)
    [NT3829], C9, 89, 93, 101, 250
    Pringle of, Turnbull of, *q.v.*
Todrick (Toddryk, Todryg, Todryk),
    David, B38, 42, C69, 218, 245,
    D160; *(same?)*, son of Robert,
    C64
    Robert, in Selkirk, C23, 75, 191,
    218, D25–27; burgess of

Mark, C135

Ralph, lord of Philiphaugh, deceased, D109–10; son of, *see* John

Ralph, of Tinnis, deceased, and Margaret Ker, his widow, C9

Ralph, C276

Robert, of Philiphaugh, C34, 103; *(same?)*, C13–14, 31, 75, 105, 161, D12; *(same?)*, of *or* in Howden, C34, 60, 80, 137, 227; *(same?)*, superior of Ladylands, C188; *(same?)*, tutor of Philiphaugh, C135, D16, 13, 36, D133, ?D109–11, ?D172; cousin of, *see* James; ?grandson of, *see* John

Robert, burgess of Selkirk, D37, 142–4, ?D105; *(same?)*, C276, D28; *(same?)* deceased, father of Margaret, D152–3

Thomas in Coldingham, deceased, C14, widow of, *see* Hunter, Janet

Thomas, of *or* in Rawflat, C20, 203

Thomas *(another)*, C12

Walter, of Minto, A35

William, of Minto, C147, 201–3, 280; son of *see* William

William, A22, C34, 39, 61, 69, 78, 107, 109, 123, 152, 164, 179, 194, 215; ?*alias* William, elder, C201, 276; *(same?)*, D160

William, son of William, of Minto, C147

Turner (Turnnor, Turnor), George, C250

James, B47

Janet (Joneta), in Stow, A56

Tushilaw (Tussilaw) [NT3018], D48 Scott, William in, *q.v.*

Tweed, river, C262

Tynnes *see* Tinnis

Uterall Burne [*now* Hutlerburn NT4123], D152–3

Vache, Vaiche *see* Veitch

Valestoun *see* Walston

Vallance (Vallanch, Vallanche, Wallance), Adam, A75, D121

George, B8, D121

John, A43

Thomas, C297

Vatsone *see* Watson

Vauch *see* Wauch; Vauchoip *see* Wauchope

Vedderburne *see* Wedderburn

Veighame *see* Wighame

Veitch (Vache, Vaiche, Veych), Adam, B26; *(same?)*, C65, 70

George, A21; *(same?)*, deceased, C143, 145; son of, *see* Walter

James, A63

John, of North Synton, C280

John *(another)*, A64; *(same?)*, B4, C142, 144–5

Thomas, C142, 249, 251

Walter, C142; son of late George, C143, 145

William, A63–64; *(same?)*, B24, C27, 142, 144–6

William, in Yair, *(same?)* A146

Vic, John, C99

Vilkeson, Vilkesoun *see* Wilkinson

Vine (Vins), John, sergeant or sheriff of Selkirk, C19–20

Vinterhop *see* Winterhope

Vod, Vods *see* Wood

Vodburne *see* Woodburn

Volson, Vollson *see* Wilson

?Vores [?Forest], Philip, C81

Vrycht *see* Wright

Vychtman *see* Wightman

Vylkesone *see* Wilkinson

Vylsone *see* Wilson

Vythman *see* Wightman

Alison, in Selkirk, C63

Elizabeth, C128

Helen (Elena), daughter of sir
    Stephen, D160

James, in Newton, D171

James, in Selkirk, C197, 204, 231,
    238–9, 240, 247–8, 261, 288,
    D11, 79, 117, 125, 147, 150;
    burgess of Selkirk, D155

Marion (Mariota), wife of George
    Michelhill, *q.v.*, C184

Patrick, C12

Stephen, *alias* sir Stephen, chap-
    lain, C42, 49, 128, 262, 286,
    D51, 128, 160; daughter of, *see*
    Helen

Thomas, A33, C289, D 90,156

Wilkynshaugh [*unidentified*, in area
    NT5543], A79

Willebush [*unidentified* in area
    NT5342], A79

William, *alias* Brother William, C297

Williamhope [NT4133], B29–30

?Williamslee (Wilyemlaw) [NT2522],
    A6, Hunter of, *q.v.*

Williamson (Williamsone), Master
    John, chaplain of Melrose, D18,
    88

Wilson (Vilson, Vollson, Vylsone,
    Wolsone), Adam, C264

  Alexander, C299

  Andrew, *alias* Dand, crofter, C86

  Helen, C86

  James, B6, 11

  Janet [*recte* Janet Smith or Mithag],
    C261

  John, in Soundhope, son of
    Thomas, C208

  John, neighbour to Scott of
    Howpasley, *q.v.* C28

  John [in Selkirk], C86, 98, 244, 264

  Robert, D22

  Simon, B6, 11

  Thomas, A49; *(same?)*, deceased,
    father of John, C208

  William, in Galashiels, C15;
    (same?), C264, 270–4

William (Voll), crofter, C86

Wilyemlaw *see* ?Williamslee

Winter (Wynter), Gilbert, A67

Winthrope (Vinterhoup, Vonterhop,
    Vynterhoup, Winterhoup,
    Wonterhope, Wynterhope),
    Andrew, in Selkirk, C25;
    deceased, C164, 185; nephew
    [or son] and heir of, *see* William

  George, in Selkirk, C164

  Henry, A67

  Marion, wife of William, D29

  Thomas, C291

  William, heir and [son?] of
    Andrew, C25, 27, 164, 185;
    (same?), *alias* William, in
    Selkirk, C19, 157, 164, 170, 185,
    246, 264, 270–4, D29, 123, 127

?Wise (?Vise, Vy[s]), James, C112

  John, D88

Wod, Wods *see* Wood

Woll (Well) [NT4621], D16; Scott of,
    q.v.

Wolson *see* Wilson

Wood (Vod, Vods, Wod), Janet
    (Joneta), C153

  John, in Selkirk, C19, 69, 78, 148,
    152–3, D6

  John *(another)*, B52

  Patrick, A38

  Thomas, C19

  William, of Hawthorn, C20

  William, A36, 76; *(same?)*, B44–6,
    C124, 244

  William, younger, *alias* 'yonge
    Voll of', A72, 75, C262; *(same?)*,
    D97, 121, 165

  William, elder, A72

  William, *(another)*, A36

Woodburn (Vodburne) [in Selkirk],
    C291

  Scott in, *q.v.*

Woodhead (Wodheid), Lauder, C81

Woucerhop *see* Wauchope

Wright (Vrycht, Wrycht, Wryth),
    John, C261

INDEX OF SUBJECTS

References are to the protocol book and instrument number as explained in the Index of Persons and Places.

Most subjects have been arranged in groups. The main groups are: Agriculture, Buildings, Clergy and Religious, Cloth and Clothing, Crops and Grains, Goods and Merchandise, Household Articles, Legal Subjects, Livestock and Animals, Occupations and Trades, Offences and Penalties and Officials and Servants.

THE STAIR SOCIETY

*Instituted in 1934 to encourage the study and
advance the knowledge of the History of Scots Law*

OFFICE-BEARERS 1993

President: PROFESSOR GORDON DONALDSON, C.B.E., MEDAL OF ST. OLAV, M.A., PH.D., D.LITT., HON.D.LITT., F.B.A., F.R.S.E.

Vice-President: THE RT. HON. LORD HOPE, P.C., B.A., LL.B., LL.D.

Chairman of Council: SHERIFF PETER G. B. McNEILL, Q.C., M.A., LL.B., PH.D.

Vice-Chairman: W. DAVID H. SELLAR, B.A., LL.B.

Council: FRANCES SHAW, M.A., PH.D.; PROFESSOR JOHN W. G. BLACKIE, B.A., LL.B.; SHERIFF IAN D. MACPHAIL, Q.C., M.A., LL.B., LL.D.; ATHOL L. MURRAY, M.A., LL.B., PH.D., F.R.HIST.S.; D. ROSS MACDONALD, B.A., LL.B.; JAMES D. CAMPBELL, LL.B; HECTOR L. MacQUEEN, LL.B., PH.D.; WILLIAM G. SIMMONS, LL.B., W.S.; SHERIFF DAVID B. SMITH, M.A., LL.B., F.S.A.SCOT.; PROFESSOR GEOFFREY D. MacCORMACK, B.A., M.A., LL.B., D.PHIL.

Literary Director: PROFESSOR WILLIAM M. GORDON, M.A., LL.B., PH.D.

Secretary and Treasurer: IVOR R. GUILD, C.B.E., W.S., 16 Charlotte Square, Edinburgh EH2 4YS

Auditor: J. MARTIN HALDANE, C.A.

Secretary for the U.S.A.: PROFESSOR W. ALAN J. WATSON, M.A., LL.B., D.PHIL., The Law School, University of Georgia

Secretary for Japan: PROFESSOR TAKESHI TSUNODA

267

CONSTITUTION

1. The Society shall be called 'The Stair Society'.

2. The object of the Society shall be to encourage the study and advance the knowledge of the history of Scots Law especially by the publication of original documents, and by the reprinting and editing of works of sufficient rarity or importance.

3. Membership of the Society shall be constituted by payment of the annual subscription, and shall cease if this be in arrear for one year.

4. The amount of the annual subscriptions shall be fixed by the Council from time to time, and shall be payable in advance on 1st January in each year.

5. The management of the affairs and funds of the society shall be vested in a Council consisting of the President, Vice-President, a Chairman, a Vice-Chairman and not more than ten ordinary elected members.

6. The President, Vice-President, Chairman and Vice-Chairman shall be elected annually at the Annual General Meeting, to hold office for the following calendar year, and shall be eligible for re-election. Those elected at the Inaugural Meeting shall hold office until 31st December, 1935.

7. The ordinary members of Council elected at the Inaugural Meeting shall hold office from that date. At every Annual General Meeting thereafter the Society shall elect members to fill any vacancies on the Council that may have occurred, or that may be due to occur at the end of the year, members so elected to hold office from the ensuring 1st of January. The original members of Council shall hold office until 31st December, 1939, and, at the Annual General Meeting to be held in November, 1939, all of these members, except two (selected by agreement or by lot), shall be eligible for re-election. The two so selected shall retire as at 31st December following, and shall not be eligible for re-election for one year. Thereafter at each Annual General Meeting two of the ordinary members of Council shall retire as at 31st December following, and shall not be eligible for re-election for one year. The two members to retire annually shall be those who have the longest continuous period of service, and, as among those of equal service, shall be selected by agreement or by lot.

8. In addition to the elected members, the Council shall have power to co-opt as additional members of Council any member of the Society who, in their opinion, may be fitted to render special service in promoting the work of the Society. Such co-opted members shall hold office for such period, not exceeding five years, as the Council may in each case determine. At no time shall the co-opted members of Council exceed three in number.

9. The Society at the Inaugural Meeting, and thereafter at the Annual General Meeting, shall appoint a Literary Director or Directors, a Secretary and a Treasurer, and such other officers as may from time to time be deemed necessary, who shall be subject to the direction of the Council in the performance of their duties, and who shall receive such remuneration as

the Council may determine. Those so appointed shall not be members of Council, but may be invited to attend any meeting of Council.

10. Any casual vacancies in the offices of President, Vice-President, Chairman, Vice-Chairman or elected members of the Council, or among the officers of the Society, may be filled up by the Council, appointments so made to be for the period till the 31st of December following the next Annual General Meeting.

11. In any year in which a volume is published each member who has paid his subscription for that year shall be entitled to receive one copy.

12. The Annual General Meeting shall be held between 1st November and 31st March at such time and place as may be fixed by the Council. If the Meeting is not held until after 31st December in any year, office-bearers and members of Council then due to retire shall remain in office until the Meeting is held. The Council may also at any time call a Special General Meeting of the Society, and shall do so on a requisition from not less than ten members, which shall specify the object for which the Meeting is to be called. Seven days' notice shall be given of all General meetings.

13. The Constitution of the Society as contained in these Rules may be amended at any General Meeting on twenty-one days' notice of the proposed amendments being given to the Secretary and included in the Agenda circulated for the Meeting.

PUBLICATIONS OF THE STAIR SOCIETY

1. *An Introductory Survey of the Sources and Literature of Scots Law.* By various authors. With an introduction by the Rt. Hon. Lord Macmillan, P.C., LL.D., Lord of Appeal in Ordinary. 1936.

1a *An Index to Volume No. 1,* compiled by James Cowie Brown, M.A., LL.B., Ph.D., was issued in 1939.

2. *Acta Curiae Admirallatus Scotiae, 6th September 1557–11th March 1561–2.* Edited by Thomas Callander Wade, M.A., LL.B., Solicitor, Falkirk. 1937.

3. *Hope's Major Practicks, 1608–1633.* Edited by the Rt. Hon. James Avon Clyde, LL.D., formerly Lord Justice-General of Scotland and Lord President of the Court of Session. Vol. I. With portrait. 1937.

4. *Hope's Major Practicks, 1608–1633.* Edited by the Rt. Hon. James Avon Clyde, LL.D., formerly Lord Justice-General of Scotland and Lord President of the Court of Session. Vol. II. 1938.

5. *Baron David Hume's Lectures, 1786–1822.* Edited and annotated by G. Campbell H. Paton, M.A., LL.B., Solicitor, and Assistant to Professor of Law in the University of Glasgow. Vol. I. With portrait. 1939.

6. *Lord Hermand's Consistorial Decisions, 1684–1777.* Edited by F. P. Walton, K.C. (Quebec), LL.D., Hon. Fellow, Lincoln College, Oxford, formerly Director, Royal School of Law, Cairo. With biographical Sketch of Lord Hermand by James Fergusson. With portrait. 1940.

7. *St. Andrews Formulare, 1514–1546.* Text transcribed and edited by Gordon Donaldson, M.A., Ph.D, and C. Macrae, M.A., D.Phil. Vol. I. 1942.

8. *Acta Dominorum Concilii, 26th March 1501–27th January 1502–3.* Transcribed by J. A. Crawford, M.A., LL.B., Advocate. Edited with an Introduction by the Rt. Hon. James Avon Clyde, LL.D., formerly Lord Justice-General of Scotland and Lord President of the Court of Session. 1943.

9. *St. Andrews Formulare, 1514–1546.* Edited by Gordon Donaldson, M.A., Ph.D., with Prefatory Note by David Baird Smith, C.B.E., LL.D. Vol II. 1944.

10. *The Register of Brieves, 1286–1386,* as contained in the Ayr MS., the Bute MS., and Quoniam Attachiamenta. Edited by the Rt. Hon. Lord Cooper, LL.D., Lord Justice-Clerk. Thomas Thomson's Memorial on Old Extent. Edited by J. D. Mackie, C.B.E., M.C., M.A., Professor of Scottish History and Literature in the University of Glasgow. 1946.

11. *Regiam Majestatem and Quoniam Atttachiamenta,* based on the text of Sir John Skene. Edited and translated with Introduction and Notes by the Rt. Hon. Lord Cooper, LL.D. 1947.

12. *The Justiciary Records of Argyll and the Isles, 1664–1705.* Transcribed and edited, with an Introduction, by John Cameron, M.A., LL.B., Ph.D, Vol.I. 1949.

13. *Baron David Hume's Lectures, 1786–1822.* Edited and annotated by G. Campbell H. Paton, M.A., LL.B., Solicitor. Vol. II. 1949.

14. *Acta Dominorum Concilii et Sessionis, 1532–1533*. Edited by Ian H. Shearer, M.A., LL.B., Advocate. 1951.
15. *Baron David Hume's Lectures, 1786–1822*. Edited and annotated by G. Campbell H. Paton, M.A., LL.B., Advocate and Lecturer in the History of Scots Law in the University of Glasgow. Vol. III. 1952.
16. *Selected Justiciary Cases, 1624–1650*. Edited and annotated by Stair A. Gillon, B.A., LL.B., Advocate. Vol. I. 1953.
17. *Baron David Hume's Lectures, 1786–1822*. Edited and annotated by G. Campbell H. Paton, M.A., LL.B., Advocate and Lecturer in the History of Scots Law in the University of Glasgow. Vol. IV. 1955.
18. *Baron David Hume's Lectures, 1786–1822*. Edited and annotated by G. Campbell H. Paton, M.A., LL.B., Advocate and Lecturer in the History of Scots Law in the University of Glasgow. Vol. V. 1957.
19. *Baron David Hume's Lectures, 1786–1822*. Edited and annotated by G. Campbell H. Paton, M.A., LL.B., Advocate and Lecturer in the History of Scots Law in the University of Glasgow. Vol. VI. 1958.
19a *A Supplement to Baron Hume's Lectures*. Edited and annotated by the Editor of the printed volumes. 1957.
20. *An Introduction to Scottish Legal History*. By various authors. With an Introduction by the Rt. Hon. Lord Normand, P.C., LL.D., Lord of Appeal in Ordinary, 1947–1953. 1958.
21. *The Practicks of Sir James Balfour of Pittendreich*. Edited by Peter G. B. McNeill, M.A., LL.B., Ph.D., Advocate. Vol. I. 1962.
22. *The Practicks of Sir James Balfour of Pittendreich*. Edited by Peter G. B. McNeill, M.A., LL.B., Ph.D., Advocate. Vol. II. 1963.
23. *The Origins and Development of the Jury in Scotland*. By Ian D. Willock, M.A., LL.B., Advocate and Professor of Jurisprudence in the University of St. Andrews. 1966.
24. *William Hay's Lectures on Marriage*. Transcribed, translated and edited by the Right Rev. Monsignor John C. Barry, M.A. (Cantab.), D.C.L. (Rome), Rector of St. Andrew's College, Drygrange, Melrose; Consultor to the Pontifical Commission for the Revision of the Code of Canon Law. 1967.
25. *The Justiciary Records of Argyll and the Isles. 1664–1742*. Edited by John Imrie. Vol. II. 1969.
26. *Miscellany I*. By various authors. With a preface by the Rt. Hon. Lord Clyde, LL.D., Lord Justice-General and Lord President of the Court of Session. 1971.
27. *Selected Justiciary Cases, 1624–1650*. Edited with an Introduction by J. Irvine Smith, M.A., LL.B., Advocate. Sheriff of Lanarkshire at Glasgow. Vol. II. 1972.
28. *Selected Justiciary Cases, 1624–1650*. Edited with an Introduction by J. Irvine SMith, M.A., LL.B., Advocate, Sheriff of Lanarkshire at Glasgow. Vol. III. 1974.
29. *The Minute Book of the Faculty of Advocates, 1661–1712*. Edited by John M. Pinkerton, Clerk of Faculty. Vol.I. 1976.

30. *The Synod Records of Lothian and Tweeddale, 1589–96, 1640–49.* Edited with an Introduction by Dr. James Kirk of the Department of Scottish History, Glasgow University. 1977.
31. *Perpetuities in Scots Law.* By Robert Burgess, LL.B., Ph.D., Senior Lecturer in Law in the University of East Anglia. 1979.
32. *The Minute Book of the Faculty of Advocates, 1713–1750.* Edited by John M. Pinkerton, late Clerk of Faculty. Vol. II. 1980.
33. *Stair Tercentenary Studies.* By various authors. Edited by David M. Walker, Q.C., M.A., LL.D., F.B.A., Regius Professor of Law at the University of Glasgow. 1981.
34. *The Court of the Official in Pre-Reformation Scotland.* By Simon Ollivant, M.A., Ph.D. 1982.
35. *Miscellany II.* By various authors. Edited by David Sellar, B.A., LL.B., of the Department of Scots Law in the University of Edinburgh. With a preface by the Rt. Hon. Lord Avonside. 1984.
36. *Formulary of Old Scots Legal Documents.* Compiled by Peter Gouldesbrough, Former Assistant Keeper in the Scottish Record Office with a Supplementary Essay on Early Scottish Conveyancing by Gordon Donaldson, H.M. Historiographer in Scotland. 1985.
37. *The Scottish Whigs and the Reform of the Court of Session 1785–1830.* By Nicholas T. Phillipson, M.A., Ph.D., of the Department of History in the University of Edinburgh. 1990.
38. *The Court Book of the Barony and Regality of Falkirk and Callendar.* Edited by Doreen M. Hunter, M.A., late of the Scottish Record Office. 1991.
39. *Miscellany III.* By various authors. Edited by William M. Gordon, M.A., LL.B., Ph.D., Douglas Professor of Civil Law at the University of Glasgow. With a preface by Professor Emeritus Gordon Donaldson, H.M. Historiographer in Scotland. 1992.

SUPPLEMENTARY SERIES

1. *The College of Justice.* Essays by R. K. Hannay. Reprinted with an Introduction and Bibliography by Hector L. MacQueen, LL.B., Ph.D., of the Department of Scots Law in the University of Edinburgh. 1990.

JOINT PUBLICATION WITH THE SALTIRE SOCIETY

The Scottish Legal Tradition. New enlarged edition by M. C. Meston, M.A., LL.B., J.D., Professor of Private Law, University of Aberdeen, W. D. H. Sellar, B.A., LL.B., Senior Lecturer in Scots Law, University of Edinburgh and the Rt. Hon. Lord Cooper, LL.D., late President of the Court of Session. Edited by Scott C. Styles, M.A., LL.B. 1991.